Department for Transport

Scottish Government Executive and Welsh Assembly Government

Transport
Statistics
Great
Britain

2009

35th EDITION

November 2009

London: TSO

Department for Transport
Great Minster House
76 Marsham Street
London SW1P 4DR
Telephone 020 7944 8300
© Crown copyright 2009

ISBN: 9780115530951

Printed in Great Britain in November 2009 on material containing at least 75% recycled fibre.

A National Statistics publication produced by Transport Statistics: DfT

National Statistics are produced to high professional standards set out in the Code of Practice for Official Statistics. They undergo regular quality assurance reviews to ensure that they meet customer needs. They are produced free from any political interference.

Contact Points: For general enquiries call the National Statistics Customer Enquiry Centre at: Room 1015, ONS, Government Buildings, Cardiff Road, Newport, Gwent, NP10 8XG. ☎ 0845 601 3034, fax 01633 652747 or E-mail: info@statistics.gov.uk

You can also obtain National Statistics from the United Kingdom Statistics Authority through the internet – go to www.statistics.gov.uk. For information relating to Transport Statistics go to www.dft.gov.uk/pgr/statistics

Prepared for publication by:
Tajbar Gul
Shawn Weekes

DfT is often prepared to sell unpublished data. Further information and queries concerning this publication should be directed to: Transport Statistics, 2/29, Great Minster House, 76 Marsham Street, London SW1P 4DR

☎ 020 7944 3098, Fax 020 7944 2165, E-mail: publicationgeneral.enq@dft.gov.uk

Cover photographs all courtesy of Alamy; from left to right: © A Ivey and Towers, © D.Burke, © Flyn Thomas, © Doug Houghton, © Steven May

Contents

Transport Statistics Contacts

Antonia Roberts
Chief Statistician (Head of Profession)
☎020-7944 4280

Statisticians

Paul Swallow
Aviation; Environment; National Statistics;
☎020-7944 4411

Jeremy Grove
Maritime Statistics – sea port traffic, inland waterways freight, shipping fleets, seafarers and port employment.
☎020-7944 4441
E-mail: maritime.stats@dft.gsi.gov.uk

Lyndsey Avery
Aviation Statistics - airport & airline statistics; international passenger survey.
☎020-7944 4276
E-mail: aviation.stats@dft.gsi.gov.uk

Annie Sorbie
Environment Statistics
☎020-7944 3775
E-mail: publicationgeneral.enq@dft.gsi.gov.uk

Dorothy Anderson
Transport Statistics for EU & other international bodies; international comparisons; survey control; GIS;
National Statistics; Transport Statistics Publication and Website Management
☎020-7944 4442
E-mail: publicationgeneral.enq@dft.gsi.gov.uk;
inter.transport.comparisons@dft.gsi.gov.uk

Stephen Reynolds
Road Freight Statistics; continuing survey of road goods transport; ad hoc surveys of vehicle transport data collection and processing unit; Survey of international road haulage.
☎020-7944 3093
E-mail: roadfreight.stats@dft.gsi.gov.uk

Fax: 020-7944-2165

Anthony Boucher
Chief Statistician – Roads and Traffic
☎020-7944 4270

Statisticians

June Bowman
Road Traffic and Road Length Statistics
☎020-7944 6573

Andy Lees
Road Traffic Statistics; National core census; London core traffic census; weigh-in-motion; Footprint environmental monitoring; computing development.
☎020-7944 6397
Email: roadtraff.manual@dft.gsi.gov.uk

Gemma Brand
Road Traffic Statistics - Annual and quarterly traffic estimates; manual traffic counts and road lengths surveys.
☎020-7944 6555
E-mail: roadtraff.stats@dft.gsi.gov.uk

Ben Coleman
Urban congestion monitoring and speed surveys.
☎020-7944 6399
E-mail: roadtraff.stats@dft.gsi.gov.uk

David Robinson
Inter urban congestion monitoring and speed surveys.
☎020-7944 6559
E-mail: roadtraff.stats@dft.gsi.gov.uk

Fax: 020-7944-2164

Barbara Noble
Chief Statistician – Road Safety Research & Statistics
☎020-7944 6642

Statisticians

Pat Kilbey
Road accident and casualty statistics; drinking and driving; car safety; international road safety; inter-modal passenger safety.
☎020-7944 6387
E-mail: roadacc.stats@dft.gsi.gov.uk

Deirdre O'Reilly
Head of Road User Safety Research
☎020-7944 2044
E-mail: roadacc.stats@dft.gsi.gov.uk

Richard Campbell
International Networks
Strategy and International Networks; End-to-end journey analysis.
☎020-7944 3291

Margaret Shaw
Rail Statistics
☎020-7944 4977
E-mail: rail.stats@dft.gsi.gov.uk

Fax: 020-7944-2160

Tim Stamp
Chief Statistician - Travel
☎020-7944 3079

Statisticians

Mouna Kehil
Bus, Coach and Taxi Statistics: patronage; receipts; subsidies; fares; vehicle distances covered; vehicle stock; concessionary travel
☎020-7944 4589
E-mail: bus.statistics@dft.gsi.gov.uk

Anna Heyworth
Regional and Local Transport Statistics: sub-national performance (including National Indicators) and funding; accessibility indicators; Labour Force Survey data; travel to school data.
☎020-7944 4746
E-mail: subnational.stats@dft.gsi.gov.uk

Daryl Lloyd
Vehicle Statistics: vehicle licensing and registrations, estimates of Vehicle Excise Duty evasion and MOT non-compliance; foreign vehicles in traffic; road maintenance
☎020-7944 6142
E-mail: vehicles.stats@dft.gsi.gov.uk
E-mail: Roadmaintenance.stats@dft.gsi.gov.uk

National Travel Survey
☎020-7944 6594
E-mail: national.travelsurvey@dft.gsi.gov.uk

Public Attitude Surveys
☎020-7944 4892
E-mail: attitudes.stats@dft.gsi.gov.uk

Fax: 020-7944-2166

2

Introduction

Welcome to the 35th edition of *Transport Statistics Great Britain.*

Transport Statistics Great Britain (TSGB) is a major publication within the scope of National Statistics and provides an accurate, comprehensive and meaningful picture of transport patronage in Great Britain.

All individual tables that make up TSGB are on the web-site in both PDF and EXCEL format, enabling users to manipulate the information to produce further tables or charts. The whole document is available as a PDF file (chapter by chapter) in a separate theme dedicated to TSGB (http://www.dft.gov.uk/transtat/tsgb).

The web-site also contains a great deal of other published statistical material, including (in PDF format) all of the recent bulletins produced by Transport Statistics. It also includes a list of forthcoming publications and their publication dates. In many cases, the bulletins produced during the course of the year provide the first release of data and these are subsequently consolidated into the TSGB tables. Thus TSGB is a snapshot of the latest data available at the time of publication. TSGB tables on the website will be updated when later data becomes available when this is possible.

I hope you find this publication useful and interesting. Any comments you may have on the contents and presentation would be welcome. Please send these to the address below or E-mail to publicationgeneral.enq@dft.gov.uk

Dorothy A Anderson
2/29 Great Minster House
76 Marsham Street
London, SW1P 4DR

Symbols and conventions

Unless otherwise stated, all tables refer to **Great Britain**.

Metric units are generally used.

Conversion factors:

1 kilometre	= 0.6214 mile
1 tonne	= 0.9842 ton
1 tonne-km	= 0.6116 ton-mile
1 billion	= 1,000 million
1 Gallon	= 4.546 litres
1 litre	= 0.220 gallons

Rounding of figures. In tables where figures have been rounded to the nearest final digit, there may be an apparent slight discrepancy between the sum of the constituent items and the total as shown.

Symbols. The symbols to the right have been used throughout.

..	= not available
.	= not applicable
-	= Negligible (less than half the final digit shown)
0	= Nil
*	= Sample size too small for reliable estimates
ow	= of which
{	= subsequent data is disaggregated
}	= subsequent data is aggregated
|	= break in the series
P	= provisional data
F	= forecast expenditure
e	= estimated outturn
n.e.s.	= not elsewhere specified
R	= Revised data

All statistics in this publication are National Statistics unless indicated otherwise on each table.

List of tables and charts

Note: *Page numbers are given in italics after the table number*

Transport Statistics Great Britain has been compiled by staff at DfT with contributions from the Scottish Executive, the Welsh Assembly Government and other Government Departments. Thanks go to those individuals and businesses who provided data for analysis in the tables. DfT are able to provide statistics other than those included in this annual compendium. Many of these are published separately in more specialised publications – available via the DfT website at: www.dft.gov.uk/pgr/statistics. Some unpublished material is available on request, as is a service (subject to availability of resources) providing customised analyses for clients. Potential customers should note that we do charge for these services and there are strict guidelines for maintaining confidentiality. Contact points for further details are shown at the bottom of each table.

1 Modal Comparisons:

Notes and Definitions

Passenger transport: 1.1

Buses and coaches: Passenger kilometres are derived from other survey data such as receipts, vehicle kilometres and patronage. Changes are estimated by deflating passenger receipts by the most appropriate price indices available. Because this proxy method has to be used, the series gives only a broad guide to trends.

Cars, vans, taxis, motor cycles and pedal cycles:

Estimates for cars (which include taxis), motorcycles (which include mopeds and scooters), and pedal cycles are derived from the traffic series (vehicle kilometres) shown in Table 7.2 and average occupancy rates (persons per vehicle) from the National Travel Survey (NTS).

Because of changes in methodology figures for the road traffic estimates, figures for 1993 have been shown calculated on the new and the old basis.

Occupancy rates for 1996 onwards are based on weighted NTS data. As data prior to 1996 has not been weighted, this produces a discontinuity in the data. This does not affect the underlying rate of growth.

Estimates for personal use of light vans are derived from the NTS.

Rail: Rail figures include National Rail, London Underground, Glasgow Underground, public metro and light rail systems (see Table 6.2 for further details).

Air: The figures are revenue passenger kilometres on scheduled and non-scheduled domestic services on UK airlines only. They exclude air taxi services, private flying and passengers paying less than 25 per cent of the full fare on scheduled and non-scheduled services.

All modes: Figures exclude travel by water.

Passenger journeys on public transport: 1.2

The data in this table is derived from –

Bus: Returns from operators to DfT;

Rail: Office of Rail Regulation;

London Underground: Transport for London;

Light rail and trams: operators;

Air: Civil Aviation Authority.

Personal travel: 1.3, 1.4 and 1.5

These tables present some basic information from the National Travel Survey (NTS). The NTS records personal travel by residents of Great Britain along the public highway in Great Britain. It records the number of trips (a one-way course of travel for a single main purpose) and the distance travelled. All modes of transport are covered, including walking more than 50 yards. Excluded from the sample are foreign visitors and people living in communal establishments (e.g. students in halls of residence). Both of these groups are likely to make a large number of public transport trips.

In Tables 1.4 and 1.5, escort trips are those where the traveller has no purpose of his/her own, other than to escort or accompany another person, e.g. take a child to school.

In 2006, a weighting strategy was introduced to the NTS. As well as adjusting for non-response bias, the weighting strategy for the NTS also adjusts for the drop-off in the number of trips recorded by respondents during the course of the travel week. The weighting strategy has been applied to NTS data from 1995 onwards.

In 2002, the drawn sample size for the NTS was nearly trebled compared with previous years, enabling key results to be presented on a single year basis for the first time since the survey became continuous. Changes to the methodology in 2002 mean that there are some inconsistencies with data for earlier years.

People entering Central London during the morning peak: 1.6

The area defined as Central London approximates to that defined as the Greater London Conurbation Centre in the Population Censuses. It is bounded by South Kensington and Paddington in the west, Marylebone Road/Euston Road in the North, Shoreditch and Aldgate in the East, Elephant and Castle and Vauxhall in the South, and includes all the main railway termini.

The survey is a count of the number of vehicle occupants (other than goods vehicles) on each road crossing the central London cordon. The cordon is situated outside the Inner Ring Road and encloses a slightly larger area than the Central London Congestion Charging Zone.

Counts are conducted for one day at each of the survey points during October/November. Taxi passengers have been counted since 1996.

Results for London Underground are derived from exit counts of people leaving the Underground stations within the Central area. Since 1996, these have been taken from automatic ticket gate data. Rail passengers are counted by observers at their last station stop before the central London cordon or, in the case of long-distance operator services, on arrival at Central London rail termini. Figures for Underground exclude people transferring from surface rail.

Casualty rates: 1.7

There have been a number of small revisions to this table but these have had little effect on the comparisons of the different modes.

For rail, figures prior to 2000 are based on financial years. Changes in reporting regulations mean that serious and minor injuries are no longer collected; only casualties taken from the scene of the accident to hospital are included in these figures.

Passenger casualty rates given in the table can be interpreted as the risk a traveller runs of being injured, per billion kilometres travelled. The coverage varies for each mode of travel and the definitions of injuries and accidents are different. Thus care should be exercised in drawing comparisons between the rates for different modes.

The table provides information on passenger casualties and, where possible, travel by drivers and other crew in the course of their work has been excluded. Exceptions are for private journeys and those in company owned cars and vans where drivers are included.

Figures for all modes of transport exclude confirmed suicides and deaths through natural causes. Figures for air, rail and water exclude trespassers and rail excludes attempted suicides. Accidents occurring in airports, seaports and railway stations that do not directly involve the mode of transport concerned are also excluded; for example, injuries sustained on escalators or falling over packages on platforms.

The following definitions are used:

Air: Accidents involving UK registered airline aircraft in UK and foreign airspace. Fixed wing and rotary wing aircraft are included but air taxis are excluded. Accidents cover UK airline aircraft around the world not just in the UK.

Rail: Train accidents and accidents occurring through movement of railway vehicles in Great Britain. As well as national rail the figures include accidents on underground and tram systems, Eurotunnel and minor railways.

Water: Figures for travel by water include both domestic and international passenger carrying services of UK registered merchant vessels.

Road: Figures refer to Great Britain and include reported personal injury accidents occurring on the public highway (including footways) in which at least one road vehicle or a vehicle in collision with a pedestrian is involved and which becomes known to the police within 30 days of its occurrence. Figures include both public and private transport. More information and analyses on road accidents and casualties can be found in Section 8: Transport accidents and casualties.

Bus or coach: Vehicles equipped to carry 17 or more passengers regardless of use.

Car: Includes taxis, invalid tricycles, three and four wheel cars and minibuses. Prior to 1999 motor caravans were also included.

Van: Vans mainly include vehicles of the van type constructed on a car chassis. These are defined as those vehicles not over 3.5 tonnes maximum permissible gross vehicle weight.

Motorcycles: Mopeds, motor scooters and motor cycles (including motor cycle combinations).

Pedal cycle: Includes tandems, tricycles and toy cycles ridden on the carriageway.

Pedestrian: Includes persons riding toy cycles on the footway, persons pushing bicycles, pushing or pulling other vehicles or operating pedestrian controlled vehicles, those leading or herding animals, occupants of prams or wheelchairs, and people who alight safely from vehicles and are subsequently injured.

Travel to work: 1.8-1.9

Tables 1.8 and 1.9 use data from the October to December 2008 quarter of the Labour Force Survey (LFS). The table is based on those people who are employed, and excludes those on Government New Deal schemes, those working from home or using their home as a working base, and those whose workplace or mode of travel to work were not known.

The questions on usual method of travel to work and usual time have been asked in each Autumn (October to December) survey since 1992. Table 1.8b gives a time series of the results from these surveys for Great Britain. The LFS is a survey of households living at private addresses in

Great Britain. In spite of its large sample size (55 thousand responding households), data for some cells in Tables 1.8 and 1.9 are not shown because they fall below the 10 thousand LFS reliability threshold.

Labour Force Survey move to Calendar Quarters (CQ's): The Labour Force Survey (LFS) moved to publishing calendar quarters from May 2006. The survey previously published seasonal quarters where March-May months covered the spring quarter, June-August was summer and so forth. This has now changed to calendar quarters as part of an EU requirement for all member states to have an LFS based on calendar quarters. LFS micro data is available for January-March (Q1), April-June (Q2), July-September (Q3) and October-December (Q4). An article on the impact and issues associated with the move to calendar quarters is available at the link:

http://www.statistics.gov.uk/cci/article. asp?ID=1546

Overseas travel and tourism, and international passenger movements: 1.10-1.12

Tables 1.10-1.12 are derived from the International Passenger Survey (IPS). In this survey, which is carried out by the Office for National Statistics, a large sample of passengers are interviewed as they enter or leave the United Kingdom by the principal air and sea routes and via the Channel Tunnel. These tables are based on IPS 'main flow' interviews, i.e. United Kingdom residents returning to, and overseas residents leaving the United Kingdom. The unit of measurement is therefore the visit and not the journey, and the mode of travel for the unit is that used by a United Kingdom resident returning or by an overseas resident departing (fly cruises are an exception to this rule as they are counted as 'sea' even though United Kingdom resident interviewed will have returned by air).

Up to 1998, the results of the IPS have been supplemented with estimates of travel between the United Kingdom and the Irish Republic provided by the Irish Central Statistics Office. In Table 1.10, estimates of road and rail visits across the land border with the Irish Republic have been included with sea trips. Since 1999, IPS interviewing has been expanded to cover trips between the United Kingdom and the Irish Republic and therefore these estimates have not been necessary. The figures given here are annual totals, but quarterly as well as annual analyses are published in Business Monitor MQ6 (Overseas Travel and Tourism) and Travel Trends (A report on the IPS), with detailed notes and definitions.

These publications are available from TSO, or through the National Statistics website. More details can be found at:

http://www.statistics.gov.uk/ssd/surveys/ international_passenger_survey.asp

The "European Union" category in Tables 1.11 and 1.12 includes all 27 member states. "Other Europe" in Tables 1.11 and 1.12 includes other central and Eastern Europe, North Cyprus, Faroe Islands, Gibraltar, Iceland, Norway, Switzerland (including Lichtenstein), Turkey, the former USSR and the states of former Yugoslavia. "Other areas" figures in Table 1.12 are mostly non-Europeans travelling from Europe.

Household Expenditure on Transport: 1.13

Data is shown to the nearest ten pence in line with usual Expenditure and Food Survey (EFS) practice. Data to the nearest penny may be obtained from the EFS contact point EFS@ons.gsi.gov.uk

The coding framework was changed for the 2001/02 survey onwards. The table has been amended to present data on the new European Standard Classification of Individual Consumption by Purpose (COICOP) basis. Changes were also made in 2006 to the weights based on the 2001 Census, for further details see Family Spending: A Report on the 2007 Expenditure and Food Survey.

Investment in transport: 1.14

The table attempts to define investment in a consistent manner for each mode but because of differences in the ways data are collected this is not always possible. Therefore, for some modes estimates have been made on the basis of limited or partial information. Some figures are subject to revision.

Roads: Sources for expenditure on road infrastructure include the Highways Agency, the Scottish Government, the Wales Assembly Government, local authorities and DBFO contractors. Figures for public investment in road infrastructure are for gross capital expenditure on national roads (i.e. motorways and trunk roads). Private investment in road infrastructure includes investment under Design, Build, Finance and Operate (DBFO) contracts. Expenditure on bus garages, stops, etc is not included. The source for expenditure on road vehicles is the Office for National Statistics.

It is not possible to separate all the private expenditure since 2002/03 from public expenditure due to the complex nature of funding.

Rail: The source for National Rail expenditure is the Office of Rail Regulation; Investment in rail infrastructure includes track renewals, new routes and electrification, signalling, buildings, and plant and equipment.

Other public investment in rail infrastructure and other rail rolling stock covers, and is sourced by, London Underground, Docklands Light Railway, Croydon Tramlink, Glasgow Underground, Manchester Metrolink light rail system, Midland Metro, Nottingham Express Transit, South Yorkshire Supertram and Tyne and Wear Metro. Eurotunnel PLC investment figures, including plant and materials, are included in other rail infrastructure. Similarly, Eurotunnel investment in rolling stock is included in other rail rolling stock. The figures for other rail rolling stock also include a tentative allowance for investment in privately owned wagons of £30 million per annum.

Central and local government expenditure on transport: 1.15

This table includes central and local government expenditure on transport and excludes, where possible, private expenditure. This differs from expenditure in Table 1.14 where we attempt to capture expenditure on infrastructure but by the private sector as well as government.

As the table shows local government expenditure on transport, the grants and other financial support provided to local government to fund this expenditure have been excluded from central government expenditure to avoid double counting.

The figures shown are compiled from various government departments. Central government expenditure in England data is compiled by the Department for Transport. Local government expenditure in England is compiled by Communities and Local Government (CLG). Expenditure in Wales comes from *Welsh Transport Statistics*, produced by the *National Assembly for Wales*. Expenditure in Scotland comes from *Scottish Transport Statistics*, a Scottish Government publication.

Where possible the current/resource figures exclude the cost of capital; that is the income that would have been earned if the assets had been sold and invested. This makes a considerable difference to reported spend by organisations such as the Highways Agency. For example the cost of capital charge alone for 2007/08 was

given as £2.833 million in the Highway Agency Annual Report. Capital expenditure includes expenditure paid by Central Government to Agencies whether or not the funding was spent in the year awarded.

Some private corporation, such as London and Continental Railways, have been reclassified as public corporations for the purposes of the National Accounts. In such cases the expenditure included in this table only includes those funds provided by Central Government and not the total expenditure of the organisation concerned.

Some revenue such as cark parking fees gained by local authorities has been included. However receipts from items such as duties on fuel and car licensing are excluded.

Transport related employment: 1.16-1.18

Details of transport-related employment by occupation are available from the Labour Force Survey (LFS). Data shown in Table 1.16 are from Q2 2008. The Labour Force Survey (LFS) moved to publishing calendar quarters in May 2006. The survey previously published seasonal quarters where March-May months covered the spring quarter, June-August was summer and so forth. This has now changed to calendar quarters as part of an EU requirement for all member states to have an LFS based on calendar quarters. LFS micro data is available for January-March (Q1), April-June (Q2), July-September (Q3) and October-December (Q4). An article on the impact and issues associated with the move to calendar quarters is available at the link: http://www.statistics.gov.uk/cci/article.asp?ID=1546

The LFS is a survey of households living at private addresses in Great Britain. In spite of its large sample size (55 thousand responding households), data for some cells in Table 1.16 are not shown because they fall below the 10 thousand LFS reliability threshold.

Table 1.16 includes people with both main and second jobs as an employee, the self-employed, those on Government employment and training programmes, and unpaid family workers. The industry totals include those working in the following industry classifications: transport via railways, other inland transport, water transport, air transport, supporting and auxiliary transport activities and the activities of travel agents, and exclude those whose occupation was not known.

By comparison, Table 6.12 relates to local bus services only, and incorporates revisions due to late returns when available.

The new Standard Occupational Classification (SOC2000) has been used instead of the previous 1990 classification for editions of *Transport Statistics Great Britain* from 2001 to 2008. SOC2000 is not directly comparable with the 1990 classifications, and it is therefore not possible to make direct comparisons with earlier editions. In addition the Transport industries are also based on the SIC200.

The Short Term Employment Surveys (STES) are the primary source for employee jobs estimates. (Tables 1.17 and 1.18) The estimates of short-term change are benchmarked to the Annual Business Inquiry (ABI/1) to maintain consistency with annual employment estimates. Prior to ABI2006 the reference period was December each year; for ABI2006 the reference period changed to September.

There is a discontinuity in the employee jobs series between December 2005 and September 2006 due to improvements to the annual benchmark. Further information can be found at:

http://www.statistics.gov.uk/CCI/article.asp?ID=1802&Pos=4&ColRank=1&Rank=224

In Table 1.18, part-time is defined as not more than normally 30 hours a week; figures are actual numbers working part-time, rather than full-time equivalents.

Retail and Consumer Prices Indices: Motoring Costs: 1.19a

These indices are taken from the published *Consumer Prices Index (CPI)* and the *Retail Prices Index (RPI)* rebased to 1998=100 for convenience. The four letter code used by the Office for National Statistics to identify the series in their time series data and publications has been included.

The operation of personal transport equipment includes spare parts and accessories, fuels and lubricants, maintenance and repairs, and other services. The main different between the operation of personal transport equipment from the CPI , the motor running costs index and the all motor index from the *Retail Prices Index* is that the latter includes the purchase of vehicle. There are some other exclusions from the CPI index such as car insurance and vehicle excise duty (regarded as a tax) but these do not have a large effect on the *Consumer Prices Index* as the weights on these are relatively small.

Retail Prices Index: transport components: 1.19b

These indices are taken from the published *Retail Prices Index*, rebased to 1998=100 for convenience. The all motor index includes purchase of a vehicle, maintenance, petrol and oil, and tax and insurance. See also notes on Table 1.19a.

Gross Domestic Product and Retail Prices Index deflators: 1.20

Gross Domestic Product deflators (at market prices) are calculated by reference to column YBGB of Table A1 of the *Quarterly National Accounts*. Consumer and Retail Prices Index deflators have been calculated directly from the published 'All Items' *Consumer and Retail Prices Index*.

Transport Statistics Great Britain 2009

1.1 Passenger transport: by mode: 1952-2008

Billion passenger kilometres/percentage

Year	Buses and coaches		Cars, vans and taxis		Motor cycles		Pedal cycles		All road		Rail [1]		Air (UK)[2]		All modes [3]	
1952	92	42	58	27	7	3	23	11	180	82	38	18	0.2	0.1	218	100
1953	93	41	64	29	7	3	21	9	185	83	39	17	0.2	0.1	225	100
1954	92	40	72	31	8	3	19	8	191	83	39	17	0.3	0.1	230	100
1955	91	38	83	35	8	3	18	8	200	84	38	16	0.3	0.1	239	100
1956	89	36	91	37	8	3	16	7	204	83	40	16	0.5	0.2	245	100
1957	84	34	92	38	9	4	16	7	201	83	42	17	0.5	0.2	244	100
1958	80	31	113	44	9	4	14	5	216	84	41	16	0.5	0.2	258	100
1959	81	30	126	46	11	4	14	5	232	85	41	15	0.6	0.2	273	100
1960	79	28	139	49	11	4	12	4	241	86	40	14	0.8	0.3	282	100
1961	76	26	157	53	11	4	11	4	255	86	39	13	1.0	0.3	295	100
1962	74	25	171	57	10	3	9	3	264	87	37	12	1.1	0.4	302	100
1963	73	23	185	59	8	3	8	3	274	88	36	12	1.3	0.4	312	100
1964	71	21	214	63	8	2	8	2	301	89	37	11	1.5	0.4	340	100
1965	67	19	231	66	7	2	7	2	312	89	35	10	1.7	0.5	349	100
1966	67	18	252	68	7	2	6	2	332	90	35	9	1.8	0.5	369	100
1967	66	17	267	70	6	2	6	2	345	91	34	9	1.9	0.5	381	100
1968	64	16	279	72	5	1	5	1	353	91	33	9	1.9	0.5	389	100
1969	63	16	286	72	5	1	5	1	359	91	35	9	1.9	0.5	395	100
1970	60	15	297	74	4	1	4	1	365	91	36	9	2.0	0.5	403	100
1971	60	14	313	75	4	1	4	1	381	91	35	9	2.0	0.5	419	100
1972	60	14	327	76	4	1	4	1	395	91	34	8	2.2	0.5	431	100
1973	61	14	345	76	4	1	4	1	414	92	35	8	2.4	0.5	452	100
1974	61	14	333	76	5	1	4	1	403	91	36	8	2.1	0.5	441	100
1975	60	14	331	76	6	1	4	1	401	92	36	8	2.1	0.5	438	100
1976	58	13	348	77	7	2	5	1	418	92	33	7	2.4	0.5	452	100
1977	58	13	354	77	7	1	6	1	425	92	34	7	2.2	0.5	461	100
1978	56	12	368	78	7	1	5	1	436	92	35	7	2.7	0.6	474	100
1979	56	12	365	77	7	2	5	1	433	92	35	7	3.0	0.6	471	100
1980	52	11	388	79	8	2	5	1	453	92	35	7	3.0	0.6	491	100
1981	48	10	394	80	10	2	5	1	458	93	34	7	2.8	0.6	495	100
1982	48	10	406	81	10	2	6	1	470	93	31	6	2.9	1.0	504	100
1983	48	9	411	80	9	2	6	1	474	93	34	7	3.0	1.0	511	100
1984	48	9	432	80	9	2	6	1	495	93	35	7	3.0	1.0	534	100
1985	49	9	441	81	8	1	6	1	504	93	36	7	3.6	0.7	544	100
1986	47	8	465	82	8	1	6	1	525	93	37	7	3.7	0.7	566	100
1987	47	8	500	83	7	1	6	1	560	93	39	6	4.0	0.7	603	100
1988	46	7	536	84	6	1	5	1	595	93	41	6	4.5	0.7	640	100
1989	47	7	581	85	6	1	5	1	639	94	39	6	4.9	0.7	683	100
1990	46	7	588	85	6	1	5	1	645	93	40	6	5.2	0.8	690	100
1991	44	6	582	86	6	1	5	1	637	94	39	6	4.8	0.7	681	100
1992	43	6	583	86	5	1	5	1	635	94	38	6	4.8	0.7	678	100
1993	44	6	584	86	4	1	4	1	636	94	37	5	5.1	0.8	677	100
1993	44	6	607	87	4	1	4	1	659	94	37	5	5.1	0.7	701	100
1994	44	6	614	87	4	1	4	1	666	94	35	5	5.5	0.8	706	100
1995	43	6	618	87	4	1	4	1	669	94	37	5	5.9	0.8	712	100
1996	43	6	622	87	4	1	4	1	674	94	39	5	6.3	0.9	719	100
1997	44	6	632	86	4	1	4	1	685	93	42	6	6.8	0.9	733	100
1998	45	6	636	86	4	1	4	1	689	93	44	6	7.0	1.0	740	100
1999	46	6	642	86	5	1	4	1	697	93	46	6	7.3	1.0	751	100
2000	47	6	640	85	5	1	4	1	695	93	47	6	7.6	1.0	749	100
2001	47	6	654	85	5	1	4	1	710	93	47	6	7.7	1.0	765	100
2002	47	6	677	86	5	1	4	1	733	93	48	6	8.5	1.1	790	100
2003	47	6	673	85	6	1	5	1	731	93	49	6	9.1	1.2	789	100
2004	48	6	678	85	6	1	4	0	736	92	50	6	9.8	1.2	796	100
2005	48	6	674	85	6	1	4	1	733	92	52	7	9.9	1.2	794	100
2006	50	6	682	85	6	1	5	1	746	92	55	7	9.9	1.2	811	100
2007	50	6	685	84	6	1	4	1	749	92	59	7	9.5	1.2	817	100
2008	..		679 P		6		5		..		51 [4]		9.0		..	

1 Financial years. National Rail, urban metros and modern trams.
2 UK airlines, domestic passengers uplifted on scheduled
  and non-scheduled flights.
3 Excluding travel by water.
4 Excluding urban metros
Notes: Bus and coach figures not available at time of going to press.
See Notes and Definitions in Sections 1 and 7
for details of discontinuity in road passenger
figures from 1993 and 1996 onwards.

Bus & coach: ☎020-7944 3076
Car, m/cycle & pedal cycle: ☎020-7944 3097
Rail: ☎020-7944 3076
Air: ☎020-7944 3088
The rail and air figures in this table
are outside the scope of National Statistics
Source - Rail: ORR; Air: CAA

1.2 Passenger journeys on public transport vehicles: 1950-2007/08

For greater detail of the years 1998/99-2008/09 see Table 6.2

Millions

Year	All local services Bus, trolleybus, or tram	Street running public transport				Rail systems [1]			Air (UK) [2]
		Local bus service	Non-local bus or coach	Trolley buses	Trams	National rail network	London Under-ground	Light rail, other rail & metros	Passengers on domestic flights
1950	16,445	12,734	260	1,961	1,750	1,010	695	..	..
1951	16,340	12,985	282	1,876	1,479	1,030	702	..	..
1952	16,039	13,049	297	1,783	1,207	1,017	670	..	0.7
1953	15,765	13,026	318	1,726	1,013	1,015	672	..	0.8
1954	15,597	13,059	293	1,663	875	1,020	671	..	1.0
1955	15,592	13,225	337	1,598	769	994	676	..	1.2
1956	15,169	13,059	341	1,503	607	1,029	678	..	1.4
1957	14,404	12,491	332	1,437	476	1,101	666	..	1.6
1958	13,513	11,879	337	1,257	377	1,090	692	..	1.5
1959	13,592	12,152	345	1,193	247	1,069	669	..	1.7
1960	13,313	12,166	367	990	157	1,037	674	..	2.2
1961	13,019	12,159	384	756	104	1,025	675	..	2.8
1962	12,648	12,045	382	557	46	965	668	..	3.3
1963	12,352	11,860	381	476	16	938	673	26	3.7
1964	11,881	11,497	386	368	16	928	674	27	4.2
1965	11,239	10,938	413	286	15	865	657	24	4.7
1966	10,609	10,407	419	188	14	835	667	24	5.1
1967	10,166	10,047	450	106	13	837	661	23	5.3
1968	9,779	9,699	455	68	12	831	655	21	5.0
1969	9,365	9,303	458	50	12	806	676	20	5.2
1970	8,687	8,643	467	34	10	824	672	18	5.4
1971	8,153	8,128	486	15	10	816	654	17	5.4
1972	7,912	7,901	512	1	10	754	655	16	5.9
1973	7,877	7,866	577	.	11	728	644	16	6.5
1974	7,716	7,706	597	.	10	733	636	15	6.1
1975	7,533	7,524	635	.	9	730	601	15	5.8
1976	7,149	7,141	648	.	8	702	546	11	6.1
1977	6,864	6,856	641	.	8	702	545	5	5.5
1978	6,625	6,617	680	.	8	724	568	3 [3]	6.4
1979	6,472	6,463	628	.	9	748	594	3 [3]	7.2
1980	6,224	6,216	559	.	8	760	559	13	7.2
1981	5,694	5,688	584	.	6	719	541	28	6.6
1982	5,518	5,512	579	.	6	630	498	51	7.0
1983	5,587	5,581	622	.	6	694	563	62	7.0
1984	5,650	5,644	587	.	6	702	672	70	8.0
1985/86	5,819	5,813	537	.	6	686	732	72	8.6
1986/87	5,500	5,494	572	.	6	738	769	60	9.3
1987/88	5,439	5,434	592	.	5	798	798	59	10.3
1988/89	5,357	5,352	563	.	5	822	815	66	11.6
1989/90	5,214	5,208	594	.	6	812	765	69	12.6
1990/91	4,980	4,974	619	.	6	809	775	66	13.1
1991/92	4,790	4,785	..	.	5	792	751	63	12.0
1992/93	4,599	4,594	..	.	5	770	728	68	12.0
1993/94	4,500	4,494	..	.	6	740	735	72	12.4
1994/95	4,533	4,528	..	.	5	735	764	78	13.3
1995/96	4,494	4,489	..	.	5	761	784	82	14.3
1996/97	4,459	4,455	..	.	5	801	772	87	15.3
1997/98	4,434	4,430	..	.	5	846	832	93	16.2
1998/99	4,355	4,350	..	.	4	892	866	100	16.9
1999/00	4,380	4,376	..	.	4	931	927	109	17.4
2000/01	4,424	4,420	..	.	4	957	970	134	18.2
2001/02	4,460	4,455	..	.	5	960	953	141	18.5
2002/03	4,554	4,550	..	.	4	976	942	150	20.2
2003/04	4,684	4,681	..	.	4	1,012	948	156	21.0
2004/05	4,741	4,737	..	.	4	1,045	976	168	22.7
2005/06	4,795	4,791	..	.	4	1,082	970	173	23.3
2006/07	5,101	5,097	..	.	3	1,151	1,040	188	23.0
2007/08	5,166	5,163 P	..	.	3	1,232	1,096	198	22.3
2008/09	5,235	5,233 P	..	.	2	1,274	1,089	201	21.0

1 Light rail and metros shown here are Glasgow Subway, Nexus (opened 1980),
Docklands Light Railway (1987), Manchester Metrolink (1992),
Stagecoach Supertram (1994), West Midlands Metro (1999)
Croydon Tramlink (2000) and Nottingham NET (2004).

2 UK airlines, domestic passengers uplifted on scheduled
and non-scheduled flights. Figures are for calendar years.

3 Glasgow Subway was closed for refurbishment in 1978 and 1979.

☎020-7944 3076
Some figures in this table are outside
the scope of National Statistics
Source - bus, coach, tram and rail operators

1.3 Average distance travelled per person per year by mode of travel and average trip length: 1995/97-2008[1]

Miles/percentage

	1995/1997	1998/2000	2002	2003	2004	2005	2006	2007	2008
By mode (miles per person per year):									
Walking (including short walks)	200	198	198	201	203	197	201	190	193
Bicycle	43	40	36	37	39	36	39	40	42
Private hire bus	106	111	124	135	132	122	94	90	94
Car/van driver	3,623	3,725	3,661	3,660	3,674	3,682	3,660	3,641	3,494
Car/van passenger	2,082	2,086	2,115	2,098	2,032	2,063	2,033	1,989	1,974
Motorcycle/moped	35	33	35	41	38	35	34	35	38
Other private (including minibuses and motorcaravans, etc.)[2]	28	32	21	28	24	34	23	21	16
Bus in London	43	44	56	60	59	67	63	67	69
Other local bus	225	218	224	230	219	212	233	239	243
Non-local bus[2]	94	100	59	87	70	75	63	71	56
London Underground	60	65	81	68	68	67	75	71	75
Surface rail	321	401	413	384	433	461	466	509	495
Taxi/minicab	46	63	59	55	51	60	52	56	54
Other public (including air, ferries, light rail, etc.)[2]	75	46	55	108	61	97	96	83	80
All modes	6,981	7,164	7,135	7,192	7,103	7,208	7,133	7,103	6,923
Percentage of mileage accounted for by car (including van/lorry)	*82*	*81*	*81*	*80*	*80*	*80*	*80*	*79*	*79*
Average trip length (miles per trip)	6.4	6.7	6.8	7.0	6.9	6.9	6.9	7.3	7.0

1 There is an apparent under-recording of short walks in 2002-03 and short trips in 2007-08 compared to other years.

2 These estimates have a large sampling error because of the small samples involved.

☎020-7944 3097
Source - National Travel Survey, DfT

1.4 Trips per person per year by main mode[1] and purpose: 2008

Trips

	Walk	Bicycle	Car driver	Car passenger	Motor-cycle	Other private	Local bus	Surface rail/under ground	Other Public	All Modes
Commuting/business	19	6	111	17	2	1	14	15	2	187
Education/escort education	41	2	22	23	-	4	11	2	1	105
Shopping	45	2	85	42	-	1	19	2	2	198
Other escort	10	-	54	29	-	-	2	-	1	96
Personal business	24	1	43	25	-	1	7	1	1	103
Leisure	40	5	94	91	1	2	13	6	7	260
Other	43	-	1	-	-	-	-	-	-	44
All purposes	221	16	410	227	4	9	65	27	14	992

1 Main mode is that used for the longest part of the trip.

☎020-7944 3097
Source - National Travel Survey, DfT

1.5 Trip distance per person per year by main mode[1] and purpose: 2008

Miles

	Walk	Bicycle	Car driver	Car passenger	Motor-cycle	Other private	Local bus	Surface rail/under ground	Other Public	All Modes
Commuting/business	15 -	18	1,333	150	18	8	74	315	38	1,970
Education/escort education	28	3	88	68	-	38	50	23	8	306
Shopping	28	3	442	281	1	3	79	31	9	877
Other escort	6	-	293	184	-	2	8	6	4	503
Personal business	14	2	263	152	2	5	27	25	12	502
Leisure	31	15	1,058	1,128	18	57	70	216	124	2,716
Other	40	-	8	1	-	-	-	-	-	48
All purposes	163	41	3,485	1,963	38	113	308	617	195	6,923

1 Main mode is that used for the longest part of the trip.

☎020-7944 3097
Source - National Travel Survey, DfT

1.6 People entering central London during the morning peak:[1] 1997-2007

People (thousands)

	1997	1998	1999	2000	2001	2002	2003	2004	2005	2006	2007
Public transport:											
Surface rail	435	448	460	465	468	451	455	452	473	491	502
London Underground & Docklands Light Railway [2]	341	360	362	383	377	380	339	344	344	379	397
Bus	68	68	68	73	81	88	104	116	115	116	113
Coach/minibus [3]	20	17	15	15	10	10	10	9	9	8	9
All public transport	863	892	905	935	935	929	909	921	940	994	1,020
Personal transport:											
Private car	142	140	135	137	122	105	86	86	84	78	75
Motor cycle	11	13	15	17	16	15	16	16	16	15	15
Pedal cycle	10	10	12	12	12	12	12	14	17	18	19
Taxi	9	8	8	8	7	7	7	7	8	7	6
All personal transport [4]	172	171	169	173	157	139	120	122	125	118	116
All transport [4]	1,035	1,063	1,074	1,108	1,093	1,068	1,029	1,043	1,065	1,113	1,137

1 0700-1000 hours. Surveys are conducted in October/November.
2 Excludes passengers transferring from surface rail services. Passengers transferring from surface rail services have been deducted from the gross Underground counts.
3 Includes commuter and tourist coaches.
4 Excludes commercial vehicles. Taxi passengers, collected since 1996 but excluded from previously published figures, have been included.

☎020-7126 4610
The figures in this table are outside
the scope of National Statistics
Source - Transport for London

1.7 Passenger casualty rates by mode: 1999-2008[1]

Per billion passenger kilometres

	1999	2000	2001	2002	2003	2004	2005	2006	2007	2008	1999-08 average
Air [2]											
Killed	0.00	0.00	0.00	0.00	0.00	0.00	0.00	0.00	0.00	0.00	0.00
KSI [3]	0.02	0.00	0.00	0.00	0.00	0.01	0.00	0.00	0.00	0.01	0.00
All [4]	0.18	0.04	0.00	0.00	0.00	0.01	0.00	0.01	0.00	0.04	0.03
Rail [5,6]											
Killed	0.9	0.3	0.3	0.4	0.2	0.2	0.1	0.1	0.1	0.0 P	0.2
Injured	19	14	13	13	13	13	12	10	11	8 P	12
Water [7]											
Killed	0.4	0.4	0.4	0.0	0.0	0.0	0.3	0.3	0.0	0.9	0.3
KSI	29	53	54	50	61	44	36	39	45	74	48
Bus or coach											
Killed	0.2	0.3	0.2	0.4	0.2	0.4	0.2	0.3	0.2	0.1	0.3
KSI	12	11	11	11	10	9	7	8	9	9	10
All	202	195	191	173	175	167	146	130	142	139	165
Car [8]											
Killed	2.7	2.7	2.8	2.7	2.7	2.6	2.6	2.4	2.2	1.9	2.5
KSI	33	32	31	29	27	25	23	22	20	18	27
All	333	335	323	304	291	282	275	259	244	227	287
Van [8]											
Killed	0.9	0.9	0.9	1.0	0.9	0.8	0.6	0.6	0.6	0.5	0.8
KSI	13	12	11	11	10	8	7	6	5	5	9
All	104	100	102	96	89	76	73	68	59	54	80
Motorcycles [8]											
Killed	113	122	112	111	114	105	97	107	97	89	106
KSI	1,423	1,493	1,405	1,367	1,264	1,194	1,109	1,155	1,116	1,089	1,254
All	5,395	5,712	5,539	5,168	4,691	4,606	4,232	4,156	3,887	3,881	4,690
Pedal cycle											
Killed	42	31	33	29	25	32	33	31	32	24	31
KSI	779	666	632	555	534	548	533	527	541	541	589
All	5,599	4,953	4,512	3,874	3,775	3,956	3,739	3,494	3,814	3,435	4,090
Pedestrian											
Killed	50	49	47	42	41	35	36	36	36	31	40
KSI	564	543	521	471	424	394	384	371	382	358	439
All	2,464	2,404	2,332	2,117	1,944	1,836	1,794	1,631	1,666	1,537	1,964

1 Figures have been revised from those published in previous years,
   see Notes and Definitions for more details.
2 Passenger casualties in accidents involving UK registered airline aircraft
   in UK and foreign airspace.
3 KSI =Killed or seriously injured
4 All = Killed, seriously and slightly injured
5 Financial year for 1999. From 2000 figures are based on calendar year basis.
6 Passenger casualties involved in train accidents and accidents occuring through movement of railway vehicles.
   Reporting regulations changed on 1 April 1996. Since then figures are only available for passenger fatalities and injuries.
   The reporting trigger for an injury is the passenger being taken to hospital directly from the scene.
7 Passenger casualties on UK registered merchant vessels.
8 Reported driver and passenger casualties.

The figures for Air, Rail and Water modes
are outside the scope of National Statistics
☎ 020-7944 6595

1.8 Main mode of transport to work and mean time taken by Government Office Region and country of workplace

a) October to December 2008									Percentage/thousands
					Rail				
Area of workplace	Car, van, minibus	Motor-cycle	Bicycle	Bus, coach	ow: National Rail	ow: Other rail [1]	All Rail	Walk	Number in employment[2]
North East	76	*	1	9	1	2	3	10	960
Tyne and Wear	70	*	*	13	*	3	5	9	458
Rest of North East	82	*	*	5	*	*	*	11	503
North West	76	-	2	7	3	-	3	11	2,691
Greater Manchester	74	*	2	9	3	1	4	10	1,025
Merseyside	72	*	*	9	7	*	7	9	464
Rest of North West	79	*	3	4	1	*	1	12	1,202
Yorkshire and the Humber	75	1	3	8	2	*	2	11	2,046
South Yorkshire	74	*	*	9	*	*	3	11	483
West Yorkshire	74	*	1	10	3	*	3	10	884
Rest of Yorks and the Humber	76	*	5	5	*	*	*	11	679
East Midlands	77	*	4	6	1	*	1	12	1,743
West Midlands	76	1	2	7	3	*	3	10	2,087
Metropolitan County	72	*	1	12	4	*	5	8	1,009
Rest of West Midlands	80	*	3	3	*	*	1	12	1,078
East of England	76	1	5	4	2	*	2	11	2,159
London	35	2	3	14	21	17	38	8	3,450
Central London	12	2	3	13	38	27	65	5	1,251
Rest of inner London	29	3	5	15	17	21	37	10	901
Outer London	62	1	2	13	6	6	12	9	1,298
South East	76	1	4	4	3	*	4	11	3,399
South West	75	1	4	4	1	*	2	14	2,138
England	69	1	3	7	5	3	8	11	20,674
Wales	82	*	2	4	2	*	2	9	1,099
Scotland	69	*	2	13	3	*	4	11	2,137
Strathclyde	67	*	*	14	6	*	6	10	898
Rest of Scotland	70	*	3	12	2	*	2	12	1,239
Great Britain	70	1	3	8	5	3	8	11	23,910

b) Great Britain: Autumn 1998 - October to December 2008[3]									Percentage/minutes
					Rail				
	Car, van, minibus	Motor-cycle	Bicycle	Bus, coach	ow: National Rail	ow: Other rail [2]	All Rail	Walk	Mean time (minutes)
Autumn 1998	71	1	3	8	4	2	6	11	24.6
Autumn 1999	70	1	3	8	4	2	6	11	24.9
Autumn 2000	70	1	3	8	4	2	6	11	25.3
Autumn 2001	70	1	3	8	4	3	7	11	25.4
Autumn 2002	71	1	3	8	4	2	6	11	25.4
Autumn 2003	71	1	3	8	4	2	6	10	25.5
Autumn 2004	71	1	3	8	4	2	6	11	25.9
Autumn 2005	71	1	3	8	4	2	7	11	25.9
October to December 2006	70	1	3	8	4	3	7	11	26.3
October to December 2007	70	1	3	8	5	3	8	11	24.3
October to December 2008	70	1	3	8	5	3	8	11	23.9

1 Includes light railway systems and trams.
2 Employment figures reflect only those people using the transport modes detailed, not all employed. This results in potential variations from previous years.
3 The Labour Force Survey (LFS) moved to publishing calendar quarters in May 2006. The survey previously published seasonal quarters where March-May months covered the spring quarter, June-August was summer and so forth. This has now changed to calendar quarters as part of an EU requirement for all member states to have an LFS based on calendar quarters. LFS micro data is available for January-March (Q1), April-June (Q2), July-September (Q3) and October-December (Q4). An article on the impact and issues associated with the move to calendar quarters is available at the link: http://www.statistics.gov.uk/cci/article.asp?ID=1546

☎020-7944 6104
Labour Force Survey Helpline: ☎01633 455 732
Source - Labour Force Survey, ONS

1.9 Time taken to travel to work by Government Office Region of workplace: October to December 2008

Area of workplace	Cumulative percentage				Mean time (minutes)
	<20 minutes	<40 minutes	<60 minutes	<90 minutes	
North East	50	86	95	99	22
Tyne and Wear	45	83	93	99	24
Rest of North East	54	90	97	99	20
North West	46	82	91	98	24
Greater Manchester	40	76	88	97	27
Merseyside	42	81	91	99	24
Rest of North West	52	86	95	99	22
Yorkshire and the Humber	45	81	92	98	24
South Yorkshire	43	81	92	98	25
West Yorkshire	41	78	90	98	26
Rest of Yorks and the Humber	52	86	94	99	22
East Midlands	49	85	95	99	22
West Midlands	46	81	92	98	24
Metropolitan County	37	75	90	98	28
Rest of West Midlands	55	87	95	98	21
East of England	49	83	92	98	23
London	17	46	67	90	44
Central London	5	28	54	85	54
Rest of Inner London	17	48	68	91	43
Outer London	31	65	80	94	34
South East	47	81	91	97	25
South West	50	85	94	98	23
England	42	76	88	96	27
Wales	51	86	95	99	21
Scotland	44	79	90	97	26
Strathclyde	40	77	91	97	26
Rest of Scotland	46	80	90	96	26
Great Britain	43	77	89	97	27

☎020 7944 6104
Labour Force Survey Helpline: ☎01633 455 732
Source - Labour Force Survey, ONS

1.10 Overseas travel: visits to and from the United Kingdom: 1998-2008

Thousands

| | Visits to the United Kingdom [1] | | | | | | Visits abroad by United Kingdom residents [2] | | | | | |
| | | Sea/Channel Tunnel | | | | | | Sea/Channel Tunnel | | | | |
Year	Air	With car [3]	With coach	Other [4]	Irish sea	Total Sea/ Channel Tunnel	Air	With car [3]	With coach	Other [4]	Irish sea	Total Sea/ Channel Tunnel
1998	17,479	2,324	2,047	3,207	688	8,266	34,283	8,575	2,751	3,202	2,061	16,589
1999 [5]	17,284	2,509	1,571	4,030	.	8,110	37,510	9,309	2,857	4,205	.	16,371
2000	17,831	1,902	1,411	4,065	.	7,378	41,392	8,453	2,627	4,364	.	15,445
2001	16,054	1,670	1,415	3,697	.	6,782	43,011	8,213	2,589	4,467	.	15,269
2002	17,098	1,901	1,336	3,845	.	7,082	43,990	7,999	3,049	4,339	.	15,387
2003	17,635	1,821	1,561	3,699	.	7,080	47,101	7,860	2,068	4,395	.	14,323
2004	20,002	1,967	1,720	4,067	.	7,753	50,435	7,125	2,290	4,344	.	13,759
2005	22,043	2,017	1,801	4,109	.	7,927	53,626	6,457	2,224	4,135	.	12,815
2006	24,588	2,039	1,735	4,351	.	8,125	56,460	5,958	2,744	4,375	.	13,076
2007	25,089	2,053	1,503	4,133	.	7,689	56,329	6,506	2,246	4,370	.	13,121
2008	24,023	2,190	1,487	4,188	.	7,864	56,041	6,057	2,283	4,630	.	12,970

1 Mode shown is that for departure from the United Kingdom.
2 Mode shown is that for return to the United Kingdom.
3 Includes motorcycles and scooters.
4 "Other" includes foot passengers, passengers with lorries and passengers with unknown vehicle type.
5 Prior to 1999, data for Irish Sea crossings were supplied separately by Irish Central Statistical Office.
   Since 1999, Irish Sea traffic is included in the International Passenger Survey.

☎020-7944 3088
Source - International Passenger Survey, ONS

1.11 Overseas travel by air:[1] visits to and from the UK: by area and purpose: 2008

(a) Visits to the United Kingdom: overseas residents by area of residence

Thousands

	North America	European Union [2]	Other Europe	Other areas	All areas
Business visit	819	3,803	550	817	5,989
Holiday - Independent [3]	938	4,137	528	1,069	6,671
Holiday - Inclusive tour [4]	105	432	75	96	708
Visiting friends and relatives	1,093	5,090	475	1,468	8,126
Miscellaneous	441	1,433	238	416	2,528
Total	3,396	14,895	1,866	3,866	24,023

(b) Visits abroad by United Kingdom residents: by area visited

Thousands

	North America	European Union [2]	Other Europe	Other areas	All areas
Business visit	770	4,939	654	1,040	7,403
Holiday - Independent [3]	1,928	16,189	1,349	2,578	22,043
Holiday - Inclusive tour [4]	847	9,916	1,424	2,510	14,696
Visiting friends and relatives	972	6,212	628	2,865	10,678
Miscellaneous	107	726	85	302	1,220
Total	4,624	37,982	4,140	9,296	56,041

1 Excludes passengers changing planes at UK airports.
2 "European Union" consists of 27 member states.
3 Not on a package holiday.
4 Excludes fly-cruise package holidays, which are included under 'other areas' in Table 1.12.

☎020-7944 3088
Source - International Passenger Survey, ONS

1.12 Overseas travel by sea and Channel Tunnel: visits to and from the United Kingdom by area, purpose and type of vehicle on board: 2008

Thousands

	(a) Visits to the United Kingdom by overseas residents: by area of residence				(b) Visits abroad by United Kingdom residents: by country visited			
	European Union [1]	Other Europe	Other areas	All areas	European Union [1]	Other Europe	Other areas	All areas
Business visit								
Without vehicle	384	8	50	442	643	0	8	650
Vehicle type:								
Car	256	2	3	262	399	3	-	402
Coach	99	3	4	106	161	0	0	161
Lorry	1,289	35	0	1,324	295	3	0	298
Motorcycle	0	0	0	0	2	0	0	2
Unknown	1	0	0	1	3	0	0	3
All	2,030	49	57	2,135	1,502	6	8	1,516
Holiday - Independent [2]								
Without vehicle	804	30	330	1,164	1,649	30	6	1,685
Vehicle type:								
Car	784	22	35	841	3,344	96	6	3,446
Coach	280	2	50	331	320	0	0	320
Lorry	0	0	0	0	6	0	0	6
Motorcycle	18	1	0	18	96	1	3	100
Unknown	10	1	-	11	15	0	-	16
All	1,895	56	414	2,366	5,431	128	15	5,574
Holiday Inclusive tour [3]								
Without vehicle	143	8	150	301	443	7	638	1,088
Vehicle type:								
Car	70	2	0	72	563	7	-	570
Coach	597	23	183	803	1,519	32	0	1,551
Lorry	0	0	0	0	0	0	0	0
Motorcycle	1	0	0	1	8	0	0	8
Unknown	0	0	0	0	0	0	-	-
All	812	33	333	1,178	2,533	46	638	3,217
Visiting friends and relatives								
Without vehicle	582	4	73	658	655	2	1	658
Vehicle type:								
Car	743	13	41	796	940	20	4	964
Coach	127	0	12	139	84	0	0	84
Lorry	0	0	0	0	2	0	0	2
Motorcycle	2	0	0	2	6	-	0	7
Unknown	5	0	0	5	0	0	0	0
All	1,459	16	125	1,600	1,687	23	5	1,714
Miscellaneous								
Without vehicle	179	12	26	217	186	2	1	189
Vehicle type:								
Car	186	1	3	190	548	0	0	548
Coach	100	5	3	107	167	0	0	167
Lorry	63	0	0	63	33	0	0	33
Motorcycle	6	0	0	6	10	0	0	10
Unknown	2	0	0	2	1	0	0	1
All	535	18	32	585	945	2	1	948
Total								
Without vehicle	2,092	62	628	2,782	3,576	41	653	4,270
Vehicle type:								
Car	2,039	40	82	2,161	5,794	126	10	5,930
Coach	1,202	34	251	1,487	2,251	32	0	2,283
Lorry	1,352	35	0	1,387	337	3	0	340
Motorcycle	28	1	0	28	122	2	3	127
Unknown	18	1	-	19	19	0	-	20
All	6,731	173	961	7,864	12,099	204	667	12,970

1 "European Union" consists of 27 member states.
2 Not on a package holiday.
3 Including UK residents on cruise and fly-cruise holidays under "other areas".

☎020-7944 3088
Source - International Passenger Survey, ONS

1.13 Household expenditure on transport: United Kingdom: 2000/01-2007

£ Per week/percentage

Transport (COICOP categories) [1]	2000/01	2001/02	2002/03	2003/04	2004/05	2005/06	2006	2006	2007
(a) Motoring and bicycle costs									
Purchase of vehicles	23.20	25.80	26.60	28.10	25.10	23.90	23.40	22.90	22.80
New cars and vans	10.60	10.70	11.30	11.40	10.10	9.60	8.30	8.00	7.80
Second-hand cars and vans	11.80	14.40	14.50	16.00	14.10	14.00	14.50	14.20	14.40
Motorcycles and scooters	0.60	0.50	0.70	0.60	0.50	..	0.30	0.30	0.40
Other vehicles (mainly bicycles)	..	0.20	0.20	0.20	0.30	0.20	0.30	0.30	0.20
Bicycle purchase	0.20	..	..	..	..	..	..	..	..
Spares, accessories, repairs and servicing	6.40	7.00	7.30	6.90	7.80	8.00	8.00	7.80	8.10
Car or van	6.00	6.80	6.90	6.60	7.50	7.70	7.70	7.50	7.80
Motorcycle	0.20	0.10	0.20	0.20	0.10	0.20	0.20	0.20	0.20
Bicycle	0.10	0.10	0.20	0.10	0.10	0.20	0.20	0.20	0.10
Petrol, diesel and other motor oils:	15.80	14.80	14.80	15.00	16.20	17.50	18.20	17.90	18.30
Petrol	14.00	12.70	12.70	12.40	13.40	14.30	14.50	14.30	14.10
Diesel	1.80	2.00	2.10	2.50	2.80	3.10	3.70	3.60	4.10
Other motor oils	0.10	0.10	0.10	0.10	0.10	0.10	0.10	0.10	0.10
Other motoring costs	1.80	1.80	1.90	1.90	2.40	2.30	2.40	2.30	2.40
All motoring and bicycle costs	47.20	49.40	50.70	51.90	51.40	51.80	52.10	50.90	51.60
(b) Transport services									
Rail and tube fares:	2.00	1.90	1.80	1.90	2.00	2.10	2.20	2.10	2.50
Season tickets	0.60	0.60	0.60	0.70	0.70	0.70	0.80	0.70	0.80
Other tickets	1.40	1.30	1.20	1.20	1.30	1.40	1.40	1.40	1.70
Bus and coach fares:	1.40	1.50	1.40	1.40	1.50	1.50	1.30	1.30	1.20
Season tickets	0.30	0.30	0.40	0.40	0.40	0.40	0.40	0.40	0.40
Other tickets	1.10	1.10	1.10	1.10	1.10	1.10	0.90	0.90	0.90
Combined tickets	0.90	1.00	0.80	0.70	0.80	1.00	1.00	1.00	1.30
Season tickets	0.70	0.80	0.60	0.50	0.60	0.80	0.80	0.80	0.90
Other tickets	0.20	0.20	0.20	0.10	0.20	0.20	0.20	0.20	0.40
Air and other travel and transport:	4.30	4.10	4.50	4.80	3.80	5.40	5.50	5.50	5.10
Air fares [2]	1.30	1.20	1.50	1.90	1.00	2.50	2.20	2.20	1.80
Other transport and travel	3.00	2.90	3.00	2.80	2.90	2.90	3.30	3.30	3.30
All transport services	8.60	8.40	8.50	8.80	8.10	9.90	10.00	9.90	10.10
All transport (excluding motor vehicle insurance and taxation and boat purchase and repairs)	55.90	57.80	59.20	60.70	59.60	61.70	62.00	60.80	61.70
All household expenditure	385.70	398.30	406.20	418.10	434.40	443.40	455.90	449.00	459.20
Percentage of household expenditure on transport	14.5	14.5	14.6	14.5	13.7	13.9	13.6	13.5	13.5
Key transport expenditure totals[3] :									
Motoring costs	55.10	58.50	61.70	62.40	62.60	63.80	62.40	61.40	62.00
Fares and other travel costs	9.50	9.50	9.70	9.60	9.50	11.10	11.10	10.90	10.90
All transport and travel	64.50	68.00	71.40	72.00	72.10	74.90	73.50	72.30	72.90
Adjusted for general inflation: 2007 prices									
Motoring costs	66.40	68.80	71.80	70.60	68.70	68.30	65.10	63.70	62.00
Fares and other travel costs	11.40	11.10	11.30	10.90	10.40	11.80	11.60	11.50	10.90
All transport and travel	77.80	79.90	83.10	81.50	79.10	80.10	76.60	75.20	72.90

1 Data for 2000/01 are based on old FES
  some items excluded under COICOP, eg motor caravans
  audio equipment, helmets (See Notes and Definitions).
  Additional changes were made in 2006, see the Survey for details.
2 Excludes air fare component of package holidays abroad.
3 Using FES classification, includes expenditure on motorcycles, bicycles,
  boats and vehicle taxation and insurance (see Notes and Definitions).

☎ 020 7944 4442
Source - Expenditure and Food Survey, ONS

For further details see *Family Spending: A Report on the 2007 Expenditure and Food Survey*
Available at:
http://www.statistics.gov.uk/downloads/theme_social/family_spending_2007/familyspending2008_web.pdf

1.14 Investment in transport: 1997/98-2007/08 [1]

											£ Million (outturn prices)
	1997/98	1998/99	1999/00	2000/01	2001/02	2002/03	2003/04	2004/05	2005/06	2006/07	2007/08
Road infrastructure											
Public [2]	3,267	2,957	3,071	3,344	3,643	3,955	3,621	4,079	4,313	4,764	4,807
Private	251	278	63	47	45	..	..	..	..	..	..
Total	3,518	3,235	3,134	3,391	3,688	3,955	3,621	4,079	4,313	4,764	4,807
Road vehicles [3]											
Cars and motor cycles: household	16,100	15,800	15,100	15,400	17,400	18,300	19,800	19,000	18,400	18,200	18,700
Cars and motor cycles: other	17,900	18,600	18,900	17,600	18,900	19,500	20,500	21,800	23,600	23,000	24,000
Cars and motor cycles: total	34,000	34,400	34,000	33,000	36,300	37,800	40,300	40,800	42,000	41,200	42,700
Other vehicles	6,900	7,100	7,300	7,400	7,800	7,500	8,400	9,100	9,600	9,500	10,500
Total	40,900	41,600	41,300	40,400	44,100	45,400	48,700	49,900	50,600	50,700	53,200
Rail infrastructure [4]											
National Rail	1,430	1,823	2,012	2,404	3,148	3,756	4,722	3,543	3,237	3,766	4,134
Other rail	898	821	1,163	386	504	485	464	729	1,219	1,276	1,433
Total	2,328	2,644	3,175	2,790	3,652	4,241	5,186	4,272	4,456	5,042	5,567
Rail rolling stock [4]											
National Rail	114	176	236	554	922	566	774	897	557	326	401
Other rail	82	85	84	75	75	75	177	165	169	124	104
Total	196	261	320	629	997	641	951	1,064	726	450	505
Ports infrastructure [4]	200	240	250	205	233	236	310	202	230	..	..
Airports											
Public [4,5]	216	140	161	163	57	71	70	62	116	..	..
Private [4]	565	542	511	566	630	784	1,373	1,434	1,662	..	..
Total	781	682	673	729	687	854	1,443	1,495	1,779	..	..

1 Some revisions have been made to the data since last year
2 Investment in road infrastructure includes all 'patching' but excludes local authority capital expenditure on car parks. Since 2002/03 it has not been possible to separately identify all the private expenditure from the total.
3 Source: Office for National Statistics
4 Partly based on figures for calendar years.
5 Prior to 2001/02 public airports investment includes air traffic control.

☎020-7944 3088
The figures in this table are outside the scope of National Statistics
Source - see Notes and Definitions

1.15 Central and local government expenditure on transport:[1] 2004/05-2008/09

				£ million (outturn prices)	
	2004/05	2005/06	2006/07	2007/08	2008/09 [2]
England	**10,024**	**10,992**	**11,855**	**14,540**	**13,790**
Central government expenditure [3, 4]	**2,446**	**2,691**	**3,062**	**2,992**	**2,941**
Capital	**1,284**	**1,354**	**1,590**	**1,368**	**1,414**
Strategic roads [5]	610	753	1,116	1,056	1,274
Olympics [6]	..	..	..	..	140
Channel Tunnel Rail Link [7]	674	601	474	312	..
Current / resource	**1,162**	**1,337**	**1,472**	**1,624**	**1,527**
Strategic roads [5]	1,146	1,284	1,347	1,353	1,343
Channel Tunnel Rail Link [7]	6	44	44	167	183
Crossrail	10	9	81	104	0
Local government expenditure	**7,578**	**8,301**	**8,793**	**11,548**	**10,850**
Capital	**2,904**	**3,461**	**3,480**	**5,912**	**4,749**
Roads	2,107	2,242	2,213	2,329	..
Car Parks	105	106	67	84	..
Public transport	682	1,103	1,186	3,465	..
Ports and Airports	11	10	14	33	..
Current / resource	**4,674**	**4,840**	**5,313**	**5,636**	**6,101**
Roads	2,336	2,569	2,619	2,708	2,740
Car Parks	-456	-490	-484	-516	-552
Revenue support to public transport	2,254	2,229	2,395	2,571	2,918
Concessionary fares [8]	539	532	783	873	994
Scotland	**1,627**	**2,175**	**2,500**	**2,710**	**2,801**
Central government expenditure [3,4]	**857**	**1,306**	**1,620**	**1,778**	**1,748**
Capital - Strategic roads	**70**	**95**	**146**	**136**	**395**
Current - Strategic roads	**255**	**218**	**260**	**265**	**..**
Subsidies to rail services in Scotland [9]	180	542	649	679	701
Subsidies to other transport industries	352	451	565	698	652
Local government expenditure	**770**	**869**	**880**	**932**	**1,054**
Capital	**271**	**334**	**448**	**485**	**504**
Roads	178	243	299	285	..
Public transport	93	91	149	199	..
Current / resource	**499**	**535**	**432**	**447**	**550**
Roads	352	380	373	388	..
Car Parks	-24	-25	-24	-24	..
Revenue support to public transport	81	85	72	76	..
Concessionary fares [8]	90	95	10	8	..
Wales	**575**	**641**	**843**	**869**	**826**
Central government expenditure [3]	**177**	**167**	**346**	**382**	**386**
Capital - rail	**113**	**105**	**128**	**144**	**134**
Capital - strategic roads	..	..	**6**	**21**	**15**
Current / resource - strategic roads	**33**	**33**	**40**	**31**	**41**
Current / resource - rail [9]	..	..	**148**	**158**	**162**
Current / resource - other transport	**31**	**28**	**25**	**28**	**35**
Local government expenditure	**398**	**474**	**497**	**486**	**440**
Capital	**141**	**203**	**214**	**186**	**135**
Roads	111	164	181	..	..
Car Parks	3	7	9	..	..
Public transport	26	33	24	..	..
Current / resource	**257**	**271**	**283**	**300**	**305**
Roads	178	186	192	205	..
Car Parks	-9	-9	-9	-9	..
Revenue support to public transport	41	46	48	..	..
Concessionary fares	46	48	52	..	..

1.15 (continued) Central and local government expenditure on transport:[1] 2004/05 - 2008/09

					£ million (outturn prices)
	2004/05	2005/06	2006/07	2007/08	2008/09 [2]
Great Britain [10]	**16,237**	**17,564**	**20,374**	**23,212**	**22,620**
Central government expenditure [3]	**7,491**	**7,920**	**10,204**	**10,245**	**10,277**
Capital	**3,731**	**3,634**	**5,074**	**4,919**	**5,653**
Allocated to individual countries [11]	**1,467**	**1,555**	**1,870**	**1,670**	**1,958**
Strategic roads[5]	793	954	1,390	1,336	1,803
Olympics	..	..	..	..	140
Channel Tunnel Rail Link [7]	674	601	474	312	..
Not allocated to individual countries	**2,264**	**2,080**	**3,204**	**3,249**	**3,696**
Rail [12]	2,185	2,019	3,134	3,197	3,635
Other roads and traffic	44	37	50	39	31
Other expenditure	34	24	21	13	30
Current / resource	**3,760**	**4,286**	**5,130**	**5,327**	**4,624**
Allocated to individual countries	**1,982**	**2,581**	**3,159**	**3,483**	**3,117**
Strategic roads[5]	1,434	1,536	1,646	1,649	1,384
Subsidies in England	16	53	125	271	183
Subsidies in Scotland	532	993	1,214	1,377	1,353
Subsidies in Wales	..	..	173	186	197
Not allocated to individual countries	**1,778**	**1,705**	**1,972**	**1,844**	**1,507**
Bus fuel duty rebates [13]	363	376	371	414	427
Rail [14]	1,034	874	1,071	860	499
Other roads and traffic	126	158	201	198	239
Air and water transport	38	49	71	101	73
Other expenditure	217	248	258	271	269
Local government expenditure	**8,746**	**9,644**	**10,170**	**12,967**	**12,343**
Capital	**3,317**	**3,998**	**4,142**	**6,583**	**5,387**
Roads	2,396	2,649	2,693	2,615	..
Car Parks	108	113	75	84	..
Public transport	801	1,227	1,360	3,665	..
Ports	11	10	14	33	..
Current / resource	**5,429**	**5,645**	**6,028**	**6,384**	**6,956**
Roads	2,867	3,135	3,185	3,301	..
Car Parks	-489	-523	-517	-549	..
Revenue support to public transport	2,376	2,360	2,515	..	..
Concessionary fares [8]	675	674	845	..	..

1   Some revisions have been made to the figures since last year. See also notes.
2   Includes provisional estimates.
3   Figures exclude grants to local authorities. For England excludes Rail expenditure.
4   Net expenditure includes EU grants treated as receipts.
5   In England, funding to Highways Agency, excluding the cost of capital.
6   Capital is mainly grants.
7   This item comprises the Government Spend on the channel tunnel rail link, including money paid to London and Continental Railways (LCR). It does not include all LCR spend.
8   From 1 April 2006 residents in England who were 60 or over and eligible disabled people were guaranteed free off-peak local bus travel within the local authority in which they lived accounting for the increase in England. As of 1 April 2006, Transport Scotland assumed responsibility for Concessionary fares, accounting for the large decrease in 2006-07 provisional outturn concessionary fares figures for Local Authorities in Scotland.
9   These figures includes grants paid to Strathclyde Passenger Transport and from 2006/07 funding for Network Rail in Scotland.
10 Great Britain total expenditure is not the sum of total expenditure for England, Scotland and Wales since it includes expenditure not allocated to individual countries.
11 Includes Welsh Rail Capital figures
12 Rail figures include direct grants to Network Rail for Great Britain to 2005/06 and England and Wales from 2006/07.
13 Mainly the Bus Service Operators Grant.
14 Net direct support for Passenger Rail Services and Grants to Passenger Transport Executives, Great Britain to 2005/06, England thereafter.

☎020-7944 4442
The figures in this table are outside the scope of National Statistics
Sources - DfT; CLG; Scottish Government; Welsh Assembly Government; HM Treasury

1.16 People in employment in transport related occupations: April to June 2008

Thousands

SOC2000[1] code	Occupation	Transport industries [2]	Other industries	All industries
1161	Transport and distribution managers	37	43	80
4134	Transport and distribution clerks	36	30	66
1232	Garage managers and proprietors	*	39	39
1226, 6212, 6219	Travel agencies and service occupations	45	49	94
3511, 3512, 8218	Air traffic controllers, pilots, operatives, etc	33	10	43
3513, 8217, 9141	Ship officers, seafarers, stevadores, dockers, etc	15	15	29
6213	Travel and tour guides	*	*	15
6214	Air travel assistants	32	*	32
6215, 8216, 3514	Rail travel assistants, operatives and train drivers	16	*	17
8213	Bus and coach drivers	116	14	130
8211	Heavy goods vehicle drivers	172	140	312
8212	Van drivers	24	189	213
8214	Taxi, cab drivers and chauffeurs	164	32	196
5231, 5233	Motor mechanics, auto engineers and electricians	20	187	207
5232, 5234	Vehicle body builders, painters and repairers	*	43	46
8135	Tyre, exhaust and windscreen fitters	*	16	16
8215	Driving instructors	*	37	39
8219	Other transport operatives	*	14	23
	Transport related occupations	731	864	1,595
	All in employment	1,337 [4]	27,300	29,314

1 Standard Occupation Classification 2000, see Notes and Definitions.
2 Based on 2000 Standard Industrial Classification (SIC2000)
    Transport, storage & communication:
  60.1 Transport via Railway
  60.2 Other inland transport
  61   Water Transport
  62   Air transport
  63   Supporting and auxiliary transport activities; activities of travel agencies.
3 Includes non transport related occupations in transport industries
NB: Data for some cells are not shown because they fall below the 10 thousand LFS reliability threshold.

☎020 7944 6104
Labour Force Survey Helpline: ☎01633 455732
Source - Labour Force Survey, ONS

1.17 Employee jobs in transport and related industries: March 1998-2009

Thousands

SIC 2003 code	Industry	1998	1999	2000	2001	2002	2003	2004	2005	2006	2007[1]	2008[1]	2009
60.1	Railways[2]	46	49	50	49	50	48	50	54	52	53	54	56
60.2, 60.3	Other land transport	443	459	455	454	460	450	458	464	477	474	488	475
61	Water transport	20	18	17	15	16	16	15	19	18	16	16	15
62	Air transport	78	85	93	90	85	88	90	85	89	89	88	75
63.1, 63.2, 63.4	Cargo handling, storage & other supporting activities	234	226	245	260	263	279	291	324	331	337	347	341
63.3	Travel agencies & tour operators	97	110	116	129	122	126	128	121	106	104	104	103
	Total: transport industries[3]	918	947	975	997	996	1,008	1,032	1,066	1,073	1,073	1,097	1,065
	Manufacture of transport equipment:												
34	Motor vehicles, trailers	236	227	221	212	206	201	196	187	172	157	155	134
35	Other transport equipment	154	162	167	171	159	150	141	140	138	143	150	148
50.1, 50.3-50.5	Retail distribution & filling stations	407	411	390	384	391	386	377	377	379	376	372	344
50.2	Maintenance and repair of motor vehicles	150	155	164	161	171	165	168	167	171	172	173	167
	Total: transport related industries[3]	947	955	942	928	926	902	882	871	860	848	993	793
	All transport and related industries and services[3]	1,864	1,902	1,918	1,925	1,922	1,909	1,914	1,937	1,933	1,921	2,090	1,858

1 The data in this table differ from those previously published. This is due to
benchmarking to the Annual Business Enquiry (ABI/1).
See the note on Tables 1.17 and 1.18 in the Notes and Definitions of Section 1.
2 See Notes and Definitions.
3 Any minor discrepancies between sub categories and totals are caused by rounding.

☎01633 456776
Source - Business Statistics Division, ONS

1.18 Employee jobs in transport and related industries: by sex and employment status: March 1990-2009

Thousands

		March 1990				March 1998				March 2008				March 2009			
		Male		Female		Male		Female		Male		Female		Male		Female	
SIC 2003 code	Industry	All	Part-time[1]	All	Part-time	All	Part-time	All	Part-time	All	Part-time	All	Part-time	All	Part-time	All	Part-time
60.1	Railways[2]	155	..	7	1	39	1	7	0	44	1	10	2	45	1	10	2
60.2, 60.3	Other land transport, and via pipelines	389	..	27	7	385	17	59	26	395	39	93	29	383	38	92	33
61	Water transport	42	..	4	0	16	0	4	1	11	2	0	1	0	2	4	1
62	Air transport	36	..	21	2	43	1	36	7	46	3	41	13	43	4	38	14
63	Miscellaneous transport and storage	216	..	84	8	212	12	119	20	291	24	160	47	282	26	161	50
	Total: transport industries[3]	838	..	143	18	695	31	225	55	787	69	308	92	764	71	305	100
	Manufacture of transport equipment:																
34	Motor vehicles, trailers	235	..	12	1	215	1	21	3	134	1	20	4	116	1	18	4
35	Other transport equipment	211	..	18	1	134	1	20	2	133	0	17	3	131	1	17	3
50.1, 50.3-50.5	Retail distribution & filling station	237	..	44	13	341	17	65	24	276	31	96	40	254	27	90	36
50.2	Maintenance & repair of motor vehicles	163	..	18	6	130	5	19	8	135	13	38	14	132	15	35	15
	Total: Transport related industries[3]	846	..	92	21	820	24	125	37	678	45	171	61	633	44	160	58
	All transport and related industries and services[3]	1,684	..	236	39	1,515	55	350	92	1,465	114	479	153	1,397	115	465	158

1 Prior to December 1991, male part-time job data were not collected.
2 See Notes and Definitions.
3 Any minor discrepancies between sub categories and totals are caused by rounding.

☎01633 456776
Source - Business Statistics Division, ONS

1.19a Retail and Consumer Prices Indices: Motoring Costs: 1998-2008

1998=100

	Consumer Prices Index		Retail Prices Index		
	All items CPI	Operation of personal transport equipment [1]	All items RPI	All motor [2]	Motoring Costs [3]
ONS Code	D7BT	D7CP	CHAW	CHBK	
1998	100.0	100.0	100.0	100.0	100.0
1999	101.3	106.3	101.5	102.4	107.1
2000	102.2	115.7	104.5	106.3	118.0
2001	103.4	115.3	106.4	105.7	117.9
2002	104.7	116.1	108.2	104.9	118.1
2003	106.1	121.9	111.3	106.3	123.4
2004	107.6	128.7	114.6	107.3	128.4
2005	109.8	137.7	117.9	108.0	135.2
2006	112.3	145.3	121.6	109.6	141.3
2007	114.9	150.7	126.8	111.0	146.6
2008	119.1	165.3	131.9	114.4	160.4

1 Operation of personal transport equipment, covering motor running costs, includes spare parts and accessories, fuels and lubricants, maintenance and repairs and other services. It excludes the purchase of a vehicle, unlike the RPI all motoring index (CHAW) given here and in Table 1.19b, and there are some other exclusions such as car insurance and vehicle excise duty, which are also included in the RPI, see Notes for further details.

2 The RPI all motor index includes purchase of a vehicle, maintenance, petrol and oil and tax and insurance, see Notes for further details.

3 The RPI motoring costs index excludes the purchase of a vehicle, but includes maintenance, petrol and oil and tax and insurance, see Notes for further details.

☎020-7944 4442
Source - Consumer Prices and Inflation Division, ONS

1.19b Retail Prices Index: transport components: 1998-2008

1998=100

		Motor vehicles						
	All items RPI	Purchase of vehicle	Mainten-ance	Petrol and oil	Tax and insurance	All motor [1]	Rail fares	Bus and Coach fares
ONS Code	CHAW	DOCS	DOCT	DOCU	DOCV	CHBK	DOCW	DOCX
1998	100.0	100.0	100.0	100.0	100.0	100.0	100.0	100.0
1999	101.5	95.7	103.9	108.4	108.1	102.4	103.6	103.6
2000	104.5	90.6	108.2	122.7	119.7	106.3	105.4	107.8
2001	106.4	89.3	113.5	116.4	126.0	105.7	109.5	112.4
2002	108.2	87.5	119.4	112.7	127.9	104.9	112.0	115.8
2003	111.3	85.1	126.5	116.8	133.4	106.3	113.9	120.6
2004	114.6	82.4	134.2	123.3	134.1	107.3	118.2	126.8
2005	117.9	78.1	142.3	134.1	132.3	108.0	123.0	135.2
2006	121.6	76.0	151.0	141.5	134.0	109.6	127.9	137.1
2007	126.8	74.0	158.8	145.3	140.1	111.0	134.5	144.9
2008	131.9	68.9	168.1	167.2	144.6	114.4	140.3	153.9

1 The RPI all motor index includes purchase of a vehicle, maintenance, petrol and oil and tax and insurance, see Notes for further details.

☎020-7944 4442
Source - Consumer Prices and Inflation Division, ONS

Transport Statistics Great Britain 2009

1.20 Gross Domestic Product, Retail Prices Index and Consumer Prices Index deflators:1998-2008

	Calendar years to 2008 price level				Fiscal years to 2008/09 price level		
Year	GDP Factor	RPI Factor	CPI Factor	Year	GDP Factor	RPI Factor	CPI Factor
1998	1.273	1.319	1.191	1998/99	1.269	1.312	1.195
1999	1.246	1.299	1.176	1999/00	1.244	1.291	1.182
2000	1.232	1.262	1.165	2000/01	1.228	1.254	1.173
2001	1.207	1.239	1.152	2001/02	1.202	1.235	1.155
2002	1.170	1.219	1.137	2002/03	1.164	1.210	1.142
2003	1.135	1.185	1.122	2003/04	1.132	1.177	1.127
2004	1.107	1.151	1.107	2004/05	1.101	1.142	1.111
2005	1.085	1.119	1.085	2005/06	1.081	1.112	1.088
2006	1.056	1.084	1.061	2006/07	1.050	1.072	1.060
2007	1.026	1.040	1.036	2007/08	1.022	1.030	1.038
2008	1.000	1.000	1.000	2008/09	1.000	1.000	1.000

☎020-7944 4442
Sources - GDP: National Expenditure and Income Division, ONS
RPI and CPI: Consumer Prices and Inflation Division, ONS

2 Aviation:

Notes and Definitions

In the *United Kingdom Airport Statistics* (annual 2008) published by the Civil Aviation Authority (CAA) the Isle of Man is now excluded from the UK total. Therefore the time series shown in tables 2.1, 2.2a, 2.2b and 2.2c has been revised to be consistent with the CAA statistics.

Some of the figures in table 2.1 are higher than the time series shown in CAA's *United Kingdom Airport Statistics* (annual 2008) due to CAA tables excluding data for airports that have ceased to handle traffic or closed, e.g. Sheffield City airport.

Tables 2.2a – 2.2c, and 2.8 are derived from the CAA publication *United Kingdom Airport Statistics* (annual). Thus;

TSGB table	CAA publication table No
2.2a	4.1 and 5
2.2b	8, 10.1 and 10.2
2.2c	13.1 and 14
2.8	12.1

Table 2.3 is derived from the CAA *Punctuality Statistics*.

Tables 2.4, 2.6 and 2.11 are derived from the CAA publication *United Kingdom Airline Statistics* (annual) and earlier volumes. Thus;

TSGB table	CAA publication table No
2.4	1.7.1/2/3/4 and 1.8.1/2/3/4
2.6	1.11.2
2.11	1.14

CAA compiles the statistics from returns submitted by United Kingdom airlines.

More information and statistics can be found at:

http://www.caa.co.uk/

Tables 2.7 and 2.12 are compiled from data supplied by the International Civil Aviation Organisation (ICAO).

Table 2.9 is compiled from data supplied by the CAA's Safety Data Unit.

Table 2.10 is compiled from data supplied by the UK Airprox Board.

Traffic at United Kingdom airports: 2.2

The table shows air transport movements (landings and take-offs of aircraft engaged in commercial air transport), terminal passengers (arrivals and departures) and freight handled (set down and picked up).

Domestic traffic (movements, passengers and freight) shown is half that published in the CAA *Airport Statistics*, to remove double counting at airport of arrival and departure. The figures for individual airports have not, however, been adjusted to eliminate double counting of domestic traffic.

Terms used in Table 2.2 are defined as follows:

Air transport movements: All scheduled movements (whether loaded or empty) and loaded charter movements, but excludes empty positioning flights by scheduled aircraft and empty charter movements.

International services: These services are flown between the United Kingdom, Isle of Man or Channel Islands and points in other countries.

Scheduled services: Those performed according to a published timetable, including those supplementary thereto, available for use by members of the public.

Non-scheduled services: Air transport movements other than scheduled services.

Terminal passengers: All revenue and non-revenue passengers joining or leaving an aircraft at a United Kingdom airport (a passenger who changes from one aircraft to another, carrying the same flight number, is counted as a terminal passenger both on arrival and departure). Transit passengers who arrive and depart on the same aircraft are not included.

Freight: Excludes mail and passengers' and crews' permitted baggage, but all other property carried on an aircraft is included. Thus excess baggage is included, as are diplomatic bags. Freight in transit through an airport on the same aircraft is excluded.

Punctuality at United Kingdom Airports: 2.3

London airports include Heathrow, Gatwick, Stansted, Luton and London City. Regional airports include Manchester, Birmingham, Glasgow, Edinburgh and Newcastle.

Transport Statistics Great Britain 2009

Main outputs of United Kingdom airlines: 2.4

Table 2.4 shows the carriage of revenue passengers, cargo (freight and mail) on services flown by United Kingdom airlines, scheduled and non-scheduled (but excluding air-taxi operations and sub-charter operations performed on behalf of United Kingdom airlines). Passenger kilometres are calculated by multiplying the number of revenue passengers carried on each flight stage by the stage distance. Passenger seat occupancy is calculated as passenger kilometres as a percentage of seat kilometres available.

Cargo (freight and mail) uplifted are calculated by counting each tonne of revenue cargo or mail on a particular journey once only and not repeatedly on each individual stage of the flight. Cargo tonne kilometres are calculated by multiplying the number of tonnes of revenue load on each stage flight by the stage distance.

Terms used in Table 2.4 are defined as follows:

Passengers: Travellers are counted as revenue passengers if the air carrier receives commercial remuneration. They are counted only once on a particular flight (with one flight number) and not for each stage of that flight.

International services: These services are flown between the United Kingdom, Isle of Man or Channel Islands and points in other countries.

Domestic services: Those entirely within the United Kingdom, Isle of Man and Channel Islands.

Scheduled services: Those performed according to a published timetable, including those supplementary thereto, available for use by members of the public.

Non-scheduled services: Air transport movements other than scheduled services.

Forecasts of air traffic demand: 2.5

The forecasts show the expected number of UK and foreign passengers passing through UK airports up to 2030, after accounting for airport capacity constraints. The underlying unconstrained forecasts are based on econometric equations which specify a relationship between passenger traffic and a number of explanatory variables which determine it. The key variables determining air traffic were found to be domestic and foreign economic growth (principally GDP); air fares; trade; and exchange rates. The relationships derived from past years' data are applied to projections of future year values of the explanatory variables to calculate forecasts of air traffic. A range of forecasts is given to reflect the uncertainties

inherent in long term forecasting. The range of unconstrained forecasts are processed in the DfT National Air Passenger Allocation Model which forecasts how passenger demand will split between UK airports taking account of likely future constraints on air transport movements (and thus passengers) at UK airports. The future constraints assume the increases to airport capacity supported in the 2003 White Paper.

United Kingdom airline fleet: 2.6

Table 2.6 gives information on the fleet size of selected larger United Kingdom airlines.

Activity at major airports: 2.7

Table 2.7 gives a comparison of the activity at some of the world's major airports. Airports are selected such that the largest 25 (as reported to ICAO) by number of terminal passengers are included. The ranking is only a guide as 'non-reporting' airports are excluded. Some airports which did not report in previous years have entered the table. A substantial proportion of the figures are estimated by ICAO on the basis of part-year data; the table is therefore of use only as a guide.

United Kingdom international passenger movements: 2.8

The Channel Islands and Isle of Man airports are included as United Kingdom airports in this table, unlike other tables in this chapter. This is consistent with CAA's airport statistics Table 12.1.

The table records the origin and destination of all revenue and non-revenue terminal passengers on air transport movement flights as reported to UK airport authorities by UK and foreign airlines.

Passengers changing planes are recorded twice, on arrival and departure. Passengers carried in aircraft chartered by British government departments, and HM and other armed forces travelling in the course of their duties are excluded. Operators are required to report, in respect of each service operated, the points of uplift and discharge of each passenger. The figures record data for direct flights only, so they may not reflect a passenger's entire air journey: the point at which a passenger disembarks from a particular service may not represent the passenger's ultimate destination.

Although operators are asked to report all passenger journeys, in some cases the actual point of uplift or discharge is not recorded. In such cases, all passengers are allocated to the aircraft's origin or ultimate destination. All identifiable diversions are reallocated to the point of intended operation.

"Former USSR" includes: Albania, Armenia, Azerbaijan, Belarus, Georgia, Kazakhstan, Kyrgyzstan, Republic Of Moldova, Russia, Turkmenistan, Ukraine, and Uzbekistan.

"Former Yugoslavia" includes: Bosnia-Herzegovina, Croatia, Serbia, Montenegro, and Macedonia.

"Rest of Europe" includes: Faroe Islands, and Iceland.

Casualties: 2.9

The table includes deaths, serious and minor injuries where an aircraft was engaged in airline, air taxi, general aviation (including private flights) and other commercial (including training) operations.

Terms used in Table 2.9 are defined as follows:

Airline: Public transport flights, which are subject to a United Kingdom Air Transport Licence. Also public transport flights which are not subject to a United Kingdom Air Transport Licence, but which utilise aircraft having a maximum take-off weight of 15 tonnes or more. Positioning flights are excluded. There are no rotary wing services by United Kingdom registered aircraft in foreign airspace, and no rotary wing or air taxi services by foreign registered aircraft in United Kingdom airspace.

Air Taxi: Public Transport flights which are not subject to a United Kingdom Air Transport Licence and which utilise aircraft having a maximum take-off weight of less than 15 tonnes. Positioning flights are excluded.

General Aviation: Includes executive, club and group, private and training flights, but does not include accidents to gliders, microlights, hang gliders or hot-air balloons.

Aircraft proximity: 2.10

Table 2.10 reflects the Civil Aviation Authority's practice, introduced in 1990, of including controller-reported incidents. Further, the term "airmiss" has been replaced by AIRPROX, meaning aircraft proximity hazard.

An AIRPROX is a situation in which, in the opinion of a pilot or controller, the distance between aircraft as well as their relative positions and speed have been such that the safety of the aircraft was or may have been compromised. AIRPROX can occur between various combinations of commercial, military and private aircraft. The numbers of AIRPROX incidents involving commercial transport aircraft are shown separately in the table.

All AIRPROX reports are assessed and, following guidelines given by the International Civil Aviation Organisation, the degrees of risk involved are categorised as 'risk of collision', 'safety not assured', 'no risk of collision', and 'risk not determined'.

Employment: 2.11

Table 2.11 shows the average number of personnel employed by United Kingdom airlines in the United Kingdom and overseas. Personnel employed by companies performing solely air-taxi operations are excluded.

Terms used in Table 2.11 are defined as follows:

Other Cockpit Personnel: Flight engineers, radio operators and navigators.

Cabin Attendants Cabins: Pursers, stewards and flight attendants.

Maintenance and Overhaul Personnel: Ground personnel, including supervising, planning and inspection personnel at Maintenance and Overhaul Personnel shops. Also includes stores and supplies personnel, time-keepers and accounts personnel at Maintenance and Overhaul Personnel workshops.

Ticketing and Sales Personnel: Personnel engaged in ticketing, sales and promotional activities.

Passenger traffic via major international airlines: 2.12

Table 2.12 gives a comparison of the major international airlines. Airlines are selected such that the largest 25 (as reported to ICAO) by passengers uplifted are included. The ranking is only a guide as 'non-reporting' airlines are excluded.

Transport Statistics Great Britain 2009

2.1 Activity at civil aerodromes: United Kingdom:[1] 1950-2008

For greater detail of the years 1998-2008 see Table 2.2

Year	Air transport movements: aircraft landings or take-offs (thousands)	Terminal passengers (thousands)	Freight handled [2] (thousand tonnes)
1950	195	2,133	31
1951	187	2,471	44
1952	195	2,776	40
1953	214	3,419	64
1954	232	4,004	84
1955	259	4,831	113
1956	293	5,617	121
1957	329	6,600	139
1958	340	6,761	167
1959	358	7,867	226
1960	402	10,075	279
1961	447	12,249	313
1962	449	13,793	344
1963	458	15,506	360
1964	480	17,649	399
1965	508	19,918	418
1966	556	22,582	517
1967	566	24,003	488
1968	560	24,845	524
1969	591	28,064	585
1970	607	31,606	580
1971	630	34,934	532
1972	669	39,125	649
1973	719	43,125	699
1974	710	40,082	717
1975	701	41,846	638
1976	740	44,666	659
1977	759	45,927	705
1978	862	52,829	748
1979	924	56,992	797
1980	954	57,823	744
1981	927	57,771	724
1982	973	58,778	693
1983	1,019	61,109	726
1984	1,079	67,572	861
1985	1,097	70,434	850
1986	1,125	75,161	881
1987	1,193	86,041	976
1988	1,280	93,162	1,088
1989	1,375	98,913	1,151
1990	1,420	102,418	1,193
1991 [3, 4]	1,353	95,297	1,122
1992 [4]	1,432	105,663	1,235
1993 [4]	1,468	111,786	1,373
1994 [4]	1,469	121,659	1,585
1995 [4]	1,534	128,857	1,700
1996 [4]	1,611	135,226	1,767
1997 [4]	1,682	145,989	1,938
1998 [4]	1,785	158,163	2,076
1999 [4]	1,877	167,695	2,186
2000 [4]	1,962	179,187	2,311
2001 [4]	2,005	180,534	2,143
2002 [4]	1,998	188,043	2,193
2003 [4]	2,059	199,211	2,206
2004 [4]	2,176	214,926	2,369
2005 [4]	2,300	227,416	2,361
2006 [4]	2,344	234,416	2,315
2007 [4]	2,379	239,968	2,325
2008	2,327	235,359	2,282

1 Includes double counting of domestic traffic, unlike Table 2.2.
2 Includes freight set down and picked up. Excludes mail and passengers' luggage.
3 Excludes air-taxi operations and Isle of Man from 1991.
4 Data for 1991-2007 have been revised to exclude the Isle of Man airport from the UK total.
 In the CAA airport statistics for 2008 the Isle of Man is now excluded from published UK totals.

☎020-7944 3088
The figures in this table are outside
the scope of National Statistics
Source - Civil Aviation Authority

2.2 Traffic at United Kingdom airports: by type of service and operator: 1998-2008

(a) Air transport movements (aircraft landings or take-offs)											Thousands
	1998	1999	2000	2001	2002	2003	2004	2005	2006	2007	2008
International (incl. traffic to/from oil rigs): [1]											
Scheduled	872	950	1,018	1,030	1,026	1,073	1,146	1,222	1,260	1,317	1,309
Non-scheduled	272	261	266	270	268	259	250	252	260	257	239
Total	1,144	1,211	1,284	1,300	1,295	1,332	1,396	1,474	1,520	1,574	1,548
Domestic: [1,2]											
Scheduled	296	308	314	328	329	343	370	393	393	386	372
Non-scheduled	24	25	25	25	23	21	20	20	19	17	18
Total	320	333	339	353	352	363	390	414	412	403	390
All traffic: [1,2]	1,464	1,544	1,623	1,654	1,647	1,695	1,786	1,887	1,932	1,976	1,938
Selected airports: [3]											
Gatwick	240	245	251	244	234	234	241	252	254	259	256
Heathrow	441	449	460	458	460	457	470	472	471	476	473
Luton	44	51	56	56	55	58	64	75	79	83	86
Stansted	102	132	144	151	152	169	177	178	190	192	177
Birmingham	88	98	108	111	112	116	109	113	109	104	103
Bristol	32	33	34	41	46	50	55	61	66	59	60
East Midlands	39	39	40	41	49	54	56	54	56	61	66
Manchester	162	169	178	182	178	192	208	218	213	207	191
Newcastle	41	42	43	46	44	42	50	55	58	58	55
Aberdeen	85	78	78	83	80	77	81	89	98	103	100
Edinburgh	72	81	86	98	105	105	112	116	116	115	114
Glasgow	83	86	88	91	87	88	92	97	97	94	87
Belfast International	37	43	41	46	38	40	43	48	48	52	54

1 In the CAA airport statistics for 2008 the Isle of Man has been excluded from the published UK totals.
  Therefore the timeseries in this table has been revised to be consistent with CAA statistics.
2 Adjusted to eliminate double counting.
3 Includes double counting.

☎020-7944 3088
The figures in this table are outside
the scope of National Statistics
Source - Civil Aviation Authority

2.2 (continued) Traffic at United Kingdom airports: by type of service and operator: 1998-2008

(b) Terminal passengers (arrivals or departures)   **Millions**

	1998	1999	2000	2001	2002	2003	2004	2005	2006	2007	2008
International (incl. traffic to/from oil rigs): [1]											
Scheduled	89.2	96.7	105.5	104.9	108.8	116.7	130.8	143.7	151.9	160.1	160.9
Non-scheduled	36.1	36.7	37.1	37.9	37.9	37.4	36.3	34.3	33.5	31.9	28.9
Total	125.3	133.4	142.6	142.8	146.7	154.1	167.1	178.0	185.4	192.0	189.8
Domestic: [1,2]											
Scheduled	16.2	17.0	18.1	18.6	20.5	22.3	23.7	24.5	24.3	23.8	22.6
Non-scheduled	0.2	0.2	0.2	0.2	0.2	0.2	0.2	0.2	0.2	0.2	0.2
Total	16.4	17.2	18.3	18.9	20.7	22.6	23.9	24.7	24.5	24.0	22.8
All traffic: [1,2]	141.7	150.5	160.9	161.7	167.3	176.7	191.0	202.7	209.9	216.0	212.6
Selected airports:											
International:											
Gatwick	26.3	27.6	29.0	28.1	26.1	26.0	27.5	28.8	30.0	31.1	30.4
Heathrow	53.2	54.8	56.9	53.8	56.4	56.6	60.2	61.0	61.3	62.1	61.3
Luton	3.3	3.9	4.4	4.8	4.7	5.1	5.9	7.5	7.9	8.4	8.9
Stansted	5.6	8.0	10.4	11.6	13.6	16.0	18.2	19.3	21.0	21.2	20.0
Birmingham	5.4	5.8	6.3	6.5	6.7	7.5	7.5	7.8	7.5	7.6	8.1
Bristol	1.4	1.6	1.7	2.1	2.5	2.8	3.3	3.8	4.3	4.6	5.1
East Midlands	1.8	1.9	1.9	2.0	2.7	3.4	3.6	3.5	4.0	4.7	4.9
Manchester	14.6	14.7	15.5	16.3	15.9	16.4	17.7	18.7	18.6	18.7	18.1
Newcastle	2.0	2.0	2.2	2.4	2.2	2.5	3.0	3.3	3.6	3.9	3.5
Aberdeen	0.9	0.8	0.8	0.9	0.9	1.0	1.0	1.2	1.3	1.5	1.5
Edinburgh	1.0	1.3	1.5	1.8	1.8	2.0	2.2	2.3	2.7	3.4	3.7
Glasgow	3.0	3.3	3.4	3.4	3.5	3.5	3.9	4.2	4.2	4.1	3.9
Belfast International	0.8	1.0	0.9	1.0	0.9	1.0	1.2	1.4	1.5	1.8	2.1
Domestic: [3]											
Gatwick	2.7	2.8	2.9	3.0	3.4	3.9	3.9	3.9	4.1	4.0	3.7
Heathrow	7.2	7.1	7.4	6.6	6.7	6.7	6.9	6.7	6.0	5.8	5.6
Luton	0.9	1.3	1.7	1.8	1.7	1.7	1.6	1.6	1.5	1.5	1.3
Stansted	1.2	1.5	1.4	2.0	2.5	2.7	2.7	2.7	2.7	2.6	2.3
Birmingham	1.2	1.1	1.2	1.2	1.2	1.4	1.3	1.5	1.5	1.5	1.5
Bristol	0.4	0.4	0.4	0.5	0.9	1.1	1.3	1.4	1.4	1.3	1.2
East Midlands	0.4	0.4	0.3	0.3	0.5	0.8	0.8	0.7	0.7	0.7	0.7
Manchester	2.6	2.7	2.8	2.8	2.7	3.1	3.3	3.4	3.5	3.2	2.9
Newcastle	0.9	0.9	1.0	1.0	1.2	1.5	1.7	1.8	1.8	1.7	1.5
Aberdeen	1.6	1.5	1.5	1.7	1.6	1.5	1.6	1.7	1.8	1.9	1.8
Edinburgh	3.5	3.7	4.0	4.3	5.1	5.5	5.8	6.1	5.9	5.6	5.3
Glasgow	3.4	3.5	3.6	3.8	4.3	4.6	4.6	4.6	4.6	4.6	4.2
Belfast International	1.8	2.1	2.2	2.6	2.7	3.0	3.2	3.4	3.5	3.4	3.1
All traffic: [3]											
Gatwick	29.0	30.4	31.9	31.1	29.5	29.9	31.4	32.7	34.1	35.2	34.2
Heathrow	60.4	61.9	64.3	60.4	63.0	63.2	67.1	67.7	67.3	67.9	66.9
Luton	4.2	5.2	6.1	6.6	6.5	6.8	7.5	9.1	9.4	9.9	10.2
Stansted	6.8	9.5	11.8	13.6	16.0	18.7	20.9	22.0	23.7	23.8	22.3
Birmingham	6.6	6.9	7.5	7.7	7.9	8.9	8.8	9.3	9.1	9.1	9.6
Bristol	1.8	2.0	2.1	2.7	3.4	3.9	4.6	5.2	5.7	5.9	6.2
East Midlands	2.2	2.3	2.2	2.3	3.2	4.3	4.4	4.2	4.7	5.4	5.6
Manchester	17.2	17.4	18.3	19.1	18.6	19.5	21.0	22.1	22.1	21.9	21.1
Newcastle	2.9	2.9	3.2	3.4	3.4	3.9	4.7	5.2	5.4	5.6	5.0
Aberdeen	2.5	2.3	2.3	2.5	2.5	2.5	2.6	3.0	3.2	3.4	3.3
Edinburgh	4.5	5.0	5.5	6.0	6.9	7.5	8.0	8.4	8.6	9.0	9.0
Glasgow	6.4	6.8	7.0	7.2	7.8	8.1	8.6	8.8	8.8	8.7	8.1
Belfast International	2.6	3.0	3.1	3.6	3.6	4.0	4.4	4.8	5.0	5.2	5.2

1 In the CAA airport statistics for 2008 the Isle of Man has been excluded from the published UK totals.
  Therefore the timeseries in this table has been revised to be consistent with CAA statistics.
2 Adjusted to eliminate double counting.
3 Includes double counting.

☎020-7944 3088
The figures in this table are outside
the scope of National Statistics
Source - Civil Aviation Authority

2.2 (continued) Traffic at United Kingdom airports: by type of service and operator: 1998-2008

(c) Freight handled [1]											Thousand tonnes
	1998	1999	2000	2001	2002	2003	2004	2005	2006	2007	2008
International (incl. traffic to/from oil rigs): [2]											
Scheduled	1,711	1,787	1,864	1,701	1,768	1,817	1,988	1,875	1,794	1,814	1,815
Non-scheduled	274	301	339	333	319	273	259	352	386	406	377
Total	1,985	2,088	2,204	2,034	2,086	2,091	2,247	2,226	2,179	2,220	2,191
Domestic: [2,3]											
Scheduled	14	14	13	11	10	14	18	9	4	4	3
Non-scheduled	31	36	41	44	44	43	43	58	63	49	42
Total	46	49	54	55	54	58	61	67	68	53	45
All traffic: [2,3]	2,031	2,137	2,258	2,089	2,140	2,148	2,308	2,294	2,247	2,272	2,237
Selected airports: [4]											
Gatwick	274	294	319	280	243	223	218	223	212	171	108
Heathrow	1,209	1,265	1,307	1,180	1,235	1,223	1,325	1,306	1,263	1,311	1,397
Luton	26	23	33	23	20	23	26	23	18	38	41
Stansted	179	174	166	166	184	199	226	237	224	204	198
Birmingham	18	29	9	12	13	12	10	13	15	14	12
East Midlands	123	128	178	195	219	227	253	267	272	275	262
Kent International	6	23	32	36	32	43	27	8	21	28	26
Liverpool	25	25	29	23	14	12	9	9	6	4	4
Manchester	101	108	117	106	113	123	149	147	149	165	142
Edinburgh	14	18	18	16	21	25	27	30	36	19	12
Glasgow	8	9	9	6	5	5	8	9	6	4	4
Prestwick	40	41	41	43	40	40	34	29	29	32	23
Belfast International	25	26	31	32	29	30	32	38	38	38	36

1 Includes freight set down and picked up. Excludes mail and passengers' luggage.
2 In the CAA airport statistics for 2008 the Isle of Man has been excluded from the published UK
   totals. Therefore the timeseries in this table has been revised to be consistent with CAA statistics.
3 Adjusted to eliminate double counting.
4 Includes double counting.

☎020-7944 3088
The figures in this table are outside
the scope of National Statistics
Source - Civil Aviation Authority

2.3 Punctuality at United Kingdom Airports: Percentage of flights on time (within 15 minutes): 1998-2008

	All reporting London airports [1]		All reporting regional airports [2]		All reporting airports		Percentage
	Scheduled	Charter	Scheduled	Charter	Scheduled	Charter	
1998	69	50	78	56	72	53	
1999	69	49	76	53	71	51	
2000	70	52	77	55	72	53	
2001	71	60	77	58	73	58	
2002	69	68	76	68	72	68	
2003	75	73	79	74	76	74	
2004	73	69	78	71	75	70	
2005	71	63	77	70	73	67	
2006	66	62	76	70	69	67	
2007	66	63	75	69	69	66	
2008	69	59	78	64	71	62	

1 Includes Heathrow, Gatwick, Stansted, Luton and London City.
2 Includes Manchester, Birmingham, Glasgow, Edinburgh and Newcastle.

☎020-7944 3088
The figures in this table are outside
the scope of National Statistics
Source - Civil Aviation Authority

2.4 Main outputs of United Kingdom airlines: by type of service:[1] 1998-2008

(a) Aircraft kilometres flown										Million kilometres	
	1998	1999	2000	2001	2002	2003	2004	2005	2006	2007	2008
International:											
Scheduled	789	827	895	920	921	965	1,059	1,178	1,251	1,333	1,371
Non-scheduled	403	427	447	437	412	431	423	414	425	444	408
Total	1,192	1,254	1,342	1,357	1,333	1,396	1,483	1,592	1,677	1,778	1,779
Domestic:											
Scheduled	118	120	121	128	126	123	138	147	148	141	137
Non-scheduled	7	7	7	8	9	8	8	7	7	6	7
Total	125	127	129	136	135	131	146	154	155	147	144
All services:											
Scheduled	886	947	1,016	1,048	1,047	1,088	1,198	1,326	1,400	1,474	1,508
Non-scheduled	410	434	455	445	421	440	431	421	432	451	414
Total	1,297	1,381	1,471	1,493	1,468	1,528	1,629	1,746	1,831	1,925	1,923

(b) Passengers uplifted											Millions
International:											
Scheduled	45	48	52	51	52	56	64	71	75	80	84
Non-scheduled	31	32	33	34	34	33	32	30	29	29	26
Total	76	81	86	85	86	89	96	101	104	108	110
Domestic:											
Scheduled	16.6	17.1	18.0	18.2	19.8	20.8	22.5	23.1	22.9	22.1	20.9
Non-scheduled	0.3	0.2	0.2	0.3	0.3	0.3	0.2	0.2	0.2	0.2	0.1
Total	16.9	17.4	18.2	18.5	20.2	21.0	22.7	23.3	23.0	22.3	21.0
All services:											
Scheduled	62	65	70	69	72	76	86	94	98	102	105
Non-scheduled	31	33	33	34	34	34	32	30	30	29	26
Total	93	98	104	104	107	110	118	124	127	131	131

(c) Passenger kilometres flown										Billion kilometres	
International:											
Scheduled	145	153	163	151	148	156	173	191	204	218	224
Non-scheduled	84	87	90	90	88	89	90	87	86	86	79
Total	229	240	253	241	236	245	263	278	290	305	302
Domestic:											
Scheduled	6.9	7.2	7.5	7.6	8.3	8.9	9.5	9.8	9.8	9.4	9.0
Non-scheduled	0.1	0.1	0.1	0.1	0.1	0.2	0.2	0.1	0.1	0.1	0.1
Total	7.0	7.3	7.6	7.7	8.5	9.1	9.8	9.9	9.9	9.5	9.0
All services:											
Scheduled	152	160	170	159	156	165	183	200	213	228	233
Non-scheduled	84	87	90	90	88	90	90	87	86	87	79
Total	236	248	261	249	244	254	273	287	300	314	311

(d) Passenger seat occupancy											Percentage
International:											
Scheduled	71.9	71.1	72.6	70.9	74.5	74.8	75.8	76.1	76.2	76.5	76.9
Non-scheduled	89.7	89.4	89.5	89.9	90.4	89.2	89.9	89.0	88.3	88.1	89.0
Total	77.5	76.8	77.9	77.0	79.7	79.5	80.1	79.7	79.4	79.5	79.7
Domestic:											
Scheduled	62.0	60.6	64.2	61.8	66.0	70.5	68.0	65.3	66.1	65.3	64.3
Non-scheduled	69.2	66.4	62.2	62.3	60.6	66.0	61.8	37.9	43.4	46.4	49.1
Total	62.1	60.7	64.9	61.8	65.9	70.4	67.9	65.0	65.9	65.1	64.2
All services:											
Scheduled	71.3	70.6	72.2	69.9	74.0	74.5	75.3	75.5	75.6	76.0	76.3
Non-scheduled	89.7	89.3	89.4	89.9	90.3	89.1	89.8	88.9	88.2	88.1	88.9
Total	76.9	76.2	77.4	75.9	79.1	79.1	79.6	79.1	78.9	79.0	79.1

2.4 (continued) Main outputs of United Kingdom airlines: by type of service:[1] 1998-2008

(e) Cargo uplifted (freight and mail)										Thousand tonnes	
	1998	1999	2000	2001	2002	2003	2004	2005	2006	2007	2008
International:											
Scheduled	800	834	873	723	752	783	879	911	938	934	974
Non-scheduled	161	178	151	114	101	105	122	104	125 [2]	220	170
Total	960	1,012	1,024	837	853	888	1,002	1,016	1,063 [2]	1,154	1,144
Domestic:											
Scheduled	32	26	25	13	17	17	15	10	8	7	6
Non-scheduled	66	71	72	75	70	64	56	80	79	72	82
Total	98	97	96	88	87	81	71	90	87	79	88
All services:											
Scheduled	831	860	897	736	769	801	895	921	946	941	980
Non-scheduled	227	249	223	189	170	169	178	185	204 [2]	292	252
Total	1,059	1,109	1,120	925	939	969	1,072	1,106	1,150 [2]	1,233	1,232

(f) Cargo tonne-kilometres flown (freight and mail)										Millions	
International:											
Scheduled	4,829	5,068	5,330	4,643	4,991	5,235	5,693	6,085	6,311	6,308	6,381
Non-scheduled	413	460	533	519	295	343	331	326	725 [2]	1,427	1,084
Total	5,242	5,528	5,863	5,162	5,286	5,578	6,024	6,411	7,036 [2]	7,735	7,465
Domestic:											
Scheduled	12	10	10	8	6	6	5	3	2	2	2
Non-scheduled	22	24	24	26	25	24	23	34	35	33	35
Total	34	34	33	34	31	30	29	37	37	35	37
All services:											
Scheduled	4,841	5,078	5,339	4,651	4,997	5,242	5,698	6,088	6,313	6,311	6,383
Non-scheduled	434	484	557	545	320	367	354	360	760 [2]	1,460	1,120
Total	5,275	5,562	5,896	5,196	5,317	5,608	6,053	6,449	7,073 [2]	7,770	7,502

1 Excludes sub-charter operations performed on behalf of UK airlines.
2 The increase in cargo in 2006 is due to a foreign airline
 registering as a UK airline in August 2006.

☎020-7944 3088
The figures in this table are outside
the scope of National Statistics
Source - Civil Aviation Authority

Transport Statistics Great Britain 2009

2.5 Forecasts of air traffic demand:[1] 2004 - 2030

					Million terminal passengers at UK airports[2]	
	2004	2010	2015	2020	2025	2030
International: [3]						
Low	.	200	220	250	290	320
Mid	175	210	250	290	325	360
High	.	210	260	300	345	385
Domestic: [4]						
Low	.	50	60	70	80	90
Mid	40	50	60	70	80	90
High	.	50	60	70	85	100
Total: [5]						
Low	.	250	280	320	370	410
Mid	215	260	310	355	405	455
High	.	260	320	370	430	480

1 Forecasts of UK terminal passengers, constrained by airport capacity, as published in the January 2009 'UK Air Passenger Demand & CO_2 Forecasts' report for a base year of 2004, assuming the additional South East capacity supported in the 2003 White Paper, i.e. a second runway at Stansted around 2015 and a third runway at Heathrow around 2020. The low-high range is found by using the minimum and maximum annual forecasts from the sensitivity tests reported (Low = High High Oil price, High = High GDP scenario).
2 Figures are rounded to the nearest 5 million terminal passengers.
3 Figures include international to international interlining passengers transferring at UK airports but not terminating in the UK.
4 Figures are on a different basis from those in Table 2.2(b) because passengers are counted at the airports at both ends of the journey and only includes passengers who start and end their journey in the UK. The total includes miscellaneous traffic, e.g. passengers to and from oil rigs.
5 Figures may not equal sum of international and domestic due to rounding to nearest 5 million.

The January 2009 'UK Air Passenger Demand & CO_2 Forecasts' report is available at: http://www.dft.gov.uk/pgr/aviation/atf/co2forecasts09/

☎020-7944 6608
The figures in this table are outside the scope of National Statistics
Source - International Networks Analysis & Support Division, DfT

2.6 United Kingdom airline fleet: 1998-2008

Aircraft in service (at end of year)											Number
	1998	1999	2000	2001	2002	2003	2004	2005	2006	2007	2008
Total [1]	837	850	889	928	903	921	945	952	963	957	967
ow:											
British Airways PLC [2]	229	217	235	235	240	240	228	232	234	234	235
EasyJet Airline Company Ltd	9	15	17	22	32	69	94	98	103	125	153
Flybe Ltd [3]	24	28	31	31	31	33	35	35	41	88	76
Thomson Airways Ltd [4]	.	.	.	.	.	.	.	.	.	.	76
Thomsonfly Ltd [4,5]	*28*	*28*	*32*	*31*	*32*	*32*	*37*	*42*	*47*	*48*	.
First Choice Airways Ltd [4,6]	*22*	*25*	*27*	*29*	*31*	*32*	*30*	*32*	*31*	*32*	.
BMI Group [7]	37	40	45	46	43	43	31	58	61	62	70
Thomas Cook Airlines Ltd [8]	.	.	.	.	.	.	.	.	.	.	42
Thomas Cook Airlines Ltd (MYT) [8,9]	21	24	31	31	34	35	31	29	25	25	.
Thomas Cook Airlines Ltd (TCX) [8,10]	.	.	17	27	24	24	24	24	24	24	.
Virgin Atlantic Airways Ltd	25	29	32	34	35	38	35	32	37	38	38
Monarch Airlines	17	20	19	22	23	22	24	28	28	31	32
Jet2.Com Ltd [11]	15	15	14	14	15	21	26	23	26	29	30
GB Airways Ltd	9	9	10	10	11	13	13	15	15	15	..
Aurigny Air Services	9	11	12	12	13	13	14	11	10	10	10
European Air Charter	16	13	11	13	13	13	12	13	6	4	4

1 Total includes only airlines who reported to the CAA in the year.
2 BA Euro Ops became part of the BA mainline fleet from 28 March 2002.
3 Prior to December 2005 known as Flybe British European.
4 First Choice Airways Ltd and Thomsonfly Ltd merged in June 2008
5 Prior to January 2006 known as Britannia Airways.
6 Prior to 2003 known as Air 2000.
7 Prior to 2005 data is for BMI British Midland.
   From 2005 data also includes BMI Regional and BMI Baby.
8 Thomas Cook Airlines Ltd (MYT) & Thomas Cook Airlines Ltd (TCX) merged in April 2008.
9 Prior to 2002 known as Airtours International Airways Ltd.
   Prior to March 2008 known as My Travel Airways.
10 Prior to April 2003 known as JMC Airlines Ltd.
   Prior to March 2008 known as Thomas Cook Airlines Ltd.
11 Prior to January 2006 known as Channel Express.

☎ 020-7944 3088
The figures in this table are outside
the scope of National Statistics
Source - Civil Aviation Authority

2.7 Activity at major airports: 2008

Country	Location	Name	Terminal passengers		Cargo handled [1]	Commercial air transport movements	
			All	ow: International	All	All [2]	ow: International [3]
			(millions)	(millions)	Tonnes (thousands)	(thousands)	(thousands)
USA	Atlanta	Hartsfield-Jackson International	89.6	9.2	655	968	..
USA	Chicago	O'Hare International	69.3	11.4	1,332	862	..
UK	London	Heathrow	66.9	61.3	1,483	473	412
Japan	Tokyo	Haneda	66.7	2.4	849	336	11
France	Paris	Charles De Gaulle	60.7	55.8	2,280	551	490
USA	Los Angeles	Los Angeles International	59.5	16.7	1,630	585	..
USA	Dallas	Dallas-Fort Worth International	57.1	5.4	660	650	..
China	Beijing	Capital	55.8	12.4	1,368	425	101
Germany	Frankfurt	Frankfurt International	53.2	46.8	2,104	477	408
USA	Denver	Denver International	51.2	2.2	251	615	..
Spain	Madrid	Barajas	50.5	30.1	359	462	252
USA	New York	J. F. Kennedy International	47.8	22.4	1,451	433	..
Netherlands	Amsterdam	Schiphol	47.4	47.3	1,603	428	426
China	Hong Kong	Hong Kong International	47.1	47.1	3,661	301	301
USA	Las Vegas	McCarran International	43.2	2.3	85	527	..
USA	Houston	G. Bush Intercontinental	41.7	8.0	412	556	..
USA	Phoenix	Sky Harbor International	39.9	1.9	250	469	..
Thailand	Bangkok	Bangkok International	37.1	30.1	1,173	246	189
USA	San Francisco	San Francisco International	37.1	9.0	494	351	..
UAE	Dubai	Dubai International	36.6	36.6	1,825	240	..
Singapore	Singapore	Changi	36.3	36.3	1,884	232	232
USA	Orlando	Orlando International	35.7	2.7	160	315	..
USA	Newark	Newark International	35.4	11.1	887	422	..
USA	Detroit	Wayne County	35.1	3.2	211	453	..
Italy	Rome	Fiumicino	34.8	21.4	153	341	..

1 Includes freight and mail.
2 All commercial movements including positioning and local movements.
3 International commercial air transport movements data for all world's major
  airports was not available at time of print.

☎020-7944 3088
The figures in this table are outside
the scope of National Statistics
Source - ICAO

2.8 United Kingdom [1] international passenger movements by air: arrivals plus departures: by country of embarkation or landing: 1998-2008

Thousands

	1998	1999	2000	2001	2002	2003	2004	2005	2006	2007	2008
European Union:											
Austria	1,191	1,201	1,257	1,278	1,443	1,508	1,749	1,796	1,788	1,877	1,826
Belgium	2,673	2,858	2,864	2,686	2,343	2,277	1,863	1,711	1,626	1,624	1,398
Denmark	1,691	1,780	1,965	1,988	2,070	2,013	2,186	2,255	2,305	2,345	2,395
France	7,059	7,580	8,235	8,435	9,657	10,232	10,941	10,994	11,560	11,785	11,676
Finland	604	666	770	753	659	702	813	799	930	944	961
Germany	7,454	8,107	8,717	8,432	8,651	9,571	10,283	10,937	11,502	11,607	11,155
Greece	4,435	5,248	5,912	6,410	6,246	6,204	5,840	5,596	5,519	5,457	5,199
Irish Republic	8,522	8,966	9,295	9,293	9,813	10,163	10,862	11,789	12,356	12,259	12,321
Italy	5,895	6,454	7,033	7,456	7,654	8,913	9,677	10,713	10,571	11,207	10,737
Luxembourg	215	224	224	203	184	159	173	182	209	251	245
Netherlands	6,477	6,777	7,096	7,313	7,804	7,780	7,933	7,888	8,256	8,352	7,660
Portugal & Madeira [2]	3,178	3,443	3,607	3,752	3,967	4,022	4,256	4,540	4,745	5,339	5,536
Spain & Canary Islands	22,089	23,803	25,923	27,576	28,952	32,230	33,478	34,558	34,877	35,535	34,558
Sweden	1,877	1,896	2,032	1,958	1,976	1,993	2,253	2,321	2,290	2,267	2,296
Bulgaria	221	194	172	187	279	382	585	771	919	953	992
Cyprus	2,034	2,333	2,670	2,962	2,683	2,787	2,776	2,989	3,006	2,969	2,951
Czech Republic	520	541	654	736	916	1,296	2,069	2,355	2,155	2,071	1,817
Estonia	29	27	28	29	38	45	83	186	178	179	157
Hungary	357	398	403	383	360	375	701	1,119	1,014	960	1,096
Latvia	68	64	51	54	58	61	126	309	461	479	464
Lithuania	51	58	51	48	48	55	95	222	319	340	359
Malta	1,045	994	1,022	1,039	1,025	1,055	1,096	1,110	1,055	1,148	1,101
Poland	419	499	498	453	467	516	998	1,845	3,328	4,352	5,023
Romania	131	118	110	109	117	135	143	157	194	333	488
Slovak Republic	1	-	-	-	2	29	127	285	470	529	716
Slovenia	58	71	69	52	48	53	116	157	183	190	168
Total EU-15	73,361	79,003	84,930	87,534	91,419	97,768	102,308	106,079	108,534	110,851	107,962
Total EU-27	78,294	84,301	90,658	93,586	97,459	104,558	111,224	117,584	121,817	125,355	123,293
Other Europe:											
Norway	1,615	1,569	1,432	1,244	1,277	1,353	1,606	1,726	1,893	1,856	1,990
Switzerland	3,228	3,631	3,926	3,829	3,983	4,108	4,184	4,501	4,957	5,142	5,416
Gibraltar	183	197	208	215	227	264	309	346	329	296	369
Turkey	2,454	2,028	2,019	2,112	2,233	2,175	2,791	3,551	3,406	3,887	4,355
Former USSR [3]	603	576	667	727	814	911	1,030	1,098	1,215	1,290	1,294
Former Yugoslavia [3]	231	151	222	269	310	351	433	548	730	848	770
Rest of Europe [3]	240	272	329	340	268	332	403	402	436	438	364
Total Other Europe	8,554	8,424	8,804	8,736	9,111	9,493	10,757	12,173	12,966	13,756	14,557
Total Europe	86,849	92,724	99,463	102,322	106,570	114,050	121,980	129,757	134,783	139,112	137,850
Rest of World:											
North Africa	1,140	1,322	1,554	1,598	1,511	1,506	2,016	2,776	3,462	3,632	3,641
Southern Africa	1,371	1,438	1,510	1,588	1,584	1,602	1,768	1,733	1,771	1,818	1,614
Rest of Africa	854	1,009	1,129	1,163	1,310	1,336	1,588	1,719	1,829	1,973	1,820
Israel	925	969	967	770	630	617	659	668	672	709	818
Persian Gulf States	377	382	404	390	431	481	534	568	610	536	557
Saudi Arabia	378	350	346	297	263	229	247	205	220	257	300
UAE	926	1,056	1,324	1,524	1,795	2,022	2,535	2,881	3,256	3,736	4,049
Rest of Near and Middle East	777	849	913	875	907	1,002	1,238	1,372	1,470	1,625	1,607
USA	17,153	18,251	19,208	17,060	16,879	16,584	18,004	18,290	18,066	18,558	18,152
Canada	3,140	3,249	3,301	3,133	2,961	2,894	3,308	3,606	3,634	3,865	3,522
South America	572	587	610	523	414	379	394	379	340	395	415
Central America	825	838	862	927	884	906	1,150	1,270	1,353	1,334	1,380
Caribbean	1,399	1,635	1,744	1,692	1,657	1,763	1,895	1,828	1,903	1,948	1,947
Australia	900	918	916	737	693	727	874	1,211	1,169	1,211	1,272
New Zealand	187	194	203	154	130	202	180	189	215	344	365
India	1,012	911	911	1,017	858	960	1,073	1,579	2,329	2,486	2,363
Pakistan	387	413	477	486	443	517	582	654	703	684	773
Rest of Indian sub-continent	536	635	713	681	682	770	856	827	832	878	833
Japan	1,440	1,325	1,416	1,131	1,209	1,046	1,189	1,184	1,085	1,031	963
Hong Kong	1,021	996	1,081	983	1,113	1,020	1,275	1,259	1,439	1,660	1,554
Singapore	863	1,011	1,144	1,209	1,203	1,150	1,169	1,158	1,272	1,230	1,248
Thailand	446	525	575	710	715	673	718	696	673	691	594
Rest of Asia	1,234	1,281	1,349	1,215	1,242	1,205	1,447	1,612	1,636	1,558	1,480
Total Rest of World [4]	37,862	40,146	42,657	39,866	39,512	39,594	44,701	47,665	49,938	52,163	51,265
Oil Rigs	693	576	586	640	628	567	564	627	713	768	763
All international air passenger movements	125,404	133,446	142,706	142,827	146,711	154,211	167,245	178,049	185,434	192,042	189,879

1 Includes Channel Islands and Isle of Man airports, unlike other tables in this chapter.
2 Includes Azores and Cape Verde Islands.
3 See Notes & Definitions for list of countries included in group.
4 Includes Greenland.

☎020-7944 3088
The figures in this table are outside the scope of National Statistics
Source - Civil Aviation Authority

2.9 Casualties caused by aviation accidents: 1998-2008

(a) Casualties caused by accidents involving United Kingdom registered aircraft in United Kingdom airspace

	1998	1999	2000	2001	2002	2003	2004	2005	2006[1]	2007[1]	2008
Airline and air taxi:											
Fixed-wing:											
Crew:											
Fatal	0	2	1	2	0	0	0	1	0	0	0
Total	0	2	4	2	0	3	0	1	1	1	4
Passengers:											
Fatal	0	6	4	0	0	0	0	1	0	0	0
Total	1	10	4	0	0	0	0	1	0	1	9
Total fixed-wing [2]	1	12	8	2	0	3	0	2	1	3	13
Rotary wing:											
Crew:											
Fatal	1	0	0	0	2	0	0	0	2	0	0
Total	3	0	1	2	3	3	0	0	2	0	0
Passengers:											
Fatal	3	0	0	0	9	0	0	0	5	0	0
Total	5	0	2	3	11	0	0	0	5	0	0
Total rotary-wing [2]	8	0	3	6	14	3	0	0	7	0	0
Other (general aviation, etc.):											
Crew:											
Fatal	15	15	20	18	9	8	12	17	7	14	8
Total	37	53	40	50	42	46	41	52	37	37	35
Passengers:											
Fatal	6	11	7	5	3	7	7	8	0	17	6
Total	24	28	22	17	14	21	14	17	21	27	25
Total other [2]	61	82	63	68	58	68	55	70	58	64	62
Overall total [2]											
Fatal	25	34	32	25	23	15	19	25	14	31	14
Total	70	94	74	76	72	74	55	70	66	67	75

(b) Casualties caused by accidents involving United Kingdom registered aircraft in foreign airspace

	1998	1999	2000	2001	2002	2003	2004	2005	2006	2007	2008
Airline and air taxi:											
Fixed-wing:											
Crew:											
Fatal	0	2	3	0	0	0	0	0	0	0	0
Total	0	3	5	0	3	4	1	0	1	0	1
Passengers:											
Fatal	0	1	0	0	0	0	0	0	0	0	0
Total	15	43	14	0	1	1	3	0	2	0	3
Total fixed-wing [2]	15	46	19	1	4	5	4	0	4	0	4
Other (general aviation, etc.):											
Crew:											
Fatal	2	4	2	4	1	1	1	0	2	2	1
Total	2	8	3	7	1	2	4	1	2	4	4
Passengers:											
Fatal	1	1	1	2	3	1	1	0	1	1	3
Total	3	6	1	3	3	2	3	0	1	3	4
Total other [2]	5	14	4	10	4	4	7	1	3	7	10
Overall total [2]											
Fatal	3	8	6	7	4	2	2	0	3	3	4
Total	20	60	23	11	8	9	11	1	7	7	14

2.9 (continued) Casualties caused by aviation accidents: 1998-2008

(c) Casualties caused by accidents involving aircraft registered overseas in United Kingdom airspace

	1998	1999	2000	2001	2002	2003	2004	2005	2006	2007	2008
Airline and air taxi:											
Fixed-wing:											
Crew:											
Fatal	0	4	0	0	0	0	0	0	0	0	0
Total	0	5	0	0	0	0	0	1 [3]	1	0	0
Passengers:											
Fatal	0	0	0	0	0	0	0	0	0	0	0
Total	1	1	0	0	0	0	0	24 [3]	0	0	0
Total fixed-wing [2]	1	6	0	0	0	0	0	25 [3]	1	0	0
Other (general aviation, etc.):											
Crew:											
Fatal	2	0	2	5	2	4	1	1	0	2	3
Total	10	2	4	9	6	5	4	5	2	4	5
Passengers:											
Fatal	2	0	4	0	3	2	0	1	0	2	4
Total	10	1	6	4	6	5	2	5	0	4	6
Total other [2]	20	3	10	13	13	11	6	10	3	8	11
Overall total [2]											
Fatal	4	4	6	5	5	6	1	2	0	4	7
Total	21	9	10	13	13	11	6	35 [3]	4	8	11

1 Some figures have been revised in 2006 and 2007.
2 These totals include 'third-party' casualties, not shown separately.
3 There were 25 minor injuries (1 crew and 24 passengers) in a single
  incident in March 2005 involving the evacuation of an aircraft.

☎020-7944 3088
The figures in this table are outside
the scope of National Statistics
Source - Civil Aviation Authority

2.10 Aircraft proximity (AIRPROX): number of incidents: 1998-2008

	1998	1999	2000	2001	2002	2003	2004	2005	2006	2007	2008
Total AIRPROX civil and military:											
Risk-bearing:											
Risk of collision	23	23	28	33	17	14	15	19	15	9	13
Safety not assured	43	49	44	42	68	58	53	51	40	39	38
Total	66	72	72	75	85	72	68	70	55	48	51
No risk of collision	132	134	123	115	129	108	131	116	103	106	100
Risk not determined	3	2	3	5	7	1	8	2	1	0	4
Total AIRPROX	201	208	198	195	221	181	207	188	159	154	155
ow:											
Commercial air transport:											
Risk-bearing:											
Risk of collision	1	4	6	0	1	0	1	1	0	0	0
Safety not assured	14	12	8	14	7	12	7	7	6	5	2
Total	15	16	14	14	8	12	8	8	6	5	2
No risk of collision	82	83	84	65	70	54	67	78	68	60	58
Risk not determined	1	0	1	4	4	0	4	1	0	0	1
Total commercial air transport	98	99	99	83	82	66	79	87	74	65	61
Commercial air transport aircraft in risk-bearing AIRPROX per 100,000 hours flown in UK airspace	*1.2*	*1.2*	*1.0*	*1.0*	*0.6*	*0.9*	*0.5*	*0.5*	*0.4*	*0.3*	*0.1*

☎020-7944 3088
The figures in this table are outside
the scope of National Statistics
Source - UK Airprox Board

2.11   Employment by United Kingdom airlines: worldwide: 1998-2008

	1998	1999	2000	2001	2002	2003	2004	2005	2006	2007	Number 2008
Pilots and co-pilots	8,548	9,244	9,443	9,984	9,933	9,758	9,798	10,064	10,671	11,259	11,534
Other cockpit personnel	460	457	332	274	209	120	102	135	158	152	111
Cabin attendants	26,967	28,465	28,819	30,461	28,548	28,398	29,634	31,120	32,718	34,369	35,267
Maintenance and overhaul personnel	12,264	12,138	12,055	11,824	11,749	11,186	9,933	9,611	9,488	9,075	8,616
Tickets and sales personnel	8,929	9,643	9,100	10,062	9,074	8,168	7,706	7,312	6,555	6,258	6,314
All other personnel	30,663	32,755	31,764	31,279	27,921	27,265	26,399	26,141	25,481	24,571	25,037
Total	87,831	92,702	91,513	93,884	87,434	84,895	83,572	84,383	85,071	85,684	86,879

☎020-7944 3088
The figures in this table are outside
the scope of National Statistics
Source - Civil Aviation Authority

2.12   Passenger traffic via major international airlines: 2008

Country	Airline	All scheduled traffic		International scheduled traffic		Charter traffic	
							ow:
		Passengers uplifted (millions)	Passenger kilometres (billions)	Passengers uplifted (millions)	Passenger kilometres (billions)	All passenger kilometres (billions)	International passenger kilometres (billions)
United States	American	92.8	211.9	21.2	80.8	0.1	-
United States	Delta	71.6	169.9	12.3	71.9	0.2	0.1
United States	United	63.1	176.7	11.4	76.5	0.4	0.4
Ireland	Ryanair	57.6	62.0	57.6	62.0	0.0	0.0
United States	US Airways	54.8	97.4	6.3	21.7	0.1	-
Germany	Lufthansa	54.7	126.3	42.2	121.1	-	-
France	Air France	50.4	131.7	32.4	121.3	0.2	0.2
United States	Northwest	48.8	114.6	10.3	56.1	0.7	0.5
China	China Southern Airlines	47.6	70.3	3.5	10.2	0.5	0.4
Japan	All Nippon Airways	47.0	57.2	4.1	19.5	0.7	0.7
United States	Continental	46.9	129.4	12.4	59.6	0.1	0.1
Japan	JAL	46.7	80.9	11.6	52.9	1.2	1.2
United Kingdom	Easyjet	37.6	42.1	32.0	39.5	0.0	0.0
China	China Eastern	36.9	53.1	4.5	14.9	0.7	0.5
China	Air China	34.2	65.7	5.3	27.0	0.4	0.2
Germany	Air Berlin	33.0	52.5	33.0	52.5	3.5	3.5
United Kingdom	British Airways	31.6	110.7	27.6	108.9	-	-
Brazil	Tam Linhas Aereas	28.0	37.8	3.6	15.6	1.8	0.3
Scandinavia	SAS	25.4	27.9	14.4	22.6	3.2	3.2
Hong Kong Sar	Cathay Pacific	25.0	91.0	25.0	91.0	0.0	0.0
Australia	Qantas	24.0	79.2	7.5	55.2	-	-
Netherlands	KLM	23.8	77.5	23.8	77.5	0.0	0.0
Canada	Air Canada	23.2	74.5	11.6	53.2	0.1	0.1
Spain	Iberia	23.1	52.8	12.8	46.1	0.0	0.0
Republic Of Korea	Korean Air	22.5	57.4	12.9	53.6	0.0	0.0

☎020-7944 3088
The figures in this table are outside
the scope of National Statistics
Source - ICAO

2.13   Major Airports in the United Kingdom

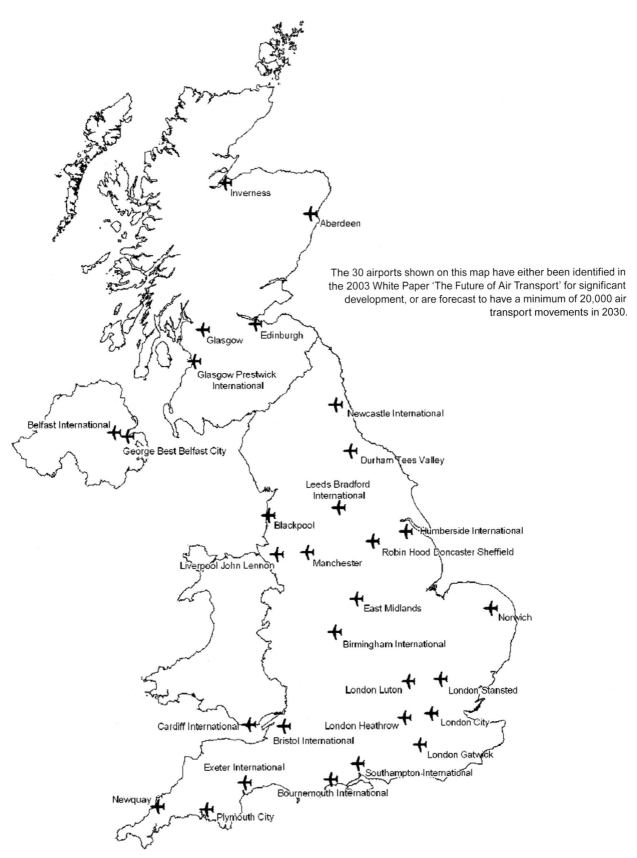

The 30 airports shown on this map have either been identified in the 2003 White Paper 'The Future of Air Transport' for significant development, or are forecast to have a minimum of 20,000 air transport movements in 2030.

Inverness

Aberdeen

Glasgow

Edinburgh

Glasgow Prestwick International

Newcastle International

Belfast International

George Best Belfast City

Durham Tees Valley

Leeds Bradford International

Blackpool

Humberside International

Liverpool John Lennon

Manchester

Robin Hood Doncaster Sheffield

East Midlands

Norwich

Birmingham International

London Luton

London Stansted

Cardiff International

London Heathrow

London City

Bristol International

London Gatwick

Exeter International

Southampton International

Newquay

Bournemouth International

Plymouth City

☎ 020-7944 3088

3 Energy and the Environment:

Notes and Definitions

Petroleum consumption: by transport mode and fuel type: 3.1

Motor spirit (All grades):
> One tonne = 300 gallons or 1,362 litres

DERV fuel (0.005% or less sulphur):
> One tonne = 264 gallons or 1,198 litres

Petroleum consumption figures are published in the *Digest of United Kingdom Energy Statistics* (DUKES) by the Department for Energy and Climate Change (DECC) at: http://www.berr.gov.uk/energy/statistics/publications/dukes/page45537.html

Road transport – Deliveries of motor spirit and DERV fuel for use in road vehicles of all kinds. As part of their work to compile the UK emissions inventory, AEA has constructed estimates for the consumption of road transport fuels by different vehicle classes. The methodology used to produce the most recent estimates has been improved. The two major changes to this methodology are the use of more detailed speed data and a more accurate fuel split between petrol and diesel cars. It now takes account of diesel cars doing more annual mileage than petrol cars and using different petrol car/diesel car mix on different road types.

A small proportion of motor spirit and diesel is not used by road vehicles, which is included in the total DECC publish for motor spirit and diesel used.

Estimates for the use of gas for road vehicles are based on information on the amounts of duty received by HM Revenue and Customs from the tax on gas used as a road fuel.

Railways – Deliveries of fuel oil, gas/diesel oil and burning oil to railways are based on estimates produced by AEA as part of their work to compile the UK Greenhouse Gas Inventory. Railway fuels include some amounts of burning oil not used directly for transport purposes.

National navigation – Fuel oil and gas/diesel oil delivered, other than under international bunker contracts, for fishing vessels, UK oil and gas exploration and production, coastal and inland shipping and for use in ports and harbours.

Air transport – Total inland deliveries of aviation turbine fuel and aviation spirit. The figures cover deliveries of aviation fuels in the United Kingdom to international and other airlines, British and foreign Governments (including armed services) and for private flying.

Energy consumption: by transport mode and source of energy: 3.2

This is the energy content of fuels delivered to consumers. The data measures the energy content of the fuels, both primary and secondary, supplied to final users. Thus it is net of fuel industry own use and conversion, transmission and distribution losses, but it includes conversion losses by final users.

Detailed data for individual fuels are converted from original units to tonnes of oil equivalent using gross calorific values and conversion factors appropriate to each category of fuel. The results are then aggregated according to the categories used in the tables. Gross calorific values represent the total energy content of the fuel, including the energy needed to evaporate the water present in the fuel.

1 tonne of oil equivalent (toe):
> = 10^7 kilocalories
> = 396.83 therms
> = 41.868 Gigajoules (GJ)
> = 11,630 Kilowatt hours (kWh).

This unit should be regarded as a measure of energy content rather than a physical quantity. There is no intention to represent an actual physical tonne of oil, and indeed actual tonnes of oil will normally have measurements in tonnes of oil equivalent which differ from units.

Gross calorific values are reviewed each year in collaboration with the fuel industries. Estimated average gross calorific values in 2008 for motor spirit and gas/diesel oil (DERV) are:

47.1 GJ per tonne of motor spirit

45.5 GJ per tonne of Gas/diesel oil (DERV)

For railways, data are based on estimates produced by AEA as part of their work to compile the UK Greenhouse Gas Inventory.

Petrol and diesel prices and duties per litre: 3.3

The price estimates are based on information provided by oil marketing companies and super/hypermarket chains and are representative of prices paid (inclusive of taxes) on or about the

15th of the month. Changes in fuel duty usually occur during the month in which a Budget is held. VAT is rebated to business users.

From 2005 the collection of Lead Replacement Petrol prices has been discontinued due to the low volume of sales.

The figures in table 3.3 differ from those in table 10.8 because of the differences in availability and timing of data collection. The international comparisons in table 10.8 (supplied by DECC, and extracted from the IEA publication 'Energy Prices and Taxes'), are based on averages over the year, whereas table 3.3 attempts to be as up to date as reasonably possible. The use of the term Tax in part (b) of table 10.8 is necessary because some other European countries impose other taxes and fees on fuel. For the UK this includes just fuel duty and VAT.

Average fuel consumption: 3.4

Passenger cars: These figures are based upon fuel consumption as recorded by participants in the National Travel Survey (NTS). This is estimated by recording the start and finish points of both the fuel gauge and the milometer, and the amount of fuel put in the vehicle in the travel week.

From the 2005 survey, NTS data has been weighted for the first time, and weights have now been applied to data from 1995. Results published here for 1995 onwards may differ from previously published figures which were based on unweighted data.

In 2002 the drawn sample size for the NTS was nearly trebled compared with previous years, enabling key results to be presented on a single year basis for the first time since the survey became continuous. Changes to the methodology in 2002 mean that there are some inconsistencies with data for earlier years. Data for earlier years are shown for a three year time period because of the smaller sample sizes for individual years.

HGVs: These figures are based on fuel consumption as recorded by participants in the Continuing Survey of Road Goods Transport (CSRGT). Respondents report the amount of fuel purchased during the survey week, with the amount of fuel at the start and end of the week assumed to balance out across the sample as a whole.

Unlike the NTS, the sample size is sufficient to report fuel consumption on a yearly basis for the whole time series. The fuel consumption figures

have not been re-weighted to the population, so the figures may not be fully representative of the HGV fleet.

The 2008 HGV data are not available at the time of publication and will be released as soon as possible at the following link: http://www.dft.gov.uk/pgr/statistics/datatablespublications/freight/goodsbyroad/.

Average new car fuel consumption: 3.5

Table 3.5 and Chart 3.5 includes separate trends for diesel and petrol cars. These trends include all types of passenger cars registered including high performance cars, 4x4's and MPV's. The data are calculated from new registration weighted average CO_2 emissions for petrol and diesel cars and the typical carbon content of petrol and diesel. This approach accounts for the relative sales of different models of car. The registration weighted average CO_2 figures are produced to monitor trends in average petrol and diesel car CO_2 emissions from year to year. The CO_2 figures for individual vehicle models are obtained under carefully controlled laboratory conditions in order to ensure repeatability and a fair comparison between models. The actual fuel consumption achieved on the road will reflect many extraneous factors such as cold starts, different driving conditions, weather conditions, different loads carried, gradients, use of electrical accessories etc. The data shown here represents fuel economy on the current standard test used to obtain comparative data on the relative fuel economy of vehicles (a drive cycle simulating urban and extra-urban driving, effectively with a single occupant, on a level road and without heaters or lights on).

Emissions for road vehicles in urban conditions: 3.6

This table takes into account emission factors for cars, light goods vehicles, heavy goods vehicles, buses and coaches and motorcycles of different ages, and indexes them against a baseline emissions from a pre-1993 petrol car without a three-way catalyst (=100). The emission factors, in units of grammes of pollutant per kilometre travelled (g/km), are from the latest version of the National Atmospheric Emissions Inventory, maintained by AEA on behalf of DEFRA and DECC, and are based on the compilation of equations derived by the Transport Research Laboratory (TRL) relating emission factor to average vehicle speed. The indices for NOx and PM are based on the latest TRL emission factors released for consultation by DfT in October 2008. The equations are derived from a database of emissions measured from actual in-service vehicles, the measurements being carried out by different laboratories in the UK and the rest of Europe over different drive cycles.

Particulate emissions (these are fine particles less than 10 micrometres or 0.01 millimetres diameter) are much lower from vehicles with petrol engines than they are from vehicles with diesel engines. For this pollutant, the index is against emissions from a pre-1993 diesel car (=100). Measurements have been made of emissions from vehicles of different sizes within each vehicle category. The figures shown here reflect average values of emission factors at a typical urban speed, weighted by the mix of sizes of vehicles in the fleet.

Since January 1993, all new cars have had to meet new EC emission standards. This resulted in the use of three way catalysts for petrol cars to meet those standards (EC Directive 91/441/EEC).

Carbon dioxide emissions and greenhouse gas emissions in the United Kingdom: 3.7 and 3.8

The data in tables 3.7 and 3.8 are presented in terms of weight of carbon dioxide emitted. To convert weight of carbon to carbon dioxide emissions, carbon figures are multiplied by a factor of 44/12.

Greenhouse gas emissions:

The basket of six greenhouse gases are carbon dioxide, methane, nitrous oxide, hydro-fluorocarbons, perfluorocarbons and sulphur hexafluoride (CO_2, CH_4, N_2O, HFC, PFC and SF_6).

Carbon dioxide:

Carbon dioxide is the most important greenhouse gas and is estimated to account for about two thirds of man made global warming. Although its global warming potential is much less per tonne than the other greenhouse gases it is present in the atmosphere in vastly greater quantities.

National Atmospheric Emissions Inventory (NAEI)

Emission figures, including more detail about the estimates and additional data, are published by the Department of Energy and Climate Change (DECC) at:

http://www.decc.gov.uk/en/content/cms/statistics/climate_change/climate_change.aspx

The NAEI figures shown in part (a) of tables 3.7 and 3.8 are based on the reporting guidelines of the Intergovernmental Panel on Climate Change (IPCC). These are the guidelines used

for international reporting of greenhouse gases. This system excludes international navigation and aviation bunker fuels from national totals, but these are shown as memo items separately from the national total.

Parts (b) and (c) show emissions based on National Communication categories.

The tables include emissions from Crown Dependencies of Jersey, Guernsey and Isle of Man, and excludes emissions from Overseas Territories.

The main difference between "by source" and "end user" emissions comes from the treatment of emissions from combustion of fossil fuels, the largest source of carbon dioxide in the UK.

By source:

The **source** breakdown splits emissions by the sector producing them.

By end user:

The **end user** breakdown also shows emissions by the sector responsible for them, but redistributes emissions from power stations and other fuel processing industries to end users on an approximate basis according to their use of the fuel. Emissions by end user are subject to more uncertainty than emissions by source and should only be used to give a broad indication of emissions by sector.

Emissions from road transport are calculated either from a combination of total fuel consumption data and fuel properties or from a combination of drive related emission factors and road traffic data. As mentioned earlier in the Notes and Definitions, changes to the methodology of the 2007 NAEI Road Transport Inventory include use of more detailed speed data and a change to the fuel split on different road types. This takes account of diesel cars doing more annual mileage than petrol cars and using different petrol car/diesel car mix on different road types. Also, revised HGV fuel consumption data from DfT have been incorporated

Further information on the UK atmospheric emissions estimates can be found at:

http://www.naei.org.uk

Environmental Accounts (EA)

The Environmental Accounts provide information on the demands that UK economic activity places on the environment and on the importance of natural resources to the economy. These demands include the emission of greenhouse gases and air pollutants.

Transport Statistics Great Britain 2009

The statistics presented in the Environmental Accounts are on a **UK residents** basis, as opposed to being based on fuel purchases in the UK. This means that they measure the emissions caused by people residing in the UK, and UK-registered businesses. The principle is that this is the same basis on which the National Accounts are produced, so environmental impacts can be directly compared with economic benefits.

The UK transport industries comprise of: railways, buses and coaches, tubes and trams, taxis, road freight, water transport, air transport, and transport via pipelines. The road freight industry covers road haulage companies as opposed to all types of road freight. Lorries owned by retailers for instance are allocated to the retail industry.

Further information on Environmental Accounts can be found on the Office for National Statistics (ONS) website at:

http://www.statistics.gov.uk/statbase/Product. asp?vlnk=3698

The main differences between the NAEI and EA's are:

- ONS apply a cross-boundary adjustment to remove purchases by overseas residents of UK fuel, and then add purchases by UK residents of foreign fuel.

- Environmental Accounts include international aviation and shipping.

- The Environmental Accounts breaks down emissions using the Eurostat industry classification, which looks at the economic sector of the person or company responsible for the activity, rather than the activity itself.

Pollutant emissions from transport in the United Kingdom: 3.9

Emission figures, including more detail about the estimates and additional data are published in the *Digest of Environmental Statistics*, by the Department for Environment, Food and Rural Affairs (DEFRA) at:

http://www.defra.gov.uk/evidence/statistics/ environment/airqual/index.htm

Figures shown in table 3.9 are based on United Nations Economic Commission for Europe (UNECE) definitions. This system, like the IPCC excludes international navigation and aviation bunker fuels from national totals, but these are shown as memo items separately from the national total.

Carbon monoxide (CO): Derived from the incomplete combustion of fuels containing carbon. It is one of the most directly toxic of substances, interfering with respiratory bio-chemistry and can affect the central nervous and cardiovascular systems. Other pollutants can exacerbate the effects. The fitting of catalytic converters to all new petrol engine vehicles made after 1992 has reduced emissions of carbon monoxide from the 1992 level.

Nitrogen oxides (NO$_x$) (expressed as nitrogen dioxide equivalent): A number of nitrogen compounds including nitrogen dioxide and nitric oxide are formed in the combustion of fossil fuel. Nitrogen dioxide is directly harmful to human health causing respiratory problems and can reduce lung function. Nitrogen oxides also contribute to the formation of ozone which is a harmful secondary pollutant in the lower atmosphere and also an important greenhouse gas contributing to global warming (high levels of ozone increase susceptibility to respiratory disease and irritate the eyes, nose, throat and respiratory system). Oxides of nitrogen can also have adverse effects on plants, reducing growth. In addition they contribute to acid rain. Emissions of nitrogen oxides from petrol engined vehicles have been reduced from the 1992 level as new vehicles built from 1992 onwards must comply with EC standards (normally by the fitting of a suitable catalytic converter).

Particulates (PM$_{10}$): Airborne particles may be measured in a number of ways. For quantifying the particles produced by transport (especially motor traffic), the most commonly used indicator relies on the use of a size-selective sampler which collects smaller particles preferentially, collecting more than 95 per cent of 5μm (0.005 millimetres) particles, 50 per cent of 10μm aerodynamic particles, and less than 5 per cent of 20μm particles. The resultant mass of material is known as PM$_{10}$. The road transport figures include emissions from tyre and brake wear.

Benzene: A known human carcinogen, the main source of benzene is the combustion and distribution of petrol. Some benzene evaporates directly into the atmosphere. Benzene is also emitted in a number of industrial processes. The large reduction in benzene emissions in 2000 was due to a reduction in the benzene content of petrol.

1,3–butadiene: A suspected human carcinogen, the main source of 1,3-butadiene is motor vehicle exhausts where 1,3-butadiene is formed from the cracking of higher olefines. 1,3-butadiene is also used in the production of synthetic rubber for tyres.

Lead (Pb): Of concern because of its effects on health, particularly that of children. The main sources of lead in air are from lead in petrol, coal combustion, and metal works. The maximum amount of lead permitted in petrol was reduced from 0.45 grams per litre to 0.40 in 1981 and then again in December 1985 to 0.15. A further step to reduce lead emissions from petrol was taken in 1986 when unleaded petrol was first sold in the United Kingdom. There was a rapid increase in the uptake of unleaded petrol in the 1990s followed by a ban on the general sale of leaded petrol at the end of 1999.

Sulphur dioxide (SO_2): An acid gas, sulphur dioxide can affect health and vegetation. It affects the lining of the nose, throat and airways of the lung, in particular, among those who suffer from asthma and chronic lung disease. The United Nations Economic Commission for Europe's (UNECE) Second Sulphur Protocol sets reduction targets for total SO_2 emissions of 50 per cent by the year 2000, 70 per cent by 2005 and 80 per cent by 2010 from a 1980 baseline. By 2000, the UK had achieved a 75 per cent reduction from 1980 baseline levels, 25 per cent ahead of the UNECE target level for that year. Road transport emissions have fallen by over 90 per cent since 1998 following a reduction in the sulphur content of fuel.

Aircraft noise: 3.10

Air transport movements are landings or take-offs of aircraft engaged in transport of passengers or cargo on commercial terms. All scheduled service movements (whether loaded or empty) are included, as well as charter movements transporting passengers or cargo. Air taxi movements are excluded.

The equivalent continuous sound level (Leq) is an index of aircraft noise exposure. It is a measure of the equivalent continuous sound level averaged over a 16 hour day from 0700 to 2300 hours BST and is calculated during the peak summer months mid-June to mid-September.

The contours referred to are broadly comparable with the previous Noise and Number Index (NNI) – The change was announced by the Minister for Aviation on 4 September 1990. 57dBA Leq represents the approximate onset of significant community disturbance (comparable with 35 NNI at the time), 63dBA Leq moderate disturbance and 69dBA Leq high disturbance. Leq is correlated with community response to aircraft noise, but it is recognised that the reactions of different individuals to aircraft noise can vary considerably. Changes in wind direction from year to year influence the area affected by aircraft noise.

The methodology underlying the calculation of the aircraft noise Leq contours is published in: *The CAA Leq Aircraft Noise Contour Model: ANCON Version 1* (DORA Report DR 9120), *The UK Civil Aircraft Noise Contour Model ANCON: Improvements in Version 2* (R&D Report 9842) and *The CAA Aircraft Noise Contour Model: ANCON Version 2.3* (ERCD Report 0606).

At the time of compilation the 2008 data for Heathrow, Gatwick and Stansted were not yet published. The on-line version of table 3.10 will be updated when data is published. Further information on the annual contour reports for Heathrow, Gatwick and Stansted can be found on DfT website at:

http://www.dft.gov.uk/pgr/aviation/
environmentalissues/nec/

An updated version of the Integrated Noise Model (INM) was used to estimate noise contours for Luton airport in 2008. As a result, any year on year comparison (2007 – 2008) should be treated with caution. Further information can be found in Luton's 'Annual Monitoring Report 2008' at:

http://www.londonluton.co.uk/en/content/8/162/
annual-monitoring-report.html

3.1 Petroleum consumption: by transport mode and fuel type: United Kingdom: 1998-2008 [1]

Million tonnes/percentage

	1998	1999	2000	2001	2002	2003	2004	2005	2006	2007	2008 [2]
Road transport:											
Motor Spirit [4]											
Cars & Taxis	20.25	20.35	20.10	19.74	19.71	18.89	18.53	17.84	17.26	16.74	15.87
Light goods	1.21	1.04	0.91	0.79	0.69	0.60	0.54	0.47	0.46	0.42	0.40
Motorcycles	0.15	0.17	0.16	0.17	0.17	0.19	0.18	0.18	0.17	0.19	0.18
Diesel [4]											
Cars & Taxis	3.91	4.36	4.61	4.86	5.36	5.74	6.33	6.82	7.25	7.68	7.51
Light goods	2.81	2.67	2.60	2.65	2.95	3.06	3.37	3.91	3.97	4.15	4.06
Heavy goods	7.42	7.61	7.65	7.82	7.83	8.12	8.04	7.83	8.03	8.30	8.12
Buses & Coaches	1.01	0.87	0.77	0.73	0.78	0.78	0.78	0.87	0.90	0.94	0.92
Propane	-	-	-	0.05	0.09	0.10	0.11	0.12	0.13	0.12	0.12
All [3]	36.76	37.06	36.80	36.81	37.58	37.50	37.87	38.04	38.17	38.55	37.19
Railways:											
Gas/diesel oil & fuel oil	0.55	0.57	0.57	0.60	0.60	0.60	0.63	0.64	0.65	0.63	0.68
Burning oil	0.01	0.01	0.01	0.01	0.01	0.01	0.01	0.01	0.01	0.01	0.00
All	0.56	0.58	0.59	0.61	0.61	0.61	0.64	0.65	0.67	0.64	0.69
Water transport:											
Gas/diesel oil	0.98	0.91	0.91	0.74	0.60	1.09	0.84	0.92	1.19	0.94	1.01
Fuel oil	0.10	0.07	0.04	0.03	0.04	0.05	0.27	0.35	0.50	0.57	0.64
All	1.09	0.98	0.95	0.78	0.65	1.14	1.11	1.27	1.69	1.51	1.65
Air:											
All aviation fuels	9.28	9.98	10.86	10.67	10.57	10.81	11.69	12.55	12.69	12.61	12.17
All petroleum used by transport [3]	47.68	48.61	49.19	48.87	49.41	50.05	51.30	52.51	53.21	53.31	51.70
All petroleum use (energy and non-energy)	78.44	77.97	77.20	76.41	76.23	77.15	79.07	80.73	79.75	77.72	75.95
Transport as a percentage of all energy and non-energy use	*61*	*62*	*64*	*64*	*65*	*65*	*65*	*65*	*67*	*69*	*68*

1 There are revisions to some of the earlier data, for details see
  "Digest of UK Energy Statistics 2009" published by DECC.
2 Figures for 2008 for road transport mode are estimated on 2007 ratios.
3 Excludes a small amount of motor spirit and diesel not used by road vehicles.
4 See the Notes and Definitions for an explanation on changes made to the fuel
  consumption estimates for 2007 and earlier.

☎020-7944 4129
Source - DECC

3.2 Energy consumption: by transport mode and source of energy: United Kingdom: 1998-2008[1]

Million tonnes of oil equivalent/percentage

	1998	1999	2000	2001	2002	2003	2004	2005	2006	2007	2008
Road transport											
Petroleum	41.02	41.40	41.07	41.10	41.94	41.82	42.22	42.39	42.51	42.85	41.33
Railways											
Petroleum	0.61	0.63	0.64	0.66	0.66	0.67	0.70	0.71	0.73	0.70	0.75
Water transport											
Petroleum	1.18	1.07	1.03	0.84	0.70	1.23	1.20	1.37	1.81	1.62	1.76
Aviation											
Petroleum	10.24	11.02	11.98	11.77	11.66	11.94	12.91	13.86	14.00	13.91	13.43
All modes											
Electricity [2]	0.73	0.74	0.74	0.76	0.73	0.71	0.73	0.76	0.71	0.70	0.73
Renewable & Waste [3]	..	..	..	..	..	..	..	..	0.19	0.36	0.82
All energy used by transport	53.77	54.85	55.46	55.14	55.68	56.37	57.75	59.08	59.94	60.13	58.81
All energy used by final users	155.92	156.53	159.21	160.93	156.48	158.03	159.82	160.19	158.33	155.33	154.81
Energy used by transport as a percentage of all energy used by final users	*34*	*35*	*35*	*34*	*36*	*36*	*36*	*37*	*38*	*39*	*38*

1 There are revisions to some of the earlier data, for details see
  "Digest of UK Energy Statistics 2009" published by DECC.
2 Includes consumption at transport premises.
3 Transport use of renewable and waste energy has been published
  in the UK's Aggregate Energy Balance since 2006 and was not collected
  before then. Therefore, there is a discontinuity in the series.

☎020-7944 4129
Source - DECC

3.3 Petrol and diesel prices and duties per litre: at April: 1999-2009

Pence/percentage

	April 1999	April 2000	April 2001	April 2002	April 2003	April 2004	April 2005	April 2006	April 2007	April 2008	April 2009 [4]
Lead replacement petrol [1]											
Price	77.8	84.5	78.2	77.8	81.4	81.3	88.5	..	..	..	..
Duty	52.9	50.9	46.8	48.8	48.8	47.1	47.1	..	..	..	..
VAT	11.6	12.6	11.7	11.6	12.1	12.1	13.2	..	..	..	..
All tax	64.5	63.5	58.5	60.4	61.0	59.2	60.3	..	..	..	..
All tax as a percentage of price	*83*	*75*	*75*	*78*	*75*	*73*	*68*	..	..	..	..
Unleaded petrol [2]											
Price	70.2	80.0	75.9	75.0	78.2	77.8	85.4	94.1	91.9	107.6	93.6
Duty	47.2	48.8	45.8	45.8	45.8	47.1	47.1	47.1	48.4	50.4	54.2
VAT	10.5	11.9	11.3	11.2	11.7	11.6	12.7	14.0	13.7	16.0	12.2
All tax	57.7	60.7	57.1	57.0	57.5	58.7	59.8	61.1	62.0	66.4	66.4
All tax as a percentage of price	*82*	*76*	*75*	*76*	*73*	*75*	*70*	*65*	*67*	*62*	*71*
Ultra low sulphur diesel [3]											
Price	73.2	81.1	77.3	76.9	80.9	79.2	89.6	97.6	94.7	116.6	101.9
Duty	50.2	48.8	45.8	45.8	45.8	47.1	47.1	47.1	48.4	50.4	54.2
VAT	10.9	12.1	11.5	11.5	12.0	11.8	13.3	14.5	14.1	17.4	13.3
All tax	61.1	60.9	57.3	57.3	57.9	58.9	60.4	61.6	62.5	67.7	67.5
All tax as a percentage of price	*83*	*75*	*74*	*74*	*72*	*74*	*67*	*63*	*66*	*58*	*66*

1 Prices prior to 2000 were for four star petrol
   Pump prices are broadly the same.
2 From April 2001, Premium unleaded prices represent Ultra Low Sulphur Petrol (ULSP)
   Pump prices are broadly the same.
3 Prices prior to 2000 were for diesel engined road vehicle fuel (DERV)
   Pump prices are broadly the same.
.. not available - the LRP series has been discontinued as it is no longer marketed.
4 VAT was reduced to 15% from 1 December 2008

☎020-7944 4129
Source - DECC

3.4 Average fuel consumption by age and type of vehicle and type of fuel: 1995/1997 to 2008

a) Passenger cars — Miles per gallon/litres per 100 km

	1995/1997	1998/2000	2002	2003	2004	2005	2006	2007	2008
Petrol cars									
Up to 2 years	32	30	31	31	32	32	32	33	32
Over 2 to 6 years	31	30	31	31	31	31	31	31	31
Over 6 to 10 years	30	30	31	31	30	30	30	30	30
Over 10 years	29	28	28	29	29	30	29	29	29
All petrol cars	31	30	30	30	30	31	31	30	31
Diesel cars [1]									
Up to 2 years	43	35	40	40	41	40	39	40	39
Over 2 years	44	39	38	38	39	38	39	37	38
All diesel cars	44	38	39	39	40	39	39	38	38
Company cars [1]	34	30	35	34	36	36	35	37	37
Private cars	32	31	31	32	32	32	32	32	32
All cars (miles/gallon)	32	31	32	32	32	33	32	32	33
All cars (litres/100 km)	8.8	9.1	8.9	8.9	8.8	8.7	8.8	8.7	8.7

b) HGVs — Miles per gallon

	1996	1999	2002	2003	2004	2005	2006	2007	2008 [2]
Rigid vehicles	9.9	10.3	9.8	9.5	9.8	10.0	9.7	9.4	..
Articulated vehicles	7.6	8.0	7.8	7.8	8.0	8.2	8.1	8.0	..

1 These estimates have a large sampling error because of the smaller sample sizes involved.
2 Data not available at time of publication

Cars: 020 7944 3097
HGVs: 020 7944 4261
Source - Passenger cars: National Travel Survey
HGVs: Continuing Survey of Road Goods Transport

3.5 Average New Car Fuel Consumption: 1998-2008
(Registration-Weighted: petrol and diesel vehicles)

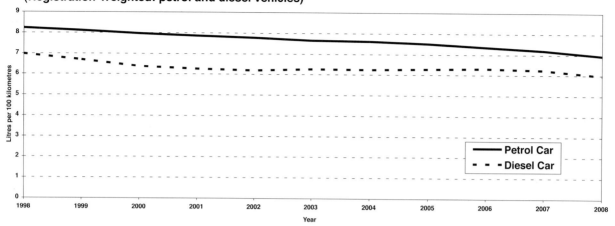

										litres per 100 km/miles per gallon	
	1998	1999	2000	2001	2002	2003	2004	2005	2006	2007	2008
Petrol Car											
litres per 100km	8.23	8.11	7.97	7.86	7.76	7.64	7.60	7.50	7.34	7.19	6.93
miles per gallon	34.32	34.84	35.46	35.94	36.40	36.99	37.16	37.66	38.46	39.28	40.73
Diesel Car											
litres per 100km	6.98	6.68	6.38	6.26	6.18	6.25	6.23	6.28	6.31	6.23	5.97
miles per gallon	40.49	42.26	44.30	45.12	45.69	45.19	45.31	45.00	44.75	45.36	47.29

☎020-7944 4129
The figures in this table are outside the scope of National Statistics
Source - Cleaner Fuels and Vehicles Division, DfT

3.6 Emissions for road vehicles (per vehicle kilometre) in urban conditions

Index: petrol car without three-way catalyst: pre 1993 = 100[1]

(a) Road vehicles (per vehicle kilometre) in urban conditions:			Carbon monoxide	Hydro-carbons[2]	Oxides of nitrogen	Particu-lates[3]	Carbon dioxide[4]
Petrol car without three-way catalyst	Pre-Euro 1	pre 1993	100	100	100	2	100
Petrol car with three-way catalyst	Euro 1	1993-1996	10	2	10	1	98
Petrol car with three-way catalyst	Euro 2	1997-2000	7	2	12	1	98
Petrol car with three-way catalyst	Euro 3	2001-2005	6	1	6	1	92
Petrol car with three-way catalyst	Euro 4	2006-	5	1	2	1	82
Diesel car	Pre-Euro 1	pre 1993	6	10	42	100	97
Diesel car	Euro 1	1993-1996	3	5	33	25	95
Diesel car	Euro 2	1997-2000	2	4	44	16	93
Diesel car	Euro 3	2001-2005	1	3	45	19	83
Diesel car	Euro 4	2006-	1	3	25	16	75
Petrol light goods vehicle without three-way catalyst	Pre-Euro 1	pre 1994	136	96	97	2	109
Petrol light goods vehicle with three-way catalyst	Euro 1	1994-1997	20	3	12	1	138
Petrol light goods vehicle with three-way catalyst	Euro 2	1998-2000	5	2	9	1	146
Petrol light goods vehicle with three-way catalyst	Euro 3	2001-2005	4	1	5	1	139
Petrol light goods vehicle with three-way catalyst	Euro 4	2006-	3	1	2	1	128
Diesel light goods vehicle	Pre-Euro 1	pre 1994	10	19	121	135	141
Diesel light goods vehicle	Euro 1	1994-1997	4	9	74	51	141
Diesel light goods vehicle	Euro 2	1998-2001	4	9	91	53	143
Diesel light goods vehicle	Euro 3	2002-2005	3	7	70	26	131
Diesel light goods vehicle	Euro 4	2006-	3	4	29	17	122
Heavy goods vehicle - Rigid	Pre-Euro I	pre 1993	25	118	604	290	
Heavy goods vehicle - Rigid	Euro I	1993-1996	14	43	402	128	See
Heavy goods vehicle - Rigid	Euro II	1997-2001	11	34	424	58	table
Heavy goods vehicle - Rigid	Euro III	2002-2005	8	23	334	58	3.6b
Heavy goods vehicle - Rigid	Euro IV	2006-	6	17	206	11	
Heavy goods vehicle - Artics	Pre-Euro I	pre 1993	29	100	1,101	325	
Heavy goods vehicle - Artics	Euro I	1993-1996	40	107	771	246	See
Heavy goods vehicle - Artics	Euro II	1997-2001	31	88	796	112	table
Heavy goods vehicle - Artics	Euro III	2002-2005	21	60	634	104	3.6b
Heavy goods vehicle - Artics	Euro IV	2006-	16	44	395	19	
Buses & coaches	Pre-Euro I	pre 1993	81	90	1,557	747	649
Buses & coaches	Euro I	1993-1996	25	67	971	363	537
Buses & coaches	Euro II	1997-2001	21	48	1,027	165	485
Buses & coaches	Euro III	2002-2005	14	33	975	153	485
Buses & coaches	Euro IV	2006-	12	33	557	41	470
Motorcycle (less than 50cc) - two stroke	Pre-Euro 1	pre 2000	236	854	2	108	42
Motorcycle (less than 50cc) - two stroke	Euro 1	2000-2004	24	188	2	44	19
Motorcycle (less than 50cc) - two stroke	Euro 2	2004-2006	24	188	1	22	19
Motorcycle (less than 50cc) - two stroke	Euro 3	2006-	24	188	1	7	19
Motorcycle (greater than 50cc) - two stroke	Pre-Euro 1	pre 2000	231	662	2	115	52
Motorcycle (greater than 50cc) - two stroke	Euro 1	2000-2004	119	458	3	46	41
Motorcycle (greater than 50cc) - two stroke	Euro 2	2004-2006	50	174	3	23	41
Motorcycle (greater than 50cc) - two stroke	Euro 3	2006-	13	60	1	7	41
Motorcycle (greater than 50cc) - four stroke	Pre-Euro 1	pre 2000	206	115	17	12	52
Motorcycle (greater than 50cc) - four stroke	Euro 1	2000-2004	69	48	18	12	45
Motorcycle (greater than 50cc) - four stroke	Euro 2	2004-2006	29	18	10	3	45
Motorcycle (greater than 50cc) - four stroke	Euro 3	2006-	8	6	5	3	45

(b) Fleet averaged CO_2 emissions for HGVs (per vehicle kilometre) in urban conditions[5]

Year	Rigid	Articulated
1990	407	677
1991	414	675
1992	414	670
1993	397	634
1994	386	607
1995	393	578
1996	387	557
1997	384	549
1998	369	516
1999	377	516
2000	376	513
2001	393	518
2002	382	512
2003	398	517
2004	384	497
2005	377	491
2006	387	493
2007	398	502

1 Particulates index is diesel car: pre 1993 =100.
2 Figures based on non-methane hydrocarbons.
3 Legislative standards exist only for diesel vehicles.
4 Legislative standards do not apply to CO_2 emissions, but average factors are available for different legislative vehicle classes based on test cycle data.
5 Based on fleet averaged fuel economy of HGVs using data from DfT survey of road goods transport, corrected for urban driving conditions for comparison with indices in Table 3.6a. These data have been revised since last year as the average miles per gallon fuel efficiency for HGVs has been updated between 1993 and 2007

☎020-7944 4129
The figures in this table are outside the scope of National Statistics
Source - AEA

3.7 Carbon dioxide emissions in the United Kingdom: 1997-2007[1]

	1997	1998	1999	2000	2001	2002	2003	2004	2005	2006	2007	Per cent of total in 2007
(a) By IPCC source category (NAEI)[2]										Million tonnes of carbon dioxide/percentage		
Transport:												
Road transport	116.7	116.0	116.9	116.1	116.1	118.5	118.3	119.5	120.0	120.4	121.6	22.4
Passenger cars	76.5	75.9	77.6	77.6	77.3	78.8	77.4	78.1	77.5	77.0	76.8	14.2
Light duty vehicles	12.6	12.7	11.7	11.1	10.9	11.5	11.6	12.3	13.8	14.0	14.5	2.7
Buses	3.3	3.2	2.8	2.4	2.3	2.5	2.5	2.5	2.7	2.8	3.0	0.6
HGVs	23.6	23.5	24.1	24.2	24.7	24.8	25.7	25.4	24.8	25.4	26.3	4.8
Mopeds & motorcycles	0.5	0.5	0.5	0.5	0.5	0.5	0.6	0.6	0.6	0.5	0.6	0.1
LPG emissions (all vehicles)	0.0	0.0	0.0	0.1	0.2	0.3	0.3	0.3	0.4	0.4	0.4	0.1
Other (road vehicle engines)	0.2	0.2	0.2	0.2	0.2	0.2	0.2	0.2	0.2	0.2	0.2	-
Other transport	7.4	7.3	7.2	7.3	6.9	6.5	8.2	8.4	9.1	10.4	9.7	1.8
Civil aviation	1.5	1.6	1.8	1.9	2.0	2.0	2.0	2.2	2.4	2.3	2.1	0.4
Railways[3]	1.7	1.8	1.8	1.8	1.9	1.9	2.0	2.1	2.1	2.2	2.2	0.4
National navigation	3.8	3.6	3.2	3.1	2.6	2.2	3.7	3.7	4.2	5.5	4.9	0.9
Other (aircraft support vehicles)	0.3	0.4	0.4	0.4	0.4	0.4	0.4	0.4	0.4	0.5	0.5	0.1
Total domestic transport	124.1	123.3	124.1	123.4	123.0	125.0	126.4	127.8	129.1	130.8	131.4	24.2
Net emissions all sources	551.6	553.6	543.0	551.1	562.5	544.9	556.2	555.9	553.2	551.1	542.6	100.0
Memo items[4]												
International bunkers - Aviation	22.7	25.3	27.5	30.3	29.6	29.0	29.7	32.5	35.1	35.6	35.0	.
International bunkers - Navigation	8.2	9.0	6.5	5.7	6.4	5.3	5.1	5.9	5.9	6.8	6.9	.
(b) By National Communication source category (NAEI)[2]										Million tonnes of carbon dioxide/percentage		
Transport:												
Road	116.7	116.0	116.9	116.1	116.1	118.5	118.3	119.5	120.0	120.4	121.6	22.4
Aviation	1.5	1.6	1.8	1.9	2.0	2.0	2.0	2.2	2.4	2.3	2.1	0.4
Railways[3]	1.7	1.8	1.8	1.8	1.9	1.9	2.0	2.1	2.1	2.2	2.2	0.4
Railways - stationary combustion	0.5	0.5	0.5	0.4	0.5	0.4	0.1	0.04	0.04	0.04	0.04	-
Shipping	3.8	3.6	3.2	3.1	2.6	2.2	3.7	3.7	4.2	5.5	4.9	0.9
Aircraft support vehicles	0.3	0.4	0.4	0.4	0.4	0.4	0.4	0.4	0.4	0.5	0.5	0.1
Military aircraft and shipping	3.6	3.2	3.1	2.9	2.9	3.1	2.8	2.9	2.8	2.7	3.5	0.6
Transport Total	128.2	127.0	127.7	126.7	126.4	128.5	129.3	130.7	131.9	133.6	134.9	24.9
Net emissions all sources	551.6	553.6	543.0	551.1	562.5	544.9	556.2	555.9	553.2	551.1	542.6	100.0
(c) By National Communication end user category (NAEI)[5]										Million tonnes of carbon dioxide/percentage		
Transport:												
Road	135.8	135.1	135.4	134.5	135.0	138.4	137.2	136.6	137.6	135.4	136.7	25.2
Aviation	1.7	1.9	2.0	2.2	2.3	2.3	2.4	2.5	2.7	2.6	2.4	0.4
Railways[3]	2.0	2.1	2.1	2.1	2.2	2.3	2.3	2.4	2.4	2.4	2.5	0.5
Railways - stationary combustion	1.9	1.9	1.8	1.8	1.9	1.8	1.5	1.5	1.5	1.7	1.6	0.3
Shipping	4.4	4.1	3.7	3.6	3.0	2.5	4.3	4.2	4.8	6.1	5.5	1.0
Aircraft support vehicles	0.4	0.4	0.4	0.4	0.4	0.4	0.5	0.5	0.5	0.5	0.5	0.1
Military aircraft and shipping	4.2	3.7	3.6	3.4	3.4	3.6	3.3	3.3	3.2	3.1	3.9	0.7
Transport Total	150.5	149.2	149.2	148.0	148.2	151.3	151.4	151.0	152.7	151.8	153.2	28.2
Net emissions all end users	551.6	553.6	543.0	551.1	562.5	544.9	556.2	555.9	553.2	551.1	542.6	100.0
(d) By industry code (Environmental Accounts)[6]										Million tonnes of carbon dioxide/percentage		
Transport industries:												
Railways[3]	1.8	1.9	1.9	1.9	2.0	2.0	2.0	2.1	2.2	2.2	2.3	0.4
Buses and coaches	3.9	3.8	3.4	3.1	2.8	3.1	3.1	3.1	3.3	3.5	3.6	0.6
Tubes and trams	0.5	0.6	0.6	0.5	0.5	0.4	0.1	-	0.05	-	-	-
Taxis operation	2.0	2.1	2.1	2.2	2.2	2.2	2.2	2.3	2.3	2.3	2.4	0.4
Freight transport by road	17.9	18.2	18.5	18.6	19.4	18.5	19.4	18.4	17.8	17.9	18.6	3.0
Transport via pipeline	0.1	0.1	0.1	0.1	0.1	0.1	0.1	0.1	0.1	0.1	0.1	-
Water transport	19.6	19.4	16.5	16.0	20.4	22.1	23.6	27.2	27.1	19.2	17.5	2.9
Air transport	27.7	31.0	33.4	36.9	36.4	35.7	36.9	39.1	42.3	43.1	43.1	7.0
All transport industries	73.5	77.0	76.5	79.3	83.8	84.2	87.5	92.4	95.2	88.4	87.7	14.3
Household use of private vehicles	63.4	63.3	64.6	64.5	65.8	68.2	67.4	68.6	68.3	68.1	67.6	11.0
Total emissions all sectors	601.7	607.7	598.0	609.4	625.8	609.9	624.4	631.1	632.2	622.4	613.1	100.0

1 Data are presented as the weight of carbon dioxide emitted.
  UK national emission estimates are updated annually and any developments in
  methodology are applied retrospectively to earlier years.
2 Source categories relate directly to the vehicle or other piece of equipment
  producing the emission. See Notes and Definitions for further details.
3 Railway emissions are those from diesel trains only.
4 Categories not included in the national total that is reported to the UNFCCC.
5 End user emissions for transport include a share of the emissions from combustion
  of fossil fuels at power stations and other fuel processing industries.
  See Notes and Definitions for further details.
6 The economic sectors are based on similar concepts and classifications of
  industries to those used in the National Accounts. See Notes and Definitions for further details.

☎020-7944 4129
Sources - AEA Energy & Environment/DECC (NAEI);
Office for National Statistics (Environmental Accounts)

3.8 Greenhouse gas emissions in the United Kingdom: 1997-2007[1]

	1997	1998	1999	2000	2001	2002	2003	2004	2005	2006	2007	Per cent of total in 2007
(a) By IPCC source category (NAEI)[2]										Million tonnes of carbon dioxide equivalent/percentage		
Transport:												
Road transport	118.9	118.1	119.0	118.1	118.0	120.3	120.0	121.1	121.5	121.8	123.0	19.3
Passenger cars	78.2	77.5	79.2	79.1	78.7	80.1	78.6	79.2	78.5	78.0	77.7	12.2
Light duty vehicles	12.7	12.8	11.8	11.2	11.0	11.6	11.7	12.5	14.0	14.1	14.6	2.3
Buses	3.4	3.3	2.8	2.5	2.4	2.5	2.5	2.5	2.8	2.9	3.0	0.5
HGVs	23.9	23.8	24.4	24.5	25.1	25.1	26.0	25.8	25.1	25.7	26.6	4.2
Mopeds & motorcycles	0.5	0.5	0.5	0.5	0.5	0.6	0.6	0.6	0.6	0.6	0.6	0.1
LPG emissions (all vehicles)	0.0	0.0	0.0	0.1	0.2	0.3	0.3	0.3	0.4	0.4	0.4	0.1
Other (road vehicle engines)	0.2	0.2	0.2	0.2	0.2	0.2	0.2	0.2	0.2	0.2	0.2	-
Other transport	7.7	7.7	7.5	7.6	7.2	6.8	8.5	8.7	9.5	10.8	10.1	1.6
Civil aviation	1.5	1.6	1.8	1.9	2.0	2.0	2.1	2.2	2.4	2.3	2.2	0.3
Railways[3]	1.9	2.0	2.1	2.1	2.2	2.2	2.2	2.3	2.4	2.4	2.5	0.4
National navigation	3.9	3.6	3.3	3.2	2.6	2.2	3.8	3.7	4.2	5.5	5.0	0.8
Other (aircraft support vehicles)	0.4	0.4	0.4	0.4	0.4	0.4	0.4	0.5	0.5	0.5	0.5	0.1
Total domestic transport	126.5	125.7	126.5	125.7	125.2	127.1	128.5	129.8	131.0	132.6	133.1	20.9
Net emissions all sources	710.7	705.8	672.9	674.9	678.3	656.2	661.0	657.9	652.1	647.5	636.2	100.0
Memo items[4]												
International bunkers - Aviation	23.0	25.6	27.8	30.6	29.9	29.3	30.0	32.9	35.4	36.0	35.3	.
International bunkers - Navigation	8.3	9.0	6.6	5.8	6.5	5.4	5.2	5.9	5.9	6.9	7.0	.
(b) By National Communication source category (NAEI)[2]										Million tonnes of carbon dioxide equivalent/percentage		
Transport:												
Road	118.9	118.1	119.0	118.1	118.0	120.3	120.0	121.1	121.5	121.8	123.0	19.3
Aviation	1.5	1.6	1.8	1.9	2.0	2.0	2.1	2.2	2.4	2.3	2.2	0.3
Railways[3]	1.9	2.0	2.1	2.1	2.2	2.2	2.2	2.3	2.4	2.4	2.5	0.4
Railways - stationary combustion	0.5	0.5	0.5	0.4	0.5	0.4	0.1	0.04	0.05	0.04	0.04	-
Shipping	3.9	3.6	3.3	3.2	2.6	2.2	3.8	3.7	4.2	5.5	5.0	0.8
Aircraft support vehicles	0.4	0.4	0.4	0.4	0.4	0.4	0.4	0.5	0.5	0.5	0.5	0.1
Military aircraft and shipping	3.7	3.2	3.2	2.9	3.0	3.1	2.8	2.9	2.8	2.8	3.5	0.6
Transport Total	130.7	129.5	130.2	129.1	128.6	130.6	131.4	132.7	133.9	135.5	136.7	21.5
Net emissions all sources	710.7	705.8	672.9	674.9	678.3	656.2	661.0	657.9	652.1	647.5	636.2	100.0
(c) By National Communication end user category (NAEI)[5]										Million tonnes of carbon dioxide equivalent/percentage		
Transport:												
Road	139.3	138.5	138.7	137.6	138.1	141.4	139.9	139.2	140.0	137.7	139.0	21.8
Aviation	1.7	1.9	2.1	2.2	2.4	2.4	2.4	2.5	2.8	2.6	2.4	0.4
Railways[3]	2.2	2.4	2.4	2.4	2.5	2.5	2.5	2.6	2.7	2.7	2.8	0.4
Railways - stationary combustion	2.0	2.0	1.9	1.9	2.0	1.9	1.6	1.6	1.6	1.7	1.7	0.3
Shipping	4.5	4.2	3.8	3.7	3.0	2.6	4.4	4.2	4.8	6.2	5.6	0.9
Aircraft support vehicles	0.4	0.5	0.5	0.5	0.5	0.5	0.5	0.5	0.6	0.6	0.6	0.1
Military aircraft and shipping	4.3	3.8	3.7	3.4	3.5	3.6	3.3	3.4	3.2	3.1	4.0	0.6
Transport Total	154.5	153.2	153.0	151.7	151.9	154.8	154.6	154.1	155.6	154.6	156.0	24.5
Net emissions all end users	710.7	705.8	672.9	674.9	678.3	656.2	661.0	657.9	652.1	647.5	636.2	100.0
(d) By industry code (Environmental Accounts)[6]										Million tonnes of carbon dioxide equivalent/percentage		
Transport industries:												
Railways[3]	2.0	2.1	2.1	2.1	2.2	2.2	2.3	2.4	2.4	2.5	2.5	0.4
Buses and coaches	4.0	3.9	3.5	3.2	2.8	3.2	3.2	3.2	3.4	3.6	3.7	0.5
Tubes and trams	0.5	0.6	0.6	0.5	0.5	0.4	0.1	0.05	0.06	0.05	0.05	-
Taxis operation	2.0	2.1	2.2	2.2	2.2	2.2	2.3	2.3	2.3	2.4	2.5	0.4
Freight transport by road	18.1	18.4	18.7	18.8	19.7	18.8	19.7	18.7	18.1	18.2	18.9	2.7
Transport via pipeline	0.1	0.1	0.1	0.1	0.1	0.1	0.1	0.1	0.1	0.1	0.1	-
Water transport	19.8	19.5	16.6	16.1	20.6	22.3	23.8	27.4	27.3	19.4	17.7	2.5
Air transport	28.0	31.4	33.8	37.3	36.8	36.1	37.3	39.5	42.8	43.6	43.5	6.2
All transport industries	74.5	78.1	77.6	80.4	84.9	85.4	88.7	93.6	96.5	89.7	88.9	12.6
Household use of private vehicles	64.9	64.8	66.2	66.1	67.3	69.7	68.9	70.1	69.7	69.4	68.9	9.8
Total emissions all sectors	760.9	760.1	728.1	733.5	741.8	721.4	729.6	733.5	731.5	719.1	707.1	100.0

1 Data are presented as the weight of carbon dioxide equivalent. UK national emission estimates are updated annually and any developments in methodology are applied retrospectively to earlier years.
2 Source categories relate directly to the vehicle or other piece of equipment producing the emission. See Notes and Definitions for further details.
3 Railway emissions are those from diesel trains only.
4 Categories not included in the national total that is reported to the UNFCCC.
5 End user emissions for transport include a share of the emissions from combustion of fossil fuels at power stations and other fuel processing industries. See Notes and Definitions for further details.
6 The economic sectors are based on similar concepts and classifications of industries to those used in the National Accounts. See Notes and Definitions for further details.
Note: The basket of six greenhouse gases are carbon dioxide, methane, nitrous oxide, hydro-fluorocarbons, perfluorocarbons and sulphur hexafluoride (CO2, CH4, N2O, HFC, PFC and SF6).

☎020-7944 4129
Sources - AEA Energy & Environment/DECC (NAEI);
Office for National Statistics (Environmental Accounts)

3.9 Pollutant emissions from transport in the United Kingdom (by UNECE source category): 1997-2007[1]

(a) Carbon monoxide (CO) — Thousand tonnes/percentage

	1997	1998	1999	2000	2001	2002	2003	2004	2005	2006	2007	Per cent of total in 2007
Transport:												
Road transport	3,706	3,355	2,997	2,480	2,093	1,807	1,541	1,305	1,058	918	786	37.2
Passenger cars	3,106	2,800	2,516	2,084	1,764	1,534	1,303	1,105	881	760	639	30.3
Light duty vehicles	406	364	287	221	168	123	91	71	56	49	45	2.1
Buses	25	21	17	13	10	8	7	5	5	5	4	0.2
HGVs	70	68	65	62	58	55	51	49	46	44	41	2.0
Mopeds & motorcycles	99	102	112	99	93	88	89	75	71	60	56	2.6
Other transport	66	67	74	81	85	74	73	80	85	83	65	3.1
Civil aviation	39	39	46	53	58	50	46	52	56	50	34	1.6
Railways	11	12	12	13	13	12	11	12	12	12	12	0.6
National navigation	9	8	7	7	6	5	8	8	9	13	11	0.5
Other mobile sources[2]	1.3	1.4	1.5	1.5	1.5	1.5	1.6	1.6	1.7	1.8	1.8	0.1
All domestic transport	3,772	3,422	3,071	2,561	2,178	1,881	1,614	1,385	1,143	1,000	851	40.2
Total	5,799	5,362	4,975	4,264	3,901	3,355	2,946	2,707	2,383	2,270	2,114	100.0
Memo items[3]												
International bunkers - Aviation	15	16	17	18	17	17	17	18	19	19	19	.
International bunkers - Navigation	19	21	15	13	15	12	12	14	13	16	16	.

(b) Nitrogen oxides (NO_x) — Thousand tonnes/percentage

	1997	1998	1999	2000	2001	2002	2003	2004	2005	2006	2007	Per cent of total in 2007
Transport:												
Road transport	891	856	808	749	693	643	594	555	514	478	441	29.7
Passenger cars	479	443	404	357	313	276	236	206	180	158	137	9.2
Light duty vehicles	87	89	86	84	83	78	75	72	67	59	55	3.7
Buses	61	60	58	54	52	51	51	48	46	47	47	3.2
HGVs	262	263	258	251	243	237	230	228	219	212	201	13.6
Mopeds & motorcycles	1.2	1.3	1.4	1.4	1.5	1.5	1.6	1.5	1.5	1.3	1.3	0.1
Other transport	128	126	123	126	115	100	133	134	148	178	166	11.2
Civil aviation	5.0	5.6	6.4	7.1	7.3	7.1	7.3	8.1	8.9	8.8	8.5	0.6
Railways	30	32	35	40	42	36	34	36	37	38	39	2.6
National navigation	84	79	71	69	56	47	82	80	92	122	109	7.4
Other mobile sources[2]	5.8	6.1	6.2	6.3	6.0	5.8	5.7	5.6	5.6	5.3	4.8	0.3
All domestic transport	1,019	982	931	875	808	743	726	689	662	656	607	40.9
Total	2,068	2,020	1,911	1,867	1,813	1,701	1,710	1,657	1,622	1,597	1,486	100.0
Memo items[3]												
International bunkers - Aviation	106	118	127	138	134	130	133	146	157	160	156	.
International bunkers - Navigation	187	203	147	129	145	121	116	132	132	153	156	.

(c) Particulates (PM_{10}) — Thousand tonnes/percentage

	1997	1998	1999	2000	2001	2002	2003	2004	2005	2006	2007	Per cent of total in 2007
Transport:												
Road transport	41.4	39.4	37.5	32.3	30.7	29.4	28.2	27.4	26.3	25.5	24.7	18.3
Passenger cars	9.4	8.9	8.8	7.1	6.9	6.8	6.5	6.3	6.2	6.1	5.9	4.4
Light duty vehicles	9.7	9.3	8.7	6.9	6.6	6.0	5.7	5.4	5.0	4.6	4.4	3.3
Buses	2.6	2.3	2.0	1.6	1.3	1.2	1.1	1.0	0.9	0.8	0.8	0.6
HGVs	11.0	10.1	9.0	7.6	6.8	6.1	5.5	5.2	4.7	4.4	3.8	2.8
Mopeds & motorcycles	0.2	0.2	0.2	0.2	0.2	0.2	0.2	0.2	0.2	0.1	0.1	0.1
Automobile tyre & brake wear	8.5	8.6	8.8	8.8	8.9	9.1	9.2	9.4	9.4	9.5	9.6	7.1
Other transport	6.1	5.8	5.4	5.1	4.5	3.8	5.6	6.4	7.4	9.5	9.1	6.7
Civil aviation	0.1	0.1	0.1	0.1	0.1	0.1	0.1	0.1	0.1	0.1	0.1	0.1
Railways	0.7	0.8	0.8	0.8	0.9	0.7	0.6	0.6	0.7	0.7	0.7	0.5
National navigation	4.8	4.4	3.9	3.7	3.0	2.6	4.4	5.2	6.2	8.3	7.9	5.9
Other mobile sources[2]	0.5	0.6	0.6	0.6	0.5	0.5	0.5	0.5	0.5	0.5	0.4	0.3
All domestic transport	47.5	45.3	42.9	37.4	35.2	33.3	33.8	33.8	33.7	35.0	33.8	25.0
Total	210	195	184	170	162	139	139	138	135	137	135	100.0
Memo items[3]												
International bunkers - Aviation	1.4	1.5	1.7	1.8	1.8	1.8	1.8	2.0	2.1	2.2	2.1	.
International bunkers - Navigation	17.0	17.3	12.4	10.5	10.9	9.3	9.5	10.9	11.5	13.2	14.0	.
Road transport resuspension[4]	18.6	19.0	19.3	19.4	19.7	20.2	20.3	20.7	20.7	21.1	21.3	.

(d) Benzene — Thousand tonnes/percentage

	1997	1998	1999	2000	2001	2002	2003	2004	2005	2006	2007	Per cent of total in 2007
Transport:												
Road transport[5]	23.8	20.6	17.6	5.7	5.3	4.6	4.0	3.4	2.8	2.5	2.2	13.2
Passenger cars	20.0	17.2	14.6	5.0	4.5	4.0	3.4	2.9	2.4	2.1	1.8	10.9
Light duty vehicles	1.6	1.4	1.1	0.3	0.3	0.3	0.2	0.2	0.2	0.2	0.2	0.9
Buses	-	-	-	-	-	-	-	-	-	-	-	
HGVs	-	-	-	-	-	-	-	-	-	-	-	0.1
Mopeds & motorcycles	0.9	0.9	1.0	0.2	0.3	0.3	0.3	0.2	0.2	0.2	0.2	1.0
Gasoline evaporation	1.3	1.0	0.9	0.2	0.2	0.1	0.1	0.1	0.1	0.1	0.0	0.2
Other transport	1.0	0.9	0.9	0.9	0.8	0.8	1.0	1.0	1.1	1.3	1.2	7.1
Civil aviation	-	-	-	-	-	-	-	-	-	-	-	0.1
Railways	0.4	0.4	0.4	0.4	0.5	0.4	0.4	0.5	0.5	0.5	0.5	3.2
National navigation	0.5	0.4	0.4	0.4	0.3	0.3	0.5	0.5	0.5	0.7	0.6	3.7
Other mobile sources[2]	-	-	-	-	-	-	-	-	-	-	-	0.1
All domestic transport	24.8	21.6	18.5	6.6	6.1	5.4	5.0	4.4	3.9	3.8	3.4	20.3
Total	39.1	35.0	31.5	18.6	17.6	16.3	15.7	16.2	16.2	16.6	16.8	100.0
Memo items[3]												
International bunkers - Aviation	0.1	0.1	0.1	0.1	0.1	0.1	0.1	0.1	0.1	0.1	0.1	.
International bunkers - Navigation	1.1	1.2	0.8	0.7	0.8	0.7	0.7	0.8	0.7	0.9	0.9	.

3.9 (Continued) Pollutant emissions from transport in the United Kingdom (by UNECE source category): 1997-2007[1]

	1997	1998	1999	2000	2001	2002	2003	2004	2005	2006	2007	Per cent of total in 2007
(e) 1,3-butadiene												Thousand tonnes/percentage
Transport:												
Road transport	6.1	5.3	4.6	3.8	3.2	2.7	2.3	1.9	1.6	1.4	1.3	53.2
Passenger cars	4.1	3.5	2.9	2.4	1.9	1.5	1.2	0.9	0.7	0.6	0.5	19.3
Light duty vehicles	0.4	0.3	0.3	0.2	0.2	0.1	0.1	0.1	0.1	0.1	0.1	3.1
Buses	0.2	0.2	0.1	0.1	0.1	0.1	0.1	0.1	0.1	0.1	0.1	2.5
HGVs	1.2	1.1	1.0	1.0	0.9	0.8	0.7	0.7	0.6	0.6	0.6	23.5
Mopeds & motorcycles	0.2	0.2	0.2	0.2	0.2	0.2	0.2	0.2	0.1	0.1	0.1	4.9
Other transport	0.2	0.2	0.2	0.2	0.2	0.2	0.2	0.2	0.2	0.2	0.2	8.6
Civil aviation	-	-	-	-	-	-	-	-	-	-	-	0.5
Railways	0.2	0.2	0.2	0.2	0.2	0.2	0.2	0.2	0.2	0.2	0.2	8.4
National navigation	..	..	..	..	..	..	..	..	..	..	..	..
Other mobile sources[2]	-	-	-	-	-	-	-	-	-	-	-	0.3
All domestic transport	6.3	5.5	4.8	4.0	3.4	2.9	2.4	2.1	1.8	1.6	1.5	61.8
Total	7.5	6.7	6.1	5.2	4.5	3.9	3.4	3.1	2.7	2.5	2.4	100.0
Memo items[3]												
International bunkers - Aviation	0.1	0.1	0.1	0.1	0.1	0.1	0.1	0.1	0.1	0.1	0.1	.
International bunkers - Navigation	..	..	..	..	..	..	..	..	..	..	..	.
(f) Lead (Pb)												Tonnes/percentage
Transport:												
Road transport[6]	780	572	301	2.2	2.0	2.0	2.0	2.0	2.1	2.1	1.7	2.4
Passenger cars	729	535	283	1.6	1.4	1.3	1.3	1.3	1.4	1.4	1.0	1.5
Light duty vehicles	45.5	32.2	14.6	0.2	0.2	0.2	0.2	0.2	0.2	0.2	0.2	0.3
Buses	0.1	0.1	-	-	-	-	-	-	-	-	-	0.1
HGVs	0.4	0.4	0.4	0.4	0.4	0.4	0.4	0.4	0.4	0.4	0.4	0.6
Mopeds & motorcycles	5.2	4.0	2.3	-	-	-	-	-	-	-	-	-
Other transport	0.6	0.6	0.6	0.6	0.5	0.5	0.7	0.7	0.8	1.0	0.9	1.3
Civil aviation	-	-	-	-	-	-	-	-	-	-	-	-
Railways	0.2	0.2	0.2	0.2	0.2	0.2	0.2	0.2	0.2	0.2	0.2	0.3
National navigation	0.4	0.4	0.3	0.3	0.3	0.2	0.4	0.4	0.5	0.7	0.6	0.9
Other mobile sources[2]	-	-	-	-	-	-	-	-	-	-	-	0.1
All domestic transport	780	572	301	2.8	2.5	2.4	2.6	2.7	2.8	3.0	2.6	3.7
Total	1,134	832	478	150	142	131	116	118	109	82	70	100.0
Memo items[3]												
International bunkers - Aviation	0.4	0.4	0.5	0.5	0.5	0.5	0.5	0.6	0.6	0.6	0.6	.
International bunkers - Navigation	1.2	1.2	0.9	0.8	0.8	0.7	0.7	0.8	0.8	1.0	1.0	.
(g) Sulphur dioxide (SO₂)												Thousand tonnes/percentage
Transport:												
Road transport	28.4	23.5	14.4	6.7	4.2	3.8	3.8	3.5	3.0	2.7	2.3	0.4
Passenger cars	18.4	13.8	12.2	5.5	3.2	2.8	2.7	2.6	2.2	2.1	1.8	0.3
Light duty vehicles	3.1	2.9	0.9	0.4	0.3	0.3	0.3	0.3	0.3	0.2	0.2	-
Buses	0.8	0.5	0.1	0.1	0.1	0.1	0.1	0.1	0.1	-	-	-
HGVs	6.0	6.2	1.1	0.6	0.6	0.6	0.6	0.6	0.5	0.4	0.3	-
Mopeds & motorcycles	0.1	0.1	0.1	-	-	-	-	-	-	-	-	-
Other transport	30.0	27.9	24.6	22.9	19.3	17.2	27.4	34.3	40.4	53.7	52.1	8.8
Civil aviation	0.5	0.5	0.4	0.4	0.5	0.4	0.5	0.6	0.6	0.7	0.6	0.1
Railways	1.5	1.6	1.6	1.5	1.4	1.4	1.9	1.9	1.9	2.0	1.9	0.3
National navigation	27.4	25.1	22.1	20.3	16.8	14.5	24.4	31.1	37.2	50.2	48.9	8.3
Other mobile sources[2]	0.3	0.3	0.3	0.3	0.3	0.3	0.4	0.4	0.4	0.4	0.4	0.1
All domestic transport	58.4	51.4	39.0	29.5	23.4	20.9	31.2	37.8	43.4	56.4	54.3	9.2
Total	1,662	1,630	1,218	1,231	1,106	979	966	813	687	671	591	100.0
Memo items[3]												
International bunkers - Aviation	7.2	8.0	6.1	6.9	7.5	6.1	7.2	8.5	9.1	11.0	9.7	.
International bunkers - Navigation	110.7	111.2	79.1	66.3	67.3	58.3	60.2	69.6	74.6	85.3	91.1	.

1 UK national emission estimates are updated annually and any developments in
   methodology are applied retrospectively to earlier years.
2 Includes machinery (Aircraft support vehicles).
3 Categories not included in the national total that is reported to UNECE.
4 Resuspension of particles caused by the turbulence of passing vehicles. Not included in totals for PM₁₀
   to avoid double-counting, but is important in reconciling roadside concentration measurements.
5 Reduction in road transport benzene emissions in 2000 mainly due to reduction in benzene content of petrol.
6 Reduction in road transport lead emissions in 2000 is mainly due to a ban on the general sale of leaded petrol.

☎020-7944 4129
Source - AEA Energy & Environment/Defra

3.10 Aircraft noise: population affected by noise around airports: 1998-2008

(a) Heathrow	1998	1999	2000	2001	2002	2003	2004	2005	2006	2007	2008 [1]
Air transport movements (thousands)	441.2	449.5	459.7	457.6	460.3	457.1	469.8	472.0	470.9	475.8	473.2
Area (sq kms) within:											
57 Leq contour	163.7	155.6	135.6	117.4	126.9	126.9	117.4	117.2	117.4	119.6	..
63 Leq contour	55.4	53.9	48.2	41.2	43.8	43.8	40.3	39.1	38.4	37.6	..
69 Leq contour	22.8	21.9	19.0	14.1	16.4	15.6	13.3	12.4	11.9	12.2	..
Population (thousands) within:											
57 Leq contour	341.0	331.6	275.2	240.4	258.3	263.7	239.7	251.7	258.0	251.9	..
63 Leq contour	82.2	91.2	71.9	54.9	64.2	64.6	55.9	51.8	51.2	45.1	..
69 Leq contour	15.5	13.8	11.5	6.8	8.6	8.0	5.7	3.9	3.6	3.7	..
(b) Gatwick											
Air transport movements (thousands)	240.2	244.7	251.2	244.0	233.6	234.5	241.2	252.0	254.4	258.9	256.4
Area (sq kms) within:											
57 Leq contour	76.8	71.4	71.9	55.9	45.2	46.1	48.0	49.3	46.7	49.0	..
63 Leq contour	28.2	26.4	26.4	19.6	15.8	16.5	16.7	16.9	15.6	16.3	..
69 Leq contour	9.7	8.9	9.0	6.0	4.6	4.8	4.8	5.1	4.6	4.9	..
Population (thousands) within:											
57 Leq contour	9.0	7.8	8.7	5.2	3.5	4.2	4.5	4.7	4.5	4.8	..
63 Leq contour	1.4	1.4	1.4	0.8	0.5	0.6	0.6	0.7	0.6	0.6	..
69 Leq contour	0.3	0.3	0.2	0.1	0.1	0.1	0.1	0.1	-	-	..
(c) Stansted											
Air transport movements (thousands)	102.2	132.3	143.6	150.6	152.4	169.2	176.8	178.0	190.0	191.5	177.3
Area (sq kms) within:											
57 Leq contour	64.5	52.3	52.4	32.1	31.7	33.3	29.9	27.4	29.3	30.8	..
63 Leq contour	22.3	20.5	20.4	11.6	11.3	11.7	9.9	8.7	8.6	8.9	..
69 Leq contour	8.7	7.9	7.6	3.6	3.4	3.5	2.8	2.4	2.3	2.5	..
Population (thousands) within:											
57 Leq contour	7.6	4.4	5.7	2.3	2.0	2.3	2.9	2.0	2.0	2.5	..
63 Leq contour	1.3	1.4	1.3	0.4	0.3	0.5	0.3	0.3	0.3	0.3	..
69 Leq contour	0.3	0.2	0.2	0.1	0.1	-	-	-	-	-	..
(d) Manchester											
Air transport movements (thousands)	161.8	169.3	177.6	182.1	177.5	191.5	208.5	218.0	213.0	206.5	191.2
Area (sq kms) within:											
57 Leq contour	53.5	48.5	46.4	43.4	40.3	39.1	39.6	40.2	37.7	37.5	35.0
63 Leq contour	16.9	17.6	15.8	14.6	12.8	13.3	13.7	14.3	13.0	12.4	11.1
69 Leq contour	6.1	5.9	5.0	4.8	4.2	4.4	4.6	4.8	4.6	4.4	3.8
Population (thousands) within:											
57 Leq contour	44.7	53.5	48.4	44.9	38.7	40.6	40.9	41.6	39.2	36.8	33.1
63 Leq contour	10.1	11.9	9.4	6.4	4.5	5.8	5.1	5.6	4.0	3.5	3.0
69 Leq contour	2.0	1.9	1.2	0.5	0.5	0.6	0.6	0.6	0.2	0.1	0.1
(e) Birmingham											
Air transport movements (thousands)	88.2	98.4	108.4	111.0	112.3	116.0	109.2	113.0	108.7	104.5	102.9
Area (sq kms) within:											
57 Leq contour	35.3	..	19.0	..	14.8	..	16.2	..	16.8	..	15.6
63 Leq contour	12.3	..	6.2	..	4.4	..	5.1	..	5.2	..	4.6
69 Leq contour	4.5	..	1.7	..	1.2	..	1.3	..	1.4	..	1.4
Population (thousands) within:											
57 Leq contour	65.6	..	33.7	..	23.7	..	26.2	..	26.8	..	22.2
63 Leq contour	16.5	..	5.5	..	2.6	..	3.8	..	3.6	..	2.4
69 Leq contour	2.5	..	0.1	..	-	..	-	..	-	..	-
(f) Luton [2]											
Air transport movements (thousands)	43.6	50.8	55.5	56.0	55.0	58.4	64.2	75.4	78.8	83.3	85.7
Area (sq kms) within:											
57 Leq contour	15.8	19.6	17.6	10.6	10.9	12.2	12.8	13.5	14.9	15.4	16.6
63 Leq contour	5.5	7.3	6.6	3.5	3.6	4.0	4.2	4.2	4.8	5.1	5.2
69 Leq contour	2.0	2.5	2.4	1.2	1.2	1.3	1.3	1.3	1.5	1.6	1.5
Population (thousands) within:											
57 Leq contour	5.8	7.4	8.1	2.3	2.4	3.2	3.8	2.6	3.0	4.4	5.3
63 Leq contour	1.1	1.2	1.7	-	0.1	0.1	0.1	0.1	0.1	0.1	0.1
69 Leq contour	0.0	0.0	0.0	0.0	0.0	0.0	0.0	0.0	0.0	0.0	0.0

1 At the time of compilation the 2008 figures for Heathrow, Gatwick and Stansted were not yet published. See DfT website for updated table.
2 An updated version of the Integrated Noise Model (INM) was used to estimate noise contours for Luton airport in 2008. As a result, any year on year comparison (2007 - 2008) should be treated with caution.

☎020-7944 4276
The figures in this table are outside the scope of National Statistics
Sources - Noise contour data: Major UK airports
Air transport movements: Civil Aviation Authority

4 Freight:

Notes and Definitions

Freight transport by mode: 4.1 – 4.3

Road: These figures include the activity of goods vehicles over 3.5 tonnes gross vehicle weight and light goods vehicles up to that weight. The estimates for heavy goods vehicles are derived from the Continuing Survey of Road Goods Transport (CSRGT) and, for light goods vehicles, from surveys carried out in 1976, 1987, 1992/93, and from 2003 to 2005 with data being interpolated for the intervening years. The light goods vehicle component of Table 4.2 has been allocated to the appropriate commodity group. In previous years it had been assumed that it should all be in the 'miscellaneous' category. Figures for 2005 onwards are therefore not strictly comparable with those previously published for earlier years.

Rail: Figures up to 1962 include free-hauled (Departmental *i.e.* goods carried by British Rail for its own purposes) traffic on revenue-earning trains (the inclusion of this traffic in 1962 would have increased the figure). Figures for rail are for each financial year.

Water: Figures from 1972 onwards are not comparable with earlier years. From 1972, water includes all UK coastwise and one-port freight movements by sea, and inland waterway traffic. Earlier years include only GB coastwise traffic and internal traffic on waterways controlled by British Waterways.

Pipeline: Pipeline estimates are for oil pipelines only (excluding offshore pipelines); data differ from those in the International Comparisons section as the latter exclude pipelines less than 50 kilometres long. The increase between 1989 and 1990 is largely due to changes in coverage.

Air: Domestic air cargo (freight and mail) within the United Kingdom, while sometimes important in terms of speed of delivery, is insignificant in volume; in 2008, domestic air cargo carried by UK airlines amounted to only 37 million tonne kilometres (see Table 2.4(f)).

Road freight transport by goods vehicles over 3.5 tonnes gross weight: 4.4-4.6

The data in these tables are derived from the Continuing Survey of Road Goods Transport.

Estimates are of domestic freight activity by GB-registered heavy goods vehicles over 3.5 tonnes gross vehicle weight. These vehicles pay the goods vehicle rates of Vehicle Excise Duty, are subject to goods vehicle 'plating' and annual testing, and require a goods operator's licence. They currently account for some 93 per cent of road freight activity, with the rest being carried by light goods vehicles up to 3.5 tonnes gross vehicle weight.

In Table 4.5, freight activity is measured in terms of the weight of goods (tonnes) handled, taking no account of the distance they are carried; this is termed 'goods lifted'. The measure in Table 4.4 is 'goods moved' (tonne kilometres) which does take account of distance. 'Goods moved', for each loaded journey, is the weight of the load multiplied by the distance it is carried. 'Goods moved' is therefore a better measure of the work done by heavy goods vehicles. In both tables activity is shown by 'mode of working', 'gross weight of vehicle' and 'commodity'.

In Tables 4.4 and 4.5 'Crude minerals' comprises *sand, gravel and clay* and *other crude minerals*. 'Building materials' comprises *cement* and *other building materials*.

The vehicle weight groups reflect some of the operating controls on goods vehicles. For rigid vehicles the maximum allowed gross vehicle weights are:

- 18 tonnes on 2 axles

- 26 tonnes on 3 axles

- 32 tonnes on 4 axles

For articulated vehicles the general limits are:

- 38 tonnes on 4 axles

- 40 tonnes on 5 axles

- 44 tonnes on 6 axles

'Mode of working' relates to whether goods are being carried on either a hire or reward or own account basis. The former relates to the carriage of goods owned by people other than the operator; the latter covers goods carried by operators in the course of their own trade or business.

The tonnes lifted and tonne kilometres estimates shown in these tables are not directly comparable to those of heavy goods vehicle kilometres derived from the traffic census in Table 7.2. Therefore, any analysis such as calculating average load (tonne kilometres/

vehicle kilometres) should use estimates published in *Road Freight Statistics 2008* which is available from DfT, available at:

http://www.dft.gov.uk/pgr/statistics/
datatablespublications/freight/goodsbyroad

The estimates are derived from the Continuing Survey of Road Goods Transport (CSRGT) which in 2008 was based on an average weekly returned sample of some 300 heavy goods vehicles. The samples are drawn from the vehicle licence records held by the Driver and Vehicle Licensing Agency (DVLA). Questionnaires are sent to the registered keepers of the sampled vehicles asking for details of its activity during the survey week. The estimates are grossed to the vehicle population and, and at the overall national level have a three per cent margin of error (at 95 per cent confidence level). Further details and results are published in *Road Freight Statistics 2008*, and previously in *Transport of Goods by Road in Great Britain*.

Methodological changes

A key component of National Statistics outputs is a programme of quality reviews carried out at least every five years to ensure that such statistics are fit for purpose and that their quality and value continue to improve. A quality review of the Department for Transport's road freight surveys, including the CSRGT, was carried out in 2003. A copy of the report can be accessed at

http://www.statistics.gov.uk/nsbase/
methods_quality/quality_review/downloads/
NSQR30FinalReport.doc

The quality review made a number of recommendations about the CSRGT. The main methodological recommendation was that, to improve the accuracy of survey estimates, the sample strata should be amended to reflect current trends in vehicle type, weight and legislative groups. These new strata are described more fully in the survey report. For practical and administrative reasons, changes were also made to the sample selection methodology. These changes have resulted in figures from 2004 onwards not being fully comparable with those for 2003 and earlier years. Detailed comparisons should therefore be made with caution.

United Kingdom Statistics Authority (UKSA) Assessment of 'Statistics on Road Freight'

In July 2009, the UK Statistics Authority confirmed that the statistics published in *Road Goods Vehicles Travelling to Mainland Europe* (quarterly series and annual bulletin), the *Survey of Foreign Vehicle Activity in Great Britain*, and *Road Freight Statistics* are designated as National Statistics, subject to the implementation of certain enhancements. The assessment report is published at:

http://www.statisticsauthority.gov.uk/
assessment/assessment-reports/assessment-
report-6---road-freight-statistics--27-july-2009.
pdf.

International Roads Goods Transport: 4.7-4.9

Note: Tables 4.7 and 4.8 were not available at time of publication but will be published on the Department's website once they are available:

http://www.dft.gov.uk/pgr/statistics/
datatablespublications/freight/goodsbyroad/

These tables show the international activity of United Kingdom registered vehicles. The statistics for GB registered vehicles are derived from the International Road Haulage Survey (IRHS), which has been conducted by the Department for Transport (and its predecessors) since 1979 in order to comply with EC Regulation 1172/98 (which replaced EC Directive 78/546 and 89/462). The Regulation requires each member state to compile statistics of the international road haulage carried out by its own goods vehicles as well as national haulage (see Tables 4.4 and 4.5).

The IRHS is carried out by asking hauliers who undertake international work to report the details of recently completed international trips travelling to mainland Europe or the Irish Republic via roll-on/roll-off ferry services or through the Channel Tunnel. Details of the sampling scheme are available from DfT.

The sample is grossed up quarterly in stages: the results, by each ferry route, are grossed to total route traffic; figures are then re-grossed to the grand total of United Kingdom powered vehicles on all ferry routes and the Channel Tunnel, to allow for routes not sampled. The ferry totals are obtained from the associated quarterly 'Ro-Ro survey'. Vehicles registered to hauliers operating in Northern Ireland are covered by the CSRGT (NI). Since 2004, this survey has been expanded to cover international activity including that across the Irish land boundary. Details of this activity are shown in Table 4.9.

A substantial amount of traffic goes by unaccompanied trailers (as well as in the foreign powered vehicles) for which statistics are not obtained in this survey. In particular, trade across the North Sea is mainly carried on unaccompanied trailers. Freight carried in foreign vehicles is not included in the IRHS (or CSRGT) tables. Other EU countries, being subject to the same Regulation, obtain comparable statistics which are published by Eurostat.

The goods classification, *Nomenclature Statistiques de Transport* (NST), the classification of commodities for transport statistics used in the European Union, is a hierarchical structure which divides the 176 headings of the classification into 10 chapters and 52 main groups. At present it is only practicable to disaggregate the IRHS data by 'chapter' apart from showing separately the two main components of chapter 9.

In Table 4.9, only 'bilateral' traffic is shown, that is traffic between the United Kingdom and another country in either United Kingdom vehicles or in those registered in that other country. The figures exclude 'cross trade', i.e. trade in vehicles registered other than in the country of loading or unloading.

National Railways Freight Traffic: 4.10-4.11

These tables summarise the performance of the freight business in terms of freight 'lifted' (measured in tonnes) and freight 'moved' (measured in tonne-kilometres). Freight 'moved' takes account of the distance the goods are carried.

In February 1996, British Rail's (BR) bulk freight operations were sold to North and South Railways, subsequently called English, Welsh and Scottish Railway (EWS). In 2007, EWS was bought by Deutsche Bahn and in January 2009 was re-named DB Schenker. The other major companies in the rail freight sector are Freightliner Ltd (formerly the BR container business), Direct Rail Services (DRS) and First GB Railfreight.

Freight moved is measured in net tonne kilometres (NTKm). This takes into account the net weight (excluding the weight of the locomotive and wagons) of the goods carried (the freight lifted, measured in tonnes) and the distance carried.

Although it is not included in the total NTKm, we have included a separate series on infrastructure traffic (goods used for railway engineering work). International comprises trains travelling through the Channel Tunnel; Domestic intermodal includes goods that have arrived by sea at ports.

Following the move of BR's bulk freight operations to the private sector there have been some changes in the way estimates of freight traffic have been compiled. In particular, the method of estimating tonne kilometres is different with the result that recent estimates are not consistent with those for earlier periods. Some revisions have been made to the series. The freight moved series now has a full commodity breakdown.

Freight lifted is the mass of goods carried on the network. It excludes the weight of the locomotives and wagons. Unlike freight moved it takes no account of the distance travelled. Data pre and post-privatisation are not directly comparable. The freight lifted table has been changed from the previous edition of TSGB to include historic data from 1986/87.

Further details can be found in *National Rail Trends* published each quarter, by the Office of Rail Regulation (ORR).

National Railways freight train movements and impacts on road haulage: 4.12

This table shows the total number of train movements (including infrastructure trains) on the network and the equivalent distance that road vehicles would need to have travelled to move the amounts of freight carried on rail.

It also shows the equivalent number of road vehicle trips necessary to move this freight. These measures provide an alternative to the traditional deadweight-based approach. These data are only available up to the 2007-08 financial year, due to the unavailability of more up-to-date road freight data.

Roll-on/roll-off: 4.13 and 4.14

Statistics on the number of lorries and unaccompanied trailers travelling from Great Britain to mainland Europe and Ireland are compiled from quarterly returns provided by roll-on/roll-off ferry operators and from monthly information supplied by Eurotunnel (unaccompanied trailers are not carried by Eurotunnel). Disaggregation by the country of registration of powered vehicles is provided by most of the ferry operators and by Eurotunnel. On some routes the operators can extract the nationality directly from the manifests or waybills, while on others each one is identified from the registration number pattern. The results are broken down by country of vehicle registration, by country of disembarkation and by GB port group. Separate figures are given for powered vehicles and unaccompanied trailers.

Powered vehicles comprise rigid vehicles, lorries with semi-trailers (articulated units) and lorries with drawbar trailers. (Some vehicles under 3.5 tonnes gross vehicle weight are also included).

Unaccompanied trailers are trailers and semi-trailers not accompanied on the ferry by a powered unit.

Up to 1978 inward traffic was also recorded, but because it was similar to outward traffic the data requirement was discontinued to save respondent effort; consequently the statistics in these tables are for outward traffic only.

Revised estimates for 2004 to 2007 were published in May 2008 following a data quality review. This resulted in a break in the series between 2003 and 2004 and comparisons by country of registration should therefore be treated with caution.

Further details of the review were published in the annual bulletin "*Roads Goods Vehicles Travelling to Mainland Europe: 2007*". More detailed analyses are provided in the quarterly bulletins of this publication; both the quarterly and annual bulletins are available on the Department's website:

http://www.dft.gov.uk/pgr/statistics/
datatablespublications/freight/secroadseur

4.1 Domestic freight transport: by mode: 1953-2008

For greater detail of the years 1998-2008 see Table 4.3

Year	Goods moved (billion tonne kilometres)					Goods lifted (million tonnes)				
	Road	Rail [1]	Water	Pipe-line	All modes	Road	Rail [1]	Water	Pipe-line	All modes
1953	32	37	20	-	89	889	294	52	2	1,237
1954	35	36	20	-	91	940	288	52	2	1,282
1955	38	35	20	-	93	1,013	279	50	2	1,344
1956	38	35	22	-	95	1,009	281	55	2	1,347
1957	37	34	21	-	92	985	279	55	2	1,321
1958	41	30	21	-	92	1,078	247	53	2	1,380
1959	46	29	21	-	96	1,164	238	53	3	1,458
1960	49	30	20	-	99	1,211	252	54	4	1,521
1961	53	29	22	1	105	1,260	242	56	6	1,564
1962	55	26	24	1	106	1,268	232	58	7	1,565
1963	57	25	25	1	108	1,407	239	60	15	1,721
1964	66	26	25	1	118	1,560	243	61	18	1,882
1965	69	25	25	1	120	1,590	232	62	26	1,910
1966	73	24	26	2	125	1,641	217	61	31	1,950
1967	75	21	25	2	123	1,651	204	57	32	1,944
1968	79	23	25	2	129	1,707	211	59	32	2,009
1969	83	23	24	3	133	1,658	211	59	36	1,964
1970	85	25	23	3	136	1,610	209	57	39	1,915
1971	86	22	22	4	134	1,582	198	52	49	1,881
1972	88	21	29 [2]	4	142	1,629	177	117 [2]	45	1,968
1973	90	23	31	5	149	1,660	196	122	50	2,028
1974	90	22	31	5	148	1,537	176	117	50	1,880
1975	92	21	28	6	147	1,511	175	108	52	1,846
1976	96	21	30	6	153	1,515	176	113	53	1,857
1977	98	20	41	9	168	1,429	171	122	75	1,797
1978	100	20	48	10	178	1,503	171	133	83	1,890
1979	103	20	56	10	189	1,499	169	140	85	1,893
1980	93	18	54	10	175	1,395	154	137	83	1,769
1981	94	18	53	9	174	1,299	154	129	75	1,657
1982	95	16	59	10	179	1,389	146 [R]	137	78	1,750 [R]
1983	96	17	60	10	183	1,358	139 [R]	143	82	1,722 [R]
1984	100	13	60	10	183	1,400	65 [R,3]	140	88	1,693 [R]
1985	103	15	58	11	187	1,452	140 [R]	142	89	1,823 [R]
1986	105	17	55	10	187	1,473	138 [R]	144	79	1,834 [R]
1987	113	18 [R]	54	11	195 [R]	1,542	144 [R]	142	83	1,911 [R]
1988	130	18	59	11	219	1,758	150	156	99	2,163
1989	138	17	58	10	222	1,812	143 [R]	155	93	2,203 [R]
1990	136	16	56	11 [4]	219	1,749	138 [R]	152	121 [4]	2,160 [R]
1991	130	15	58	11	214	1,600	136	144	105	1,985
1992	127	16 [R]	55	11	209 [R]	1,555	122	140	106	1,923
1993	135	14	51	12	211	1,615	103	134	125	1,977
1994	144	13	52	12	221	1,689	97	140	161	2,087
1995	150	13	53	11	227	1,701	101	143	168	2,113
1996	154	15 [5]	55	12	236	1,730	102	142	157	2,131
1997	157	17	48	11	234	1,740	105	142	148	2,135
1998	160	17	57	12	246	1,727	102	149	153	2,131
1999	158	18 [6]	59	12	246	1,664	96 [R,6]	144	155	2,059 [R]
2000	159	18	67	11	256	1,693	96	137	151	2,077
2001	159	19	59	12	248	1,682	94	131	151	2,058
2002	159	19	67	11	256	1,734	87	139	146	2,106
2003	162	19	61	11	252	1,753	89	133	141	2,116
2004	163 [7]	20	59	11	253	1,863 [7]	100 [8]	127	158	2,249
2005	163	22	61	11	257	1,868	105 [9]	133	168	2,275
2006	167	22	52	11	251	1,940	108	126	159	2,333
2007	173	21	51	10	255	2,001	102 [10]	126	146	2,376
2008	163	21	50	10 [11]	244	1,868	103	123	147 [11]	2,241

1 Figures for rail are for financial years.
2 Figures from 1972 onwards are not comparable with earlier years. From 1972, water includes all UK coastwise and one-port freight movements by sea, and inland waterway traffic. Earlier years inlcude only GB coastwise traffic and internal traffic on BWB waterways.
3 The figure is low because the amount of coal lifted was significantly reduced due to the UK miner's strike in 1984/85.
4 The increase compared to the corresponding figure for 1989 is largely due to changes in coverage.
5 There is a break in the series between 1995 and 1996 due to a change in the method of data collection.
6 There is a break in the series between 1998 and 1999 due to a change in the source data.
7 See footnote 2 Table 4.4.
8 Break in the series, increase largely due to changes in data collection method.
9 Break in the series, because figures from 2005 onwards include some of the tonnes lifted by GB railfreight.
10 Break in the series, because coal data was not supplied by GB Railfreight prior to 2007-08.
11 Some data based on estimates – this survey is currently under review by DECC to improve data quality.

Rail: ☎020-7944 8874
Road: ☎020-7944 3180
Water: ☎020-7944 3087
Pipeline: ☎020-7215 2718
The rail figures in this table are outside the scope of National Statistics
Source - Rail - ORR
Pipeline - DECC

4.2 Domestic freight moved: by commodity: 2008

Billion tonne kilometres/percentage

Commodity group (NST[3] Chapter)	Road[1] Billion tonne-kms	Percentage	Rail[2] Billion tonne-kms	Percentage	Pipeline Billion tonne-kms	Percentage
0 Agricultural products and live animals	13.4	8	..	..	0.0	0
1 Foodstuffs and animal fodder	37.5	23	..	..	0.0	0
2 Solid mineral fuels	1.1	1	7.9	38	0.0	0
3 Petroleum products	6.5	4	1.5	7	10.2	100
4 Ores and metal waste	1.8	1	..	..	0.0	0
5 Metal products	5.7	3	1.5	7	0.0	0
6 Crude and manufactured minerals and building materials	22.4	14	2.7	13	0.0	0
7 Fertilisers	1.9	1	..	..	0.0	0
8 Chemicals	7.3	4	..	..	0.0	0
9 Machinery, transport equipment, manufactured articles and miscellaneous articles	66.0	40	..	..	0.0	0
All commodities	163.5	100	20.6	100	10.2	100

1 All goods vehicles, including those up to 3.5 tonnes gross vehicle weight.
2 Figures for rail are for financial years e.g. 2008/09.
  Rail categories do not all match those recorded by ORR,
  so the components do not sum to the total.
3 Standard EC classification for transport. See Notes.

Rail: ☎020-7944 8874
Road: ☎020-7944 3180
Pipeline: ☎020-7215 2718
The rail figures in this table are
outside the scope of National Statistics
Source - Rail - ORR
Pipeline - DECC

4.3 Domestic freight transport: by mode: 1998-2008

(a) Goods moved — Billion tonne kilometres/percentage

	1998	1999	2000	2001	2002	2003	2004	2005	2006	2007	2008
Petroleum products											
Road [1]	5.2	5.0	6.4	5.8	5.2	5.5	5.7	5.5	5.6	5.1	6.5
Rail [2]	1.6	1.5 [3]	1.4	1.2	1.2	1.2	1.2	1.2	1.5	1.6	1.5
Water [4]	45.2	48.6	52.7	43.5	51.7	46.9	46.9	47.2	37.8	36.4	36.4
ow: coastwise	36.4	33.3	26.0	23.1	24.2	23.3	26.6	30.3	22.7	25.0	26.5
Pipeline	11.7	11.6	11.4	11.5	10.9	10.5	10.7	10.8	10.8	10.2	10.2 [10]
All modes	63.7	66.7	71.9	62.0	69.0	64.1	64.5	64.7	55.8	53.3	54.6
Coal and coke											
Road [1]	2.0	2.2	1.5	2.1	1.5	1.5	1.2	1.5	1.3	1.6	1.0
Rail [2]	4.5	4.8 [3]	4.8	6.2	5.7	5.8	6.7	8.3	8.6	7.7	7.9
Water [4]	0.5	0.5	0.2	0.5	0.3	0.5	0.3	0.4	0.5	0.5	0.5
All modes	7.0	7.5	6.5	8.8	7.5	7.9	8.5	10.2	10.4	9.8	9.5
Other traffic											
Road [1]	153.1	150.5	151.5	150.6	152.7	154.7	155.6	156.4	159.7	166.4	156.0
Rail [2]	11.3 [R]	11.9 [3]	12.0 [R]	12.0	11.7	11.9	12.5	12.2	11.8	11.9	11.2
Water [4]	11.2	9.6	14.6	14.8	15.2	13.5	12.3	13.3	13.5	13.9	12.7
All modes	175.6 [R]	172.0	178.1 [R]	177.4	179.6	180.0	180.4	181.9	185.0	192.2	179.9
All traffic											
Road [1]	160.3	157.7	159.4	158.5	159.4	161.7	162.5 [6]	163.4	166.7	173.1	163.5
Rail [2]	17.3	18.2 [3]	18.1	19.4	18.5	18.9	20.3	21.7	21.9	21.2	20.6
Water [4]	56.9	58.7	67.4	58.8	67.2	60.9	59.4	60.9	51.8	50.8	49.7
Pipeline	11.7	11.6	11.4	11.5	10.9	10.5	10.7	10.8	10.8	10.2	10.2
All modes	246.2	246.2	256.3	248.2	256.0	252.0	253.0	256.9	251.3	255.3	244.0
Percentage of all traffic											
Road [1]	65	64	62	64	62	64	64	64	66	68	67
Rail [2]	7	7	7	8	7	7	8	8	9	8	8
Water [4]	23	24	26	24	26	24	23	24	21	20	20
Pipeline	5	5	4	5	4	4	4	4	4	4	4
All modes	100	100	100	100	100	100	100	100	100	100	100

(b) Goods lifted — Million tonnes/percentage

	1998	1999	2000	2001	2002	2003	2004	2005	2006	2007	2008
Petroleum products											
Road [1]	61	61	75	74	59	64	67	70	69	71	80
Rail [2]	..	..	..	..	..	..	..	..	..	..	..
Water [4]	76	72	72	60	67	64	63	66	57	56	58
ow: coastwise	55	52	40	34	36	35	38	42	34	35	36
Pipeline	153	155	151	151	146	141	158	168	159	146	147 [10]
All modes [5]	290	288	298	285	272	269	288	304	285	274	285
Coal and coke											
Road [1]	26	28	22	21	17	22	14	21	17	24	15
Rail [2]	45	36 [3]	35	39 [R]	34	35	43 [7]	48 [8]	49	43 [9]	47
Water [4]	3	3	3	3	2	2	1	2	2	2	2
All modes	70	75	60	63 [R]	53	59	67	72	68	69	63
Other traffic											
Road [1]	1,640	1,575	1,596	1,587	1,658	1,667	1,782	1,777	1,854	1,906	1,773
Rail [2]	57	61 [3]	60	54 [R]	53	54	57 [7]	58 [8]	59	59 [9]	56
Water [4]	70	70	62	68	70	67	63	65	66	68	63
All modes	1,767	1,706	1,718	1,709 [R]	1,781	1,788	1,902	1,901	1980	2,032	1,892
All traffic											
Road [1]	1,727	1,664	1,693	1,682	1,734	1,753	1,863 [6]	1,868	1,940	2,001	1,868
Rail [2]	102	96 [R,3]	96	94	87	89	100 [7]	105 [8]	108	102 [9]	103
Water [4]	149	144	137	131	139	133	127	133	126	126	123
Pipeline	153	155	151	151	146	141	158	168	159	146	147
All modes	2,131	2,059 [R]	2,077	2,058	2,106	2,116	2,249	2,275	2,333	2,376	2,241
Percentage of all traffic											
Road [1]	81	81	82	82	82	83	83	82	83	84	83
Rail [2]	5	5	5	5	4	4	4	5	5	4	5
Water [4]	7	7	7	6	7	6	6	6	5	5	5
Pipeline	7	8	7	7	7	7	7	7	7	6	7
All modes	100	100	100	100	100	100	100	100	100	100	100

1 All goods vehicles, including those up to 3.5 tonnes gross vehicle weight. See Notes and Definitions.
2 Figures for rail are for financial years (e.g. 1998 will be 1998/99 etc.)
3 There is a break in the series between 1998-99 and 1999-00 due to a change in the source data.
4 Figures for water are for UK traffic.
5 Excludes rail.
6 See footnote 2 Table 4.4.
7 Break in the series, increase largely due to changes in data collection method.
8 Break in the series, because figures from 2005 onwards include some of the tonnes lifted by GB railfreight.
9 Break in the series, because coal data was not supplied by GB Railfreight prior to 2007-08.
10 Some data based on estimates – this survey is currently under review by DECC to improve data quality

Rail: ☎020-7944 8874
Road: ☎020-7944 3180
Water: ☎020-7944 3087
Pipeline: ☎020-7215 2718
The rail figures in this table are outside the scope of National Statistics
Source - Rail - ORR
Pipeline - DECC

4.4 Freight transport by road: goods moved by goods vehicles over 3.5 tonnes:[1] 1998-2008

Billion tonne kilometres

(a) By mode of working	1998	1999	2000	2001	2002	2003	2004[2]	2005	2006	2007	2008
Mainly public haulage	114.3	110.9	113.0	114.7	110.6	114.3	110.8	109.7	112.1	115.6	102.9
Mainly own account	37.6	38.3	37.5	34.7	39.2	37.4	41.4	43.0	43.5	45.9	48.9
All modes	151.9	149.2	150.5	149.4	149.8	151.7	152.2	152.7	155.6	161.5	151.7
(b) By gross weight of vehicle											
Rigid vehicles:											
Over 3.5 tonnes up to 17 tonnes	17.8	17.9	15.8	13.1	11.9	10.1	9.1	8.1	7.2	5.8	5.5
Over 17 tonnes up to 25 tonnes	4.2	4.3	4.8	5.7	6.3	6.8	7.9	8.3	8.6	9.5	8.3
Over 25 tonnes	14.7	15.3	15.4	15.6	17.3	18.3	18.9	20.3	20.8	22.5	20.3
All rigids	36.6	37.5	36.0	34.5	35.6	35.2	35.9	36.7	36.6	37.8	34.1
Articulated vehicles:											
Over 3.5 tonnes up to 33 tonnes	14.4	14.0	14.0	12.8	9.9	8.8	7.0	6.3	6.1	5.6	5.2
Over 33 tonnes	100.9	97.7	100.4	102.1	104.4	107.7	109.4	109.7	112.9	118.1	112.5
All artics	115.3	111.7	114.4	114.9	114.3	116.5	116.4	116.0	119.0	123.7	117.6
All vehicles:											
Over 3.5 tonnes up to 25 tonnes	22.5	22.7	21.3	19.3	18.7	17.3	17.3	16.7	16.3	15.7	14.1
Over 25 tonnes	129.4	126.5	129.2	130.1	131.1	134.4	134.9	136.0	139.3	145.8	137.6
All weights	151.9	149.2	150.5	149.4	149.8	151.7	152.2	152.7	155.6	161.5	151.7
(c) By commodity											
Food, drink and tobacco	42.5	41.5	44.3	41.4	43.1	42.2	41.7	40.6	42.0	45.1	43.7
Wood, timber and cork	3.6	3.8	3.7	3.9	3.8	4.1	4.5	4.7	4.1	3.3	4.0
Fertiliser	1.2	1.4	1.2	1.2	1.2	1.2	0.8	1.1	0.8	0.9	1.3
Crude minerals	13.3	12.7	12.4	13.0	13.9	13.8	14.1	14.8	15.4	16.0	13.3
Ores	1.1	1.3	1.2	1.2	1.1	1.2	1.4	1.7	1.4	1.8	1.8
Crude materials	2.6	2.6	2.6	2.3	2.7	2.3	3.3	2.4	2.7	2.6	2.3
Coal and coke	2.0	2.2	1.5	2.1	1.5	1.5	1.2	1.5	1.3	1.6	1.0
Petrol and petroleum products	5.2	5.0	6.4	5.8	5.2	5.5	5.7	5.5	5.7	5.1	6.5
Chemicals	7.9	7.4	6.8	7.2	6.5	6.8	6.3	7.6	6.2	7.0	6.1
Building materials	10.7	10.6	10.6	11.7	10.9	12.0	12.1	10.9	11.5	11.6	11.0
Iron and steel products	7.7	6.8	6.8	5.7	5.3	5.4	5.4	5.2	4.7	6.4	4.1
Other metal products n.e.s.	1.7	1.7	1.7	1.4	1.5	1.5	1.9	2.1	2.1	2.0	1.8
Machinery and transport equipment	9.1	8.7	9.1	8.9	8.5	8.7	8.9	9.3	9.4	9.5	8.9
Miscellaneous manufactures n.e.s.	15.9	15.7	15.1	15.4	16.2	15.8	16.3	15.5	16.3	16.4	12.6
Miscellaneous articles n.e.s. (incl. commodity not known)	27.5	27.9	27.1	28.2	28.4	29.5	28.8	29.8	31.7	32.2	33.3
All commodities	151.9	149.2	150.5	149.4	149.8	151.7	152.2	152.7	155.6	161.5	151.7

1 Rigid vehicles or articulated vehicles (tractive unit and trailer) with gross vehicle weight over 3.5 tonnes.

2 Figures for 2004 onwards are not fully comparable with those for 2003 and earlier years.
  Detailed comparisons should therefore be made with caution. See Notes and Definitions.

☎020-7944 3180

4.5 Freight transport by road: goods lifted by goods vehicles over 3.5 tonnes:[1] 1998-2008

Million tonnes

(a) By mode of working	1998	1999	2000	2001	2002	2003	2004[2]	2005	2006	2007	2008
Mainly public haulage	1,041	991	1,038	1,052	1,019	1,053	1,101	1,079	1,127	1,145	986
Mainly own account	589	576	556	529	608	590	643	667	685	724	748
All modes	1,630	1,567	1,593	1,581	1,627	1,643	1,744	1,746	1,813	1,869	1,734
(b) By gross weight of vehicle											
Rigid vehicles:											
Over 3.5 tonnes up to 17 tonnes	268	254	229	203	188	159	160	135	130	109	103
Over 17 tonnes up to 25 tonnes	106	86	87	86	90	100	113	118	120	130	122
Over 25 tonnes	401	408	424	443	491	506	539	559	598	629	532
All rigids	776	748	741	733	768	765	812	812	849	868	757
Articulated vehicles:											
Over 3.5 tonnes up to 33 tonnes	125	113	107	97	81	69	60	51	50	50	46
Over 33 tonnes	729	706	746	751	778	809	872	883	914	952	931
All artics	854	819	852	848	859	878	932	934	964	1,001	977
All vehicles:											
Over 3.5 tonnes up to 25 tonnes	382	346	325	294	283	265	277	257	256	245	230
Over 25 tonnes	1,248	1,221	1,268	1,287	1,343	1,378	1,467	1,489	1,557	1,624	1,504
All weights	1,630	1,567	1,593	1,581	1,627	1,643	1,744	1,746	1,813	1,869	1,734
(c) By commodity											
Food, drink and tobacco	346	333	346	321	339	333	351	339	360	373	370
Wood, timber and cork	27	28	26	28	28	32	42	36	30	29	35
Fertiliser	9	11	10	9	11	12	7	14	7	9	22
Crude minerals	327	297	308	298	333	327	364	370	380	390	317
Ores	18	20	16	16	17	21	22	23	19	22	24
Crude materials	20	20	18	20	21	19	25	22	23	23	20
Coal and coke	26	28	22	21	17	22	14	21	17	24	15
Petrol and petroleum products	61	61	75	74	59	64	67	70	69	71	80
Chemicals	53	47	49	50	41	47	46	53	48	48	45
Building materials	161	159	165	165	167	165	185	169	180	175	177
Iron and steel products	54	48	49	44	39	41	43	42	41	47	33
Other metal products n.e.s.	18	17	16	14	14	16	19	19	21	20	20
Machinery and transport equipment	73	67	69	70	68	66	70	76	79	83	75
Miscellaneous manufactures n.e.s.	96	91	97	97	105	98	111	109	112	113	95
Miscellaneous articles n.e.s. (incl. commodity not known)	342	340	328	353	367	379	378	384	426	440	406
All commodities	1,630	1,567	1,593	1,581	1,627	1,643	1,744	1,746	1,813	1,869	1,734

1 Rigid vehicles or articulated vehicles (tractive unit and trailer) with gross vehicle weight over 3.5 tonnes.
2 Figures for 2004 onwards are not fully comparable with those for 2003 and earlier years.
  Detailed comparisons should therefore be made with caution. See Notes and Definitions.

☎020-7944 3180

4.6 Freight transport by road: length of haul by goods vehicles over 3.5 tonnes:[1] 1998-2008

										Million tonnes	
(a) Goods lifted	1998	1999	2000	2001	2002	2003	2004[2]	2005	2006	2007	2008
Not over 100 kilometres	1,132	1,073	1,093	1,083	1,129	1,132	1,223	1,228	1,286	1,320	1,211
Over 100 kilometres	497	494	501	496	498	509	521	518	527	549	523
All distances	1,630	1,567	1,593	1,581	1,627	1,643	1,744	1,746	1,813	1,869	1,734

(b) Goods moved									Billion tonne kilometres		
Not over 100 kilometres	38.6	36.9	38.1	36.8	38.8	39.4	41.7	42.9	44.4	45.9	43.8
Over 100 kilometres	113.3	112.3	112.4	112.6	111.0	112.0	110.6	109.8	111.1	115.6	107.9
All distances	151.9	149.2	150.5	149.4	149.8	151.7	152.2	152.7	155.6	161.5	151.7

(c) Average length of haul by gross weight of vehicle										Kilometres	
Rigid vehicles:											
Over 3.5 tonnes up to 17 tonnes	66	68	69	65	63	63	57	60	55	53	54
Over 17 tonnes up to 25 tonnes	40	50	56	67	70	68	70	71	72	73	68
Over 25 tonnes	37	37	36	35	35	36	35	37	35	36	38
All rigids	47	50	49	47	46	46	44	45	43	44	45
Articulated vehicles:											
Over 3.5 tonnes up to 33 tonnes	115	124	131	132	122	128	118	121	122	113	112
Over 33 tonnes	138	138	135	136	134	133	125	124	123	124	121
All artics	135	136	134	136	133	133	125	124	123	124	120
All vehicles	93	95	94	94	92	92	87	87	86	86	87

1 Rigid vehicles or articulated vehicles (tractive unit and trailer) with gross vehicle weight over 3.5 tonnes.
2 Figures for 2004 onwards are not fully comparable with those for 2003 and earlier years.
  Detailed comparisons should therefore be made with caution. See Notes and Definitions

☎020-7944 3180

4.7 International road haulage by United Kingdom registered powered vehicles over 3.5 tonnes gross vehicle weight: goods carried: by country of loading or unloading:[1] 2007[2]

Country	Outward journey				Inward journey			
	Tonnes (thousand)	Per cent	Tonne-kms (million)	Per cent	Tonnes (thousand)	Per cent	Tonne-kms (million)	Per cent
Austria	9	-	14	-	12	-	17	-
Belgium	884	17	416	10	1,327	22	645	14
Denmark	13	-	10	-	4	-	5	-
Finland	-	-	-	-	-	-	-	-
France	1,871	37	1,276	30	2,456	40	1,369	31
Germany	636	12	582	14	620	10	547	12
Greece	13	-	37	1	3	-	9	-
Irish Republic	335	7	133	3	138	2	49	1
Italy	263	5	415	10	292	5	449	10
Luxembourg	55	1	32	1	50	1	29	1
Netherlands	492	10	289	7	628	10	363	8
Portugal	8	-	18	-	7	-	16	-
Spain	364	7	670	16	453	7	829	19
Sweden	22	-	33	1	3	-	5	-
EU15 (excl. United Kingdom)	4,966	97	3,926	93	5,994	98	4,331	97
Bulgaria	0	0	0	0	0	0	0	0
Cyprus	5	-	16	-	3	-	9	-
Czech Republic	4	-	5	-	4	-	5	-
Estonia	0	0	0	0	0	0	0	0
Hungary	2	-	5	-	1	-	1	-
Latvia	0	0	0	0	0	0	0	0
Lithuania	12	-	0	0	0	0	0	0
Malta	0	0	0	0	0	0	0	0
Poland	5	-	10	-	-	-	1	-
Romania	1	-	3	-	1	-	3	-
Slovakia	3	-	6	-	0	0	0	0
Slovenia	-	-	-	-	-	-	-	-
New Member States[3]	32	1	45	1	9	-	20	-
European Union	4,998	98	3,970	94	6,002	98	4,350	97
Switzerland	59	1	70	2	87	1	101	2
Norway	1	-	1	-	0	0	0	0
Other countries	61	1	179	4	5	-	13	-
All countries	5,119	100	4,222	100	6,094	100	4,464	100

1 Excludes vehicles travelling between Northern Ireland and the Republic of Ireland only, i.e. where the whole journey is confined to the island of Ireland.

2 2008 data not available at time of publication.

3 New Member State countries that joined the EU since 1 May 2004.

☎020-7944 3180

4.8 International road haulage by United Kingdom registered powered vehicles over 3.5 tonnes gross weight by type of transport and commodity: [1] 2007[2]

(a) Outward journey

Commodity group (NST[3] Chapter	Total traffic				ow: Hire or reward			
	Tonnes (thousand)	Per cent	Tonne-kms (million)	Per cent	Tonnes (thousand)	Per cent	Tonne-kms (million)	Per cent
0 Agricultural products and live animals	166	3	108	3	164	3	106	3
1 Foodstuffs and animal fodder	990	19	941	22	947	19	907	22
2 Solid mineral fuels	24	-	12	-	24	-	12	-
3 Petroleum products	36	1	20	-	36	1	20	-
4 Ores and metal waste	20	-	11	-	20	-	11	-
5 Metal products	162	3	148	4	162	3	148	4
6 Crude and manufactured minerals and building materials	66	1	58	1	66	1	58	1
7 Fertilisers	3	-	2	-	3	-	2	-
8 Chemicals	573	11	452	11	570	11	450	11
9 Miscellaneous	1,695	33	1,369	32	1,637	33	1,312	32
ow:								
Machinery and engines	836	16	718	17	804	16	675	16
Leather and textiles	514	10	450	11	500	10	442	11
All unclassified	1,384	27	1,101	26	1,378	28	1,097	27
All commodities	5,119	100	4,222	100	5,006	100	4,123	100

(b) Inward journey

Commodity group (NST[3] Chapter	Total traffic				ow: Hire or reward			
	Tonnes (thousand)	Per cent	Tonne-kms (million)	Per cent	Tonnes (thousand)	Per cent	Tonne-kms (million)	Per cent
0 Agricultural products and live animals	531	9	457	10	510	9	442	10
1 Foodstuffs and animal fodder	1,855	30	1,184	27	1,814	30	1,163	27
2 Solid mineral fuels	21	-	15	-	21	-	15	-
3 Petroleum products	23	-	18	-	23	-	18	-
4 Ores and metal waste	22	-	12	-	22	-	12	-
5 Metal products	82	1	48	1	82	1	48	1
6 Crude and manufactured minerals and building materials	144	2	174	4	144	2	174	4
7 Fertilisers	3	-	1	-	3	-	1	-
8 Chemicals	372	6	256	6	372	6	256	6
9 Miscellaneous	1,568	26	1,289	29	1,538	26	1,246	28
ow:								
Machinery and engines	765	13	609	14	743	12	576	13
Leather and textiles	469	8	357	8	461	8	348	8
All unclassified	1,473	24	1,009	23	1,467	24	1,005	23
All commodities	6,094	100	4,464	100	5,995	100	4,381	100

1 Excludes vehicles travelling between Northern Ireland and the Republic of Ireland only, i.e. where the whole journey is confined to the island of Ireland.
2 2008 data not available at time of publication.
3 Standard EC classification for transport. See Notes.

☎020-7944 3180

4.9 Bilateral[1] traffic, between the United Kingdom and European Union countries, in vehicles registered in the United Kingdom and the corresponding European Union country: 2007 [2]

Thousand tonnes/percentage

Country of loading/unloading	Goods loaded in the United Kingdom			Goods unloaded in the United Kingdom		
	In UK vehicles	In vehicles registered in the country of unloading	UK hauliers' share (percentage)	In UK vehicles	In vehicles registered in the country of loading	UK hauliers' share (percentage)
Austria	83	175	32	49	402	11
Belgium	907	1,153	44	1,339	1,741	43
Denmark	13	53	20	15	165	8
Finland	-	0	100	-	4	7
France	1,886	3,853	33	2,479	5,256	32
Germany	691	2,204	24	712	3,201	18
Greece	13	38	25	3	112	3
Irish Republic	8,740	3,473	72	2,856	3,852	43
Italy	282	814	26	296	1,599	16
Luxembourg	55	31	64	50	85	37
Netherlands	520	1,152	31	656	2,358	22
Portugal	8	853	1	7	318	2
Spain	371	1,085	25	457	2,479	16
Sweden	23	5	83	3	4	43
EU15 (excl. United Kingdom)	13,594	14,890	48	8,923	21,574	29
Bulgaria	129	19	87	70	6	92
Cyprus	5	1	88	3	2	61
Czech Republic	4	271	1	4	526	1
Estonia	0	19	0	0	24	0
Hungary	2	217	1	1	304	-
Latvia	0	7	0	0	3	0
Lithuania	8	75	9	50	91	35
Malta	45	0	-	20	0	-
Poland	10	853	1	37	1,169	3
Romania	1	272	-	1	465	-
Slovakia	3	93	4	0	189	0
Slovenia	142	54	72	107	151	41
New Member States[3]	349	1,880	16	292	2,930	9
European Union	13,942	16,770	45	9,215	24,504	27

1 Excluding 'cross trade', i.e. trade in vehicles registered elsewhere than in the country of loading or unloading.
2 All figures are for 2007, as these are the most recent available for foreign vehicles.
3 New Member State countries that joined the EU since 1 May 2004.

☎020-7944 3180
The figures in this table are outside the scope of National Statistics
Source: Eurostat

4.10 National Railways freight moved by commodity: 1986/87-2008/09

Billion net tonne-kilometres

	Coal	Metals	Construction	Oil & petroleum	International	Domestic intermodal	Other	Total[1]	Infrastructure[2]
1986/87	5.0	2.5	2.9	2.1	..	..	4.0	16.6	..
1987/88	4.6	2.7	2.9	2.0	..	..	5.2	17.5	..
1988/89	4.8	2.8	3.3	2.2	..	..	4.9	18.1	..
1989/90	4.6	2.5	3.2	2.1	..	..	4.2	16.7	..
1990/91	5.0	2.3	2.7	2.0	..	..	3.8	16.0	..
1991/92	5.0	2.4	2.5	2.0	..	..	3.4	15.3	..
1992/93	5.4	2.3	2.5	2.0	..	..	3.3	15.5	..
1993/94	3.9	2.1	2.3	1.9	..	..	3.5	13.8	..
1994/95	3.3	1.7	2.5	1.8	..	..	3.8	13.0	..
1995/96	3.6	1.7	2.3	1.8	..	..	3.9	13.3	..
1996/97[3]	3.9	..	..	..	..	..	11.2	15.1	..
1997/98	4.4	..	..	..	..	..	12.5	16.9	..
1998/99	4.5	2.1	2.1	1.6	1.1	3.5	2.5	17.3	1.2
1999/00[4]	4.8	2.2	2.0	1.5	1.0	3.9	2.7	18.2	1.2
2000/01	4.8	2.1	2.4	1.4	1.0	3.8	2.6	18.1	1.2
2001/02	6.2	2.4	2.8	1.2	0.6	3.5	2.6	19.4	1.3
2002/03	5.7	2.6	2.5	1.2	0.5	3.4	2.7	18.5	1.2
2003/04	5.8	2.4	2.7	1.2	0.5	3.5	2.8	18.9	1.2
2004/05	6.7	2.6	2.9	1.2	0.5	4.0	2.5	20.3	1.3
2005/06	8.3	2.2	2.9	1.2	0.5	4.3	2.3	21.7	1.4
2006/07	8.6	2.0	2.7	1.5	0.4	4.7	1.9	21.9	1.4
2007/08	7.7	1.8	2.8	1.6	0.4	5.1	1.7	21.2	1.7
2008/09	7.9	1.5	2.7	1.5	0.4	5.2	1.4	20.6	1.6

1 Infrastructure not included in total.
2 This series excludes some possession trains used during engineering works.
3 There is a break in the series between 1995–96 and 1996–97 due to a change in the method of data collection.
4 There is a further break in the series between 1998-99 and 1999-00 due to a change in the source data.

☎020-7944 8874
The figures in this table are outside the scope of National Statistics
Source - ORR

4.11 National Railways Freight lifted by commodity: 1986/87-2008/09

Million tonnes

	Coal	Metals	Construction	Oil & petroleum	Other	Total[1]
1986/87	77.2	17.3	18.1	9.8	16.0	138.4
1987/88	78.8	19.6	19.5	10.1	16.3	144.4
1988/89	79.2	20.6	22.9	10.8	16.1	149.5
1989/90	75.8	18.9	23.5	10.2	14.7	143.1
1990/91	74.7	18.0	20.2	10.0	15.1	138.2
1991/92	75.1	17.8	17.7	10.0	15.3	135.8
1992/93	67.9	15.9	15.8	9.5	13.2	122.4
1993/94	48.9	15.8	16.1	9.0	13.4	103.2
1994/95	42.5	16.9	16.8	8.1	13.0	97.3
1995/96	45.2	15.1	11.5	6.3	22.6	100.7
1996/97[2]	52.2	..	..	..	49.6	101.8
1997/98	50.3	..	..	..	55.1	105.4
1998/99	45.3	..	..	..	56.8	102.1
1999/00[3]	35.9	..	..	..	60.6	96.5
2000/01	35.3	..	..	..	60.3	95.6
2001/02	39.5	..	..	..	54.5	93.9
2002/03	34.0	..	..	..	53.0	87.0
2003/04	35.2	..	..	..	53.7	88.9
2004/05[4]	43.3	..	..	..	56.8	100.1
2005/06[5]	47.6	..	..	..	57.7	105.3
2006/07	48.7	..	..	..	59.5	108.2
2007/08[6]	43.3	..	..	..	59.1	102.4
2008/09	46.6	..	..	..	56.1	102.7

1 Any minor discrepancies between sub categories and totals
  are caused by rounding.
2 No data breakdown available for Metals, Construction and
  Oil & petroleum from 1996/97.
3 Break in series from 1999/00. See Notes and Definitions.
4 Break in series, with most of the increase due to changes in data collection method.
5 Break in series from 2005/06 as some GB Railfreight tonnes lifted now included.
6 Break in series from 2007/08 as GB Railfreight coal data now included.

☎020-7944 8874
The figures in this table are outside
the scope of National Statistics
Source - ORR

4.12 National Railways freight,
Number of freight train movements and impacts on road haulage: 2002/03-2008/09

(a) Number of freight train movements[1,2]

	2002/03	2003/04	2004/05	2005/06	2006/07	2007/08	Thousands 2008/09
Total number of freight trains movements	374.4	416.1	382.0	455.6	364.9	332.2	316.7

(b) Impacts on road haulage

	2002/03	2003/04	2004/05[5]	2005/06	2006/07	2007/08	Billions 2008/09[6]
Road vehicle kilometres equivalent[3]	1.4	1.4	1.2	1.2	1.4	1.4	..
							Millions
Road vehicle journeys equivalent[4]	5.6	5.9	7.0	6.7	6.6	6.7	..

1 Figures have been sourced from Network Rail.
2 Measures the total number of train movements (including infrastructure trains)
  on the network.
3 The equivalent distance that road vehicles would need to have
  travelled to move the amounts of freight carried on rail, which is
  affected more by volume than by weight.
4 The equivalent number of road vehicle trips necessary to move this freight.
5 Data from 2004-05 are not directly comparable with previous data due to
  a change in the method of data collection to the underlying information
  (Freight Lifted data series).
6 No data available for 2008/09.

☎020-7944 8874
The figures in this table are outside
the scope of National Statistics
Source - ORR, Network Rail

**4.13   Roll-on/roll-off ferry and Channel Tunnel traffic; road goods vehicles outward
to mainland Europe: by country of registration: 1998-2008**

Thousands

	1998	1999	2000	2001	2002	2003	2004	2005	2006	2007	2008
Powered vehicles:											
United Kingdom	544.3	562.7	544.8	517.6	493.3	473.9	440.6	417.8	405.9	399.7	382.3
Austria	10.1	14.7	17.1	42.0	45.8	42.9	39.0	36.4	30.9	34.5	30.0
Belgium }	72.7	96.7	114.1	119.3	121.4	104.3 {	121.7	116.7	107.8	112.5	99.5
Luxembourg }							3.7	3.7	3.9	5.0	5.5
Denmark	7.3	8.7	9.5	12.0	16.9	13.7	25.8	23.0	22.6	22.3	20.1
Finland	0.6	0.7	0.9	3.1	2.0	1.1	0.2	0.3	0.6	0.6	0.7
Germany	52.4	73.1	111.5	132.0	148.2	155.7	233.2	213.9	211.6	218.4	199.9
France	272.4	319.1	338.8	352.4	363.1	363.2	224.3	214.0	204.8	197.2	178.7
Greece	1.9	2.6	2.9	2.6	2.8	3.6	10.7	9.5	8.3	7.6	5.9
Irish Republic	38.8	44.7	48.5	46.6	44.6	30.8	59.5	56.2	56.6	55.8	46.3
Italy	35.3	45.8	67.8	91.1	127.8	132.4	99.2	92.5	87.8	81.7	60.7
Netherlands	125.4	153.3	185.1	187.5	186.3	210.2	263.8	251.6	244.0	251.9	243.7
Spain	56.3	67.7	81.8	93.9	102.2	105.9	134.2	128.5	129.2	124.8	112.5
Sweden	10.3	1.0	1.4	1.8	1.8	1.4	1.5	1.4	1.8	1.7	1.6
Portugal	6.7	9.2	10.7	10.2	11.0	9.4	26.5	24.5	25.9	26.1	24.2
EU15											
(excluding											
United Kingdom)	690.2	837.3	990.0	1,094.5	1,173.9	1,174.6	1,243.4	1,172.2	1,135.7	1,140.2	1,029.3
Cyprus	..	0.1	0.2	0.1	0.2	0.2	0.1	0.1	0.1	0.1	-
Czech Republic	..	5.4	5.2	6.8	7.8	13.1	27.5	46.1	57.8	70.0	77.1
Estonia	..	0.0	0.1	0.2	0.3	0.3	1.3	1.4	2.2	2.7	3.0
Hungary	..	6.9	8.0	11.1	12.4	12.7	22.3	43.9	60.7	79.5	71.9
Latvia	..	0.3	0.3	0.1	0.2	0.2	0.4	1.0	1.4	1.6	2.7
Lithuania	..	0.9	1.4	1.0	0.7	1.6	5.5	11.8	21.7	29.2	33.2
Malta	..	0.2	0.3	0.3	0.3	0.2	0.2	0.2	0.2	0.2	0.1
Poland	..	7.0	10.4	12.5	12.0	14.2	58.2	100.3	146.6	204.5	256.3
Slovakia	..	0.2	0.2	0.4	1.0	2.4	9.4	18.1	29.6	37.2	35.0
Slovenia	..	1.5	1.9	3.5	4.7	4.7	8.6	11.6	16.5	19.3	20.3
Romania	..	..	..	..	..	8.3	10.4	15.6	19.2	25.9	53.0
Bulgaria	..	..	..	..	..	8.6	8.3	11.0	7.9	12.5	25.3
NMS[1,2]	.. {	22.5	28.0	36.2	39.5	49.5	152.3	261.0	363.9	482.8	577.9
	{										
Other countries in Europe	35.4 {										
and elsewhere	{										
	{	24.9	24.9	43.2	76.7	97.6	50.6	79.5	106.5	95.9	65.1
Unknown	4.8	6.3	17.7	20.5	18.1	19.1	10.0	10.4	9.2	10.9	5.0
All countries	1,274.8	1,453.7	1,605.4	1,711.9	1,801.5	1,814.7	1,896.9	1,940.8	2,021.2	2,129.5	2,059.7
Unaccompanied trailers	737.5	737.8	712.9	686.4	726.0	780.4	787.5	762.8	784.0 R	771.9 R	708.6
Powered vehicles											
and unaccompanied											
trailers	2,012.3	2,191.4	2,318.3	2,398.3	2,527.5	2,595.1	2,684.4	2,703.6	2,805.2 R	2,901.4 R	2,768.3

1 Data for 2004 - 2007 includes 12 New Member State countries as at 1st January 2007
   (Includes Romania and Bulgaria)
2 Data for 1997 - 2003 includes the 10 states that joined the EU in 2004 (omits Romania and Bulgaria).

☎0207-944 4131

4.14 Roll-on/roll-off ferry and Channel Tunnel traffic: road goods vehicles outward to mainland Europe: [1] **1998-2008**

(a) By country of disembarkation[2]   Thousands

	1998	1999	2000	2001	2002	2003	2004	2005	2006	2007	2008
Powered vehicles:											
Belgium	132	132	152	144	144	76	88	100	87	100	92
France	1,024	1,210	1,330	1,435	1,520	1,601	1,651	1,693	1,789	1,883	1,814
Netherlands	103	107	119	125	128	129	149	139	136	138	144
Others	15	4	4	8	9	7	8	8	10	9	10
All countries	1,275	1,454	1,605	1,712	1,802	1,815	1,897	1,941	2,021	2,129	2,060
Unaccompanied trailers:											
Belgium	267	289	263	251	263	266	240	240	247	227	198
France	86	64	57	57	47	54	54	50	41	46	42
Netherlands	281	279	281	275	312	344	366	350	369	378	348
Others	104	107	112	103	105	116	127	123	127 [R]	126 [R]	121
All countries	738	738	713	686	726	780	787	763	784 [R]	772 [R]	709
All vehicles	2,012	2,191	2,318	2,398	2,527	2,595	2,684	2,704	2,805 [R]	2,901 [R]	2,768

(b) By Great Britain port area[3,4,5]

	1998	1999	2000	2001	2002	2003	2004	2005	2006	2007	2008
Powered vehicles:											
North Sea	132	129	144	152	155	157	174	166	161	162	163
Strait of Dover	1,018	1,207	1,350	1,446	1,531	1,525	1,589	1,646	1,740	1,846	1,773
English Channel	124	117	112	114	116	132	133	129	121	121	123
All ports	1,275	1,454	1,605	1,712	1,802	1,815	1,897	1,941	2,021	2,129	2,060
Unaccompanied trailers:											
North Sea	601	641	634	610	667	730	732	702	731 [R]	713 [R]	656
Strait of Dover	91	53	44	43	30	22	27	32	33	35	30
English Channel	46	44	36	33	29	28	28	28	21	25	22
All ports	738	738	713	686	726	780	787	763	784 [R]	772 [R]	709
All vehicles	2,012	2,191	2,318	2,398	2,527	2,595	2,684	2,704	2,805 [R]	2,901 [R]	2,768

1 For details of revisions to the figures for the years 2004 to 2007 see DfT Statistical
  Bulletin 'Roads Goods Vehicles travelling to Mainland Europe: 2007'
2 For Channel Tunnel traffic, France is the country of disembarkation.
3 North Sea: all ports on east coast north of and including the Thames estuary.
4 Dover Strait: Dover, Folkestone, Ramsgate and the Channel Tunnel.
5 English Channel: all ports on south coast, west of Folkestone.

☎020-7944 4131

5 Maritime:

Notes and Definitions

Ports traffic: 5.1 – 5.7

These tables relate to foreign, coastwise and one-port traffic through ports in the United Kingdom.

More details are available in the annual Transport Statistics Report *Maritime Statistics,* published by The Stationery Office, and also available free on the DfT web site.

The data are derived as follows:

(a) from 2000,

    (i) detailed quarterly returns from shipping lines or their agents of all freight traffic at major UK ports;

    (ii) quarterly returns of inwards and outwards weight and units by port authorities or other undertakings at major ports;

    (iii) annual returns of inwards and outwards traffic only by port authorities or other undertakings at minor ports.

(b) prior to 2000,

    (i) detailed annual traffic returns made by port authorities or other undertakings at major ports;

    (ii) annual returns of inwards and outwards traffic from port authorities or other undertakings at minor ports

The major ports include all ports with cargo volumes of at least 1 million tonnes in 2000 (2 million tonnes under the previous system between 1995 and 1999) and a few other smaller ports. The breakdowns of traffic for 1995 and later years in the tables include major ports traffic and are supplemented by estimates for the minor ports.

Definitions used:

Port groups: For statistical purposes, ports of Great Britain are grouped geographically as shown in map 5.9.

Weights: All weights reported for port and waterborne freight statistics include crates and other packaging. The tare weights of containers and other items of transport equipment are excluded.

Foreign traffic: Traffic between ports in the United Kingdom (Great Britain and Northern Ireland), and foreign countries, that is countries outside Great Britain, Northern Ireland, the Isle of Man and the Channel Islands.

Domestic traffic: The sum of coastwise and one-port traffic.

Coastwise traffic: Goods loaded or unloaded at ports in the United Kingdom, and transported to or from another port in the United Kingdom.

One-port traffic: One-port traffic comprises:

- dredged sand, gravel, etc. landed at a port for commercial purposes;

- traffic to and from off-shore installations. Fuel shipped to oil rigs is included in 'Other traffic – outwards'; and

- material shipped for dumping at sea (this practice has now ceased).

Container and roll-on traffic (commonly known as 'unitised traffic'): Includes road goods vehicles, unaccompanied trailers and other goods carried on roll-on/roll-off shipping services, containers carried on all types of shipping services and rail wagons and barges carried on ships. Goods carried on 'unitised' services constitute a subset of total traffic and are reported in tables 5.4 and 5.5.

Coastwise routes: Coastwise routes (table 5.6) are the ferry services between mainland Great Britain and Northern Ireland, the Isle of Man, the West of Scotland island of Lewis (between Ullapool and Stornoway), the Orkneys and Shetlands, and the Channel Islands. Short ferry routes between Scottish islands, and those across river estuaries and to the Isle of Wight, are excluded. Only in the case of ferry routes between mainland Great Britain and the Orkneys and Shetlands is traffic counted at both ends of the route. In other cases, traffic is counted at the mainland Great Britain port only.

Domestic waterborne freight traffic: 5.8 and 5.10

These tables present estimates of goods lifted (tonnes) and goods moved (tonne -kilometres) in the United Kingdom by coastal shipping (coastwise and one-port traffic) and on inland waters. The data are based on annual studies for DfT by MDS-Transmodal.

The definitions of inland waters were devised for the first survey of waterborne transport carried out in 1980, and slightly updated in 2004. The definitions were produced from the perspective of measuring freight traffic travelling on inland waters, which could travel by another surface mode within the UK. There are two boundary definitions used to measure the amount of traffic:

Inland waterways: all water areas available for navigation that lie inland of a boundary defined as the most seaward point of any estuary which might reasonably be bridged or tunnelled – this is taken to be where the width of water surface area is both less than 3 km at low water and less than 5 km at high water on spring tides.

Inland waters: all waters within the *Smooth Water Line,* that is, the outermost limit of Category D waters in the Maritime and Coastguard Agency (MCA) inland waters classification, "tidal rivers and estuaries where significant wave height could not be expected to exceed 2m at any time". This is generally much further seaward than the inland waterways boundary. Prior to 2004 a broadly similar limit was used – the summer boundary of the Partially Smooth Water Area (PSWA) – waters within this limit are known as *sheltered waters.*

For the purpose of estimating tonnes and tonne-kilometres, all traffic *wholly within* inland waters (i.e. internal traffic) is counted. Tonnes is then simply tonnes lifted, and tonne-kilometres is tonnes lifted multiplied by the distance travelled.

Traffic which crosses the inland waters boundary and which also goes upstream of the inland waterways boundary, is counted as well; but traffic which is essentially *seagoing traffic* to and from major *seaboard* ports is specifically excluded.

Where traffic is included, tonnes is then tonnes lifted and tonne-kilometres is tonnes lifted multiplied by the distance travelled but calculated from the point at which the vessel crosses the *inland waterways* boundary.

Detailed statistics for 2008 are available in the annual Statistics Bulletin*, Waterborne Freight in the UK 2008,* and further details of the inland waterway network in freight use, its wharves and its craft, in the occasional report *Waterborne Freight Benchmark Report 2007,* both published by DfT and available on the DfT web site.

United Kingdom International sea passenger movements: 5.11 and 5.12

These tables have been compiled from statistics collected monthly from shipping operators by DfT and cover travel between the UK and other countries. Domestic passengers are excluded. The figures do include drivers of lorries, coaches and other vehicles. Short sea routes in these tables are generally routes between the UK and Belgium, Denmark, Faroe Isles, Finland, France, Germany, Ireland, Netherlands, Norway, Spain and Sweden.

United Kingdom and Crown Dependency registered trading vessels: 5.13

Until the end of 1986, United Kingdom registered fleet figures were derived from DfT records of trading vessels of 500 gross tons or over registered at ports in the United Kingdom, the Channel Islands and the Isle of Man. A different ship type classification was also in use. For 1986 only, for purposes of comparison, it shows figures from both sources giving the composition of the fleet on the basis of both the 'old' and 'new' ship type classifications.

The United Kingdom owned and registered merchant fleets: 5.14 and 5.15

The figures given in these tables are derived from Lloyd's Register-Fairplay data and cover trading vessels of 500 gross tons or above. Table 5.15 covers vessels owned by UK companies wherever the vessels are registered, while Table 5.14 covers vessels registered in the United Kingdom and Crown Dependencies (Isle of Man, Channel Islands), excluding those owned by the Government.

Trading vessels are those carrying cargo or passengers for commercial purposes. This excludes offshore supply vessels, non-cargo vessels, tugs, fishing vessels, dredgers, river and other non seagoing vessels. For more data and background information see the Transport Statistics Report, *Maritime Statistics,* available from The Stationery Office and the DfT web site.

Gross tonnage: Under the International Convention on the Tonnage Measurement of Ships, 1969 gross tonnage (gt) is defined as the following function of the total volume of all enclosed spaces in the ship (V), in cubic metres:

$$GT = K_1 V$$
where $K_1 = 0.2 + 0.02 \log_{10} V.$

Deadweight tonnes: The term deadweight tonnes, or 'dwt', is a measurement of the weight of cargo, stores, fuel, passengers and crew carried by the ship when loaded to her maximum summer loadline.

Tankers: Include oil, gas, chemical and other specialised tankers.

Bulk carriers: Large and small carriers including combination – ore/oil and ore/bulk/oil – carriers.

Specialised carriers: Includes vessels such as livestock carriers, car carriers and chemical carriers.

Fully cellular container: Figures include only container vessels of this type.

Ro-Ro: These are for passenger and cargo Ro-Ro vessels.

Other general cargo vessels: These include reefer vessels, general cargo/passenger vessels, and single and multi-deck general cargo vessels.

Passenger vessels: These are cruise liner and other passenger vessels.

UK shipping industry revenue and expenditure from international activities: 5.16

The revenue and expenditure figures in this table are derived from the results of annual inquiries carried out by the Chamber of Shipping (CoS). The United Kingdom shipping industry is defined as United Kingdom resident companies which own or operate ships irrespective of their flag of registry.

This includes companies, which are United Kingdom subsidiaries of overseas parent companies, and excludes overseas resident subsidiaries of United Kingdom companies.

This treatment arises from the primary purpose of the CoS inquiries, which is to provide estimates for the sea transport account of the United Kingdom Balance of Payments. In the Balance of Payments the revenue from overseas resident subsidiary companies is treated as investment income, not part of the sea transport account.

International activities cover the activities of ships either owned by the United Kingdom industry or operated by the industry on charter. The activities covered are:

- carriage of UK imports and exports;

- carriage of trade between two foreign countries (cross trades);

- carriage of passengers on international ferry routes and sea cruises;

- chartering ships to overseas operators.

The passenger revenue series includes revenue from overseas residents only and is consistent with data published in *The Pink Book* (United Kingdom Balance of Payments). Associated expenditure includes:

- payment for bunkers uplifted abroad;

- disbursements in overseas ports: cargo handling, port dues, crews' expenses, agency fees, light dues etc.;

- charter payments to overseas ship owners.

Marine accident casualties: 5.17

The information is derived from accidents reported to the UK Marine Accident Investigation Branch (MAIB) in compliance with the Merchant Shipping (Accident Reporting and Investigation) Regulations (SI 2005 No.881). The role of the MAIB is to prevent future accidents through investigation of the causes and circumstances of accidents.

The data in part (a) refer to accidents to persons on UK registered merchant vessels of greater than or equal to 100 gross tons only, including accidents during access. Such vessels have a duty to report accidents to the MAIB, wherever in the world they occur.

The data in part (b) refer to all recorded accidents in UK 12-mile territorial waters. Requirements to report such accidents to the MAIB vary. Broadly, most UK registered commercial vessels have a duty to report; certain small UK craft or hired pleasure craft are only required to report certain types of accident; non-commercial UK pleasure craft are largely exempt; non-UK flagged vessels are only required to report such accidents if they are in a UK port/harbour or if carrying passengers to/from a UK port. However, the MAIB will record, and may investigate, any significant accidents of which they are notified by other bodies such as the Coastguard or harbour or inland waterway authorities.

For further information see the MAIB website www.maib.gov.uk.

HM Coastguard Statistics: 5.18

HM Coastguard, part of the Maritime and Coastguard Agency (MCA), initiates and co-ordinates Civil Maritime Search and Rescue operations within the UK Search and Rescue Region (UKSRR).

Machinery and equipment failure, the inability to cope when the weather deteriorates, diving incidents and failure to inform relatives or other agents ashore when likely to be overdue have been the major causes of SAR incidents.

Definitions of terms used are:

Commercial vessels: All Merchant Vessels (including ferries and cruise ships), tugs, barges, dredgers, offshore installations, tenders, supply vessels, support vessels, research vessels, cable layers, mega-yachts, hovercraft etc.

Fishing vessels: All registered fishing vessels.

Pleasure craft: Yachts (except mega-yachts), sailing dinghies, cabin cruisers, speedboats, diving support boats, sail training craft, square riggers, rowing boats and inflatable craft. From 1994 data also includes canoes/kayaks, sailboards and jet-skis (personal watercraft) previously included in 'others'.

Incidents to persons: Includes man-overboard, divers, swimmers, missing persons, persons cut off by tides, persons stuck on cliffs, etc.

Medical evacuations: Incidents where injured persons taken from vessels at sea to shore for medical treatment, or injured cliff walkers evacuated to hospital, etc.

Others: Includes incidents involving military vessels, military aircraft, civilian aircraft, animal rescue, etc.

Distress reports: Includes all Distress, Urgency, Pyrotechnic and EPIRB/ELT signals and those reports subsequently found to be false alarms or hoaxes.

5.1 United Kingdom ports:[1] foreign, coastwise and one-port traffic: 1965-2008

Million tonnes

Year	Foreign			Coastwise			One-port			Total		
	Imports	Exports	All	Inwards	Outwards	All	Inwards	Outwards [2]	All	Inwards	Outwards	All
Great Britain												
1965	153.4	35.7	189.1	54.1	60.4	114.5	7.2	8.5	15.7	214.7	104.6	319.2
1966	157.1	38.2	195.3	54.2	59.7	113.9	6.8	8.5	15.3	218.1	106.4	324.5
1967	161.7	38.0	199.7	53.1	56.9	110.0	6.6	8.5	15.1	221.4	103.4	324.8
1968	175.6	41.7	217.3	51.1	56.6	107.7	7.8	8.5	16.3	234.5	106.8	341.3
1969	185.5	43.3	228.8	52.1	56.9	109.0	8.3	8.5	16.8	245.9	108.7	354.6
1970	196.2	48.0	244.2	51.8	56.2	108.0	9.2	8.6	17.8	257.2	112.8	370.0
1971	202.0	48.7	250.7	46.0	52.0	98.0	10.9	8.6	19.5	258.9	109.3	368.2
1972	205.0	49.7	254.7	45.4	51.8	97.2	16.0	8.8	24.8	266.4	110.3	376.7
1973	219.5	53.5	273.0	46.4	57.3	103.7	13.9	8.9	22.8	279.8	119.7	399.5
1974	211.1	51.1	262.2	48.5	56.9	105.4	13.1	10.1	23.2	272.7	118.1	390.8
1975	175.3	50.2	225.5	41.5	48.9	90.4	13.0	11.2	24.2	229.8	110.3	340.1
1976	180.0	62.8	242.8	41.1	50.9	92.0	14.4	11.2	25.6	235.5	124.9	360.3
1977	158.2	77.6	235.8	44.1	56.3	100.4	21.7	12.3	34.0	224.0	146.2	370.2
1978	152.8	90.7	243.5	47.5	62.2	109.7	26.5	12.8	39.3	226.8	165.7	392.4
1979	157.1	107.5	264.6	52.7	67.0	119.7	29.5	12.9	42.4	239.3	187.5	426.8
1980	131.2	117.1	248.3	57.4	67.7	125.1	24.6	14.0	38.6	213.2	198.8	412.0
United Kingdom												
1980	133.4	117.5	250.8	64.8	69.8	134.6	24.6	14.0	38.6	222.8	201.3	424.1
1981	125.7	126.1	251.8	60.2	68.2	128.4	22.3	13.6	35.8	208.2	207.8	416.1
1982	122.9	130.7	253.6	67.2	71.3	138.5	24.6	13.4	37.9	214.7	215.4	430.1
1983	121.9	136.8	258.7	68.9	71.3	140.1	26.6	13.0	39.6	217.5	221.1	438.5
1984	143.5	142.1	285.5	64.2	66.3	130.5	28.5	12.3	40.9	236.3	220.7	456.9
1985	143.3	148.2	291.5	63.2	66.3	129.6	28.1	13.7	41.8	234.7	228.2	462.9
1986	150.6	150.7	301.3	60.9	63.7	124.6	27.2	13.4	40.6	238.7	227.8	466.5
1987	154.9	151.0	305.9	59.8	61.2	121.0	31.8	12.9	44.7	246.6	225.0	471.6
1988	169.7	142.2	311.9	66.3	65.1	131.3	34.2	14.6	48.8	270.2	221.9	492.1
1989	174.6	127.5	302.1	64.1	64.8	128.9	35.0	14.8	49.8	273.7	207.1	480.9
1990	183.5	136.2	319.6	61.0	61.5	122.3	34.1	15.9	50.0	278.4	213.6	492.0
1991	182.1	143.2	325.3	61.7	62.8	124.4	29.8	15.1	44.9	273.6	221.0	494.6
1992	182.6	150.2	332.8	58.2	60.8	119.0	29.0	14.9	43.9	269.8	225.9	495.7
1993	189.5	157.5	346.9	59.4	62.0	121.5	23.8	14.0	37.8	272.7	233.5	506.2
1994	190.1	179.0	369.1	63.3	64.8	128.1	28.6	12.4	41.0	281.9	256.2	538.1
1995	190.3	178.8	369.1	67.9	72.1	140.0	26.7	12.4	39.1	284.9	263.3	548.2
1996	192.7	175.8	368.5	69.9	75.3	145.2	25.1	12.4	37.5	287.7	263.5	551.2
1997	205.7	179.3	385.0	67.5	72.0	139.5	21.8	12.2	34.0	295.0	263.5	558.5
1998	209.3	181.7	390.9	70.7	71.9	142.7	26.1	8.8	34.9	306.1	262.4	568.5
1999	203.6	184.4	387.9	67.0	71.1	138.1	36.4	3.2	39.6	307.0	258.7	565.6
2000	220.9	193.1	414.0	57.4	61.9	119.3	38.0	1.7	39.8	316.3	256.7	573.1
2001	238.4	180.4	418.7	57.3	54.9	112.2	33.3	2.2	35.4	328.9	237.5	566.4
2002	220.9	178.2	399.1	57.8	57.3	115.2	41.7	2.0	43.7	320.5	237.5	557.9
2003	229.3	174.0	403.3	56.9	56.1	113.0	37.2	1.7	39.0	323.4	231.9	555.3
2004	250.4	169.6	420.0	58.3	59.7	117.9	33.4	1.4	34.8	342.1	230.6	572.8
2005	262.3	163.7	426.0	61.4	64.9	126.2	30.4	1.9	32.3	354.0	230.5	584.5
2006	278.9	160.6	439.5	56.7	56.5	113.2	29.0	1.6	30.6	364.7	218.6	583.3
2007	273.3	164.5	437.9	57.6	57.2	114.8	26.9	2.0	28.9	357.8	223.7	581.5
2008	266.1	156.0	422.1	56.2	57.9	114.1	24.1	1.9	26.0	346.5	215.7	562.2

1 Great Britain only prior to 1980.
2 Estimated prior to 1974.

☎020-7944 3087

5.2 United Kingdom ports: foreign, coastwise and one port traffic by type of cargo: 1998-2008

Thousand tonnes

	1998	1999	2000	2001	2002	2003	2004	2005	2006	2007	2008
Foreign traffic											
Liquid bulk traffic											
Imports	61,346	56,528	70,788	74,495	62,811	66,447	75,897	76,988	85,530	83,442	82,214
Exports	106,041	110,591	118,509	110,321	107,516	100,772	95,974	87,995	82,883	84,563	76,383
All	167,387	167,120	189,297	184,816	170,327	167,218	171,871	164,983	168,412	168,005	158,597
Dry bulk traffic											
Imports	68,333	65,219	65,652	77,360	67,575	72,644	76,625	87,546	92,846	85,936	85,966
Exports	20,840	18,905	19,739	17,206	18,026	20,559	18,098	18,010	18,113	17,725	18,288
All	89,173	84,124	85,391	94,565	85,600	93,203	94,722	105,557	110,959	103,661	104,254
Container and roll-on traffic											
Imports	61,191	64,272	64,753	65,721	68,371	69,199	75,520	77,431	80,288	84,519	81,730
Exports	49,029	49,616	49,323	47,334	47,313	47,291	49,869	51,045	52,801	54,418	54,239
All	110,220	113,889	114,076	113,054	115,685	116,490	125,390	128,476	133,089	138,937	135,969
Semi-bulk traffic											
Imports	16,878	15,967	17,174	17,059	18,523	17,284	18,413	16,766	16,706	17,016	13,608
Exports	4,897	4,519	4,411	3,737	3,613	3,848	4,342	5,287	5,299	6,511	5,355
All	21,775	20,486	21,584	20,796	22,136	21,131	22,755	22,054	22,005	23,527	18,963
Conventional traffic											
Imports	1,531	1,595	2,500	3,730	3,645	3,699	3,990	3,529	3,555	2,399	2,609
Exports	854	735	1,145	1,786	1,705	1,535	1,314	1,393	1,456	1,321	1,704
All	2,385	2,330	3,645	5,515	5,349	5,234	5,304	4,922	5,012	3,720	4,313
All foreign traffic											
Imports	209,279	203,581	220,866	238,364	220,924	229,273	250,445	262,261	278,925	273,312	266,127
Exports	181,661	184,367	193,127	180,383	178,173	174,003	169,597	163,731	160,552	164,539	155,969
All	390,940	387,948	413,993	418,747	399,097	403,276	420,042	425,992	439,477	437,851	422,096
Coastwise traffic											
Liquid bulk traffic											
Inwards	51,514	48,164	36,677	37,008	38,631	36,901	39,183	41,261	35,429	36,440	35,622
Outwards	52,622	51,966	41,696	36,049	37,535	35,371	38,788	42,477	33,941	34,893	36,755
All	104,136	100,131	78,373	73,058	76,166	72,273	77,971	83,738	69,370	71,333	72,377
Dry bulk traffic											
Inwards	7,599	6,792	8,243	8,032	7,245	7,956	6,453	6,717	7,914	6,861	7,126
Outwards	7,882	7,229	8,201	7,112	7,785	8,438	7,814	8,366	8,675	7,761	7,598
All	15,480	14,021	16,444	15,144	15,030	16,395	14,268	15,083	16,589	14,622	14,724
Container and roll-on traffic											
Inwards	11,236	11,542	12,186	11,797	11,539	11,458	12,253	12,910	12,872	13,434	12,923
Outwards	10,660	11,396	11,506	11,064	11,341	11,426	12,026	12,995	12,988	13,785	13,056
All	21,895	22,938	23,692	22,861	22,880	22,884	24,280	25,905	25,860	27,219	25,979
Semi-bulk traffic											
Inwards	176	203	247	364	324	373	320	217	351	479	444
Outwards	477	221	311	570	546	544	519	565	373	443	291
All	653	424	558	934	870	917	838	783	725	922	735
Conventional traffic											
Inwards	212	274	96	74	99	194	73	278	167	345	132
Outwards	306	285	139	131	124	368	518	451	482	328	154
All	518	559	236	206	223	562	591	729	649	673	287
All coastwise traffic											
Inwards	70,736	66,975	57,448	57,276	57,838	56,883	58,282	61,382	56,734	57,559	56,249
Outwards	71,946	71,098	61,853	54,926	57,331	56,147	59,665	64,854	56,459	57,210	57,853
All	142,682	138,073	119,302	112,202	115,168	113,030	117,947	126,237	113,193	114,769	114,102

☎020-7944 3087

5.2 (continued) United Kingdom ports: foreign, coastwise and one port traffic by type of cargo: 1998-2008

Thousand tonnes

	1998	1999	2000	2001	2002	2003	2004	2005	2006	2007	2008
One-port traffic											
Liquid bulk traffic											
Inwards	10,587	20,220	24,937	18,245	25,886	22,328	19,152	16,169	14,171	10,816	9,551
Outwards	4,365	126	485	647	693	563	361	421	336	494	457
All	14,951	20,346	25,422	18,892	26,579	22,892	19,513	16,590	14,506	11,310	10,009
Dry bulk traffic											
Inwards	14,436	15,051	12,503	14,362	15,197	14,389	13,821	13,476	14,189	15,311	13,882
Outwards	98	41	41	68	67	70	28	52	32	67	75
All	14,534	15,092	12,544	14,430	15,264	14,460	13,849	13,529	14,221	15,378	13,957
Non-oil traffic with UK off-shore installations											
Inwards	1,063	1,136	589	643	606	490	414	724	672	801	682
Outwards	4,332	3,019	1,199	1,452	1,234	1,112	995	1,470	1,249	1,395	1,320
All	5,394	4,155	1,789	2,095	1,840	1,602	1,409	2,194	1,921	2,196	2,002
All one-port traffic											
Inwards	26,085	36,407	38,030	33,250	41,688	37,208	33,388	30,369	29,031	26,928	24,115
Outwards	8,794	3,186	1,725	2,167	1,994	1,745	1,383	1,944	1,617	1,956	1,853
All	34,880	39,593	39,755	35,417	43,682	38,953	34,771	32,313	30,648	28,884	25,968
Foreign and domestic traffic											
Liquid bulk traffic											
Inwards	123,446	124,913	132,402	129,748	127,328	125,676	134,232	134,417	135,129	130,699	127,388
Outwards	163,028	162,684	160,690	147,017	145,744	136,706	135,123	130,894	117,159	119,950	113,596
All	286,474	287,597	293,092	276,765	273,072	262,382	269,355	265,311	252,289	250,649	240,983
Dry bulk traffic											
Inwards	90,367	87,062	86,398	99,754	90,016	94,990	96,899	107,739	114,949	108,109	106,974
Outwards	28,820	26,175	27,981	24,386	25,878	29,067	25,940	26,429	26,820	25,553	25,961
All	119,187	113,237	114,379	124,140	115,894	124,057	122,839	134,168	141,769	133,661	132,936
Container and roll-on traffic											
Inwards	72,427	75,814	76,939	77,518	79,910	80,657	87,774	90,341	93,160	97,953	94,654
Outwards	59,689	61,013	60,829	58,398	58,654	58,717	61,896	64,040	65,789	68,203	67,295
All	132,115	136,827	137,768	135,915	138,565	139,374	149,669	154,381	158,949	166,156	161,948
Semi-bulk traffic											
Inwards	17,054	16,170	17,421	17,423	18,847	17,657	18,733	16,984	17,057	17,495	14,052
Outwards	5,374	4,740	4,721	4,307	4,159	4,392	4,860	5,853	5,672	6,954	5,646
All	22,428	20,910	22,142	21,730	23,006	22,049	23,593	22,836	22,729	24,449	19,698
Conventional traffic											
Inwards	1,744	1,869	2,596	3,804	3,744	3,893	4,063	3,807	3,722	2,744	2,742
Outwards	1,159	1,020	1,284	1,917	1,828	1,903	1,832	1,843	1,938	1,649	1,858
All	2,903	2,889	3,880	5,721	5,572	5,796	5,895	5,651	5,660	4,393	4,599
Non-oil traffic with UK off-shore installations											
Inwards	1,063	1,136	589	643	606	490	414	724	672	801	682
Outwards	4,332	3,019	1,199	1,452	1,234	1,112	995	1,470	1,249	1,395	1,320
All	5,394	4,155	1,789	2,095	1,840	1,602	1,409	2,194	1,921	2,196	2,002
All foreign and domestic traffic											
Inwards	306,100	306,963	316,344	328,890	320,450	323,364	342,115	354,012	364,690	357,800	346,491
Outwards	262,402	258,651	256,706	237,477	237,497	231,896	230,645	230,529	218,627	223,704	215,675
All	568,502	565,614	573,050	566,366	557,947	555,260	572,760	584,541	583,318	581,504	562,166

☎020-7944 3087

5.3 United Kingdom ports: foreign and domestic traffic by port: 1998-2008

Thousand tonnes

	1998	1999	2000	2001	2002	2003	2004	2005	2006	2007	2008
Aberdeen	3,786	3,368	3,377	3,845	3,645	3,233	3,888	4,609	4,663	5,131	4,833
Ayr	346	229	283	274	241	291	401	418	419	553	557
Barrow	275	247	231	225	279	241	206	151	145	192	206
Barry	433	445	597	586	547	457	403	443	515	456	465
Belfast	12,510	12,862	12,484	13,402	12,825	13,201	13,559	13,500	13,514	13,416	13,040
Berwick	139	135	146	110	89	134	89	76	94	83	94
Blyth	1,135	807	933	761	786	885	892	915	1,147	1,464	1,069
Boston	1,258	1,179	1,265	847	766	1,035	705	767	834	836	961
Bridgwater	67	59	84	104	86	101	105	106	91	50	46
Brightlingsea	140	142	65	248	76	125	138	118	97	103	82
Bristol	7,710	7,615	9,647	10,895	10,083	11,439	10,759	11,206	12,261	11,178	11,527
Cairnryan	2,504	2,437	2,283	2,014	2,099	2,328	2,849	3,274	3,145	3,163	2,928
Cardiff	2,452	2,661	2,699	2,739	2,209	2,287	2,504	2,450	2,873	3,057	2,596
Clyde (incl. Ardrossan)	8,127	8,495	7,224	11,069	9,733	9,214	11,507	15,737	14,981	12,063	14,338
Colchester	330	207	163	-	-	-	-	-	-	-	-
Coleraine	21	7	21	45	54	54	53	67	55	74	61
Cowes IOW	310	412	434	480	213	281	193	179	235	266	252
Cromarty Firth	4,456	2,336	2,329	2,145	2,658	3,501	3,208	3,325	3,206	3,502	2,252
Dover	17,690	19,387	17,434	19,074	20,212	18,796	20,753	21,145	23,805	25,144	24,344
Dundee	1,061	1,072	1,047	1,101	1,103	1,016	1,058	1,222	1,202	1,035	978
Exmouth (incl. Exeter)	52	-	-	-	-	-	-	-	-	-	-
Falmouth	484	398	598	471	406	438	352	570	697	753	722
Felixstowe	30,025	31,466	29,686	28,354	25,119	22,282	23,413	23,144	24,370	25,685	24,988
Fishguard	387	395	421	341	408	474	522	513	597	572	560
Fleetwood	1,106	1,368	1,530	1,608	1,521	1,624	1,662	1,635	1,670	1,772	1,571
Folkestone	634	462	560	251	-	112	77	94	13	25	-
Forth	44,400	45,396	41,143	41,607	42,202	38,752	34,892	34,218	31,556	36,681	39,054
Fowey	1,624	1,451	1,527	1,535	1,453	1,447	1,330	1,270	1,103	1,121	935
Garston	572	522	472	462	443	433	511	532	570	515	467
Glensanda	5,140	5,217	5,899	5,471	5,846	5,322	5,189	5,439	6,004	7,050	6,336
Gloucester & Sharpness	410	427	598	541	564	552	539	498	458	490	467
Goole	2,648	2,650	2,711	2,633	2,265	1,913	2,174	2,623	2,215	2,281	2,159
Great Yarmouth	1,865	1,216	757	666	711	778	607	763	950	900	784
Grimsby & Immingham	48,387	49,757	52,501	54,831	55,731	55,931	57,616	60,686	64,033	66,279	65,267
Harwich	3,281	4,059	3,990	2,623	3,495	4,330	4,264	4,221	4,176	3,784	3,739
Heysham	3,585	3,370	3,723	3,824	3,705	4,083	3,539	3,676	4,014	3,586	3,185
Holyhead	3,407	3,437	3,444	3,229	3,288	3,329	3,945	4,147	4,153	3,468	3,419
Hull	10,249	10,119	10,722	10,586	10,298	10,529	12,443	13,363	12,785	12,497	12,249
Inverness	763	783	724	714	686	727	726	665	671	684	697
Ipswich	2,184	2,391	2,925	2,924	3,336	3,888	3,557	3,578	3,505	2,797	2,572
King's Lynn	883	945	1,069	873	1,019	1,052	718	1,008	613	578	771
Lancaster	126	112	135	117	130	156	115	111	146	123	113
Larne	3,389	4,032	4,508	3,520	4,295	4,319	4,984	5,496	5,489	5,464	5,166
Lerwick	559	486	521	979	653	616	590	622	541	615	658
Littlehampton	128	173	188	210	224	174	93	61	71	72	78
Liverpool	30,357	28,913	30,421	30,288	30,413	31,684	32,233	33,775	33,550	32,258	32,204
London	57,311	52,206	47,892	50,654	51,185	51,028	53,289	53,843	51,911	52,739	52,965
Londonderry	1,127	1,216	1,133	1,060	1,065	1,172	1,392	1,151	1,690	1,934	1,839
Lowestoft	269	456	439	319	309	370	242	242	323	237	169
Manchester	7,409	7,825	7,687	7,879	6,279	6,088	6,634	7,222	8,049	8,079	7,438
Medway	15,528	13,973	15,292	14,853	14,840	15,619	14,535	15,470	18,957	15,417	14,971
Milford Haven	28,783	32,187	33,768	33,792	34,543	32,737	38,452	37,547	34,307	35,496	35,875
Mistley Quay	217	144	150	163	116	116	135	155	160	174	161
Montrose	561	614	721	675	728	798	777	697	640	582	609
Mostyn	326	359	310	309	871	944	656	203	180	154	139
Neath	506	474	466	504	369	383	416	406	464	420	274
Newhaven	1,012	461	578	998	863	949	929	876	1,046	1,003	1,196
Newport	2,628	2,532	2,673	2,980	3,111	2,790	3,448	3,971	3,846	2,843	3,195
Orkney	16,156	16,998	22,798	18,407	18,812	14,422	17,934	14,534	11,249	10,592	4,789
Par	549	605	558	485	479	348	337	315	209	58	-

☎020-7944 3087

5.3 (continued) United Kingdom ports: foreign and domestic traffic by port, 1998-2008

Thousand tonnes

	1998	1999	2000	2001	2002	2003	2004	2005	2006	2007	2008
Perth	240	242	266	218	176	144	159	139	148	144	141
Peterhead	2,818	2,209	1,123	1,339	1,343	1,051	676	928	947	790	871
Plymouth	1,310	1,671	1,799	1,877	1,854	2,053	2,167	2,308	2,452	2,486	2,322
Poole	1,700	1,581	1,296	1,819	1,798	1,640	1,754	1,712	1,806	1,405	1,518
Port Talbot	13,302	11,821	11,725	8,271	4,971	7,819	8,555	8,573	8,659	9,052	8,147
Portsmouth	4,527	4,317	4,521	4,282	4,365	4,222	4,940	4,931	4,205	3,961	3,937
Ramsgate	1,869	1,207	1,237	1,432	1,848	1,789	1,702	1,872	1,704	2,015	1,968
River Ouse	412	247	302	197	181	236	238	217	234	282	226
River Trent	2,360	2,193	2,450	2,396	2,346	2,309	2,329	1,924	2,062	2,207	1,984
Rivers Hull and Humber	10,197	8,830	9,015	7,846	8,902	10,025	9,242	9,843	9,774	9,370	9,351
Seaham	521	493	506	536	314	459	434	505	530	554	499
Shoreham	1,811	1,708	1,762	1,804	1,786	1,725	1,686	1,828	1,797	1,989	1,792
Silloth	155	231	168	141	134	155	168	170	171	180	148
Southampton	34,259	33,289	34,773	35,689	34,156	35,773	38,431	39,947	40,556	43,815	40,974
Stranraer	1,780	1,690	1,506	1,404	1,273	1,274	1,277	1,165	1,222	1,231	1,190
Sullom Voe	31,109	37,680	38,204	31,166	29,376	26,360	23,939	20,541	19,447	16,573	14,539
Sunderland	999	1,037	934	1,021	928	1,020	1,117	920	904	1,024	805
Sutton Bridge	913	846	817	695	669	746	571	534	593	609	530
Swansea	3,137	1,650	1,014	1,261	1,069	848	721	695	634	683	589
Tees and Hartlepool	51,454	49,316	51,473	50,842	50,447	53,842	53,819	55,790	53,348	49,779	45,436
Teignmouth	665	654	657	660	641	641	569	595	683	639	589
Tyne	2,136	2,210	2,391	2,469	2,656	2,763	2,973	3,357	4,077	4,613	5,417
Wallasea	120	128	146	149	165	175	176	196	233	221	162
Warrenpoint	1,563	1,715	1,676	1,480	1,826	1,880	1,967	2,436	2,307	1,999	2,119
Whitby and Scarborough	65	62	39	-	-	-	4	-	-	-	-
Whitehaven	-	-	-	-	-	2	-	-	-	-	-
Whitstable	306	153	170	189	159	129	103	81	121	79	70
Wisbech	61	59	50	54	59	49	57	75	112	63	58
Workington	623	563	636	418	430	258	180	246	200	182	132
Other ports	4,313	4,118	4,412	5,014	4,589	4,543	4,269	3,961	4,131	4,016	4,242
England	367,560	357,652	363,212	366,645	362,409	370,138	378,872	392,286	400,573	399,085	386,534
Wales	56,150	56,578	57,892	54,734	52,020	52,613	60,051	59,310	56,673	56,598	55,790
Scotland	124,713	130,100	130,512	123,820	122,156	110,535	110,444	108,890	101,587	101,952	96,346
Great Britain	548,423	544,330	551,616	545,199	536,585	533,287	549,367	560,486	558,833	557,636	538,669
Northern Ireland	20,079	21,284	21,434	21,167	21,363	21,973	23,393	24,055	24,485	23,868	23,497
All UK ports	568,502	565,614	573,050	566,366	557,947	555,260	572,760	584,541	583,318	581,504	562,166

☎020-7944 3087

5.4 United Kingdom ports: foreign and domestic unitised traffic[1] 1998-2008

(a) Units											Thousands
	1998	1999	2000	2001	2002	2003	2004	2005	2006	2007	2008
Containers on Lo-Lo and conventional services [2,3]	3,722	3,918	4,325	4,464	4,506	4,533	4,919	4,754	4,883	5,381	5,269
Containers on Ro-Ro services [2]	528	550	-	-	-	-	-	-	-	-	-
Road goods vehicles	3,206	3,182	3,118	3,317	3,479	3,547	3,857	3,906	4,183	4,295	4,342
Unaccompanied trailers	2,312	2,533	2,742	2,687	2,760	2,781	2,734	2,840	2,944	2,989	2,700
Rail wagons, shipborne port-to-port trailers and barges [3]	-	-	361	344	348	374	383	665	668	744	657
All main freight units	9,769	10,182	10,546	10,811	11,094	11,235	11,893	12,165	12,678	13,408	12,968
Other unitised freight:											
Import/export vehicles	3,135	3,251	3,095	3,313	3,662	3,736	3,953	3,978	3,906	4,022	3,592
Other units	..	..	277	225	167	163	145	208	186	244	145
All freight units	12,904	13,433	13,918	14,349	14,923	15,133	15,991	16,351	16,770	17,674	16,705

(b) Tonnage											Thousand tonnes
Containers on Lo-Lo and conventional services [2,3]	46,680	49,600	51,613	51,814	51,178	51,413	56,502	53,949	54,493	60,718	59,734
Containers on Ro-Ro services [2]	8,830	8,800	-	-	-	-	-	-	-	-	-
Road goods vehicles [4]	71,802	73,519	35,852	37,706	39,119	38,759	42,896	44,854	46,592	48,233	48,694
Unaccompanied trailers	..	..	38,408	35,678	36,843	37,361	38,087	38,600	39,658	38,534	36,114
Rail wagons, shipborne port-to-port trailers and barges [3]	-	-	6,166	4,846	5,294	5,505	5,483	10,064	10,837	11,099	10,800
All main freight units	127,312	131,919	132,039	130,043	132,434	133,038	142,969	147,468	151,580	158,583	155,342
Other unitised freight:											
Import/export vehicles	3,812	3,965	4,083	4,023	4,693	4,839	5,268	5,400	5,566	5,932	5,144
Other unitised freight	992	942	1,646	1,849	1,437	1,497	1,433	1,513	1,803	1,641	8,907
All unitised traffic	132,115	136,827	137,768	135,915	138,565	139,374	149,669	154,381	158,949	166,156	169,392

1 Includes estimates for traffic at minor ports.
2 From 2000, containers on Ro-Ro services are mainly classified to rail wagons, shipborne port-to-port trailers and barges.
3 More accurate recording of container/shipborne port-to-port trailers movements from 2005 means that figures for 2005 onwards are not directly comparable with 2000-2004; in 2005 approximately 300,000 container units were reported under rail wagons, shipborne port-to-port trailers and barges, which would previously have been erroneously reported under the Containers on Lo-Lo and conventional services.
4 Including unaccompanied trailers prior to 2000.

☎020-7944 3087

5.5 United Kingdom ports: foreign and domestic main freight units by port:[1,2] 1998-2008

(a) Units											Thousands
	1998	1999	2000	2001	2002	2003	2004	2005	2006	2007	2008
Aberdeen	10	10	12	39	40	42	45	51	49	50	52
Belfast	448	456	471	444	422	448	470	472	488	500	469
Boston	20	16	17	4	3	7	11	11	4	7	2
Bristol	21	27	32	49	57	60	69	73	64	63	52
Cairnryan	170	171	157	165	179	193	211	231	237	240	226
Cardiff	25	24	29	29	24	28	33	34	42	28	20
Clyde	55	59	53	48	33	45	36	36	37	43	34
Cromarty Firth	6	5	4	1	-	-	-	-	-	-	-
Dover	1,499	1,652	1,625	1,774	1,856	1,786	1,982	2,047	2,325	2,364	2,299
Felixstowe	2,150	2,246	2,330	2,247	2,058	1,817	1,936	1,945	2,095	2,281	2,150
Fishguard	31	32	34	27	33	36	40	47	54	53	49
Fleetwood	91	108	116	125	120	126	125	131	134	147	136
Forth	63	66	79	90	117	143	165	171	168	164	171
Goole	67	68	70	70	51	18	27	61	44	36	37
Grimsby and Immingham	411	449	478	560	637	747	718	732	777	835	821
Harwich	212	215	246	199	258	323	404	408	330	322	292
Heysham	273	275	259	257	253	324	240	250	281	250	228
Holyhead	191	193	185	208	215	231	272	296	315	337	324
Hull	318	303	324	293	298	327	358	376	385	409	372
Ipswich	2	6	37	65	88	106	114	93	89	39	40
Larne	299	311	301	317	345	339	365	385	390	402	381
Liverpool	590	667	737	769	724	747	810	837	878	946	928
London	768	852	831	827	912	890	948	962	951	1,130	1,117
Manchester	1	-	1	-	-	-	1	7	3	1	-
Medway	333	326	324	310	325	314	377	413	354	307	454
Milford Haven	46	53	55	61	58	61	68	71	84	94	86
Newhaven	24	1	-	9	24	37	31	34	50	39	47
Newport	4	3	-	-	-	-	-	-	-	-	-
Orkney	11	12	4	16	22	22	22	22	21	34	27
Plymouth	8	7	6	7	7	8	11	13	12	14	10
Poole	82	81	73	70	75	73	67	69	75	79	83
Portsmouth [3]	302	288	292	327	328	331	323	305	291	298	285
Ramsgate	100	60	83	95	135	147	143	153	152	148	162
Shoreham	-	-	-	-	-	-	-	-	-	-	-
Southampton [3]	559	604	713	745	793	849	894	857	904	1,111	960
Stranraer	146	146	155	139	122	117	127	105	112	116	115
Swansea	22	21	14	6	4	5	5	7	4	-	-
Tees & Hartlepool	237	207	234	213	219	228	226	232	254	275	272
Tyne	30	31	24	35	51	47	55	47	50	59	64
Warrenpoint	67	65	68	63	68	65	68	94	104	104	98
Other ports of UK	79	66	71	108	142	145	97	87	71	83	105
England	8,143	8,525	8,896	9,071	9,272	9,323	9,876	10,064	10,509	11,171	10,826
Wales	318	326	318	342	397	430	438	455	498	512	479
Scotland	493	499	492	574	590	628	676	695	689	718	715
Great Britain	8,955	9,350	9,706	9,987	10,259	10,382	10,991	11,214	11,696	12,402	12,019
Northern Ireland	814	832	840	824	835	853	903	951	982	1,007	949
All ports of UK	9,769	10,182	10,546	10,811	11,094	11,235	11,893	12,165	12,678	13,408	12,968

1 Includes containers, road goods vehicles, unaccompanied trailers,
  rail wagons, shipborne port to port trailers and barges only.
2 Includes estimates of traffic at minor ports.
3 Excludes traffic to and from the Isle of Wight.

☎020-7944 3087

(continued) 5.5 United Kingdom ports: foreign and domestic main freight units by port, [1,2] 1998-2008

(b) Tonnage										Thousand tonnes of goods	
	1998	1999	2000	2001	2002	2003	2004	2005	2006	2007	2008
Aberdeen	90	88	102	235	261	272	309	343	309	328	353
Belfast	5,928	6,068	5,727	5,944	5,658	5,926	6,095	6,258	6,406	6,637	6,405
Boston	270	238	229	47	39	87	85	111	59	56	20
Bristol	307	370	457	695	770	810	942	1,030	993	1,092	912
Cairnryan	2,502	2,436	2,116	1,834	1,915	2,138	2,662	3,062	2,948	2,979	2,766
Cardiff	283	239	290	307	247	205	238	248	265	235	160
Clyde	533	530	779	534	346	426	406	370	398	469	439
Cromarty Firth	44	45	30	10	-	-	-	-	-	-	-
Dover	17,162	18,782	17,017	18,627	19,694	18,261	20,170	20,663	23,341	24,582	23,888
Felixstowe	29,321	30,859	28,881	27,388	24,250	21,439	22,547	22,717	24,076	25,601	24,931
Fishguard	382	391	417	336	405	470	518	506	594	568	557
Fleetwood	1,106	1,368	1,469	1,542	1,470	1,561	1,599	1,615	1,648	1,763	1,558
Forth	900	985	607	832	1,687	2,077	2,383	2,351	2,398	2,572	2,622
Goole	1,071	980	966	920	684	294	383	887	636	559	518
Grimsby and Immingham	7,107	7,592	7,928	9,142	9,993	11,793	11,290	11,879	12,487	13,342	14,188
Harwich	2,485	3,211	3,121	1,992	2,858	3,517	4,030	3,582	3,539	3,194	3,017
Heysham	3,390	3,199	3,471	3,422	3,352	3,745	3,232	3,303	3,699	3,289	3,004
Holyhead	3,116	3,148	3,019	2,896	2,974	2,981	3,596	3,768	3,794	3,128	3,135
Hull	4,524	4,452	4,771	4,145	4,156	4,502	4,799	4,971	4,983	5,245	4,791
Ipswich	35	83	414	712	1,039	1,294	1,410	1,151	1,096	453	407
Larne	3,372	4,016	4,159	3,211	4,020	3,957	4,692	5,168	5,127	5,221	4,950
Liverpool	7,723	8,429	9,429	9,513	8,856	9,494	10,382	10,873	11,200	11,967	11,673
London	10,444	10,282	10,711	10,986	12,015	12,233	14,355	14,590	14,485	15,062	15,110
Manchester	9	6	8	-	-	-	20	23	5	3	-
Medway	4,205	3,984	4,142	3,572	3,556	3,280	3,796	4,269	3,506	2,975	4,445
Milford Haven	567	712	717	797	760	794	886	1,059	1,086	1,224	1,116
Newhaven	326	20	-	251	300	450	416	468	687	560	830
Newport	37	44	-	-	1	9	6	2	7	3	-
Orkney	101	105	91	84	129	69	115	114	115	149	160
Plymouth	118	92	78	76	69	78	110	148	137	157	108
Poole	1,043	1,012	602	1,048	1,118	902	1,021	1,041	1,120	990	1,044
Portsmouth [3]	3,765	3,639	3,771	3,549	3,400	3,312	3,874	3,757	2,884	3,108	2,920
Ramsgate	1,834	1,096	1,187	1,356	1,848	1,758	1,668	1,842	1,648	1,971	1,941
Shoreham	-	-	-	1	3	2	1	1	-	-	-
Southampton [3]	4,710	5,430	6,396	6,724	7,030	7,299	7,894	7,799	8,327	10,617	8,689
Stranraer	1,780	1,690	1,505	1,404	1,273	1,273	1,277	1,165	1,222	1,231	1,190
Swansea	174	159	100	31	39	50	51	75	36	5	-
Tees & Hartlepool	4,304	3,969	4,930	3,362	3,388	3,441	3,382	3,657	3,876	4,153	4,191
Tyne	322	333	433	434	510	518	514	486	470	634	626
Warrenpoint	1,033	1,088	1,160	1,046	1,196	1,205	1,363	1,837	1,646	1,513	1,693
Other ports of UK	889	749	808	1,039	1,126	1,120	451	279	326	952	984
England	106,247	109,933	111,006	109,789	110,120	109,820	117,704	120,571	124,589	131,490	128,948
Wales	4,559	4,693	4,543	4,498	5,179	5,337	5,535	5,658	5,782	5,163	4,968
Scotland	6,173	6,122	5,444	5,555	6,262	6,793	7,580	7,976	8,030	8,560	8,378
Great Britain	116,979	120,747	120,993	119,842	121,561	121,950	130,819	134,205	138,402	145,213	142,294
Northern Ireland	10,332	11,172	11,046	10,201	10,873	11,088	12,150	13,263	13,178	13,370	13,048
All ports of UK	127,312	131,919	132,039	130,043	132,434	133,038	142,969	147,468	151,580	158,583	155,342

1 Includes containers, road goods vehicles, unaccompanied trailers,
  rail wagons, shipborne port to port trailers and barges only.
2 Includes estimates of traffic at minor ports.
3 Excludes traffic to and from the Isle of Wight.

☎020-7944 3087

5.6 United Kingdom ports: accompanied passenger vehicles on foreign and coastwise routes:[1] 1998-2008

Thousand vehicles

(a) Cars	1998	1999	2000	2001	2002	2003	2004	2005	2006	2007	2008
France	4,453	3,954	3,524	3,619	3,727	3,669	3,720	3,449	3,563	3,734	3,712
Belgium	87	244	260	115	120	111	112	124	129	132	118
Netherlands	351	405	422	383	420	390	379	336	330	290	241
Germany	44	40	22	27	32	19	24	23	-	-	-
Irish Republic	886	854	876	833	878	879	837	773	751	781	723
Denmark	25	27	23	26	27	22	23	21	48	26	21
Scandinavia and Baltic	52	36	26	15	36	44	31	39	19	21	61
of which:											
Norway	..	..	14	6	15	29	9	20	9	21	61
Sweden	..	..	11	8	20	15	21	18	10	-	-
Spain	83	84	83	93	104	80	81	94	85	88	95
All overseas routes	5,982	5,644	5,235	5,111	5,344	5,213	5,207	4,861	4,927	5,072	4,972
Channel Tunnel [2]	*3,351*	*3,260*	*2,784*	*2,530*	*2,336*	*2,279*	*2,101*	*2,047*	*2,046*	*2,142*	*1,907*
Coastwise routes by ship: [3]											
Northern Ireland [4]	1,179	1,282	1,108	1,078	1,082	1,104	1,138	1,054	1,007	1,089	1,026
Isle of Man	98	137	140	136	166	159	157	75	147	183	152
Orkney and Shetland [4]	122	127	128	104	125	155	156	163	170	196	206
Channel Islands	103	112	159	162	179	128	111	104	90	89	94
Other	34	34	36	39	42	44	48	48	47	49	49
All coastwise routes	1,536	1,692	1,570	1,520	1,594	1,591	1,611	1,444	1,461	1,605	1,526
All cars	7,518	7,336	6,806	6,631	6,939	6,804	6,818	6,305	6,388	6,677	6,498
(b) Buses and coaches											
France	166	167	157	153	155	141	152	128	114	110	106
Belgium	3	3	2	2	1	4	4	4	3	4	3
Netherlands	8	7	7	6	8	7	5	8	7	7	5
Germany	-	-	-	-	-	-	1	-	-	-	-
Irish Republic	19	18	19	16	17	16	16	17	15	15	14
Denmark	-	-	-	-	-	-	1	-	-	-	-
Scandinavia and Baltic	1	1	-	-	1	1	1	1	-	-	1
Spain	1	1	-	1	1	1	1	1	1	1	1
All overseas routes	198	196	187	178	183	169	181	159	142	137	131
Channel Tunnel [2]	*96*	*82*	*79*	*75*	*72*	*72*	*63*	*77*	*67*	*65*	*61*
Coastwise routes by ship: [3]											
Northern Ireland [4]	15	14	15	14	16	17	17	15	15	15	10
Isle of Man	1	1	1	1	1	1	-	-	-	-	-
Orkney and Shetland [4]	-	-	-	-	-	1	1	1	1	1	2
Channel Islands	-	-	-	-	-	-	-	-	1	-	-
Other	-	-	-	-	-	-	-	1	-	-	-
All coastwise routes	16	16	16	16	17	19	18	16	18	16	12
All buses and coaches	214	212	203	194	201	188	199	175	159	153	143

1 Includes estimates for traffic at minor ports.
2 Shown here for comparison but not included in total.
3 Excludes traffic to the Isle of Wight.
4 Vehicles counted at both ends of route.

☎020-7944 3087

5.7 United Kingdom ports: accompanied passenger vehicles on foreign and coastwise routes by port:[1] 1998-2008

Thousand vehicles

	1998	1999	2000	2001	2002	2003	2004	2005	2006	2007	2008
Cars:											
Belfast	400	454	437	397	400	403	406	315	316	328	288
Cairnryan	183	182	151	140	153	139	137	140	134	156	154
Dover	3,047	2,758	2,433	2,396	2,466	2,418	2,507	2,470	2,648	2,838	2,729
Fishguard	178	187	194	180	183	157	156	144	140	152	143
Forth	-	-	-	-	28	43	44	43	28	31	21
Harwich	256	273	285	272	280	254	244	207	182	119	109
Heysham	52	121	123	97	86	75	76	67	83	94	82
Holyhead	481	454	500	464	488	501	481	465	452	480	445
Hull	205	215	217	197	186	167	165	173	176	189	186
Larne	187	196	155	149	164	175	174	206	199	232	221
Liverpool	130	125	37	133	148	162	162	129	135	160	152
Medway	-	-	-	-	-	-	-	-	-	-	-
Milford Haven	124	119	130	114	117	118	111	97	101	120	107
Newhaven	136	78	73	76	78	90	91	44	74	91	99
Orkney	49	51	50	40	49	62	64	67	69	99	86
Plymouth	178	178	175	176	192	187	189	194	176	183	190
Poole	202	163	176	200	234	216	186	119	126	141	156
Portsmouth [2]	939	973	934	976	1,011	915	891	770	666	610	678
Ramsgate	21	-	-	-	-	-	3	11	29	27	28
Southampton	-	-	-	-	-	-	-	-	-	-	-
Stranraer	372	338	270	248	257	239	275	239	250	257	239
Swansea	48	45	41	38	41	41	40	36	29	-	-
Tyne	71	98	73	63	121	123	113	112	113	103	99
Other ports	260	326	351	274	258	319	301	260	262	270	288
All cars	7,518	7,336	6,806	6,631	6,939	6,804	6,818	6,305	6,388	6,677	6,498
Buses and coaches:											
Dover	154	157	148	145	148	125	128	108	106	105	98
Holyhead	13	12	13	12	12	12	12	13	12	12	11
Portsmouth	11	10	8	7	7	15	24	20	8	4	8
Other ports	36	33	33	30	33	35	35	34	33	32	26
All buses and coaches	214	212	203	194	201	188	199	175	159	153	143

1 Includes estimates for traffic at minor ports.
2 Excludes traffic to the Isle of Wight

☎020-7944 3087

5.8 Waterborne transport within the United Kingdom: 1998-2008

(a) Goods moved										Billion tonne-kilometres	
	1998	1999	2000	2001	2002	2003	2004	2005	2006	2007	2008
UK inland waters traffic											
Non-seagoing traffic											
Internal	0.2	0.2	0.2	0.2	0.2	0.2	0.2	0.2	0.2	0.1	0.2
Seagoing traffic (by route)											
Coastwise	0.2	0.2	0.2	0.2	0.2	0.2	0.2	0.2	0.2	0.2	0.2
Foreign	1.3	1.3	1.0	1.1	1.1	1.0	1.0	1.1	1.1	1.2	1.1
One-port	0.3	0.3	0.2	0.3	0.3	0.2	0.2	0.2	0.2	0.2	0.2
Total	2.0	1.9	1.7	1.8	1.7	1.6	1.5	1.6	1.7	1.7	1.7
Coastwise traffic between UK ports [1]	45.0	40.6	36.5	34.1	35.1	33.3	35.4	39.4	32.4	34.5	35.1
One-port traffic of UK ports [1]	10.0	16.2	29.7	23.3	30.8	26.4	22.9	20.3	18.2	15.0	13.3
All traffic [1,2]	56.9	58.7	67.4	58.8	67.2	60.9	59.4	60.9	51.8	50.8	49.7

(b) Goods lifted [1]										Million tonnes	
UK inland waters traffic											
Non-seagoing traffic											
Internal	4.3	4.3	4.3	4.3	4.0	3.2	2.6	3.4	3.6	3.4	3.7
Seagoing traffic (by route)											
Coastwise	9.6	8.7	9.3	8.8	6.8	7.4	7.2	8.6	8.5	8.0	7.7
Foreign	35.3	33.9	30.8	33.4	32.0	31.8	30.1	32.0	34.0	34.9	35.2
One-port	8.2	7.0	4.5	7.0	6.2	5.0	4.7	4.8	4.9	5.7	5.4
Total	57.3	53.8	49.0	53.5	49.0	47.4	44.6	48.7	51.0	52.0	51.9
Coastwise traffic between UK ports [1]	77.3	73.0	63.1	58.5	59.5	58.5	59.8	65.1	58.1	58.8	58.1
One-port traffic of UK ports [1]	32.6	33.3	39.3	35.1	43.7	39.0	34.8	32.3	30.6	28.9	26.0
All traffic [1,2]	149.4	144.5	137.4	131.3	139.1	132.5	127.2	132.8	126.3	125.9	123.0

1 More accurate recording of the origin and destination of crude oil traffic from 2000 onwards has meant that figures for coastwise and one-port traffic are not directly comparable with previous years.
2 The 'All traffic' figures in part (a) from 2000 onwards and in part (b) for all years are calculated by the addition of the totals for coastwise traffic, one-port traffic, and the internal and foreign components of inland waters traffic.

☎020-7944 3087

5.9 Principal ports, port groups and freight waterways

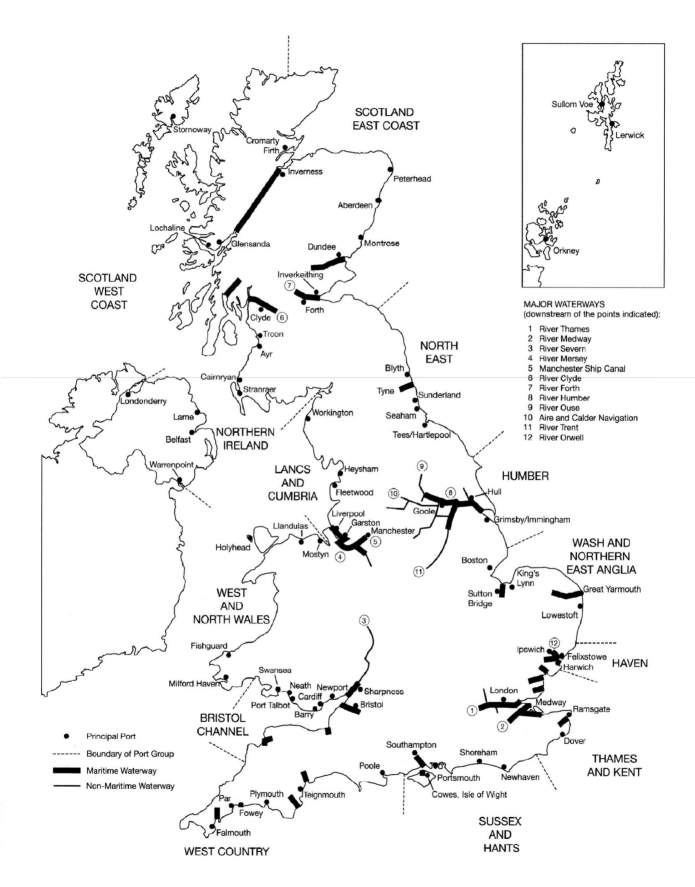

SCOTLAND
EAST COAST

Stornoway
Cromarty
Firth
Inverness
Peterhead
Aberdeen
Lochaline
Glensanda
Dundee
Montrose
SCOTLAND
WEST
COAST
Inverkeithing
⑦
Forth
Clyde ⑥
Troon
Ayr
NORTH
EAST
Blyth
Cairnryan
Stranraer
Tyne
Sunderland
Londonderry
Seaham
Workington
Tees/Hartlepool
Larne
NORTHERN
IRELAND
Belfast
Warrenpoint
Heysham
LANCS
AND
CUMBRIA
Fleetwood
HUMBER
⑨
⑩
Hull
Goole
⑧
Liverpool
Garston
Grimsby/Immingham
Llandulas
Manchester
⑤
Holyhead
Mostyn ④
Boston
WASH AND
NORTHERN
EAST ANGLIA
⑪
WEST
AND
NORTH WALES
King's
Lynn
Great Yarmouth
Sutton
Bridge
Lowestoft
Fishguard
③
Ipswich ⑫
Felixstowe
HAVEN
Swansea
Harwich
Milford Haven
Neath Newport
Sharpness
London
Cardiff
Medway
Port Talbot
Bristol
①
Ramsgate
Barry
②
BRISTOL
CHANNEL
Dover
Southampton
Shoreham
Poole
Portsmouth
Newhaven
THAMES
AND KENT
Par
Plymouth
Teignmouth
Cowes, Isle of Wight
Fowey
SUSSEX
AND
HANTS
Falmouth
WEST COUNTRY

Inset (top right):
Sullom Voe
Lerwick
Orkney

MAJOR WATERWAYS
(downstream of the points indicated):

1 River Thames
2 River Medway
3 River Severn
4 River Mersey
5 Manchester Ship Canal
6 River Clyde
7 River Forth
8 River Humber
9 River Ouse
10 Aire and Calder Navigation
11 River Trent
12 River Orwell

Legend:
● Principal Port
- - - Boundary of Port Group
▰ Maritime Waterway
— Non-Maritime Waterway

☎ 020-7944 3087

5.10 Traffic on major rivers and other inland waterway routes: 2002-2008

	Internal Traffic							Seagoing Traffic						
(a) Goods moved													**Billion tonne-kilometres**	
	2002	2003	2004	2005	2006	2007	2008	2002	2003	2004	2005	2006	2007	2008
River Thames	0.10	0.11	0.09	0.09	0.09	0.08	0.10	0.67	0.60	0.53	0.61	0.67	0.74	0.71
River Medway	-	-	-	-	-	-	0.01	0.04	0.05	0.04	0.03	0.04	0.04	0.03
River Severn	-	-	-	-	-	-	-	0.01	0.01	0.01	0.01	0.01	0.01	0.01
River Mersey	-	-	-	-	-	-	-	0.09	0.09	0.10	0.10	0.11	0.11	0.10
Manchester Ship Canal	0.01	0.01	0.01	0.01	0.01	0.01	0.01	0.09	0.09	0.09	0.09	0.09	0.08	0.06
River Clyde	-	-	-	-	-	-	-	0.05	0.06	0.05	0.07	0.06	0.09	0.11
River Forth	-	-	-	-	-	-	-	0.18	0.18	0.18	0.18	0.18	0.17	0.20
River Humber	0.01	0.01	0.01	0.02	0.01	0.01	0.01	0.23	0.21	0.22	0.22	0.21	0.22	0.21
River Ouse	0.01	0.01	0.01	0.01	0.01	-	-	0.03	0.03	0.04	0.05	0.04	0.04	0.04
Aire and Calder Nav'n	0.02	0.01	0.01	0.01	0.01	0.01	0.01	-	-	-	-	-	-	-
River Trent	0.02	0.02	0.02	0.02	0.02	-	-	0.03	0.03	0.03	0.03	0.03	0.03	0.03
River Orwell	-	-	-	-	-	-	-	0.06	0.07	0.06	0.06	0.06	0.05	0.05
All above waterways	0.17	0.17	0.15	0.16	0.16	0.12	0.15	1.50	1.43	1.35	1.45	1.50	1.59	1.54
All waterways	0.18	0.18	0.15	0.17	0.16	0.14	0.16	1.51	1.44	1.37	1.46	1.52	1.60	1.55
(b) Goods lifted													**Million tonnes**	
River Thames	2.09	2.02	1.54	1.81	2.09	1.94	2.18	17.16	16.03	14.19	17.13	18.67	20.06	19.49
River Medway	0.58	0.56	0.37	0.44	0.35	0.24	0.55	2.38	2.74	2.02	1.45	2.13	2.22	1.77
River Severn	-	-	-	0.21	0.19	0.26	0.23	0.56	0.55	0.54	0.50	0.46	0.49	0.47
River Mersey	0.23	0.22	0.23	0.24	0.32	0.30	0.33	5.51	5.08	5.63	6.13	6.57	6.42	5.78
Manchester Ship Canal	0.23	0.22	0.23	0.24	0.32	0.30	0.33	5.51	5.08	5.63	6.13	6.57	6.42	5.78
River Clyde	0.01	-	-	-	-	-	-	1.29	1.34	1.29	1.59	1.53	2.08	2.53
River Forth	-	-	-	-	-	-	-	8.53	8.58	8.52	8.47	8.49	8.28	9.52
River Humber	0.40	0.35	0.44	0.58	0.44	0.34	0.29	5.53	5.29	5.51	5.79	5.32	5.67	5.50
River Ouse	0.41	0.43	0.37	0.52	0.43	0.29	0.29	2.45	2.15	2.41	2.84	2.45	2.56	2.39
Aire and Calder Nav'n	1.06	0.50	0.37	0.40	0.40	0.30	0.29	-	-	-	-	-	-	-
River Trent	0.30	0.26	0.26	0.25	0.24	0.17	0.18	2.35	2.31	2.33	1.92	2.06	2.21	1.98
River Orwell	-	-	-	-	-	-	-	3.34	3.90	3.56	3.58	3.51	2.80	2.57
All waterways [1]	3.96	3.18	2.60	3.40	3.56	3.36	3.69	44.99	44.21	42.02	45.33	47.42	48.65	48.22

1 Where goods are carried on more than one inland
waterway route, the tonnage lifted is counted on
each route travelled. The 'All Waterways' figures
exclude all such double counting.

☎020-7944 3087

Transport Statistics Great Britain 2009

5.11 United Kingdom international sea passenger movements by country of embarkation or landing:[1] 1998-2008

Thousands

	1998	1999	2000	2001	2002	2003	2004	2005	2006	2007	2008
Ro-Ro ferry passengers on short sea routes											
Belgium	1,749	1,592	1,507	1,379	1,129	740	739	778	748	751	676
Denmark	195	188	164	156	132	88	97	91	89	96	90
France	23,912	22,454	19,755	19,485	20,555	19,077	18,565	16,834	16,925	17,377	16,844
Germany	246	222	188	164	161	92	117	98	1	1	1
Irish Republic	4,606	4,343	4,234	3,882	3,880	3,802	3,656	3,380	3,221	3,291	3,069
Netherlands	1,768	1,939	2,031	2,026	2,209	2,094	2,002	1,848	1,897	1,636	1,667
Norway	188	208	225	230	241	235	231	200	149	153	120
Spain	373	346	320	355	341	308	310	378	372	357	370
Sweden	186	87	89	73	73	81	75	79	59	5	4
Other Europe	4	3	3	4	3	7	7	8	6	1	-
Total	33,226	31,381	28,517	27,753	28,726	26,523	25,799	23,693	23,465	23,668	22,840
Passengers on long sea journeys	23	26	26	27	32	25	40	52	58	68	72
Passengers on cruises beginning or ending at UK ports[2]	..	445	461	469	540	702	767	935	1,013	1,064	1,341
All international passengers[3]	33,249	31,852	29,003	28,249	29,298	27,250	26,605	24,680	24,537	24,800	24,254

1 For details of Channel Tunnel passenger numbers please see Table 6.8. ☎020-7944 4121
2 Cruise passengers, like other passengers, are included at both departure. and arrival if their journey begins and ends at a UK seaport.
3 Excluding cruise passengers in 1998.

5.12　United Kingdom international sea passenger movements by port and port area:[1] 1998-2008

Thousands

	1998	1999	2000	2001	2002	2003	2004	2005	2006	2007	2008
Ro-Ro ferry passengers on short sea routes [2]											
Thames and Kent											
London	12	16	15	14	13	11	14	13	12	11	7
Ramsgate	161	50	76	88	117	137	148	193	214	233	222
Dover	19,330	18,324	16,078	15,857	16,329	14,631	14,275	13,359	13,799	14,258	13,783
Folkestone	905	653	440	5	-	-	-	-	-	-	-
All Thames and Kent	20,408	19,043	16,609	15,964	16,459	14,780	14,437	13,566	14,025	14,503	14,012
South Coast											
Newhaven	621	337	313	337	379	397	361	167	270	329	284
Portsmouth	3,509	3,487	3,176	3,344	3,406	3,116	3,077	2,631	2,166	2,084	2,087
Southampton	-	-	-	-	-	-	5	3	-	-	-
Poole	414	472	455	586	620	623	520	398	479	469	474
Weymouth	53	56	60	-	8	15	20	21	18	19	15
Plymouth	642	627	583	583	631	603	617	636	564	575	571
All South Coast	5,240	4,980	4,587	4,851	5,044	4,754	4,600	3,856	3,498	3,476	3,431
West Coast											
Swansea	158	133	124	122	121	118	116	100	81	-	-
Milford Haven	512	495	463	388	387	384	378	321	333	379	345
Fishguard	810	830	832	687	662	645	614	590	584	597	554
Holyhead	2,775	2,541	2,518	2,380	2,371	2,333	2,262	2,173	2,057	2,138	1,996
Mostyn	-	-	-	5	44	48	10	-	-	-	-
Liverpool	343	337	293	298	291	269	270	190	162	173	172
Fleetwood	-	-	-	-	-	-	-	-	-	-	-
Other ports	9	7	4	3	4	5	5	5	4	3	2
All West Coast	4,606	4,343	4,234	3,882	3,880	3,802	3,656	3,380	3,221	3,291	3,069
East Coast											
Lerwick	7	6	6	6	7	13	14	11	10	1	-
Forth	-	-	-	-	105	195	192	183	112	110	74
Tyne	466	626	667	745	816	829	767	699	648	638	595
Hull	1,027	1,022	972	1,006	1,041	994	976	964	1,017	1,010	966
Grimsby and Immingham	10	9	12	13	38	43	43	44	49	63	81
Ipswich	-	-	5	6	6	6	7	8	8	4	2
Felixstowe	77	78	86	80	58	19	19	19	16	15	15
Harwich	1,384	1,272	1,335	1,196	1,268	1,085	1,085	959	857	553	593
Other ports	2	2	3	4	3	3	3	4	4	4	4
All East Coast	2,973	3,016	3,086	3,056	3,342	3,188	3,106	2,891	2,722	2,398	2,329
All port areas	33,226	31,381	28,517	27,753	28,726	26,523	25,799	23,693	23,465	23,668	22,840
Passengers on long sea journeys	23	26	26	27	32	25	40	52	58	68	72
Passengers on cruises beginning or ending at UK ports [3]	..	445	461	469	540	702	767	935	1,013	1,064	1,341
of which:											
Southampton	..	211	281	295	331	438	476	637	658	716	889
Dover	..	136	119	100	120	139	154	141	188	175	223
Harwich	..	70	43	68	69	97	91	84	104	104	126
Other ports	..	28	17	4	20	28	46	71	64	69	103
All international passengers [4]	33,249	31,852	29,003	28,249	29,298	27,250	26,605	24,680	24,537	24,800	24,254

1 For details of Channel Tunnel passenger numbers please see Table 6.8.

2 See Notes and Definitions.

3 Cruise passengers, like other passengers, are included at both departure.
　and arrival if their journey begins and ends at a UK seaport.

4 Excluding cruise passengers in 1997 and 1998.

☎020-7944 4121

5.13 United Kingdom and Crown Dependency registered trading vessels of 500 gross tons and over: summary of tonnage by type[1]: 1950-1986 and 1986-2008

For greater detail of the years 1998-2008 see Table 5.14

End of year	Passenger 000 Gt	Cargo liners 000 Gt	Container 000 Gt	Tramps 000 Gt	Bulk carriers 000 Gt	Tankers 000 Gt	Total 000 Gt	Total Number [2]
1950	2,936	5,949	-	..	4,366	3,946	17,198	3,092
1951	2,992	5,933	-	..	4,084	4,187	17,196	3,056
1952	2,935	6,063	-	..	3,836	4,430	17,264	3,014
1953	2,825	6,066	-	..	3,939	4,637	17,467	3,016
1954	2,998	6,007	-	..	3,965	5,046	18,016	3,041
1955	3,012	6,080	-	..	3,979	5,138	18,208	3,041
1956	3,013	6,300	-	..	3,841	5,329	18,484	3,041
1957	2,958	6,540	-	..	3,696	5,638	18,833	3,031
1958	2,843	6,545	-	..	3,837	6,021	19,245	3,007
1959	2,749	6,605	-	..	3,706	6,745	19,805	2,950
1960	2,814	6,568	-	..	3,762	7,058	20,202	2,902
1961	2,771	6,294	-	..	4,143	7,288	20,497	2,808
1962	2,495	6,133	-	..	4,441	7,486	20,554	2,689
1963	2,342	5,939	-	..	4,328	7,788	20,396	2,538
1964	2,244	5,936	-	..	4,444	7,804	20,428	2,473
1965	2,115	5,894	-	..	4,687	7,685	20,382	2,401
1966	1,971	5,898	..	2,666	2,130	7,857	20,522	2,319
1967	1,709	5,576	..	2,521	2,661	7,908	20,375	2,181
1968	1,605	5,398	..	2,173	2,974	8,580	20,730	2,058
1969	1,245	5,452	194	1,904	3,265	10,215	22,274	2,002
1970	1,230	5,233	418	1,621	3,710	11,849	24,061	1,977
1971	1,101	4,444	683	1,425	4,219	13,304	25,177	1,875
1972	1,010	3,895	1,162	1,222	6,152	13,500	26,940	1,798
1973	920	3,749	1,346	1,060	7,366	14,665	29,106	1,776
1974	855	3,656	1,365	1,027	7,694	16,199	30,795	1,767
1975	748	3,330	1,363	958	8,022	17,069	31,489	1,682
1976	661	3,148	1,349	910	8,030	15,742	29,839	1,573
1977	654	2,923	1,624	882	8,181	15,797	30,061	1,545
1978	614	2,546	1,827	743	7,174	15,173	28,078	1,421
1979	606	2,248	1,651	613	6,555	13,558	25,232	1,305
1980	617	1,992	1,600	554	6,428	14,578	25,769	1,275
1981	604	1,589	1,600	470	5,985	11,870	22,117	1,118
1982	582	1,340	1,580	409	5,101	10,221	19,233	985
1983	602	1,099	1,543	372	3,911	8,367	15,894	866
1984	636	893	1,572	349	3,398	7,463	14,312	777
1985	616	728	1,489	335	2,851	6,191	12,208	693
1986	588	564	1,369	244	1,864	3,083	7,711	545

End of year	Passenger 000 Gt	Other cargo 000 Gt	Ro-Ro 000 Gt	Container 000 Gt	Specialised carriers 000 Gt	Bulk carriers 000 Gt	Tankers 000 Gt	Total 000 Gt	Total Number [2]
1986	259	510	561	1,369	95	2,003	3,249	8,046	546
1987	259	410	591	1,335	132	1,322	3,010	7,059	506
1988	259	332	586	1,335	128	1,301	2,661	6,603	482
1989	242	277	510	1,368	122	1,253	2,252	6,025	450
1990	269	257	555	1,275	118	828	2,210	5,512	427
1991	271	242	604	1,091	99	489	2,166	4,963	409
1992	276	174	632	1,015	100	446	2,188	4,831	363
1993	272	145	657	1,017	124	293	2,161	4,670	344
1994	281	212	874	1,236	110	294	2,481	5,488	360
1995	360	282	910	1,326	52	485	2,346	5,761	365
1996	360	269	1,068	1,110	49	819	2,383	6,057	377
1997	361	254	1,093	1,113	49	831	3,407	7,108	392
1998	358	307	1,123	1,379	49	854	2,977	7,048	416
1999	363	293	1,161	1,502	103	761	3,253	7,436	421
2000	762	321	1,332	2,140	151	844	3,971	9,521	471
2001	746	502	1,431	2,362	151	946	4,516	10,653	534
2002	945	570	1,617	3,303	100	1,491	4,472	12,497	610
2003	1,130	825	1,637	4,548	121	1,729	5,991	15,982	723
2004	711	830	1,608	5,072	165	2,302	6,214	16,902	754
2005	539	885	1,589	5,539	345	2,926	6,978	18,801	795
2006	472	936	1,466	5,900	604	2,839	7,536	19,753	814
2007	627	763	1,534	6,304	925	3,050	7,401	20,603	816
2008	592	707	1,531	7,503	1,072	3,081	8,187	22,673	842

1 See Notes for change of classification in 1986.
2 Number of vessels (units).

☎020-7944-4119

The figures in this table are outside
the scope of National Statistics
Source (from 1986) - Lloyds Register - Fairplay

5.14 United Kingdom and Crown Dependency registered trading vessels of 500 gross tons and over: summary of tonnage by type of vessel: 1998 - 2008 (end of year)

	1998	1999	2000	2001	2002	2003	2004	2005	2006	2007	2008
Number:											
Tankers	145	141	141	166	195	224	244	263	273	268	275
Bulk carriers	26	22	26	28	34	38	49	60	58	63	64
Specialised carriers	11	15	16	16	13	13	14	16	21	26	30
Fully cellular container	45	51	67	71	99	137	146	160	170	177	202
Ro-Ro (passenger & cargo)	92	94	105	110	118	120	118	113	108	110	110
Other general cargo	86	87	100	127	131	169	169	172	174	160	150
Passenger	11	11	16	16	20	22	14	11	10	12	11
All vessels	416	421	471	534	610	723	754	795	814	816	842
Gross tonnage (thousand tons):											
Tankers	2,977	3,253	3,971	4,516	4,472	5,991	6,214	6,978	7,536	7,401	8,187
Bulk carriers	854	761	844	946	1,491	1,729	2,302	2,926	2,839	3,050	3,081
Specialised carriers	49	103	151	151	100	121	165	345	604	925	1,072
Fully cellular container	1,379	1,502	2,140	2,362	3,303	4,548	5,072	5,539	5,900	6,304	7,503
Ro-Ro (passenger & cargo)	1,123	1,161	1,332	1,431	1,617	1,637	1,608	1,589	1,466	1,534	1,531
Other general cargo	307	293	321	502	570	825	830	885	936	763	707
Passenger	358	363	762	746	945	1,130	711	539	472	627	592
All vessels	7,048	7,436	9,521	10,653	12,497	15,982	16,902	18,801	19,753	20,603	22,673
Thousand deadweight tonnes:											
Tankers	5,163	5,737	7,069	7,885	7,567	9,446	9,660	11,112	11,920	11,540	12,655
Bulk carriers	1,563	1,404	1,545	1,738	2,782	3,245	4,375	5,580	5,409	5,791	5,823
Specialised carriers	29	47	65	65	44	48	59	109	181	272	314
Fully cellular container	1,543	1,682	2,365	2,597	3,691	5,124	5,663	6,241	6,673	7,160	8,569
Ro-Ro (passenger & cargo)	364	366	474	522	607	605	591	574	535	554	556
Other general cargo	414	402	430	706	799	1,121	1,126	1,193	1,265	1,039	976
Passenger	56	58	98	95	111	131	92	76	70	82	77
All vessels	9,132	9,695	12,045	13,608	15,602	19,719	21,566	24,885	26,053	26,438	28,971

☎020-7944-4119
The figures in this table are outside
the scope of National Statistics.
Source - Lloyds Register - Fairplay

5.15 Shipping: United Kingdom owned trading vessels of 500 gross tons and over: summary of tonnage by type of vessel: 1998-2008 (end of year)

	1998	1999	2000	2001	2002	2003	2004	2005	2006	2007	2008
Number:											
Tankers	127	124	133	114	113	124	145	144	149	143	145
Bulk carriers	29	29	29	38	35	43	51	60	60	63	70
Specialised carriers	10	14	10	10	10	9	9	11	17	19	23
Fully cellular container	62	57	73	77	72	92	78	75	91	101	104
Ro-Ro (passenger & cargo)	91	99	103	103	105	109	106	102	98	105	107
Other general cargo	148	153	139	116	115	124	138	146	146	158	157
Passenger	19	17	16	18	20	26	15	19	18	23	25
All vessels	486	493	503	476	470	527	542	557	579	612	631
Gross tonnage (thousand tons):											
Tankers	2,408	1,565	2,952	2,579	2,620	3,601	4,497	4,139	4,668	5,246	5,827
Bulk carriers	1,230	825	904	1,845	1,772	1,913	2,287	2,753	2,614	2,786	3,214
Specialised carriers	42	192	53	100	100	82	81	261	594	798	960
Fully cellular container	1,841	1,641	2,240	2,525	2,509	3,552	3,035	3,297	4,254	4,893	4,886
Ro-Ro (passenger & cargo)	991	1,145	1,260	1,355	1,423	1,589	1,472	1,404	1,334	1,445	1,450
Other general cargo	526	546	492	409	570	793	940	912	963	1,070	1,095
Passenger	541	585	604	636	725	1,092	588	919	915	1,088	1,360
All vessels	7,577	6,499	8,505	9,449	9,720	12,622	12,900	13,685	15,341	17,327	18,792
Thousand deadweight tonnes:											
Tankers	4,411	2,662	5,205	4,646	4,690	5,529	6,687	6,054	6,080	6,474	7,265
Bulk carriers	2,254	1,479	1,636	3,495	3,377	3,594	4,300	5,345	4,922	5,228	5,994
Specialised carriers	29	80	32	45	45	42	40	90	189	241	293
Fully cellular container	1,948	1,774	2,433	2,734	2,785	3,993	3,349	3,708	4,758	5,491	5,523
Ro-Ro (passenger & cargo)	285	349	423	414	454	543	514	504	478	513	531
Other general cargo	713	735	660	569	807	1,113	1,323	1,233	1,296	1,464	1,499
Passenger	86	86	80	82	87	130	64	117	114	139	153
All vessels	9,727	7,164	10,469	11,985	12,245	14,945	16,277	17,052	17,836	19,551	21,257

☎020-7944 4119
The figures in this table are outside
the scope of National Statistics
Source - Lloyds Register - Fairplay

5.16 United Kingdom shipping industry: international revenue and expenditure: 1998-2008

(a) Revenue £ Million

	1998	1999	2000	2001	2002	2003	2004	2005	2006	2007	2008
Dry cargo and passenger vessels: (including ferries)											
Freight on:											
Imports	482	522	484	541	534	501	547	619	390 [1]	423	436
Exports	322	375	400	406	481	525	444	544	530 [1]	552	636
Cross-trades	1,602	1,511	1,453	1,609	1,844	2,069	3,180	3,874	2,831 [1]	2,744	3,082
Total freight revenue	2,406	2,408	2,337	2,556	2,859	3,095	4,171	5,037	3,751	3,719	4,154
Charter receipts	109	99	148	106	129	196	676	963	1,086	1,564	2,014
Passenger revenue	462	463	630	488	569	993	846	608	444	430	469
Total revenue	2,977	2,970	3,115	3,150	3,557	4,284	5,693	6,608	5,281	5,713	6,637
Wet (tankers and liquefied gas carriers):											
Freight on:											
Imports	29	20	3	46	47	44	48	52	79	87	86
Exports	60	59	98	82	96	126	173	174	130	142	219
Cross-trades	442	350	458	497	420	742	1,305	1,194	1,222	1,395	2,530
Total freight revenue	531	429	559	625	563	912	1,526	1,420	1,431	1,624	2,835
Charter receipts	70	87	104	336	162	247	472	748	603	554	763
Total revenue	601	516	663	961	725	1,159	1,998	2,168	2,034	2,178	3,598
All vessels:											
Freight on:											
Imports	511	542	487	587	581	545	595	671	469	510	522
Exports	382	434	498	488	577	651	617	718	660	694	855
Cross-trades	2,044	1,861	1,911	2,106	2,264	2,811	4,485	5,068	4,053	4,139	5,612
Total freight revenue	2,937	2,837	2,896	3,181	3,422	4,007	5,697	6,457	5,182	5,343	6,989
Charter receipts	179	186	252	442	291	443	1,148	1,711	1,689	2,118	2,777
Passenger revenue	462	463	630	488	569	993	846	608	444	430	469
Total revenue	3,578	3,486	3,778	4,111	4,282	5,443	7,691	8,776	7,315	7,891	10,235

(b) Expenditure £ Million

	1998	1999	2000	2001	2002	2003	2004	2005	2006	2007	2008
Dry cargo operations:											
Bunkers	149	165	288	321	377	429	537	701	463	255	407
Other disbursements	1,367	1,060	1,143	1,284	1,618	1,646	1,962	2,759	1,405	1,373	1,646
Charter payments	239	146	173	335	255	236	692	577	317 [1]	106	185
Total expenditure	1,755	1,371	1,604	1,940	2,250	2,311	3,191	4,037	2,185	1,734	2,238
Wet cargo operations:											
Bunkers	70	81	141	146	134	171	195	319	278	399	540
Other disbursements	150	132	115	141	135	284	276	523	236	408	385
Charter payments	181	89	172	176	140	184	359	636	655	721	1,257
Total expenditure	401	302	428	463	409	639	830	1,478	1,169	1,528	2,182
All cargo operations:											
Bunkers	219	246	429	467	511	600	732	1,020	741	654	947
Other disbursements	1,517	1,192	1,258	1,425	1,753	1,930	2,238	3,282	1,641	1,781	2,031
Charter payments	420	235	345	511	395	420	1,051	1,213	972	827	1,442
Total expenditure	2,156	1,673	2,032	2,403	2,659	2,950	4,021	5,515	3,354	3,262	4,420

1 Following a restructuring in the UK shipping industry trading in dry freight and in chartering-in of dry vessels fell significantly during 2006.

☎ 020-7014 2023
Source - ONS

5.17 Marine accident fatalities and injuries reported: 1998-2008

(a) United Kingdom registered merchant vessels of 100 gross tons and over, any location
Number

	1998	1999	2000	2001	2002	2003	2004	2005	2006	2007	2008
Deaths of passengers, crew members and others by cause											
Deaths from accidents to vessels	1	0	0	0	1	0	0	1	1	3	1
Deaths from accidents on board	1	2	2	1	5	1	3	1	3	9	5
Deaths from persons overboard	2	3	2	4	0	2	1	2	2	0	2
Total	4	5	4	5	6	3	4	3	6	12	8
Deaths and injuries to passengers by type of injury											
Deaths	2	1	1	1	0	0	0	1	1	0	2
Fractures	108	66	88	111	110	138	114	79	82	79	90
Other injuries	10	13	48	26	24	48	32	29	31	27	78
Total	120	80	137	138	134	186	146	109	114	106	170
Deaths and injuries to crew members by type of injury											
Deaths	2	4	3	3	5	3	4	2	3	12	5
Fractures	68	62	66	71	78	81	68	61	57	65	57
Other injuries	260	222	232	222	219	204	235	183	171	165	163
Total	330	288	301	296	302	288	307	246	231	242	225
Deaths and injuries to others (e.g. pilots, surveyors)											
Deaths	0	0	0	1	1	0	0	1	2	0	1
Fractures	3	7	6	4	3	4	5	2	4	4	6
Other injuries	5	1	4	0	3	1	2	3	2	2	2
Total	8	8	10	5	7	5	7	6	8	6	9

(b) Deaths of passengers, crew members and others, any vessels in UK waters[1]
Number

	1998	1999	2000	2001	2002	2003	2004	2005	2006	2007	2008
By location											
Coastal waters	27	18	9	8	16	19	14	25	32	35	15
Port/harbour area	10	11	11	4	9	5	4	7	6	5	10
River/canal	4	4	3	5	2	4	1	4	13	12	7
Non-tidal waters	0	1	0	2	4	0	0	5	2	11	1
Total	41	34	23	19	31	28	19	41	53	63	33
By vessel type											
UK merchant vessel 100gt & over	2	5	1	2	3	2	1	2	1	5	2
UK merchant vessel under100gt	8	2	1	3	2	4	3	2	6	5	2
UK fishing vessel	13	6	7	6	8	9	9	6	12	5	7
UK pleasure craft (non-commercial)[2]	7	11	4	3	8	10	3	23	27	46	18
UK other (non-commercial)	0	0	0	0	0	0	0	0	0	1	0
Non UK merchant vessel 100gt & over	7	6	8	5	5	2	2	4	5	0	4
Non UK other	4	4	2	0	5	1	1	4	2	1	0
Total	41	34	23	19	31	28	19	41	53	63	33
Deaths of passengers, crew members and others by cause											
Deaths from accidents to vessels	28	18	8	5	14	17	10	29	30	34	15
Deaths from accidents on board	7	9	9	6	8	5	3	5	9	9	6
Deaths from persons overboard	6	7	6	8	9	6	6	7	14	20	12
Total	41	34	23	19	31	28	19	41	53	63	33

1 Marine accidents recorded by the MAIB. The requirement on vessels to report accidents
to the MAIB varies by vessel type and location (see Notes). However, the MAIB will record details of, and may
investigate, significant accidents of which they are notified by bodies such as the Coastguard.   ☎023 8039 5500
2 A special exercise in 2005-2007 to research pleasure craft deaths resulted in higher recording of deaths.

For further details see the *Annual Report* by the
Marine Accident Investigation Branch. Available at:
www.maib.gov.uk

The figures in this table are outside
the scope of National Statistics.
Source: MAIB, DfT

5.18 HM Coastguard statistics: search and rescue operations: United Kingdom:[1,2] 1998-2008

Number

	1998	1999	2000	2001	2002	2003	2004	2005	2006	2007	2008
Incidents involving vessels where assistance rendered:											
Commercial vessels	308	458	537	569	597	512	961	1,207	672	..	..
Fishing vessels	715	624	647	670	627	589	521	624	360	..	..
Pleasure craft	3,328	3,334	3,267	3,529	3,679	3,748	3,924	4,101	2,933	..	..
Incidents involving persons where assistance rendered:											
Incidents involving persons	1,359	1,202	1,693	1,872	2,241	2,436	2,169	3,237	2,169	..	..
Medical evacuations	370	427	403	473	460	585	481	513	458	..	..
Reports received:											
Distress reports	1,627	2,548	2,353	2,208	2,357	..	..	..	..	..	..
Hoaxes	269	258	221	206	260	232	301	406	529	691	475
Number of persons involved in incidents where assistance rendered:											
Persons assisted	14,366	17,535	14,717	16,487	19,984	25,118	21,929	22,477	23,113	..	..
Persons rescued	4,685	5,215	5,217	4,852	5,851	5,689	4,947	4,790	4,809	..	..
Lives lost	249	251	236	284	319	316	364	376	360	313	314
Total number of incidents where assistance rendered	6,328	6,581	6,703	7,242	7,604	8,070	8,056	7,252	6,592	..	..
Total number of incidents	11,553	12,220	12,016	12,514	13,395	13,849	14,240	16,754	17,185	18,180	18,759

1 HM Coastguard revised its statistical collection and collation procedures in 1998 and again in a phased programme between 2003 and 2005. Continuing ongoing refinements to the data collection, recording and analyses may make comparisons with previous years difficult. e.g. A change to data collection procedures in 2006 has resulted in a fall in the number of vessels recorded as 'assisted'.
2 Due to industrial action by some HM Coastguard staff, figures for 2007 and 2008 are incomplete.

☎023 8032 9487
The figures in this table are outside the scope of National Statistics
Source - MCA

6 Public Transport:

Notes and Definitions

National Rail/London Underground passenger traffic: 6.1

The figures shown for national rail passenger traffic during 1919 and 1923 include all journeys on those 'London Railways' subsequently taken over by the London Passenger Transport Board in 1933. Additionally, in 1919 a journey using the services of more than one company was reported by each of them, with consequent duplication in the figures. The figures for journeys on the London Underground from 1948 include those originating on the former British Railways network (approximately 70 million journeys in 1948), and on those lines transferred to the London Transport Passenger Executive on 1 January 1948 (estimated at 62 million journeys in 1947).

Electrified route: Pre 1947 figures refer to track length, not route length, and include electrified sidings. In 1947, there were 3,370 electrified track kilometres.

National Railways passenger journeys and kilometres: Figures from 1986 are assessed on the All Purpose Ticket Issuing System (APTIS) and are not comparable with earlier years. The rail series for passenger data changes after privatisation in 1994, with possible double counting of some journeys where a route is shared with more than one operator. Both series have been revised from 1999/00. More detail is given in sections 6.3 and 6.4.

London Underground passenger kilometres: From 1965, passenger kilometres are those actually travelled. Prior to 1965, a different method of estimation was used, leading to slight overestimates of the order of 0.1 billion passenger kilometres per year.

Rail systems: 6.2

National Rail

Data up to 1994/95 show services by the former British Rail. From 1995/96 data these show the transition to services provided by the privatised passenger train operators on the national network.

For the loaded train kilometres series, a new methodology was used from 2002/03 quarter 2. Previously loaded train kilimetres was published using data sourced from DfT. However, ORR has revised the methodology behind these data, and is now using more comprehensive data supplied

by ATOC to generate these statistics. These data include non-franchised Train Operating Companies (TOC) information. Further details can be found in National Rail Trends Yearbook, published by ORR.

London Underground

Summary data are shown here. Further detail appears in Table 6.7.

Glasgow Underground

The series shown is for the underground loop line which serves Glasgow. Suburban rail services in Strathclyde PTE are excluded.

Docklands Light Railway

The series shows the growth of the DLR. The Lewisham extension under the Thames at Greenwich was completed in 1999. A new line for London City Airport opened in December 2005. A further extension to Woolwich Arsenal was completed in January 2009 with a further extension under construction.

Tyne and Wear Metro

The system has been extended in stages. Heworth to South Shields was opened on 24th March 1984. The extension from Bankfoot to Callerton and Newcastle Airport opened in November 1991. The 24km extension from Pelaw to Sunderland and South Hylton opened in March 2002. Part of that route shares some stations with national rail services.

Blackpool Trams

The traditional Victorian street-running tramway serves Blackpool Unitary Authority and Fleetwood, Lancashire.

Manchester Metrolink

Converted and extended from suburban rail, in 1991/92, 26 kilometres and 16 stations were transferred from the national network to the light rail system. It has a mix of segregated track and on-street running. Metrolink was opened in 1992, with the first section running between Bury and Manchester Victoria Station. The Eccles extension opened in 2000.

Sheffield Supertram

The Supertram was opened in 1994 between Sheffield and Meadowhall. Further lines came into service from Malin Bridge to Halfway and Cathedral to Herdings Park. In December 1997, operations were transferred to Stagecoach Plc.

Midland Metro

This rapid transit system was constructed by the Altram consortium, making use of former rail alignments. The line from Wolverhampton to Birmingham Snow Hill opened in 1999.

Croydon Tramlink

A modern three line tram network in south London, opened in May 2000. It is operated by FirstGroup for TfL.

Nottingham NET

NET is a modern street running tram system running north-south through the city. It runs parallel to suburban rail north of the centre. It was opened in March 2004.

National Rail receipts and passenger traffic: 6.3 and 6.4

Passenger Revenue: Passenger revenue includes all ticket revenue and miscellaneous charges associated with passenger travel e.g. car park charges. For journeys involving some travel on London Underground, receipts have been apportioned appropriately. Revenue does not include government support or grants.

Passenger Kilometres: Estimates of passenger kilometres are made from ticket sales. Travel on season tickets assumes appropriate factors for the number of journeys per ticket. Results are compiled in respect of 13 four week periods per year, so quarterly figures are derived from these.

There is some underestimation of passenger journeys and kilometres from 1997/98. This is because, for technical reasons, the passenger kilometres represented by certain new ticket types were not being captured by the operators' ticket system.

The figures were reviewed and revised by the Strategic Rail Authority to include best estimates for this missing element. This exercise was backdated to the start of 1999/00, and is now repeated annually by the Office of Rail Regulation, who have taken over responsibility for rail statistics. Passenger revenue data are unaffected by these adjustments.

For the passenger kilometres series, new methodologies were applied in 2003/04 and in 2007/08 to improve the categorisation of ticket type. Further details can be found in *National Rail Trends Yearbook,* published by ORR (previously the responsibility of the SRA).

Route and station/depots open to traffic: 6.5

In 1991/92, 16 stations transferred from the national network to Manchester Metrolink. From 1994/95 the number of stations shown include only those on the national network. Eighteen other stations, mainly on the London Underground, are included in the figures for earlier years.

Recent revisions to the 'length of route' infrastructure series represented in table 6.5 reflect improvements in the technology used to measure route kilometres. Up until 2003-04 the data were collected on a semi-manual basis from various systems. From 2004-05 the principal track engineers' database, GEOGIS, has been used. The apparent drop from 2004-05 to 2005-06 does not reflect an actual reduction in route km open for traffic but is due to improvements in data collection and data quality that resulted in a restatement of route length. 2007-08 data are not consistent with earlier years as a new methodology has been introduced because of revisions to route classification data.

Public Performance Measure (PPM): 6.6

The PPM was introduced in 2000 by the then Shadow Strategic Rail Authority, replacing the Passengers' Charter as a means of measuring passenger train performance. Unlike the Charter measure that only covered particular services, PPM covers all scheduled services and combines the previously individual punctuality and reliability results into a single performance measure. PPM is measured against the planned timetable, which makes allowance for specific delays (e.g. engineering works), which might differ from the previously published timetable. Table 6.6 shows the Charter results for years in which it applied, and also PPM results from the time it was introduced. Passenger Charter figures are displayed regularly by individual train operators.

From 2006/07, the rail industry has re-classified TransPennine Express (TPE) to the long distance sector. Hence, TPE services are now considered 'on time' if they arrive within 10 minutes of the scheduled arrival time (not within 5 minutes as was the case up to 2005/06).

London Underground: 6.7

Data obtained from the London Underground Directors Report and Accounts each year up to 2002-03. Responsibility for the Underground transferred to Transport for London in July 2003. TfL's *Annual Report* provides further detail.

Traffic receipts data are provided by TfL in 13 four week periods per year. These include revenue from car parking and penalty fares. Season ticket journeys are those estimated to have been made in each year, irrespective of when the ticket was sold. The cost per train kilometre includes renewals and depreciation. It excludes reorganisation and restructuring costs within TfL.

Other income includes property rents received, and commercial advertising receipts.

The number of stations is for those currently owned and operated by London Underground. Some suburban stations on the national rail network in London are also served by London Underground trains but are managed by the local rail franchise holder.

Channel Tunnel: 6.8

The Channel Tunnel opened for freight traffic in June 1994 and for passenger services in November of that year. Passenger shuttle services opened in December. Four different types of service operate through the Channel Tunnel as follows:

- *Freight Shuttles*: carrying road freight vehicles between Folkestone and Calais.

- *Tourist Shuttles*: carrying passenger vehicles between Folkestone and Calais.

- *Freight Trains*: through freight trains between Great Britain and Europe.

- *Eurostar Trains*: carrying passengers between London, France and Belgium.

Commercial traffic is fare-paying traffic using the tunnel. *Non-commercial traffic* is non-fare-paying traffic (e.g. staff and authorised agents). Figures for 1996-97 & 1997-98 were affected by a fire on 16 November 1996 which suspended services on both freight and tourist shuttles. Tourist shuttle resumed services on 10 December 1996 with full freight services resuming in June 1997.

Bus and coach industry: 6.9-6.16

Tables for the bus and coach industry refer to the activities of all holders of Public Service Vehicle (PSV) operators' licences. These vehicles are generally classified in the Bus Tax Class. An operator wishing to run bus or coach services is normally required to possess a PSV licence.

However, certain vehicles and types of service are exempt from licensing and are excluded from the tables, such as community buses and local services operated by taxis. Taxis are generally classified in the Private Light Goods tax class, with private cars, so they are excluded from the PSV tables. Most of the information in these tables, which mainly refer to local bus services, is derived from annual returns made to DfT by a sample of holders of PSV operators' licences.

A local bus service is a stopping service available to the general public, where the route is registered with the Traffic Commissioner, which is eligible for Bus Service Operators Grant.

Bus and coach services which comprise contract, private hire, tours, excursions and express journeys are generally classified as "non-local" or "other" work. Some services, such as long distance coach services, might contain a mixture of local work and non-local express work.

Some important changes have been made to the legal framework under which the industry operates.

Outside London:

- from 1 April 1986, the Passenger Transport Authorities in metropolitan areas were subjected to precept control

- local bus services outside London were deregulated on 26 October 1986, introducing on-the-road competition

- widespread privatisation of public sector bus operations took place from 1986. There are fewer bus operators in the public sector.

Within London:

- responsibility for London (Regional) Transport transferred from the former Greater London Council to the Secretary of State for Transport from 29 June 1984. On 1 April 1985, a separate operating subsidiary, London Buses Ltd, was established

- progressive tendering of local bus services in London was introduced in July 1985

- the former operating divisions of London Buses Ltd were privatised by the end of 1994

- from July 2000, Transport for London (TfL) was established as a successor body to London Transport, with strategic control of local buses through the Greater London Authority (GLA) under an elected Mayor of London.

Outside London, after bus deregulation in 1986, general subsidy was no longer feasible as most services were provided on a purely commercial basis, with on-the-road competition for routes.

Public transport support was restricted to unprofitable but socially necessary services, the operation of which was generally put out to tender.

In London, nearly all local bus services are operated by the private sector under contract to TfL. Bus routes, once awarded to a contractor after a tendering process, are then protected from on-the-road competition.

Bus and coach vehicle kilometres: 6.9

Service kilometres operated are measured by DfT's annual sample PSV survey of operators, and, for the bus contractors in London, by TfL. The majority of local bus service kilometres are run on a commercial basis. Subsidised local service kilometres are around a fifth of the local service total. Non-local service kilometres include long distance coaching, private hire, school contract work, excursions and tours.

Bus and coach stock: 6.10

After deregulation many large buses were replaced by smaller ones. In recent years, with the emphasis on passenger accessibility, more full size, low floor single deck buses have entered service. Operators have been buying more new vehicles, which has increased the fleet size and reduced the overall age of the PSV fleet.

Passenger receipts: 6.11

Receipts comprise amounts paid by, or for, all passengers carried. They include payments for season tickets and travel passes, and concessionary fare reimbursement from local authorities. Receipts exclude public transport support, Rural Bus Subsidy Grant (RBSG) and Bus Service Operator Grant (BSOG, formerly Fuel Duty Rebate).

Local authorities and passenger transport authorities run concessionary fare schemes for groups such as the elderly, the disabled and children. From April 2006, schemes in England had to offer, as a minimum, free off-peak bus travel to elderly and disabled residents in their local area. Local authorities reimburse operators for revenue lost as a result of their participation in concessionary fare schemes after taking account of any income from the extra travel generated. The reimbursement should be seen as an incentive to the passenger to travel more.

The operators should not lose, or gain, revenue through such schemes. From April 2008, the scheme has been extended across England to allow elderly and disabled residents to travel anywhere in England, in line with the national schemes already in place in Scotland and Wales.

Staff employed: 6.12

There was a fall in staff employed in the mid 1990s reflecting the widespread use of driver-only buses and the contracting out of an increased proportion of activities such as fleet maintenance. In recent years, as the bus fleet has grown, staff numbers have increased. Staff members may have more than one role, so the tables show those classified according to their main occupation.

Local passenger journeys by area: 6.13

These are collected through DfT's annual sample PSV survey of operators and, for London, from TfL. They are a count of boardings of each vehicle, so a trip which requires a change from one bus to another would show two boardings. TfL obtains data on boardings from on-bus surveys. This information is useful as a check on DfT's annual PSV survey results for the capital. Over the last year, further bus patronage data have been obtained from local authorities, which they have used in their Local Transport Plans. This extra information has allowed DfT to revise its series of boardings. The main change has been an adjustment which gives a reduction in the allocation to London, with an increase in the surrounding counties.

Local authority support: 6.14

Public transport support, also known as "revenue support" covers forms of local authority current expenditure on public transport (not concessionary fare reimbursement). It includes payments to operators for the operation of subsidised services, and local authority administrative costs associated with bus operations, such as the tendering process itself and publicity. The Transport Act 1985 restricted support to unprofitable "socially necessary" services.

Subsidised bus services are run under contract to local transport authorities, usually following competitive tendering. Outside London, from 1998-99, Rural Bus Subsidy Grant (RBSG) has been paid by central government to many local authorities to encourage bus service provision in their more rural parts. RBSG is therefore included in the support table. In London, support takes a different form, as nearly all bus services are run on a commercial basis, under contract to TfL. Contracts for particular routes are awarded to operators after competitive tendering. The contract payments take into account the high level of service provision required in London, including services that run later in the evenings and at weekends.

Local bus fares indices: 6.15

Information required for the calculation of the index of local bus fares is obtained from a DfT survey of a panel of bus operators, who account for about 85 per cent of receipts from passengers on local bus services. Operators supply information about the size of each fare change, each quarter. Indices for groups of operators in different areas of GB are obtained by averaging changes, using weights based on receipts from passengers from DfT's PSV annual survey (receipts used for the index exclude concessionary fare reimbursement from local authorities). The DfT local bus fares index is a small part of the Retail Prices Index.

The index is intended to measure the change in the average cost to the fare-paying passenger. In practice, as the operators select the basket of fare changes to report each quarter and as cash-less transactions become more common (e.g. pre-paid travel passes) the index can only give a broad guide to fare changes. Also, fare changes outside London are frequent, so adjustments must be made to the index each quarter. Bus fare changes in London usually take place once a year, in January.

There is a trend towards simpler fare structures, with operators charging flat fares or zoned fares, and the use of pre-payment through stored value tickets, which speed up boarding.

Operating costs per local bus kilometre: 6.16

Costs per bus kilometre are higher in London and metropolitan areas than elsewhere. Greater traffic congestion, more frequent services and the need to use larger buses for busy services all contribute to higher costs.

Other costs, such as the cost of tendering and publicity associated with bus services, borne by local authorities or TfL rather than the operators, are not shown in this table.

Taxi industry: 6.17

A taxi, or hackney carriage, is a vehicle with fewer than 9 passenger seats which is licensed to "ply for hire" (i.e. it may stand at ranks or be hailed in the street by members of the public). This distinguishes taxis from Private Hire Vehicles (PHVs), which must be booked in advance through an operator and may not ply for hire (taxis may also be pre-booked). Taxis must normally be hired as a whole (i.e. separate fares are not charged to each passenger). However, taxis may charge separate fares when a sharing scheme is in operation, when they are run as a bus under a special PSV operators' licence or when pre-booked (PHV operators may also charge passengers separately if they share a journey).

In England and Wales, taxis and PHVs are licensed by district or borough councils, unitary authorities or, in London, the Public Carriage Office (PCO) which is part of TfL. The licensing authority is usually the body which sets taxi fares, although fare changes may be requested by the taxi trade. PHV fares are set by the operator. TfL is implementing the Private Hire Vehicles (London) Act 1998 for the licensing of London PHV operators, drivers and vehicles. PHV operators in London must be licensed.

Taxi and PHV use has grown so there has been a large increase in the numbers of licensed taxis and PHVs.

The data on vehicles and drivers come from several sources. The London figures are from data held by TfL in the PCO. The statistics relating to provincial England and Wales come from surveys of district councils and unitary authorities.

6.1 Rail: length of national railway [1] route at year end, and passenger travel by national railway [1] and London Underground: 1900-2008/09

For greater detail of the years 1998/99-2008/09 see Table 6.2

Year	Length of National Rail route (kilometres)			National Rail		London Underground	
	Total route	Electrified [2] route	Open to Passenger traffic	Passenger journeys (million)	Passenger kilometres (billion)	Passenger journeys (million)	Passenger kilometres (billion)
1900	29,783	..	..	..	..	..	..
1919	32,420	1,321	..	2,064	..	..	..
1923	32,462	1,122	..	1,772	..	..	..
1928	32,565	1,901	..	1,250	..	..	..
1933	32,345	2,403	..	1,159	..	..	..
1938	32,081	3,378	..	1,237	30.6	492	..
1946	31,963	..	..	1,266	47.0	569	..
1947	31,950	1,455	..	1,140	37.0	554	5.4
1948	31,593	1,455	..	1,024	34.2	720	6.2
1949	31,500	1,489	..	1,021	34.0	703	6.1
1950	31,336	1,489	..	1,010	32.5	695	6.0
1951	31,152	1,487	..	1,030	33.5	702	5.6
1952	31,022	1,508	..	1,017	32.9	670	5.4
1953	30,935	1,508	..	1,015	33.1	672	5.4
1954	30,821	1,577	..	1,020	33.3	671	5.7
1955	30,676	1,577	23,820	994	32.7	676	5.6
1956	30,618	1,624	23,612	1,029	34.0	678	5.5
1957	30,521	1,621	23,532	1,101	36.4	666	5.4
1958	30,333	1,622	23,621	1,090	35.6	692	5.3
1959	29,877	1,799	22,632	1,069	35.8	669	5.1
1960	29,562	2,034	22,314	1,037	34.7	674	5.2
1961	29,313	2,234	22,043	1,025	33.9	675	5.1
1962	28,117	2,511	20,785	965	31.7	668	4.9
1963	27,330	2,556	20,328	938	30.9	674	4.9
1964	25,735	2,659	18,781	928	32.0	674	4.9
1965	24,011	2,886	17,516	865	30.1	657	4.7
1966	22,082	3,064	16,359	835	29.7	667	4.8
1967	21,198	3,241	15,904	837	29.1	661	4.8
1968	20,080	3,182	15,242	831	28.7	655	4.7
1969	19,470	3,169	15,088	805	29.6	676	5.0
1970	18,989	3,162	14,637	824	30.4	672	5.1
1971	18,738	3,169	14,484	816	30.1	654	5.2
1972	18,417	3,178	14,499	754	29.1	655	5.3
1973	18,227	3,462	14,375	728	29.8	644	5.2
1974	18,168	3,647	14,373	733	30.9	636	5.2
1975	18,118	3,655	14,431	730	30.9	601	4.8
1976	18,007	3,735	14,407	702	28.4	546	4.4
1977	17,973	3,767	14,413	702	29.3	545	4.3
1978	17,901	3,716	14,396	724	30.0	568	4.5
1979	17,735	3,718	14,412	748	30.7	594	4.5
1980	17,645	3,718	14,394	760	30.3	559	4.2
1981	17,431	3,729	14,394	719	29.7	541	4.1
1982	17,229	3,753	14,371	630	27.2	498	3.7
1983	16,964	3,750	14,375	695	29.5	563	4.3
1984/85	16,816	3,798	14,304	701	29.5	672	5.4
1985/86	16,752	3,809	14,310	686	30.4	732	6.0
1986/87	16,670	4,156 [R]	14,304	738 [3]	30.8 [3]	769	6.2
1987/88	16,633	4,207	14,302	798	32.4	798	6.3
1988/89	16,599	4,376	14,309	822	34.3	815	6.3
1989/90	16,587	4,546	14,318	812	33.3	765	6.0
1990/91	16,584	4,912	14,317	809	33.2	775	6.2

6.1 (continued) Rail: length of national railway [1] route at year end, and passenger travel by national railway [1] and London Underground: 1900-2008/09

For greater detail of the years 1998/99-2008/09 see Table 6.2

Year	Length of National Rail route (kilometres)			National Rail		London Underground	
	Total route	Electrified [2] route	Open to Passenger traffic	Passenger journeys (million)	Passenger kilometres (billion)	Passenger journeys (million)	Passenger kilometres (billion)
1991/92	16,588	4,886	14,291	792	32.5	751	5.9
1992/93	16,528	4,910	14,317	770	31.7	728	5.8
1993/94	16,536	4,968	14,357	740	30.4	735	5.8
1994/95	16,542	4,970	14,359	735	28.7	764	6.1
1995/96	16,666	5,163	15,002	761	30.0	784	6.3
1996/97	16,666	5,176	15,034	801	32.1	772	6.2
1997/98	16,656	5,166	15,024	846	34.7	832	6.5
1998/99	16,659	5,166	15,038	892	36.3	866	6.7
1999/00	16,649	5,167	15,038	931 [4]	38.5 [4]	927	7.2
2000/01	16,652	5,167	15,042	957	38.2	970	7.5
2001/02	16,652	5,167	15,042	960	39.1	953	7.5
2002/03	16,670	5,167	15,042	976	39.7	942	7.4
2003/04	16,493	5,200	14,883	1,012	40.9	948	7.3
2004/05	16,116 [5]	5,200 [5]	14,328 [5]	1,045	41.8	976	7.6
2005/06	15,810	5,205	14,356	1,082	43.2	970	7.6
2006/07	15,795	5,250	14,353	1,151	46.2	1,040	8.0
2007/08	15,814 [6]	5,250 [6]	14,484 [6]	1,232	49.0	1,096	8.4
2008/09	15,814	5,250	14,494	1,274	50.7	1,089	8.6

1 From 1994/95 route length is for the former Railtrack.
 'From 1995/96 data are for National Rail, former British Rail and
 'Train Operating Companies. Excludes rail routes managed by PTEs.
2 Pre-1947 figures refer to track length, not route length,
 and include electrified sidings. In 1947 electrified track kilometres totalled 3,370.
3 Break in series. From 1986/87 figures include an element of double counting,
 as a journey involving more than one operator is scored against each operator.
 This contrasts with former British Rail data for which a through ticket journey was counted only once.
4 Break in series due to a change in methodology.
5 Break in series due to a change in methodology.
6 Break in series due to a change in methodology.

☎Rail: 020-7944 8874
☎London Underground: 020-7944 3076
The figures in this table are outside
the scope of National Statistics
Sources - ORR,
London Underground

6.2 Rail systems: 1998/99-2008/09

(a) Passenger journeys
Millions

	1998/99	1999/00	2000/01	2001/02	2002/03	2003/04	2004/05	2005/06	2006/07	2007/08	2008/09
National Rail network [1]	892	931	957	960	976	1,012	1,045	1,082	1,151	1,232	1,274
London Undergound	866	927	970	953	942	948	976	970	1,040	1,096	1,089
Glasgow Underground	15	15	14	14	13	13	13	13	13	14	14
Docklands Light Railway	28	31	38	41	46	48	50	54	64	67	68
Tyne & Wear Metro [2]	34	33	33	33	37	38	37	36	38	40	41
Blackpool Trams [3]	4	4	4	5	4	4	4	4	3	3	2
Manchester Metrolink [4]	13	14	17	18	19	19	20	20	20	20	21
Sheffield Supertram	10	11	11	11	12	12	13	13	14	15	15
Midland Metro [5]	.	5	5	5	5	5	5	5	5	5	5
Croydon Tramlink [6]	.	.	15	18	19	20	22	23	25	27	27
Nottingham NET [7]	.	.	.	.	.	-	8	10	10	10	10
All light rail	104	113	138	146	154	160	172	177	192	201	203
All rail	1,862	1,971	2,065	2,059	2,072	2,119	2,193	2,229	2,383	2,529	2,566

(b) Passenger kilometres
Millions

	1998/99	1999/00	2000/01	2001/02	2002/03	2003/04	2004/05	2005/06	2006/07	2007/08	2008/09
National Rail network	36,280	38,472	38,179	39,141	39,678	40,906 R	41,762	43,211	46,218 R	49,007	50,698
London Undergound	6,716	7,171	7,470	7,451	7,367	7,340	7,606	7,586	7,947	8,352	8,646
Glasgow Underground	47	47	46	44	43	43	43	42	42	46	45
Docklands Light Railway	144	172	200	207	232	235	245	257	301	326	318
Tyne & Wear Metro	238	230	229	238	275	284	283	279	295	313	319
Blackpool Trams	..	13	13	15	14	11	12	11	10	9	7
Manchester Metrolink	117	126	152	161	167	169	204	206	208	210	221
Sheffield Supertram	35	37	38	39	40	42	44	44	42	44	45
Midland Metro	.	50	56	50	50	54	52	54	51	51	50
Croydon Tramlink	.	.	96	99	100	105	112	117	128	141	144
Nottingham NET	.	.	.	.	.	2	37	42	43	44	42
All Light rail	581	675	830	854	920	945	1,033	1,052	1,120	1,185	1,191
All rail	43,577	46,318	46,479	47,446	47,965	49,191	50,401	51,849	55,285	58,544	60,535

(c) Passenger revenue
£ million (at current prices)

	1998/99	1999/00	2000/01	2001/02	2002/03	2003/04	2004/05	2005/06	2006/07	2007/08	2008/09
National Rail network	3,089	3,368	3,413	3,548	3,663	3,901	4,158	4,493	5,012 R	5,555	6,004
London Undergound	977	1,058	1,129	1,151	1,138	1,161	1,241	1,309	1,417	1,525	1,615
Glasgow Underground	9	10	10	10	10	10	11	11	13	13	14
Docklands Light Railway	20	22	29	32	36	37	40	46	54	62	63
Tyne & Wear Metro	23	24	24	25	29	31	33	34	38	32	32
Blackpool Trams	4	4	4	5	5	4	4	4	5	4	3
Manchester Metrolink	..	..	18	20	21	21	22	23	24	22	23
Sheffield Supertram	6	7	7	8	10	9	11	10	13	11	12
Midland Metro	.	..	3	4	5	5	5	6	6	4	5
Croydon Tramlink	.	.	12	13	15	16	18	19	20	15	14
Nottingham NET	.	.	.	.	.	..	6	7	8	7	8
All Light rail	63	68	108	117	131	135	151	161	180	171	173
All rail	4,128	4,493	4,650	4,815	4,931	5,197	5,550	5,963	6,609	7,251	7,792

(d) Route kilometres open for passenger traffic
Number

	1998/99	1999/00	2000/01	2001/02	2002/03	2003/04	2004/05	2005/06	2006/07	2007/08	2008/09
National Rail network [8]	15,038	15,038	15,042	15,042	15,042	14,883	14,328	14,356	14,353	14,484	14,494
London Undergound	392	408	408	408	408	408	408	408	408	408	408
Glasgow Underground	11	11	11	11	11	11	11	10	10	10	10
Docklands Light Railway	22	26	26	26	26	26	26	30	31	32	33
Tyne & Wear Metro	59	59	59	78	78	78	78	78	78	78	78
Blackpool Trams	18	18	18	18	18	18	18	18	18	18	18
Manchester Metrolink	31	39	39	39	39	39	39	39	39	42	39
Sheffield Supertram	29	29	29	29	29	29	29	29	29	29	29
Midland Metro	.	20	20	20	20	20	20	20	20	20	20
Croydon Tramlink	.	.	28	28	28	28	28	28	28	28	28
Nottingham NET	.	.	.	.	.	14	14	15	14	14	14
All Light rail	170	202	230	249	249	263	263	268	267	271	269
All rail	15,600	15,648	15,680	15,699	15,699	15,554	14,999	15,032	15,028	15,163	15,171

6.2 (continued) Rail systems: 1997/98-2008/09

(e) Stations or stops served

Number

	1998/99	1999/00	2000/01	2001/02	2002/03	2003/04	2004/05	2005/06	2006/07	2007/08	2008/09
National Rail network	2,499	2,503	2,508	2,508	2,508	2,507	2,508	2,510	2,520	2,516	2,516
London Undergound	269	274	274	274	274	274	274	274	273	268	270
Glasgow Underground	15	15	15	15	15	15	15	15	15	15	15
Docklands Light Railway	29	34	34	34	34	34	34	38	34	39	40
Tyne & Wear Metro	46	46	46	58	58	58	58	59	59	60	60
Blackpool Trams	124	124	124	124	124	124	124	124	121	121	121
Manchester Metrolink	26	36	36	36	37	37	37	37	37	37	37
Sheffield Supertram	47	47	47	48	48	48	48	48	48	48	48
Midland Metro	.	23	23	23	23	23	23	23	23	23	23
Croydon Tramlink	.	.	38	38	38	38	38	39	39	38	39
Nottingham NET	.	.	.	.	.	23	23	23	23	23	23
All Light rail	287	325	363	376	377	400	400	406	399	404	406
All rail	3,055	3,102	3,145	3,158	3,159	3,181	3,182	3,190	3,192	3,188	3,192

(f) Loaded train or tram kilometres

Millions

	1998/99	1999/00	2000/01	2001/02	2002/03	2003/04	2004/05	2005/06	2006/07	2007/08	2008/09
National Rail network [9]	405.1	418.4	427.2	435.9	443.3	448.4 R	446.8 R	459.5 R	464.0 R	459.1 R	479.3
London Underground	61.2	63.1	63.8	65.4	65.9	68.5	69.5	68.8	69.8	70.5	70.6
Glasgow Underground	1.1	1.2	1.2	1.2	1.1	1.1	1.1	1.2	1.2	1.2	1.2
Docklands Light Railway	2.6	2.9	2.9	2.9	3.2	3.4	3.3	3.4	4.4	4.4	3.9
Tyne & Wear Metro	4.8	4.8	4.7	4.7	6.3	6.3	5.6	5.5	5.8	6.2	5.6
Blackpool Trams	1.2	1.2	1.2	1.3	1.1	0.9	0.8	0.8	0.9	0.7	0.7
Manchester Metrolink	3.4	3.6	4.4	4.5	4.6	4.6	4.4	4.4	3.8	4.0	3.9
Sheffield Supertram	2.4	2.4	2.4	2.4	2.5	2.5	2.4	2.4	2.4	2.4	2.5
Midland Metro	.	.	1.9	1.6	1.7	1.7	1.6	1.7	1.6	1.5	1.7
Croydon Tramlink	.	.	2.1	2.4	2.5	2.5	2.4	2.4	2.5	2.2	2.2
Nottingham NET	.	.	.	.	.	0.2	1.0	1.2	1.2	1.2	1.1
All Light rail	15.5	16.1	20.8	21.0	23.0	23.2	22.8	23.0	23.8	24.0	22.9
All rail	481.8	497.6	511.8	522.3	532.2	540.1	539.0	551.3	557.6	553.6	573

(g) Passenger carriages or tramcars

Number

	1998/99	1999/00	2000/01	2001/02	2002/03	2003/04	2004/05	2005/06	2006/07	2007/08	2008/09
National Rail network [10]	..	..	..	..	..	..	..	..	..	..	..
London Underground	3,923	3,954	3,954	3,954	3,954	3,959	3,959	4,070	4,070	4,070	4,070
Glasgow Underground	41	41	41	41	41	41	41	41	41	44	44
Docklands Light Railway	70	70	70	74	94	94	94	94	94	94	112
Tyne & Wear Metro	90	90	90	90	90	90	90	90	90	102	102
Blackpool Trams	77	75	81	75	76	76	76	76	79	78	77
Manchester Metrolink	26	32	32	32	32	32	32	32	32	34	34
Sheffield Supertram	25	25	25	25	25	25	25	25	25	28	29
Midland Metro	.	16	16	16	16	16	16	16	16	23	18
Croydon Tramlink	.	24	24	24	24	24	24	24	24	26	24
Nottingham NET	.	.	.	.	.	15	15	15	15	16	16
All Light rail	329	373	379	377	398	413	413	413	416	445	456
All rail	..	..	..	..	..	..	..	..	..	..	

1 Franchised train operating companies from February 1996 following rail privatisation.
2 Tyne & Wear Metro extension to Sunderland opened in March 2002.
3 Blackpool Trams shown as a self-contained system.
4 Transfer of 20 stations from the rail network to Manchester Metrolink.
5 Midland Metro opened in 1999.
6 Croydon Tramlink opened in 2000.
7 Nottingham Express Transit opened in March 2004.
8 Breaks in series due to changes in methodology (see notes and definitions section 6.5)
9 Breaks in series due to changes in methodology (see notes and definitions section 6.5)
10 No data available for National Rail leased rolling stock after rail privatisation.

☎London Underground: 020-7944 3076
☎Rail: 020-7944 8874
The National Rail and Underground figures in this
table are outside the scope of National Statistics
Source - Network Rail, former Railtrack, ORR, TfL,
light rail operators and PTEs

Transport Statistics Great Britain 2009

6.3 National railways: receipts:[1] 1998/99-2008/09

											£ Million
	1998/99	1999/00	2000/01	2001/02	2002/03	2003/04 [2]	2004/05	2005/06	2006/07	2007/08 [3]	2008/09
All Passenger Operators											
Ordinary fares	2,242	2,463	2,463	2,585	2,693	2,890	3,088	3,323	3,714	4,120	4,443
Season tickets	847	905	950	964	970	1,011	1,071	1,170	1,298	1,434	1,561
All tickets (current prices)	3,089	3,368	3,413	3,548	3,663	3,901	4,158	4,493	5,012	5,555	6,004
All tickets (2008/09 prices)	3,934	4,207	4,208	4,279	4,280	4,433	4,597	4,876	5,283	5,691	6,004

1 Includes British Rail services and those provided by private operators.
  Adjusted to 2008/09 prices using the GDP market price deflator.
2 Break in series due to change in methodology.
3 Break in series due to change in methodology.

☎020-7944 8874
The figures in this table are outside
the scope of National Statistics
Source - ORR

6.4 Passenger kilometres on national railways:[1] 1998/99-2008/09

											Billions
	1998/99	1999/00 [2]	2000/01	2001/02	2002/03	2003/04	2004/05	2005/06	2006/07	2007/08 [3]	2008/09
All Passenger Operators:											
Ordinary fare	26.4	28.0	27.2	28.1	28.4	28.9	29.4	30.0	32.9	33.9	35.2
Season ticket	9.8	10.4	10.9	11.0	11.3	12.0	12.4	13.2	13.3	15.1	15.5
All tickets	36.3	38.5	38.2	39.1	39.7	40.9	41.8	43.2	46.2	49.0	50.7

1 Estimates of passenger kilometres are derived from ticket sales.
  Travel on season tickets assumes appropriate factors for the
  number of journeys made per ticket.
2 Break in series due to change in methodology (see notes and definitions Section 6).
3 Break in series due to change in methodology (see notes and definitions Section 6).

☎020-7944 8874
The figures in this table are outside
the scope of National Statistics
Source - ORR

6.5 National railways: route and stations open for traffic at end of year: 1998/99-2008/09

											Kilometres/number
	1998/99	1999/00	2000/01	2001/02	2002/03	2003/04	2004/05 [2]	2005/06	2006/07	2007/08 [3]	2008/09
Route open for traffic:											
Electrified	5,166	5,167	5,167	5,167	5,167	5,200	5,200	5,205	5,250	5,250	5,250
Non-electrified	11,493	11,482	11,485	11,485	11,485	11,293	10,916	10,605	10,545	10,564	10,564
All routes:	16,659	16,649	16,652	16,652	16,652	16,493	16,116	15,810	15,795	15,814	15,814
Open for passenger traffic	15,038	15,038	15,042	15,042	15,042	14,883	14,328	14,356	14,353	14,484	14,494
Open for freight traffic only	1,621	1,610	1,610	1,610	1,610	1,610	1,788	1,454	1,442	1,330	1,320
Passenger stations: [1]	2,499	2,503	2,508	2,508	2,508	2,507	2,508	2,510	2,520	2,516	2,516

1 The number of stations shown are those on the national network.
  Metro stations and stations shared with London Underground are excluded.
2 Break in series due to change in methodology (see notes and definitions Section 6).
3 Break in series due to change in methodology (see notes and definitions Section 6).

☎020-7944 8874
The figures in this table are outside
the scope of National Statistics
Source - Network Rail, formerly Railtrack

6.6 National railways: punctuality and reliability: 1998/99-2008/09

											Percentage
	1998/99	1999/00	2000/01	2001/02	2002/03	2003/04	2004/05	2005/06	2006/07[2]	2007/08	2008/09
Public Performance Measure (PPM)[1]	87.9	87.8	79.1	78.0	79.2	81.2	83.6	86.4	88.1	89.9	90.6
Punctuality	91.5	91.9	..	..	..	..	..	..	..	..	..
Reliability	98.8	98.8	..	..	..	..	..	..	..	..	..

1 The PPM is a measure of the percentage of
  trains arriving on time, combining punctuality
  and reliability. It replaced the former
  Passenger's Charter measures from June 2000.
2 Break in the series due to change in methodology (see notes and defintions Section 6)

☎020-7944 8874
The figures in this table are outside the scope of National Statistics
Source - ORR

6.7 London Underground: 1998/99-2008/09

	1998/99	1999/00	2000/01	2001/02	2002/03	2003/04	2004/05	2005/06	2006/07	2007/08	2008/09
Passenger Journeys (millions)											
Ordinary [1]	463	477	486	491	495	491	486	460	519	581	616
Season ticket	403	450	484	462	446	457	490	510	521	515	473
All journeys	866	927	970	953	942	948	976	970	1,040	1,096	1,089
Passenger kilometres (millions)	6,716	7,171	7,470	7,451	7,367	7,340	7,606	7,586	7,947	8,352	8,646
Receipts (£ million)											
Ordinary [1]	546	579	610	636	628	625	663	678	782	880	961
Season ticket	430	479	519	515	510	536	578	629	635	645	654
Traffic receipts	977	1,058	1,129	1,151	1,138	1,161	1,241	1,309	1,417	1,525	1,615
Traffic receipts at 2008/09 prices [2]	1,244	1,321	1,392	1,388	1,329	1,319	1,372	1,420	1,494	1,562	1,615
Costs (£ million)											
Rail operations [3,4]	869	962	1,115	1,341	1,628	..	..	..	..	..	..
Other operations	18	33	42	30	36	..	..	..	..	..	..
Depreciation, renewals, severance [3]	267	299	341	344	336	..	..	..	..	..	..
All costs (current prices)	1,154	1,294	1,497	1,715	2,000	..	..	..	..	..	..
All costs 2008/09 prices [2]	1,464	1,611	1,839	2,061	2,329	..	..	..	..	..	..
Loaded train kilometres (millions)	61	63	64	65	66	69	69	69	70	70	71
Passenger place kilometres (billions)	55	57	57	58	58	..	..	..	..	..	..
Receipts per journey (£)	1.13	1.14	1.16	1.21	1.21	1.22	1.27	1.35	1.36	1.39	1.48
Receipts per jny at 2008/09 prices [2]	1.43	1.42	1.43	1.45	1.41	1.39	1.40	1.46	1.43	1.42	1.48
Costs per train kilometre (£)	19	21	23	26	31	..	..	..	..	..	..
Costs per km at 2008/09 prices [2]	24	26	29	32	36	..	..	..	..	..	..
Average no. passengers per train	110	114	117	114	113	107	110	110	114	118	122
Loss before grants and tax (£ m)	177	236	368	564	863	..	..	..	..	..	..
Loss at 2008/09 prices [2]	225	294	452	678	1,004	..	..	..	..	..	..
Operational data (number)											
Rail staff	16,032	16,462	16,956	18,679	17,214	..	..	..	..	..	..
Stations	269	274	274	274	274	274	274	274	273	268	270
Rail carriages	3,923	3,954	3,954	3,954	3,954	3,959	3,959	4,070	4,070	4,070	4,070
Route kilometres	392	408	408	408	408	408	408	408	408	408	408

1 Ordinary journeys include daily travelcards and those where concessionary fares apply.
2 Adjustment to 2008/09 values using the GDP Deflator. 'Other' income no longer available on the same basis as previously published.
3 From 1998/99, following a change in London Underground's accounting policy, expenditure that had previously been treated as renewals was either charged to the cost of operations or capitalised as an addition to fixed assets.
4 The cost of rail operations includes most of the costs of London Underground's PFI and PPP contracts that are delivering a modernised tube network.

☎020-7944 3076
The figures in this table are outside the scope of National Statistics
Source - Transport for London

6.8 Channel Tunnel: traffic to and from Europe: 1998-2008

											Thousands
	1998	1999	2000	2001	2002	2003	2004	2005	2006	2007	2008
Vehicles carried on Le Shuttle:											
Passenger	3,448	3,342	2,864	2,605	2,408	2,351	2,165	2,124	2,089	2,207	1,963
Freight	705	839	1,133	1,198	1,231	1,285	1,281	1,309	1,296	1,415	1,254
All vehicles	4,153	4,181	3,997	3,803	3,639	3,636	3,446	3,433	3,385	3,622	3,218
Passengers on Eurostar and Le Shuttle	18,405	17,550	17,018	16,313	15,252	14,699	15,064	15,527	15,501	16,164	16,305
Through-train freight tonnes	3,141	2,865	2,947	2,447	1,487	1,743	1,889	1,588	1,569	1,214	1,239

☎020-7944 8874
The figures in this table are outside the scope of National Statistics
Sources - Eurotunnel, Eurostar and EWS International/DB Schenker

6.9 Bus and coach services: vehicle kilometres: 1998/99-2008/09

(a) Local bus services by area
Millions

	1998/99	1999/00	2000/01	2001/02	2002/03	2003/04	2004/05	2005/06	2006/07	2007/08[1]	2008/09[1]
London	358	362	371	381	404	444	457	461	465	475	485
English metropolitan areas	684	661	654	646	630	596	575	565	584	586 P	589 P
English non metropolitan areas	1,123	1,160	1,134	1,102	1,088	1,069	1,077	1,070	1,141	1,095 P	1,072 P
England	2,165	2,183	2,158	2,129	2,122	2,109	2,109	2,096	2,190	2,156 P	2,146 P
Scotland	358	363	369	368	374	369	357	357	377	381 P	383 P
Wales	118	123	126	126	123	113	116	120	116	127 P	125 P
Great Britain	2,642	2,670	2,653	2,622	2,619	2,590	2,581	2,573	2,682	2,664 P	2,654 P
All outside London	2,284	2,308	2,282	2,241	2,215	2,146	2,124	2,112	2,217	2,189 P	2,169 P

(b) Local bus services outside London by area
Millions

	2006/07			2007/08[1]			2008/09[1]		
	Comm-ercial	Sub-sidised	Total	Comm-ercial	Sub-sidised	Total	Comm-ercial	Sub-sidised	Total
English metropolitan areas	512	72	584	..	..	586 P	..	..	589 P
English non metropolitan areas	867	274	1,141	..	..	1,095 P	..	..	1,072 P
Scotland	301	76	377	..	..	381 P	..	..	383 P
Wales	79	37	116	..	..	127 P	..	..	125 P
All outside London	1,759	459	2,218	..	..	2,189 P	..	..	2,169 P

(c) All services
Millions

	1998/99	1999/00	2000/01	2001/02	2002/03	2003/04	2004/05	2005/06	2006/07	2007/08[1]	2008/09[1]
Local bus services	2,642	2,670	2,653	2,622	2,619	2,590	2,581	2,573	2,682	2,664 P	2,654 P
Other (non-local) services	1,590	1,451	1,507	1,479	1,336	1,398	1,343	1,395	1,284	1,511 P	..
All services	4,232	4,121	4,160	4,101	3,955	3,988	3,924	3,968	3,967	4,175 P	..

1 Break in local bus series (outside London) due to changes in estimation methodology. These figures are provisional.   ☎020-7944 3076

6.10 Bus and coach services: vehicle stock: 1998/99-2007/08

Thousands

	1997/98	1998/99	1999/00	2000/01	2001/02	2002/03	2003/04	2004/05	2005/06	2006/07	2007/08[3]
Single deckers:											
up to 16 seats	10.5	10.9	11.5	10.8	11.3	11.7	14.2	14.4	15.6	13.0	11.9
17-35 seats	13.6	14.4	13.9	15.0	13.0	12.9	..	..	..	..	..
36 plus seats	34.9	36.4	37.5	37.5	39.2	37.9	..	..	..	..	..
All single deckers[1]	59.0	61.7	62.9	63.3	63.5	62.5	63.7	64.0	65.5	63.8	64.1
All double deckers	17.1	17.0	16.8	16.0	16.0	16.3	16.5	16.6	15.5	16.2	16.3
All vehicles [2]	76.2	78.7	79.7	79.2	79.5	78.8	80.1	80.6	81.0	80.0	80.4

1 "Single deckers", in this context, includes minibuses and coaches as well as single-decker buses   ☎020-7944 3076
2 Public Service Vehicles in tax classes 34 and 38. Taken from DfT's annual surveys.
3 2008/09 estimates not available at the time of the publication.

6.11 Bus and coach services: passenger receipts
(Including concessionary fare reimbursement): 1998/99-2006/07

(a) Local bus services by area (current prices)

£ Million

Area	1996/97	1997/98	1998/99	1999/00	2000/01	2001/02	2002/03	2003/04	2004/05	2005/06	2006/07[1]
London	561	599	626	652	674	695	715	767	871	939	1,003
English metropolitan areas	672	719	718	704	747	764	786	815	846	907	914
English other areas	866	906	930	972	1,038	1,074	1,135	1,281	1,311	1,424	1,709
England	2,099	2,224	2,274	2,328	2,459	2,533	2,635	2,863	3,029	3,270	3,626
Scotland	290	296	300	314	332	321	354	358	381	385	424
Wales	83	81	85	88	99	98	105	105	110	114	124
Great Britain	2,472	2,601	2,659	2,731	2,890	2,952	3,094	3,326	3,519	3,769	4,173
All outside London	1,911	2,002	2,033	2,078	2,216	2,257	2,379	2,559	2,648	2,830	3,170

(b) All services at current prices

£ Million

	1996/97	1997/98	1998/99	1999/00	2000/01	2001/02	2002/03	2003/04	2004/05	2005/06	2006/07
Local bus services	2,472	2,601	2,659	2,731	2,890	2,952	3,094	3,326	3,519	3,769	4,173
Other (non-local) services [2]	1,067	1,144	1,260	1,390	1,556	1,606	1,535	1,586	1,603	..	..
All services	3,539	3,745	3,919	4,121	4,446	4,558	4,629	4,912	5,122	..	..

(c) All services at 2008/09 prices [3]

£ Million

	1996/97	1997/98	1998/99	1999/00	2000/01	2001/02	2002/03	2003/04	2004/05	2005/06	2006/07
Local bus services	3,299	3,383	3,387	3,411	3,563	3,560	3,615	3,779	3,891	4,090	4,399
Other (non-local) services	1,424	1,488	1,605	1,736	1,918	1,937	1,793	1,802	1,772	..	..
All services	4,723	4,871	4,992	5,148	5,482	5,497	5,408	5,582	5,663	..	..

1 2007/08 and 2008/09 estimates not available at the time of publication.
2 Passenger receipts for non-local services are no longer collected.
3 Prices for the series are adjusted for general inflation to 2008/09 prices, using the GDP market price deflator.

☎020-7944 3076

6.12 Bus and coach services: staff employed: 1997/98-2007/08

Thousands

Staff	1997/98	1998/99	1999/00	2000/01	2001/02	2002/03	2003/04	2004/05	2005/06	2006/07	2007/08 [2]
Drivers & crew	108.7	113.6	117.1	116.8	117.9	118.0	122.0	126.0	126.0	127.3	131.9
Maintenance	19.9	20.0	19.8	19.6	20.8	19.3	19.7	20.6	20.1	20.3	20.9
Other	17.3	18.1	17.9	19.5	21.5	17.9	20.7	20.0	20.4	20.0	21.0
All staff [1]	145.9	151.6	154.8	156.0	160.2	155.2	162.4	166.6	166.5	167.6	173.8

1 The full-time equivalents of all part time staff and all
  working proprietors are classified according to their main occupation.
2 2008/09 estimates were not available at the time of publication.

☎020-7944 3076

6.13 Local bus services: passenger journeys by area: 1998/99-2008/09

Millions

Area	1998/99	1999/00	2000/01	2001/02	2002/03	2003/04	2004/05	2005/06	2006/07	2007/08[1]	2008/09[1]
London	1,266	1,294	1,347	1,422	1,527	1,692	1,802	1,881	1,993	2,089	2,149
English metropolitan areas	1,256	1,213	1,203	1,196	1,182	1,162	1,128	1,111	1,141	1,104 P	1,111 P
English other areas	1,286	1,297	1,292	1,263	1,255	1,233	1,210	1,204	1,336	1,328 P	1,335 P
England	3,808	3,804	3,842	3,881	3,964	4,087	4,140	4,196	4,470	4,522 P	4,594 P
Scotland	424	455	458	466	471	478	479	477	506	517 P	515 P
Wales	118	117	119	108	115	116	118	118	122	124 P	124 P
Great Britain	4,350	4,376	4,420	4,455	4,550	4,681	4,737	4,791	5,097	5,163 P	5,233 P
All outside London	3,084	3,082	3,073	3,033	3,023	2,989	2,935	2,910	3,104	3,074 P	3,084 P

1 Break in local bus series (outside London) due to changes in estimation methodology.
  These figures are provisional.

☎020-7944 3076

6.14 Local bus services: Local authority support by area: 1997/98-2007/08

(a) Concessionary fare reimbursement: by area (current prices)

£ Million

	1997/98	1998/99	1999/00	2000/01	2001/02	2002/03	2003/04	2004/05	2005/06	2006/07	2007/08[2]
London	110	121	124	126	129	129	137	135	157	178	186
English metropolitan areas	176	176	185	189	190	184	188	188	189	251	265
England: other areas	104	103	106	108	122	123	132	132	141	315	368
England	390	401	415	423	441	436	457	455	487	743	819
Scotland	42	42	41	40	39	65	91	90	95	154	163
Wales	8	8	10	11	13	30	37	41	48	52	57
All Great Britain	440	451	466	475	493	531	585	585	630	949	1,039
All outside London	330	330	341	349	364	402	448	451	473	772	853

(b) Public transport support: by area (current prices)

£ Million

	1997/98	1998/99	1999/00	2000/01	2001/02	2002/03	2003/04	2004/05	2005/06	2006/07	2007/08[2]
London[1]	1	12	10	57	201	368	516	546	596	617	662
English metropolitan areas	98	109	109	104	110	106	113	104	116	130	134
England: other areas	86	110	127	133	147	170	196	212	240	230	238
England	185	231	246	294	458	644	825	862	952	977	1,034
Scotland	23	22	25	28	33	35	36	38	45	48	51
Wales	9	11	14	16	20	21	25	27	28	29	30
All Great Britain	218	265	284	337	511	700	885	927	1,026	1,054	1,115
All outside London	217	253	274	280	310	332	369	381	430	437	453

(c) All Great Britain at 2008/09 prices [1]

£ Million

	1997/98	1998/99	1999/00	2000/01	2001/02	2002/03	2003/04	2004/05	2005/06	2006/07	2007/08[2]
Concessionary fare reimbursement	572	574	582	585	595	620	665	647	684	1,001	1,064
Public transport support	283	337	354	415	616	818	1,006	1,025	1,113	1,111	1,142

1 Adjusted for general inflation to 2008/09 prices using the GDP deflator.
2 2008/09 estimates not available at the time of publication.

☎020-7944 3076

6.15 Local bus services: fare indices by area: 1998/99-2008/09

1995=100

Area	1998/99	1999/00	2000/01	2001/02	2002/03	2003/04	2004/05	2005/06	2006/07	2007/08	2008/09
London	113.8	117.2	117.3	115.5	114.8	116.9	126.8	139.7	151.5	159.5	160.2
English metropolitan areas	117.9	123.5	128.6	135.5	140.7	146.7	153.3	166.0	168.3	178.3	190.3
English other areas	117.3	122.6	129.2	136.1	142.4	149.0	155.9	166.2	159.5	168.0	178.6
England	116.4	121.4	125.8	130.3	134.3	139.4	147.2	159.4	160.1	169.1	177.4
Scotland	121.2	124.1	129.1	131.1	133.8	136.1	140.0	143.9	151.0	155.7	166.7
Wales	116.0	121.9	128.4	135.7	142.3	147.2	153.7	159.9	169.7	177.8	188.1
Great Britain	117.1	121.8	126.4	130.6	134.5	139.2	146.5	157.5	159.0	167.6	176.2
All outside London	118.2	123.2	129.0	135.1	140.4	146.0	152.3	162.2	160.7	169.1	180.1
Retail Prices Index	109.8	111.6	114.9	116.6	119.1	122.4	126.2	129.5	134.4	139.9	144.1

☎020-7944 4139

6.16 Local bus services: operating costs per vehicle-kilometre: 1996/97-2006/07

(a) At current prices										Pence per vehicle kilometre [1]	
	1996/97	1997/98	1998/99	1999/00	2000/01	2001/02	2002/03	2003/04	2004/05	2005/06	2006/07[4]
London [2]	154	152	155	157	168	178	203	210	221	238	251
English PTE areas	94	90	90	92	101	105	105	114	118	130	148
English other areas	74	76	79	81	87	94	89	100	94	98	111
England	91	92	94	96	105	111	114	127	128	138	151
Scotland	73	74	77	73	78	84	80	80	86	90	100
Wales	65	71	74	74	76	77	84	83	82	86	93
Great Britain	88	89	91	92	100	105	108	118	120	129	141
All outside London	79	81	84	82	89	95	92	99	98	105	118

(b) At 2008/09 prices [3]										Pence per vehicle kilometre [1]	
London [2]	206	198	197	196	207	215	237	239	244	258	265
English PTE areas	125	117	115	115	125	127	123	130	130	141	156
English other areas	99	99	101	101	107	113	104	114	104	107	117
England	121	120	120	120	129	134	133	144	142	149	159
Scotland	97	96	98	91	96	101	93	91	95	98	105
Wales	87	92	94	92	94	93	98	94	91	93	98
Great Britain	117	116	116	115	123	127	126	134	133	140	149
All outside London	105	105	107	102	110	115	107	112	108	114	124

1 Net of Bus Service Operators Grant. Includes depreciation of vehicles.
2 Routes operated under contract to Transport for London
   on the London bus network and other scheduled local services.
3 Adjusted for general inflation to 2008/09 prices using the GDP Deflator.
4 2007/08 and 2008/09 estimates not available at the time of the publication.

☎020-7944 3076

6.17 Taxis: vehicles, drivers and fares: England and Wales: 1997-2007/08

										Thousands/Index	
	1997	1998	1999	2000	2001	2002	2003/04	2004/05	2005/06	2006/07	2007/08[4]
London											
Number of licensed taxis[1]	18.9	19.4	19.2	20.9	20.5	20.5	20.8	20.7	21.4	21.6	21.8
Number of licensed drivers	22.3	22.7	23.3	23.7	24.5	24.5	24.8	24.7	24.7	24.6	24.7
Taxi fare index 1995=100[2]	109	113	118	125	140	150	..	..	..	..	..
Private Hire Vehicles	..	..	..	..	..	..	..	32.4	39.9	44.4	46.9
Outside London											
Number of licensed taxis[1]	36.5	..	42.1	..	42.6	..	46	47	..	52	..
Number of licensed drivers[3]	83.2	..	98.2		96.4	..	48	48	..	47	..
Taxi fare index 1995=100[2]	109	116	122	..	130	..	..	..	..	..	..
Private Hire Vehicles	66.2	..	..	..	..	..	80.8	..	..	85.7	..

1 Data for London are from TfL. Outside London they are from surveys of
   district councils and unitary authorities.
2 Fare changes are not collected each year. Fare rises usually
   take place in the spring in London, or at various times of the
   year outside London, so these indices can only give a guide.
3 Dual licensing of drivers for both taxis and PHVs may have overstated the figures from 1994 to 2001.
4 2008/09 estimates not available at the time of the publication.

☎020-7944 3076

7 Roads and Traffic:

Notes and Definitions

Road traffic: 7.1, 7.2, 7.3 and 7.4

Special Note

Quality Review

1. The Review of Road Traffic and Road Length Statistics (National Statistics Quality Review Series Report 49) was published in January 2007 and is available from the National Statistics website:

http://www.ons.gov.uk/about-statistics/ methodology-and-quality/quality/nat-stats-qual-revs/full-list-of-completed-quality-reviews/index. html

Work is now taking place through the Traffic Estimates Improvement Programme to implement the recommendations in the review. In addition other areas for development have been identified and explored.

Methodological Note

2. A revised short paper (How National Traffic Estimates are Made) outlining the full methodology used by the Department to calculate traffic estimates is now available online at

http://www.dft.gov.uk/pgr/statistics/ datatablespublications/roadstraffic/ notesdefinitions/nattraffestimatesmade.pdf or by request from:

Department for Transport, Statistics Roads 2 Division, Zone 3/17, Great Minster House, 76 Marsham Street, London SW1P 4DR.

Local Authority level statistics

3. Estimates of road traffic at local authority level, together with corresponding figures for casualties in road accidents, will be made available on the DfT website. They are provided to enable the calculation and monitoring of road casualty rates for individual local authorities. These traffic figures are less robust than the regional and national totals and are not classed as National Statistics.

Revisions to data

4. The road traffic estimates for 'light vans' and 'larger buses and coaches' for 2007 have been revised.

5. There are step changes in the minor road length figures in 2004 and 2006 due to changes in the base data. In 2004, amendments were made to the data for private roads in Scotland which had been incorrectly recorded as public roads. Since 2006, minor road length estimates have been made using Ordnance Survey's Integrated Transport Network (ITN) dataset, rather than the OSCAR dataset. This change in methodology leads to an increase in minor road lengths due to the greater accuracy of ITN.

End of Special Note

The total activity of traffic on the road network in Great Britain is measured in vehicle kilometres. In Table 7.2, road traffic is given by vehicle class and year. The traffic for each year is a function of the length of the public road network (kilometres) and the traffic flow (vehicles).

The Department produces estimates of annual average daily flow (AADF) for each link of the major road network. They are produced using 12-hour manual data counts from a large number of sites and traffic profiles derived from automatic counters at about 190 sites. The AADFs are available from

www.dft.gov.uk/matrix

The definitions for the vehicle types included in the traffic census are given below:

All motor vehicles: All vehicles except pedal cycles.

Cars and taxis: Includes passenger vehicles with nine or fewer seats, three wheeled cars and four wheel-drive 'sports utility vehicles'. Cars towing caravans or trailers are counted as one vehicle. The definition used for traffic statistics therefore differs from that used in the vehicle licensing statistics shown in Tables 9.1-9.8.

Motorcycles etc: Includes motorcycles, scooters and mopeds and all motorcycle or scooter combinations.

Larger buses and coaches: Includes all public service vehicles and works buses which have a gross weight greater than 3.5 tonnes.

Light vans: Goods vehicle not exceeding 3.5 tonnes gross vehicle weight. Includes all car-based vans and those of the next largest carrying capacity such as transit vans. Also included are ambulances, pickups and milk floats.

Heavy goods vehicles (HGV): Includes all goods vehicles over 3.5 tonnes gross vehicle weight.

Rigid HGV with two axles: Includes all rigid heavy goods vehicles with two axles. Includes tractors (without trailers), road rollers, box vans and similar large vans. A two axle motor tractive unit without trailer is also included.

Rigid HGV with three axles: Includes all non articulated goods vehicles with three axles irrespective of the position of the axles. Excludes two axle rigid vehicles towing a single axle caravan or trailer. Three axle motor tractive units without a trailer are also included.

Rigid HGV with four or more axles: Includes all non articulated goods vehicles with four axles, regardless of the position of the axles. Excludes two or three axle rigid vehicles towing a caravan or trailer.

Articulated heavy goods vehicles: When a heavy goods vehicle is travelling with one or more axles raised from the road (sleeping axles) then the vehicle is classified into the class of the number of axles on the road, and not to the class of the total number of axles. Articulated goods vehicles with three and four axles are merged into one category, as they are not differentiated during manual traffic counts.

Articulated HGV with three axles (or with trailer): Includes all articulated goods vehicles with three axles. The motor tractive unit will have two axles and the trailer one. Also included in this class are two axle rigid goods vehicles towing a single axle caravan or trailer.

Articulated HGV with four axles (or with trailer): Includes all articulated vehicles with a total of four axles regardless of the position of the axles, i.e. two on the tractive unit with two on the trailer, or three on the tractive unit with one on the trailer. Also includes two axle rigid goods vehicles towing two axle close coupled or drawbar trailers.

Articulated HGV with five axles (or with trailer): This includes all articulated vehicles with a total of five axles regardless of the position of the axles. Also includes rigid vehicles drawing close coupled or drawbar trailers where the total axle number equals five and articulated vehicles where the motor tractive unit has more than one trailer and the total axle number equals five.

*Articulated HGV with six or more axles (or with trailer):*This includes all articulated vehicles with a total of six or more axles regardless of the position of the axles. Also includes rigid vehicles drawing close coupled or drawbar trailers where the total axle number equals six or more and articulated vehicles where the motor tractive unit has more than one trailer and the total axle number equals six or more.

Pedal cycles: Includes all non motorised cycles.

Forecasts of Road Traffic: 7.5

The forecasts in Table 7.5 are taken from the modelling and analytical work undertaken by the National Transport Model that lay behind the Department's publication entitled 'Road Transport Forecasts for England 2007'. The forecasts show traffic growth in England, disaggregated by vehicle type. The figures in the table are based to 2003 = 100. Further details of the Department's National Transport Model, the forecasts paper and separate forecasts for each English region can be found on the DfT web site. Full details of the Plan and underlying assumptions are given in Transport 2010: The 10 Year Plan and Background Analysis. A technical paper describing the improvements to the 1997 NRTF modelling framework will be made available shortly.

http://www.dft.gov.uk/pgr/economics/ntm/

Road network: 7.6, 7.8 and 7.9

The lengths of major roads are obtained from the major roads database maintained by the Department for Transport using information from the Government Offices, local authorities, the Scottish Government, the Welsh Assembly Government and Ordnance Survey. Road length information for minor 'B', 'C' and unclassified roads are obtained from Ordnance Survey roads data (the Integrated Transport Network dataset), local authorities, the Scottish Government and the Welsh Assembly Government. All figures given in Tables 7.8 and 7.9 are road lengths at the 1st April of each year. The road definitions are as follows:

Major roads: Include motorways and all class 'A' roads. These roads usually have high traffic flows and are often the main arteries to major destinations.

Motorways (built under the enabling legislation of the Special Roads Act 1949, now consolidated in the Highways Acts of 1959 and 1980): Are major roads of regional and urban strategic importance, often used for long distance travel. They are usually three or more lanes in each direction and generally have the maximum speed limit of 70mph.

'A' Roads: Can be trunk or principal roads. These are often described as the 'main' roads and tend to have heavy traffic flows though not as high as motorways.

Trunk roads (designated by the Trunk roads Acts 1936 and 1946): Most motorways and many of the long distance rural 'A' roads are trunk roads. The responsibility for their maintenance lies with the Secretary of State and they are managed by the Highways Agency in England, the National Assembly of Wales in Wales and the Scottish Executive in Scotland (National Through Routes).

Strategic Road Network (SRN): Consists of motorways and trunk 'A' roads (dual and single carriageway) in England that are managed by the Highways Agency, as well as the M6 Toll.

Non-trunk roads: Roads for which local authorities are highway authorities. The Secretary of State, the Scottish Government, and the Welsh Assembly Government have power to classify non-trunk roads in agreement with the local highway authority. Non-trunk roads are therefore either classified or unclassified, the former being of two types, principal and non-principal. The classified principal roads are class 'A' roads, except for a few local authority motorways, and are of regional and urban strategic importance. The non-principal roads are those which distribute traffic to urban and regional localities. The non-principal classified roads are sub-divided into 'B' and 'C' classes. Unclassified roads are those in the least important categories, i.e. local distributor and access roads.

Principal roads: Major roads are maintained by local authorities. These are mainly 'A' roads, though some local authorities do have responsibility for some motorways).

Minor Roads: These are 'B' and 'C' classified roads and unclassified roads (all of which are maintained by the local authorities), as referred to above. Class III (later 'C') roads were created in April 1946. 'B' roads in urban areas can have relatively high traffic flows, but are not regarded as being as significant as 'A' roads, though in some cases may have similarly high flows. They are useful distributor roads often between towns or villages. 'B' roads in rural areas often have markedly low traffic flows compared with their 'A' road counterparts. 'C' Roads are regarded as of lesser importance than either 'B' or 'A' roads, and generally have only one carriageway of two lanes and carry less traffic. They can have low traffic flows in rural areas. Unclassified roads include residential roads both in urban and rural situations and rural lanes, the latter again normally having very low traffic flows. Most unclassified roads will have only two lanes, and in rural areas may only have one lane with "passing bays" at intervals to allow for two-way traffic flow.

Urban roads: Are major and minor roads within an urban area with a population of 10,000 or more. The definition is based on the 2001 Communities and Local Government definition of Urban Settlements. The definition for 'urban settlement' is in Urban and rural area definitions: a user guide which can be found on the Communities and Local Government web site.

Rural roads: Are major and minor roads outside urban areas (these urban areas have a population of more than 10,000 people).

Private Roads: Are included in the major roads as these private roads (usually toll roads, tunnels or bridges) are accessible to the general public, whereas private minor roads, not usually being accessible to the general public, are not included.

Vehicle speeds: 7.10 and 7.11

The types of vehicle analysed in the urban and non-urban survey are motor cycles, cars, cars towing, LGVs, buses/coaches, rigid 2 axle HGVs, rigid 3 and rigid 4 axles HGVs, 4 axles articulated HGVs and 5 or more axles articulated HGVs. The automatic counters identify rigid 2 axle lorries but cannot distinguish between vehicles weighing less than 7.5 tonnes gross and those weighing more. The weight of this type of vehicle determines its speed limit on non-urban roads. Consequently it is impossible to tell how many rigid 2 axle HGVs are speeding. For further details of speed limits for different types of vehicle on different classes of non-built up road, see Table 4.1 of the Road Statistics 2008 bulletin, produced by Transport Statistics DfT.

Non-urban roads (Table 7.10): The speeds indicated are average traffic speeds from 27 motorway sites, 7 dual carriageway sites and 26 single carriageway sites.

Urban roads (Table 7.11): Speed measurements were taken from 26 sites with speed limits of 30 mph and from 10 sites with speed limits of 40 mph.

Congestion on the Strategic Road Network in England: 7.12

The Strategic Road Network (SRN) in England consists of motorways and trunk 'A' roads (dual and single carriageway) that are managed by the Highways Agency, as well as the M6 Toll.

For monitoring purposes, the network has been split into 103 recognisable routes (for instance the A46 from Leicester to Lincoln). Each route has two directions, so there is a total of 206 route-directions. Following a review of data quality in 2008, the number of routes included in the journey time reliability measure increased from 91 to 95 routes for the year ending March 2008 onwards, and there is a small discontinuity with earlier periods. The remaining eight routes are excluded from the measure due to data quality considerations.

The Department monitors reliability using the average vehicle delay on the slowest 10% of journeys on the SRN. This indicator is used to measure performance against the Department's Public Service Agreement (PSA). For the Spending Review 2004, there was a target to improve reliability between the baseline year ending July 2005 and the year ending March 2008. For the Comprehensive Spending Review 2007, the baseline is the year ending March 2008. The measure will be monitored until March 2011, though there is no specific numerical target.

Average vehicle delay is derived from the difference between observed journey times and a reference journey time (the time that could theoretically be achieved when the traffic is free flowing), weighting by traffic flows for each route of the network. The slowest 10% of journeys are selected for each 15-minute departure time between 6am and 8pm for each day of the week, on each of the 91 routes. The indicator therefore reflects journeys experienced on all types of route on all days at all times of the day.

The data used for the measure are from the Highways Agency's Traffic Information System, which brings together journey time and traffic flow data from several different sources.

Details of the methodology used for the measure are provided online:

http://www.dft.gov.uk/pgr/
statistics/datatablespublications/
roadstraffic/speedscongestion/
congestiononthestrategicroad5359

Regional expenditure on roads: 7.13

Whereas the figures in Table 1.15 relate to net expenditure, those in Table 7.13 relate to gross expenditure. For this reason, and because of certain differences in coverage (in particular the treatment of professional and technical services), England totals differ from those in Tables 1.14 and 1.15.

The local roads figure for new construction/ improvement plus structural maintenance includes expenditure on technical surveys. These figures include both expenditure recorded on local authority capital expenditure returns and also structural maintenance recorded on the revenue returns. Structural maintenance includes reconstruction, overlay, resurfacing, patching, surface dressing, drainage, footways, bridges, earthworks and fences. Routine maintenance includes verge maintenance, sweeping, gullies, signals, signs and marking. Winter maintenance includes salting, snow clearance and the maintenance and operation of ice detection equipment.

Figures for motorways and trunk roads are not directly comparable with previously published data for years earlier than 2001/02, as the Highways Agency is now using a resource accounting system. The introduction of the new accounting systems has led to changes in categorisation and slight adjustments to the way some figures are calculated.

Road construction tender price index: 7.14

The index measures the movement of prices in competitive tenders for road construction contracts in Great Britain. It includes new road construction and major maintenance works of a value exceeding £250,000. Contribution to the data from which this index is calculated is by way of the completion of survey forms and submission of priced bills of quantities. The contributors are the Highways Agency and the highways departments of the local authorities of England, Scotland and Wales. The published annual figures are the derived from a quarterly series produced published by the Building Cost Information Service of the Royal Institution of Chartered Surveyors for Construction Market Intelligence Division of the Department for Business, Innovation and Skills.

Further information on thus index can be found in the Construction Statistics Annual notes and definitions available at http://www.statistics.gov.uk/StatBase/Product.asp?vlnk=284

Road Tax Revenue: 7.15

Information on fuel tax revenues is collected by HMRC. Information on vehicle excise duty is collected by the Driver and Vehicle Licensing Agency (DVLA) and reported in financial returns and the motor tax account. These figures do not include revenues from trade plates but do include revenue from duties that are subsequently refunded. Vehicle numbers are averages based on quarterly analyses and therefore differ from the end year statistics given in Chapter 9.

Latest estimates on the level of revenue loss from vehicle excise duty evasion is available from a DfT report – 'Vehicle Excise Duty Evasion 2008' or at www.dft.gov.uk/pgr/ statistics/datatablespublications/vehicles/ excisedutyevasion

New road construction and improvements: 7.16

The lane km quoted are net km – this is the total length of new lane kms added to the strategic network including additional lanes (widening), bypasses, carriageway alignment etc. less the total length of lane kms removed from the strategic road network.

Start figures from 1996/97 onwards include schemes under Design, Build Finance and Operate (DBFO) contracts. These contracts, which are a part of the Private Finance Initiative, involve the private sector in the provision and improvement of sections of trunk road, or in a few cases of motorway, and in the management of both their own works and contiguous stretches of road over a lengthy period. The private sector provides the funding and is reimbursed by Government through payments linked to usage and performance.

In 1997/98, there were no new starts for any national schemes (including PFI schemes see above) that involved the construction of additional lane kilometres. This reflected policy decisions taken by the previous and present governments. There were no completions in 2001/02.

7.1 Road traffic by type of vehicle: 1949-2008
For greater detail for the years 1998-2008 see Table 7.2

Billion vehicle kilometres

Year	Cars and taxis	Motor cycles etc	Larger buses and coaches	Light vans [1]	Goods vehicles [2]	All motor vehicles	Pedal cycles
1949	20.3	3.1	4.1	6.5	12.5	46.5	23.6
1950	25.6	4.4	4.1	7.8	11.2	53.1	19.9
1951	29.3	5.6	4.2	8.2	11.7	58.9	20.8
1952	30.6	6.0	4.2	8.7	11.3	60.8	22.9
1953	33.4	6.7	4.2	9.1	11.5	64.9	20.8
1954	37.2	6.9	4.2	9.3	12.2	69.7	18.8
1955	42.3	7.5	4.2	9.8	13.2	77.0	18.2
1956	46.2	7.4	4.2	10.0	13.0	80.8	16.2
1957	45.2	8.3	4.0	10.3	12.5	80.3	16.1
1958	55.4	8.4	3.9	11.9	13.5	93.0	14.1
1959	62.2	9.8	4.0	13.7	14.6	104.2	13.6
1960	68.0	10.0	3.9	15.0	15.3	112.3	12.0
1961	76.9	9.7	4.0	16.4	15.5	122.4	10.9
1962	83.7	8.7	4.0	16.6	15.4	128.3	9.3
1963	91.4	7.6	4.0	17.6	15.7	136.3	8.2
1964	105.7	7.5	4.0	17.7	17.4	152.3	8.0
1965	115.8	6.7	3.9	19.0	17.3	162.7	7.0
1966	126.5	6.0	3.9	19.0	17.5	172.9	6.3
1967	135.1	5.2	3.8	18.7	17.2	180.0	5.6
1968	142.7	4.7	3.8	18.9	17.6	187.7	5.0
1969	147.9	4.2	3.8	19.3	17.4	192.5	4.6
1970	155.0	4.0	3.6	20.3	17.6	200.5	4.4
1971	165.1	3.9	3.6	21.3	18.1	212.0	4.3
1972	174.7	3.7	3.6	22.2	18.4	222.5	3.9
1973	184.0	3.9	3.5	23.3	19.3	234.0	3.7
1974	180.0	4.2	3.3	23.6	18.6	229.7	3.8
1975	181.6	5.1	3.2	23.5	18.3	231.7	4.4
1976	190.4	6.3	3.3	24.2	19.2	243.5	5.0
1977	194.1	6.2	3.2	24.5	18.8	246.8	6.1
1978	202.4	6.1	3.3	25.2	19.5	256.5	5.1
1979	201.5	6.4	3.3	25.1	19.6	255.9	4.6
1980	215.0	7.7	3.5	26.1	19.7	271.9	5.1
1981	219.5	8.9	3.5	26.2	18.9	276.9	5.4
1982	227.3	9.2	3.5	26.0	18.4	284.5	6.4
1983	231.2	8.3	3.7	26.1	18.8	288.1	6.4
1984	244.0	8.1	3.9	27.5	19.6	303.1	6.4
1985	250.5	7.4	3.7	28.6	19.6	309.7	6.1
1986	264.4	7.1	3.7	30.0	20.1	325.3	5.5
1987	284.6	6.7	4.1	32.7	22.3	350.5	5.7
1988	305.4	6.0	4.3	36.2	23.8	375.7	5.2
1989	331.3	5.9	4.5	39.7	25.5	406.9	5.2
1990	335.9	5.6	4.6	39.9	24.9	410.8	5.3
1991	335.2	5.4	4.8	41.7	24.5	411.6	5.2
1992	338.0	4.5	4.6	41.2	23.8	412.1	4.7
1993 [3]	338.1	3.8	4.6	41.6	24.3	412.3	4.0
1994	345.0	3.8	4.6	43.3	24.8	421.5	4.0
1995	351.1	3.7	4.9	44.5	25.4	429.7	4.1
1996	359.9	3.8	5.0	46.2	26.2	441.1	4.1
1997	365.8	4.0	5.2	48.6	26.9	450.3	4.1
1998	370.6	4.1	5.2	50.8	27.7	458.5	4.0
1999	377.4	4.5	5.3	51.6	28.1	467.0	4.1
2000	376.8	4.6	5.2	52.3	28.2	467.1	4.2
2001	382.8	4.8	5.2	53.7	28.1	474.4	4.2
2002	392.9	5.1	5.2	55.0	28.3	486.5	4.4
2003	393.1	5.6	5.4	57.9	28.5	490.4	4.5
2004	398.1	5.2	5.2	60.8	29.4	498.6	4.2
2005	397.2	5.4	5.2	62.6	29.0	499.4	4.4
2006	402.6	5.2	5.4	65.2	29.1	507.5	4.6
2007 [4]	404.1	5.6	5.5	68.4	29.4	513.0	4.2
2008	401.7	5.1	5.2	68.1	28.7	508.9	4.7

1 Not exceeding 3,500 kgs gross vehicle weight, post 1982.
2 Over 3,500 kgs gross vehicle weight, post 1982.
3 Data for 1993 onwards are not directly comparable with the figures for 1992 and earlier.
4 Data for 'light vans' and 'Larger buses & coaches' for 2007 have been revised.

☎020-7944 3095

7.2 Road Traffic: by type of vehicle: 1998-2008

Billion vehicle kilometres

	1998	1999	2000 [1]	2001 [2]	2002	2003	2004	2005	2006	2007 [3]	2008
Cars and taxis	370.6	377.4	376.8	382.8	392.9	393.1	398.1	397.2	402.6	404.1	401.7
Motor cycles etc	4.1	4.5	4.6	4.8	5.1	5.6	5.2	5.4	5.2	5.6	5.1
Larger buses and coaches	5.2	5.3	5.2	5.2	5.2	5.4	5.2	5.2	5.4	5.5	5.2
Light vans [4]	50.8	51.6	52.3	53.7	55.0	57.9	60.8	62.6	65.2	68.4	68.1
Goods vehicles [5]											
2 axles rigid	11.1	11.6	11.7	11.5	11.6	11.7	11.7	11.5	11.3	11.1	10.7
3 axles rigid	1.9	1.7	1.7	1.8	1.8	1.8	1.9	1.9	1.9	2.0	2.0
4 or more axles rigid	1.6	1.5	1.5	1.5	1.5	1.6	1.6	1.7	1.7	1.8	1.9
3 and 4 axles artic	3.0	3.0	2.7	2.5	2.3	2.2	2.2	2.0	1.9	1.8	1.6
5 axles artic	7.3	7.2	6.7	6.4	6.4	6.2	6.5	6.4	6.6	6.6	6.5
6 or more axles artic	2.9	3.3	4.1	4.5	4.8	5.0	5.4	5.5	5.7	6.1	6.0
All	27.7	28.1	28.2	28.1	28.3	28.5	29.4	29.0	29.1	29.4	28.7
All motor vehicles	458.5	467.0	467.1	474.4	486.5	490.4	498.6	499.4	507.5	513.0	508.9
Pedal cycles	4.0	4.1	4.2	4.2	4.4	4.5	4.2	4.4	4.6	4.2	4.7

1 The decline in the use of cars and taxis in 2000 was due to the fuel dispute. ☎020-7944 3095
2 Figures affected by the impact of Foot and Mouth disease during 2001.
3 Data for 'light vans' and 'Larger buses and coaches' for 2007 have been revised.
4 Not exceeding 3,500 kgs gross vehicle weight.
5 Over 3,500 kgs gross vehicle weight.

7.3 Motor vehicle traffic: by road class: 1998-2008

Billion vehicle kilometres

	1998	1999	2000 [1]	2001 [2]	2002	2003	2004	2005	2006	2007	2008
Motorways	85.7	87.8	88.4	90.8	92.6	93.0	96.6	97.0	99.4	100.6	100.1
Rural 'A' roads: [3]											
Trunk [5]	63.3	64.7	64.2	65.9	64.6	61.5	59.7	58.0	59.2	58.6	58.6
Principal [5]	65.4	66.0	65.8	67.4	71.8	77.7	81.6	83.3	84.4	84.9	84.2
All rural 'A' roads	128.7	130.7	130.0	133.3	136.4	139.3	141.3	141.3	143.6	143.5	142.8
Urban 'A' roads: [4]											
Trunk [5]	13.8	14.0	14.0	7.6	7.4	6.7	6.0	5.5	5.6	5.4	5.5
Principal [5]	67.5	67.9	67.7	74.2	74.8	75.1	76.8	76.2	76.9	75.9	74.6
All urban 'A' roads	81.3	81.9	81.7	81.8	82.2	81.7	82.8	81.7	82.5	81.3	80.1
All Major roads	295.7	300.4	300.0	305.9	311.2	314.0	320.7	320.1	325.5	325.4	323.0
Minor roads:											
Minor rural roads	60.4	61.3	61.5	61.6	64.5	64.4	65.9	66.8	69.3	72.0	72.2
Minor urban roads	102.4	105.3	105.5	106.9	110.8	111.9	112.0	112.5	112.7	115.5	113.7
All minor roads	162.8	166.6	167.0	168.5	175.3	176.4	177.9	179.3	182.0	187.5	185.9
All roads	458.5	467.0	467.1	474.4	486.5	490.4	498.6	499.4	507.5	513.0	508.9

1 The decline in the use of cars and taxis in 2000 was due to the fuel dispute. ☎020-7944 3095
2 Figures affected by the impact of Foot and Mouth disease during 2001.
3 Rural roads: Major and minor roads, from 1993 onwards, are defined as being outside an urban area (see definition below).
4 Urban roads: Major and minor roads, from 1993 onwards, are defined as within an urban area with a population
   of 10,000 or more. These are based on the 2001 urban settlements. The definition for 'urban settlement' is in
   Urban and rural area definitions: a user guide which can be found on the Communities and Local Government
   web site at:
   http://www.communities.gov.uk/publications/planningandbuilding/urbanrural
5 Figures for trunk and principal 'A' roads in England, from 2001 onwards, are affected by the detrunking programme.

7.4   Road traffic: by type of vehicle and class of road: 2008

Billion vehicle kilometres

| | Cars and taxis | Motor cycles etc. | Larger buses and coaches | Light vans [2] | Goods vehicles [1] | | | | | | All Goods vehicles | All motor vehicles | Pedal cycles |
| | | | | | Rigid by number of axles | | | Articulated by number of axles | | | | | |
					2	3	4 or more	3 + 4	5	6 or more			
Motorways:	74.8	0.4	0.5	12.3	3.2	0.5	0.5	0.7	3.9	3.3	12.1	100.1	-
Rural 'A' roads: [3]													
Trunk [4]	44.4	0.4	0.3	7.8	1.7	0.3	0.3	0.4	1.5	1.5	5.7	58.6	-
Principal [4]	67.3	0.8	0.6	11.0	2.0	0.4	0.4	0.3	0.7	0.7	4.5	84.2	0.1
All rural 'A' roads:	111.7	1.2	0.9	18.8	3.7	0.7	0.8	0.7	2.2	2.2	10.2	142.8	0.2
Urban 'A' roads: [5]													
Trunk [4]	4.3	-	-	0.7	0.1	-	-	-	0.1	0.1	0.4	5.5	-
Principal [4]	61.1	0.9	1.1	9.0	1.4	0.2	0.3	0.1	0.2	0.2	2.4	74.6	0.7
All urban 'A' roads:	65.5	0.9	1.1	9.7	1.5	0.3	0.3	0.1	0.3	0.3	2.8	80.1	0.7
Minor roads:													
Minor rural roads	56.5	0.9	0.7	12.2	1.2	0.3	0.2	0.1	0.1	0.1	2.0	72.2	1.0
Minor urban roads	93.3	1.7	2.0	15.1	1.2	0.2	0.1	-	-	0.1	1.7	113.7	3.0
All minor roads:	149.8	2.6	2.7	27.3	2.4	0.5	0.3	0.1	0.1	0.2	3.6	185.9	3.9
All roads:	401.7	5.1	5.2	68.1	10.7	2.0	1.9	1.6	6.5	6.0	28.7	508.9	4.7

1   Over 3,500 kgs gross vehicle weight.
2   Not exceeding 3,500 kgs gross vehicle weight.
3   Rural roads: Major and minor roads, from 1993 onwards, are defined as being outside an urban area.
4   Figures for trunk and principal 'A' roads in England are affected by the detrunking programme.
5   Urban roads: Major and minor roads, from 1993 onwards, are defined as within an urban area with a population
    of 10,000 or more. These are based on the 2001 urban settlements. The definition for 'urban settlement' is in
    Urban and rural area definitions: a user guide which can be found on the Communities and Local
    Government web site at:
    http://www.communities.gov.uk/publications/planningandbuilding/urbanrural

☎020-7944 3095

7.5 Forecasts of road traffic in England and vehicles in Great Britain:[1] 2010-2025

Index: 2003 = 100

	2003	2010	2015	2025
Vehicle kilometres: England:				
Cars and taxis	100	103	115	130
Goods vehicles [2]	100	99	106	114
Light goods vehicles	100	111	132	163
Buses and coaches	100	100	100	100
All motor traffic (except two wheelers)	100	104	117	132
Car ownership: Great Britain:				
Cars per person	100	107	110	116
Number of cars	100	111	119	133

1   The traffic forecasts are central forecasts taken from the Department's Road
    Transport Forecasts for England 2008. The paper also contains: a forecast
    range reflecting uncertainties in the key forecasting assumptions that
    affect travel demand; and a break down of the forecasts by region.
2   Over 3.5 tonnes gross vehicle weight.
3   Car Ownership Data is taken from TEMPRO (Ver 5.4).

☎020-7944 6197
The figures in this table are outside
of the scope of National Statistics
Source - Integrated Transport, Economics

7.6 Roads lengths: Great Britain: 1914-2008

For greater detail for the years 1998-2008 see Table 7.8 or 7.9.

Kilometres

Year	Trunk	Class 1 or principal	Class 2 or B	Class 3 or C	Unclassified	All	ow: motorways Trunk	ow: motorways Principal	ow: motorways Total
1914	.	..	..	.	..	284,843	.	.	.
1923	.	37,383	23,720	.	224,265	285,369	.	.	.
1928	.	40,457	25,244	.	221,996	287,697	.	.	.
1933	.	42,784	26,786	.	215,842	285,412	.	.	.
1938	4,953	39,276	27,418	.	217,799	289,446	.	.	.
1943	7,176	37,305	28,532	.	..	..	.	.	.
1947	13,181	31,410	28,498	77,768	143,735	294,592	.	.	.
1951	13,275	31,435	28,481	78,346	145,929	297,466	.	.	.
1952	13,274	31,484	28,471	78,340	147,002	298,570	.	.	.
1953	13,284	31,464	28,485	78,364	148,161	299,758	.	.	.
1954	13,309	31,519	28,469	78,409	149,305	301,012	.	.	.
1955	13,309	31,553	28,479	78,505	150,863	302,710	.	.	.
1956	13,309	31,656	28,398	78,565	152,297	304,226	.	.	.
1957	13,311	31,762	28,333	78,615	153,998	306,018	.	.	.
1958	13,372	31,714	28,329	78,621	155,583	307,620	.	.	.
1959	13,401	31,744	28,329	78,653	158,573	310,700	13	.	13
1960	13,580	31,765	28,334	78,718	160,106	312,502	153	.	153
1961	13,628	31,780	28,357	78,740	161,667	314,171	209	10	219
1962	13,654	31,797	28,349	78,785	163,064	315,649	233	10	243
1963	13,745	31,860	28,337	78,829	166,611	319,382	312	10	322
1964	13,885	31,902	28,368	78,837	168,463	321,455	470	10	480
1965	13,993	31,971	28,392	78,855	170,357	323,568	557	10	566
1966	14,030	32,053	28,376	78,858	171,865	325,182	616	13	629
1967	14,159	32,543	..	279,479 [1]	..	326,180	747	11	761 [2]
1968	14,354	32,536	..	281,288 [1]	..	328,178	869	11	884 [2]
1969	14,439	32,533	107,254 [3]	..	166,089	320,315	946	18	964
1970	14,463	32,584	107,285 [3]	..	168,152	322,484	1,022	35	1,057
1971	14,668	32,737	107,388 [3]	..	169,872	324,665	1,235	35	1,270
1972	15,060	32,825	107,404 [3]	..	172,428	327,717	1,609	60	1,669
1973	15,011	32,859	27,409	79,791	172,060	327,131	1,660	70	1,730
1974	15,119	32,942	27,500	80,062	173,443	329,036	1,776	92	1,869
1975	15,240	33,088	27,606	80,156	173,949	330,039	1,881	94	1,975
1976	15,502	33,225	27,812	80,512	175,794	332,846	2,062	93	2,155
1977	15,223	33,598	27,875	80,693	177,874	335,263	2,131	106	2,237
1978	14,820	34,199	27,874	80,545	178,826	336,264	2,287	107	2,394
1979	14,805	34,430	27,866	80,599	180,278	337,978	2,340	116	2,455
1980	14,949	34,187	28,151	80,736	181,610	339,633	2,445	111	2,556
1981	14,915	34,656	28,232	80,398	184,119	342,320	2,524	123	2,647
1982	14,901	34,700	28,451	80,358	185,531	343,942	2,561	131	2,692
1983	14,972	34,819	28,537	80,327	187,121	345,776	2,609	132	2,741
1984	15,057	34,862	29,036	80,123	188,511	347,589	2,678	108	2,786
1985	15,014	34,908	29,042	80,460	189,276	348,699	2,705	108	2,813
1986	15,359	34,969	29,121	80,360	191,267	351,076	2,820	101	2,920
1987	15,394	35,089	29,766	80,004	192,442	352,695	2,874	101	2,975
1988	15,472	35,041	29,681	80,165	193,957	354,315	2,891	102	2,992
1989	15,618	35,131	29,706	80,542	195,606	356,602	2,903	92	2,995
1990	15,666	35,226	29,838	80,716	196,588	358,034	2,993	77	3,070
1991	15,356	35,649	30,106	81,073	197,783	359,966	3,033	68	3,102
1992	15,358	35,712	30,227	81,334	199,679	362,310	3,063	71	3,133
1993 [4]	14,819	34,514	30,229	83,816	221,461	384,839	3,139	72	3,211
1994	14,815	34,574	30,225	83,931	222,012	385,557	3,170	72	3,242
1995	14,840	34,732	30,221	84,046	222,562	386,401	3,197	72	3,269
1996	14,967	34,522	30,217	84,162	223,115	386,983	3,253	45	3,298
1997	15,131	34,603	30,213	84,277	223,668	387,893	3,333	45	3,378
1998	15,058	34,758	30,209	84,392	224,225	388,641	3,376	44	3,421
1999	15,102	34,916	30,205	84,509	224,783	389,515	3,404	45	3,449
2000	15,123	34,951	30,200	84,624	225,339	390,237	3,422	45	3,467
2001	14,800 [5]	35,330 [5]	30,196	84,742	225,901	390,969	3,431	45	3,476
2002	14,112	36,040	30,192	84,858	226,462	391,663	3,433	45	3,478
2003	13,047	37,083	30,188	84,976	227,048	392,342	3,432	46	3,478
2004	12,625	37,567	30,178 [6]	84,223 [6]	223,082 [6]	387,674 [6]	3,478	46	3,523
2005	12,148	38,028	30,189	84,459	223,184	388,008	3,466	54	3,519
2006	12,226	38,085	30,018 [6]	84,469 [6]	229,605 [6]	394,409 [6]	3,503	53	3,555
2007	12,201	38,101	30,265	84,423	229,889	394,879	3,518	41	3,559
2008	12,152	38,098	30,161	84,574	229,482	394,467	3,518	41	3,559

1 Includes 'B' and unclassified roads.
2 Includes other motorways i.e. those not at the time allocated to either the Department for Transport or local authorities.
3 Includes 'C' roads.
4 A number of minor revisions have been made to the lengths of major roads from 1993 onwards.
5 Figures for trunk and principal 'A' roads in England, from 2001 onwards, are affected by the detrunking programme.
6 New information from 2004 and from 2006 has enabled better estimates of Road lengths to be made - see notes and definitions.

☎020-7944 3095

7.7 Motorway and trunk 'A' road network of England, Scotland and Wales: March 2009

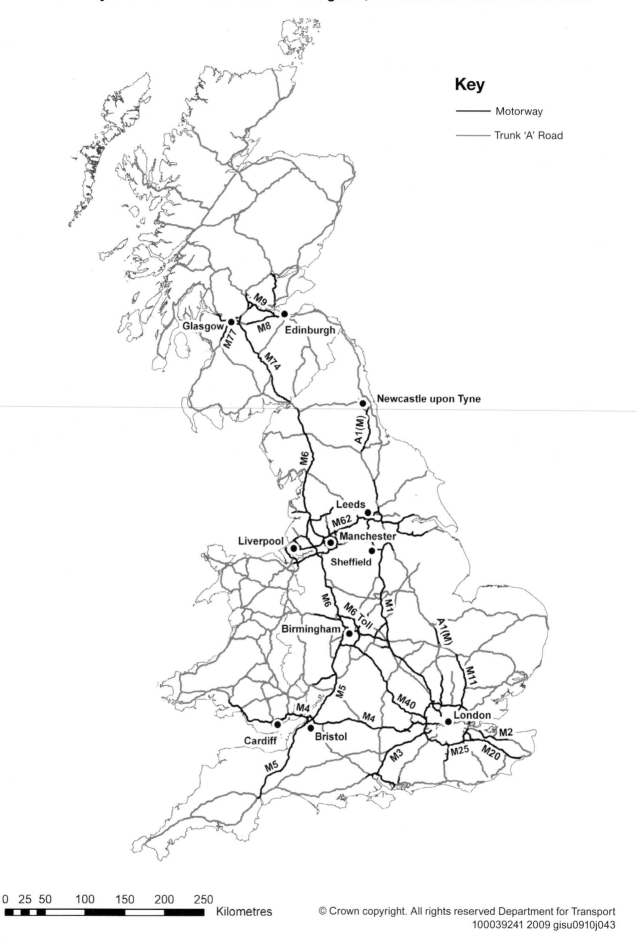

Key

── Motorway

── Trunk 'A' Road

0 25 50   100   150   200   250
Kilometres

7.8 Public road length: by road type: 1998-2008 [1]

	1998	1999	2000	2001	2002	2003	2004	2005	2006 [6]	2007	2008
											Kilometres
Trunk motorway	3,376	3,404	3,422	3,431	3,433	3,432	3,478	3,466	3,503	3,518	3,518
Principal motorway	44	45	45	45	45	46	46	54	53	41	41
Rural 'A' roads: [2]											
Trunk [3]	10,585	10,611	10,627	10,607	9,973	9,027	8,641	8,239	8,277	8,258	8,213
Principal [3]	24,783	24,852	24,866	24,915	25,559	26,498	26,889	27,312	27,336	27,346	27,372
All rural 'A' roads:	35,369	35,463	35,493	35,522	35,532	35,525	35,530	35,550	35,612	35,603	35,586
Urban 'A' roads: [4]											
Trunk [3]	1,096	1,087	1,074	762	705	587	506	444	446	425	420
Principal [3]	9,931	10,019	10,040	10,370	10,436	10,539	10,632	10,663	10,696	10,714	10,685
All urban 'A' roads:	11,027	11,106	11,114	11,132	11,141	11,127	11,138	11,107	11,143	11,139	11,105
Minor rural roads: [5]											
B roads	24,586	24,579	24,570	24,562	24,554	24,547	24,640	24,639	24,574	24,795	24,685
C roads	73,405	73,500	73,593	73,688	73,783	73,878	73,363	73,581	73,548	73,480	73,582
Unclassified	111,132	111,350	111,568	111,787	112,006	112,231	109,561	109,426	115,250	115,365	115,032
All minor rural roads	209,123	209,429	209,731	210,037	210,343	210,656	207,565	207,646	213,371	213,641	213,299
Minor urban roads: [5]											
B roads	5,622	5,626	5,630	5,633	5,638	5,641	5,538	5,550	5,445	5,470	5,476
C roads	10,986	11,009	11,031	11,054	11,076	11,098	10,859	10,878	10,921	10,942	10,992
Unclassified	113,093	113,432	113,772	114,114	114,456	114,816	113,520	113,757	114,355	114,524	114,450
All minor urban roads	129,702	130,068	130,432	130,802	131,169	131,556	129,917	130,186	130,721	130,936	130,918
All major roads	49,816	50,018	50,074	50,130	50,152	50,130	50,192	50,176	50,310	50,302	50,250
All minor roads: [5]	338,825	339,496	340,163	340,838	341,512	342,212	337,482	337,832	344,092	344,577	344,217
All roads	388,641	389,515	390,237	390,969	391,663	392,342	387,674	388,008	394,402	394,879	394,467

1 A number of minor revisions have been made to the lengths of major roads from 1993 onwards.
2 Rural roads: Major and minor roads, from 1993 onwards, are defined as being outside an urban area.
3 Figures for trunk and principal 'A' roads in England, from 2001 onwards, are affected by the detrunking programme.
4 Urban roads: Major and minor roads, from 1993 onwards, are defined as within an urban area with a population of 10,000 or more. These are based on the 2001 urban settlements. The definition for 'urban settlement' is in *Urban and rural area definitions: a user guide* which can be found on the Communities and Local Government web site at:
http://www.communities.gov.uk/publications/planningandbuilding/urbanrural
5 New information from 2004 and from 2006 has enabled better estimates of minor road lengths to be made - see notes and definitions

☎020-7944 3095

7.9 Public road length: by class of road and country: 2008

Kilometres

	England	Wales	Scotland	Great Britain
Motorways:				
Trunk	2,970	141	407	3,518
Principal	41	-	-	41
Dual Carriageway:				
Trunk urban [1,2]	196	19	50	265
Trunk rural [1,3]	2,421	329	456	3,205
Principal urban [1,2]	2,356	104	185	2,646
Principal rural [1,3]	1,631	97	92	1,820
Single Carriageway:				
Trunk urban [1,2]	88	29	38	156
Trunk rural [1,3]	1,575	1,170	2,263	5,008
Principal urban [1,2]	7,040	365	634	8,040
Principal rural [1,3]	16,948	2,051	6,553	25,552
B roads [4]	19,853	2,989	7,319	30,161
C roads [4]	64,358	9,797	10,419	84,574
Unclassified roads [4]	181,489	16,766	31,226	229,482
Total	300,967	33,858	59,642	394,467

1 Figures for trunk and principal 'A' roads in England, from 2001 onwards, are affected by the detrunking programme.

☎020-7944 3095

2 Urban roads: Major and minor roads, from 1993 onwards, are defined as within an urban area with a population of 10,000 or more. These are based on the 2001 urban settlements. The definition for 'urban settlement' is in *Urban and rural area definitions:* a user guide which can be found on the Communities and Local Government web site at:
http://www.communities.gov.uk/publications/planningandbuilding/urbanrural

3 Rural roads: Major and minor roads, from 1993 onwards, are defined as being outside an urban area.

4 New information from 2004 and from 2006 has enabled better estimates of minor road lengths to be made - see notes and definitions.

7.10 Vehicle speeds on non-built-up roads by road type and vehicle type: Great Britain: 2008

Per cent

(a) Motorways [1]	Motor-cycles [7]	Cars	Cars towing	Light Goods [4]	Buses/ Coaches	Heavy goods vehicles [5]				
						Rigid			Articulated	
						2 axles [6]	3 axles	4 axles	3 or 4 axles	5+ axles
Under 50 mph	5	5	16	5	7	8	13	15	10	10
50-59 mph	24	14	54	15	44	52	79	83	87	89
60-64 mph	9	13	18	13	26	11	6	1	1	1
65-69 mph	13	19	8	18	8	10	1	0	1	0
70-74 mph	15	20	3	19	7	9	0	0	1	0
75-79 mph	13	15	1	14	4	6	0	0	0	0
80-89 mph	15	12	0	13	3	4	0	0	0	0
90 mph and over	5	2	0	3	1	1	0	0	0	0
Speed limit (mph)	70	70	60	..	70	..	60	60	60	60
Percentage more than 10 mph over limit	20	15	4	..	4	..	1	1	1	0
Average speed (mph)	69	69	57	69	61	60	54	53	54	53
Number observed (thousands)	3,382	442,152	3,214	68,719	4,636	28,833	2,798	1,810	7,821	42,327
(b) Dual carriageways [2]										
Under 30 mph	0	0	1	0	0	0	0	0	0	0
30-39 mph	1	1	1	1	1	1	2	2	1	1
40-49 mph	5	4	16	4	8	9	18	19	16	13
50-59 mph	17	17	51	19	49	50	67	77	78	85
60-64 mph	10	16	17	16	24	13	12	1	3	1
65-69 mph	14	20	8	19	7	11	0	0	1	0
70-79 mph	30	31	4	30	8	13	0	1	1	0
80 mph and over	22	10	0	11	2	3	0	0	0	0
Speed limit (mph)	70	70	60	..	60	..	50	50	50	50
Percentage more than 10 mph over limit	22	10	5	..	10	..	12	2	5	2
Average speed (mph)	70	67	56	67	59	60	53	53	53	54
Number observed (thousands)	330	40,623	329	5,501	262	2,084	231	141	376	1,869
(c) Single carriageways [3]										
Under 20 mph	1	0	2	0	0	1	1	1	1	0
20-29 mph	3	2	7	2	3	3	5	6	6	2
30-39 mph	10	15	18	14	19	18	23	26	21	18
40-49 mph	29	41	49	40	50	45	50	46	48	49
50-59 mph	30	31	22	31	25	28	20	21	24	31
60-64 mph	9	6	2	6	2	3	0	0	0	1
65-69 mph	6	2	0	3	1	1	0	0	0	0
70 mph and over	11	2	0	2	0	1	0	0	0	0
Speed limit (mph)	60	60	50	..	50	..	40	40	40	40
Percentage more than 10 mph over limit	11	2	2	..	3	..	20	22	24	31
Average speed (mph)	53	48	43	49	46	47	43	44	44	46
Number observed (thousands)	529	45,823	499	5,851	396	2,205	295	201	365	1,707

1 Average vehicle speeds from 27 motorway sites.
2 Average vehicle speeds from 7 dual carriageway sites.
3 Average vehicle speeds from 26 single carriageway sites.
4 Goods vehicles 3.5 tonnes gross weight and under.
5 Goods vehicles over 3.5 tonnes gross weight.
6 Speed limit depends on loading which cannot be determined.
7 Motorcycles include mopeds and other types of two wheeled motor vehicles.

☎020-7944 6397

7.11: Vehicle speeds on built-up roads by speed limit and vehicle type: Great Britain: 2008

(a) 30 mph speed limit roads [1]   Per cent

| | Motor-cycles [3] | Cars | Cars towing | Light goods [4] | Buses/ Coaches | Heavy goods vehicles [5] | | | | |
| | | | | | | Rigid | | | Articulated | |
						2 axles	3 axles	4 axles	3 or 4 axles	5+ axles
Under 20 mph	8	5	5	6	11	8	7	4	6	3
20-29 mph	39	46	50	42	63	46	50	44	48	48
30-34 mph	27	31	33	31	20	29	33	39	33	37
35-39 mph	14	13	9	15	5	12	8	10	10	10
40-44 mph	6	4	2	5	1	4	1	2	2	2
45-49 mph	3	1	0	1	0	1	0	0	0	0
50 mph and over	2	0	0	1	0	1	0	0	0	0
Percent over 35 mph	26	18	11	21	7	17	10	13	13	12
Average speed (mph)	31	30	29	30	27	29	29	30	29	30
Number observed (thousands)	641	56,950	141	5,928	555	1,761	115	134	88	177

(b) 40 mph speed limit roads [2]   Per cent

| | Motor-cycles [3] | Cars | Cars towing | Light goods [4] | Buses/ Coaches | Heavy goods vehicles [5] | | | | |
| | | | | | | Rigid | | | Articulated | |
						2 axles	3 axles	4 axles	3 or 4 axles	5+ axles
Under 20 mph	3	2	4	3	3	4	4	3	5	2
20-29 mph	16	17	22	16	21	18	20	14	17	15
30-34 mph	19	26	27	24	30	26	24	20	25	24
35-39 mph	26	31	31	30	32	30	34	37	34	40
40-44 mph	19	16	12	16	10	14	15	19	14	15
45-49 mph	10	6	3	7	2	5	3	5	4	3
50-59 mph	6	2	1	3	1	2	1	2	1	1
60 mph and over	2	0	0	1	0	0	0	0	0	0
Percent over 45 mph	18	9	4	11	4	8	4	7	6	4
Average speed (mph)	38	36	34	36	34	35	34	36	35	35
Number observed (thousands)	734	48,546	195	5,642	528	1,781	205	170	167	444

1 Average vehicle speeds from 26 sites.
2 Average vehicle speeds from 10 sites.
3 Motorcycles includes mopeds and other types of two wheeled motor vehicles.
4 Goods vehicles 3.5 tonnes gross weight and under.
5 Goods vehicles over 3.5 tonnes gross weight.

☎020-7944 6397

**7.12 Journey time reliability measure[1] on the Strategic Road Network: England
Years ending July 2005 to July 2009**

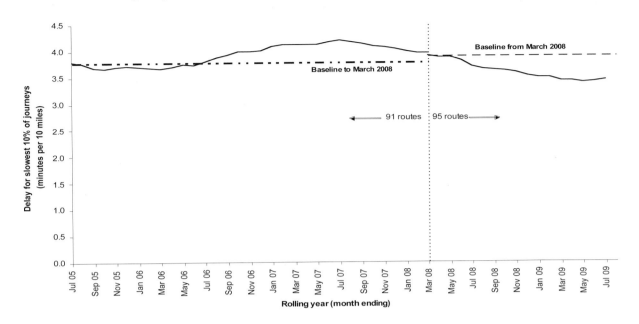

[1] Average vehicle delay for the slowest 10% of journeys.

☎020-7944 6392

7.13   Regional expenditure on roads: 2007/08

£ Million

	North East	Yorkshire and the Humber	North West	East Midlands	West Midlands	East of England	South East	London	South West	England
Motorways and trunk roads: [1]										
New construction/improvement and structural maintenance	53.2	98.5	228.3	197.2	196.3	212.6	306.0	15.6	236.8	1,544.6
Current maintenance, including routine and winter maintenance [2]	23.2	21.5	73.5	62.9	83.1	73.7	98.6	6.5	91.6	534.7
DBFO shadow tolls [3]	34.2	71.9	-	-	14.1	23.3	35.2	-	46.3	225.1
Local Roads: [4]										
New construction/improvement for highways, lighting, road safety and structural maintenance [5]	172.9	304.6	428.6	265.8	385.4	461.2	443.4	472.9	319.2	3,254.0
Revenue expenditure on bridge structural maintenance and strengthening	2.9	3.5	5.7	2.4	6.9	4.4	8.7	12.4	5.7	52.7
Routine and winter maintenance	38.1	101.1	139.5	89.5	105.2	108.4	168.4	265.2	106.3	1,121.6
Revenue expenditure on road safety	9.5	12.9	23.1	21.5	45.1	38.1	41.5	287.7	19.8	499.2
Revenue expenditure on public lighting	39.0	49.2	72.7	33.6	44.2	40.8	54.8	60.0	38.6	433.0
All road expenditure	373.2	663.2	971.4	672.9	880.5	962.5	1,156.6	1,120.4	864.3	7,664.9

1 Figures are now collected on a resource accounting basis and cannot be compared with data prior to 2001/02.
   Until 2001/02, associated costs of investment (including depreciation and capital costs) were not included within
   these figures. Apportionment between the Government Office Regions involves an estimation process.
2 Until 2001/02 this table showed figures for 'routine and winter maintenance and public lighting'
   Highways Agency is no longer able to separately identify this expenditure and this now falls within the wider category
   'Current maintenance including routine & winter maintenance
3 Payments to contractors under Design, Build, Finance & Operate (DBFO) schemes.
4 Local authority expenditure excludes car parks.
5 Includes expenditure on 'patching'.

☎020-7944 6142

Sources - Highways Agency Financial Accounts and local authority returns to CLG

7.14 Road construction tender price index[1]: 1998-2008

1995=100

Year	1998	1999	2000	2001	2002	2003	2004	2005	2006	2007	2008
All roads	99	100	114	117	121	121	122	135	150	153	145 [P]

1 This table has been revised so that the index is 1995 = 100

☎020-7944 6142
The figures in this table are outside
the scope of National Statistics

7.15 Road taxation revenue in 2007/08

	Road taxes (£million)	
(a) Vehicle Excise Duty classified by vehicle taxation group	Number of vehicles (thousand)	Vehicle excise duty
Private and light goods	30,327	5,080
Motorcycles, scooters and mopeds	1,133	54
Buses and coaches	110	31
Goods	445	296
Other	2,142	57
All vehicles	34,158	5,518

(b) Fuel tax classified by propulsion type	Petrol	Diesel	Total[1]
	11,736	12,650	24,905

1 Total fuel tax by propulsion includes oil and gas.

☎020-7944 3077
The road tax figures in this table are outside the scope of National Statistics
Source - HMRC and DVLA

7.16 New road construction and improvement: motorways and all purpose trunk roads: England: 1998/99-2008/09

(a) Starts	1998/99 [1]	1999/00	2000/01	2001/02	2002/03	2003/04	2004/05	2005/06	2006/07	2007/08	2008/09
Route kilometres	10	20	23	5	21	51	30	69	65	59	35 [P]
Lane kilometres	65	126	95	18	65	195	82	153	178	104	97 [P]
(b) Completions											
Route kilometres	96	40	38	0 [2]	56	113	49	37	50	42	84 [P]
Lane kilometres	559	160	197	0 [2]	191	446	172	108	110	109	127 [P]

1 Starts and completions for 1996/97 onwards include DBFO schemes.
2 See comments on Table 7.16 in the Notes and Definitions of Section 7.

☎020-7944 6142
The figures in this table are outside the scope of National Statistics
Source - Highways Agency

8 Transport Accidents and Casualties:

Notes and Definitions

Reported road accidents and casualties: 8.1-8.5

The statistics in these tables refer to personal injury accidents occurring on the public highway (including footways) in which at least one road vehicle or a vehicle in collision with a pedestrian is involved and which become known to the police within 30 days of its occurrence. The vehicle need not be moving and accidents involving stationary vehicles and pedestrians or users are included. One accident may give rise to several casualties. "Damage only" accidents are not included in this publication. Further information about reported road casualty statistics can be found at:

http://www.dft.gov.uk/pgr/statistics/ datatablespublications/accidents/

Very few, if any, fatal accidents do not become known to the police. However, research conducted on behalf of the Department in the 1990s has shown that a significant proportion of non-fatal injury accidents are not reported to the police. In addition some casualties reported to the police are not recorded and the severity of injury tends to be underestimated. The most recent work on levels of reporting was published by the Department in Article 5 of Reported Road Casualties Great Britain: 2008 Annual Report, which can be found at:

http://www.dft.gov.uk/pgr/statistics/ datatablespublications/accidents/casualtiesgbar/ rrcgb2008

Definitions of terms used in the tables:

Accident: Involves personal injury occurring on the public highway (including footways) in which at least one road vehicle or a vehicle in collision with a pedestrian is involved and which becomes known to the police within 30 days of its occurrence. The vehicle need not be moving and accidents involving stationary vehicles and pedestrians or users are included. One accident may give rise to several casualties. "Damage only" accidents are not included in this publication.

Adults: Persons aged 16 years and over (except where otherwise stated).

Cars: Includes taxis, estate cars, three and four wheel cars and minibuses except where otherwise stated. Also includes motor caravans prior to 1999.

Bus or coach: Vehicles equipped to carry 17 or more passengers regardless of use.

Casualty: A person killed or injured in an accident. Casualties are sub-divided into killed, seriously injured and slightly injured.

Children: Persons under 16 years of age (except where otherwise stated).

Drivers: Persons in control of vehicles other than pedal cycles, motorcycles and ridden animals (see riders). Other occupants of vehicles are passengers.

Failed breath test: Drivers or riders tested with a positive result, or who failed or refused to provide a specimen of breath.

Fatal accident: An accident in which at least one person is killed.

Goods vehicles: These are divided into two groups according to vehicle weight (see below). They include tankers, tractor units travelling without their semi-trailers, trailers, articulated vehicles and pick-up trucks.

Heavy goods vehicles (HGV): Goods vehicles over 3.5 tonnes maximum permissible gross vehicle weight (gvw).

Light goods vehicles (LGV): Goods vehicles, mainly vans (including car derived vans), not over 3.5 tonnes maximum permissible gross vehicle weight (gvw).

Killed: Human casualties who sustained injuries which caused death less than 30 days(before 1954, about two months) after the accident. Confirmed suicides are excluded.

Motorcycles: Mopeds, motor scooters and motor cycles (including motor cycle combinations).

Motorways: "M" roads and "A"(M) roads.

Other roads: All "B", "C" class and unclassified roads, unless otherwise noted.

Other vehicles: Other motor vehicles include ambulances, fire engines, trams, refuse vehicles, road rollers, agricultural vehicles, excavators, mobile cranes, electric scooters and motorised wheelchairs etc. Other non motor vehicles include those drawn by animal, ridden horses, invalid carriages without a motor, street barrows etc.

Passengers: Occupants of vehicles, other than the person in control (the driver or rider). Includes pillion passengers.

Pedal cycles: Includes tandems, tricycles and toy cycles ridden on the carriageway.

Pedal cyclists: Riders of pedal cycles, including any passengers. From 1983 the definition includes a small number of cycles and tricycles with battery assistance with a maximum speed of 15 mph..

Pedestrians: Includes children riding toy cycles on the footway, persons pushing bicycles, pushing or pulling other vehicles or operating pedestrian controlled vehicles, those leading or herding animals, occupants of prams or wheelchairs, and people who alight safely from vehicles and are subsequently injured.

Riders: Persons in control of pedal cycles, motorcycles or ridden animals. Other occupants of these vehicles are passengers.

Rural roads: Major roads and minor roads outside urban areas and having a population of less than 10 thousand.

Severity: Of an accident: the severity of the most severely injured casualty (fatal, serious or slight). Of a casualty: killed, seriously injured or slightly injured.

Serious accident: One in which at least one person is seriously injured but no person (other than a confirmed suicide) is killed.

Serious injury: an injury for which a person is detained in hospital as an "in patient", or any of the following injuries whether or not they are detained in hospital: fractures, concussion, internal injuries, crushings, burns (excluding friction burns), severe cuts, severe general shock requiring medical treatment and injuries causing death 30 or more days after the accident. An injured casualty is recorded as seriously or slightly injured by the police on the basis of information available within a short time of the accident. This generally will not reflect the results of a medical examination, but may be influenced according to whether the casualty is hospitalised or not.

Slight accident: One in which at least one person is slightly injured but no person is killed or seriously injured.

Slight injury: An injury of a minor character such as a sprain (including neck whiplash injury), bruise or cut which are not judged to be severe, or slight shock requiring roadside attention. This definition includes injuries not requiring medical treatment.

Speed limits: Permanent speed limits applicable to the roadway.

Urban roads: Major and minor roads within an urban area with a population of 10 thousand or more. The definition is based on the 1991 Office of the Deputy Prime Minister definition of urban settlements. The urban areas used for these tables are based on 2001 census data.

Users of a vehicle: All occupants, i.e. driver (or rider) and passengers, including persons injured while boarding or alighting from the vehicle.

Motoring offences: 8.6 – 8.7

Breath tests: Section 25 and Schedule 8 of the Transport Act 1981 amended the drinking and driving provisions of the Road Traffic Act 1972. These sections of the Act were renumbered (but otherwise unchanged) in the Road Traffic Act 1988. The police can require a person to take a screening breath test if they have reasonable cause to suspect that the person has been driving or attempting to drive or had been in charge of a vehicle with alcohol in his or her body, or that he or she has committed a moving traffic offence, or that he or she has been involved in an accident. A person failing to provide a breath test without reasonable excuse is guilty of an offence.

For the purposes of evidence in court, breath analysis was introduced in May 1983. The prescribed alcohol limit is 80 milligrams (mg) of alcohol in 100 millilitres (ml) of blood or 107mg per 100ml urine. The equivalent breath alcohol limit is expressed as 35 micrograms of alcohol per 100ml breath. In April 1996 the Association of Chief Police Officers recommended that drivers in all injury accidents should be breath tested.

An evidential breath test is required to be taken at a police station after a positive screening test, or where a screening test was refused or could not be provided. It may also be required after arrest for impairment or in certain other cases, e.g. where a person arrested for theft of a motor vehicle is suspected of having consumed alcohol.

A suspect will normally be asked to provide two specimens of breath to establish the amount of alcohol in his or her body. The lower result is taken as evidence of the person's breath alcohol concentration. Where the lower result is between 36 and 50 micrograms the suspect may request a blood or urine test. In certain limited circumstances a suspect can be required to provide a specimen of blood or urine instead of breath.

Findings of guilt at all courts: Includes all motoring offences which have resulted in a finding of guilt either after a summary trial at Magistrates' Court or else at the Crown Court. A person appearing in court can be dealt with for more than one offence at that appearance, and in this table the number of offences is counted, not the number of persons appearing at court.

Fixed penalty notices: A large number of motoring offences are dealt with by fixed penalty notices. Under the extended fixed penalty system introduced by the Transport Act 1982, now incorporated in Part III of the Road Traffic Offenders Act 1988, the police can issue fixed penalty notices for a wide range of offences. The court can automatically register an unpaid notice as a fine without any court appearance.

Offences for which a fixed penalty notice cannot be given include causing death or bodily harm, dangerous driving, driving after consuming alcohol or taking drugs, careless driving, accident offences, unauthorised taking or theft of a motor vehicle, certain driving licence and record keeping offences, and vehicle test offences. When court proceedings are instituted following non-payment of a fixed penalty, the offence may be included twice in the table.

Written warnings: These include cautions given in lieu of prosecutions for offences where there would have been enough evidence to support a prosecution. Informal warnings and advice, whether oral or written, are not included.

Obstruction, waiting and parking offences are dealt with both by fixed penalty notices and penalty charge notices. Penalty Charge Notices are issued by Local Authorities under Civil Parking Enforcement powers. The fall in fixed penalty notices issued by the police can be attributed mainly to more local authorities issuing Penalty Charge Notices. Data collated by the Department for Transport estimated that in 2007 around 8.2 million Penalty Charge Notices were issued by Local Authorities in England and Wales, up from 8.0 million in 2006. Further information on Penalty Charge Notices can be found at:

http://www.dft.gov.uk/epdf/162469/221412/2215 35/224295/282930/451959/busoctdec08.pdf

Motor insurance (formerly 8.8)

The data previously published in Table 8.8 are no longer routinely available. For further information see the Association of British Insurers web site at: www.abi.org.uk or Standard and Poor's SynThesys Non-Life database of returns

Railway accidents: 8.8- 8.10

These tables give the number of train accidents and casualties on all railway undertakings in Great Britain. Railway undertakings are required to report accidents, failures and dangerous occurrences to the Secretary of State for Transport under the regulatory safety legislation. As well as Network Rail and London Transport railways, the tables also cover accidents on Eurotunnel, tram systems and minor railways.

Incident reports are recorded within a database called SIGNAL. From 2008, safety data have been collated directly from the SIGNAL database. Previously, data were exported from SIGNAL and manually manipulated to produce tabular information. This revised approach allows data collation to be more up-to-date as the data can be refreshed in real-time, rather than a one-off manual export of data. Furthermore, this approach reduces the potential for human error by automating the process. The approach has been extended to update 2007 data. Previously this year would have been copied directly from the previous year's reports. Data prior to 2007 remain as previously published, but may be updated after further investigation.

The 2008 data were extracted in June 2009. They should be treated as provisional since they will be subject to change next year as more information becomes available. Some of the reasons for potential changes are listed below:

- Incident reports may be received after publication; these reports will be entered into SIGNAL and updated in the publication the following year;

- All non-natural cause fatalities which occur within the railway network are required to be reported. However, possible suicides in England and Wales cannot be confirmed until the receipt of a coroner's verdict, which can take up to 12 months. This can result in fatalities changing category;

- Changes to existing reports following updated information will result in SIGNAL being updated. For example, if an incident previously recorded as an injury subsequently becomes a death within three months of the original accident, this will be updated within the tables.

Casualty figures in Table 8.8 are shown in the categories below. Casualty figures are subdivided into casualties resulting from:

- Train accidents;

- Accidents through movement of railway vehicles (but excluding train accidents), e.g. boarding or alighting from trains, opening or closing carriage doors at stations;

- Accidents on railway premises not connected with movement of railway vehicles, e.g. falling on steps at stations, slipping on platforms;

- Injuries and fatalities of trespassers and suicides on railway land.

Table 8.9 is based on passenger casualties owing to train accidents and movement accidents. This is the basis for comparisons with other modes of transport. Under the new Accidents Reporting Regulations (RIDDOR 95) brought into force on 1 April 1996, there is no distinction between major and minor injury to members of the public. All injuries to members of the public are now shown as either minor injuries or killed. The reporting trigger for minor injuries is that the person is taken to hospital for treatment.

Table 8.10 shows the total number of train accidents (collisions, derailments, etc.) reported irrespective of whether personal injury was involved. The figures include accidents on non-passenger lines and lines closed to normal traffic while engineering work took place.

Due to European regulations on the reporting of rail transport statistics, the rail accidents data now covers calendar years, rather than financial years. As such, there is overlap between the 2002/03 data and the 2003 data, with accidents from 1 January 2003 to 31 March 2003 reported in both. However, each represents 12 full months.

8.1 Reported road accidents and casualties: 1950-2008

For greater detail of the years 1997-2008 see Table 8.2 or 8.3

		Casualties										
		Killed (number)					Injured (thousands)				Casualty rate per 100 million vehicle kilometres	All traffic (billion vehicle km)
Year	Accidents (thousands)	Pedest-rians	Pedal cyclists	Motor cyclists	All other road users	All	Serious	Slight	All	All casualties (thousands)		
1950	167	2,251	805	1,129	827	5,012	49	148	196	201	276	73
1951	178	2,398	800	1,175	877	5,250	52	159	211	216	272	80
1952	172	2,063	743	1,142	758	4,706	50	153	203	208	248	84
1953	186	2,233	720	1,237	900	5,090	57	165	222	227	265	86
1954	196	2,226	696	1,148	940	5,010	57	176	233	238	269	89
1955	217	2,287	708	1,362	1,169	5,526	62	200	262	268	281	95
1983	243	1,914	323	963	2,245	5,445	71	233	303	309	105	294
1984	253	1,868	345	967	2,419	5,599	73	246	319	324	105	309
1985	246	1,789	286	796	2,294	5,165	71	241	312	318	101	316
1986	248	1,841	271	762	2,511	5,385	69	247	316	321	97	331
1987	239	1,703	280	723	2,419	5,125	64	242	306	311	87	356
1988	247	1,753	227	670	2,402	5,052	63	254	317	322	85	381
1989	261	1,706	294	683	2,690	5,373	63	273	336	342	83	412
1990	258	1,694	256	659	2,608	5,217	60	275	336	341	82	416
1991	236	1,496	242	548	2,282	4,568	52	255	307	311	75	417
1992	233	1,347	204	469	2,209	4,229	49	257	307	311	75	417
1993 [1]	229	1,241	186	427	1,960	3,814	45	257	302	306	74	416
1994	234	1,124	172	444	1,910	3,650	47	265	312	315	74	426
1995	231	1,038	213	445	1,925	3,621	46	262	307	311	72	434
1996	236	997	203	440	1,958	3,598	44	272	317	321	72	445
1997	240	973	183	509	1,934	3,599	43	281	324	328	72	454
1998	239	906	158	498	1,859	3,421	41	281	322	325	70	462
1999	235	870	172	547	1,834	3,423	39	278	317	320	68	471
2000	234	857	127	605	1,820	3,409	38	279	317	320	68	471
2001	229	826	138	583	1,903	3,450	37	273	310	313	65	479
2002	222	775	130	609	1,917	3,431	36	263	299	303	62	491
2003	214	774	114	693	1,927	3,508	34	253	287	291	59	495
2004	207	671	134	585	1,831	3,221	31	246	278	281	56	503
2005	199	671	148	569	1,813	3,201	29	239	268	271	54	504
2006	189	675	146	599	1,752	3,172	29	227	255	258	50	512
2007	182	646	136	588	1,576	2,946	28	217	245	248	48	517
2008	171	572	115	493	1,358	2,538	26	202	228	231	45	514

1 See Notes and Definitions in Section 7 for details of discontinuity in road traffic figures from 1993 onwards. From 1993 the data has been estimated using the expansion factors and the new methodology for measuring road lengths, they are not directly comparable with the figures for 1992 and earlier.

☎020-7944 6595

8.2 Reported road accident casualties by road user type and severity: 1998-2008

											Number
	1998	1999	2000	2001	2002	2003	2004	2005	2006	2007	2008
Child pedestrians: [1]											
Killed	103	107	107	107	79	74	77	63	71	57	57
KSI[2]	3,737	3,457	3,226	3,144	2,828	2,381	2,339	2,134	2,025	1,899	1,784
All severities	17,971	16,876	16,184	15,819	14,231	12,544	12,234	11,250	10,131	9,527	8,648
Adult pedestrians: [3]											
Killed	803	760	750	712	688	695	589	604	602	585	515
KSI	6,592	6,221	6,112	5,745	5,644	5,422	5,005	4,847	4,894	4,900	4,724
All severities	25,827	24,806	24,481	23,463	23,258	22,531	21,404	20,725	19,774	19,676	19,013
Child pedal cyclists: [1]											
Killed	32	36	27	25	22	18	25	20	31	13	12
KSI	915	950	758	674	594	595	577	527	503	522	417
All severities	6,930	7,290	6,260	5,451	4,809	4,769	4,682	4,286	3,765	3,633	3,306
Adult pedal cyclists: [3]											
Killed	126	135	98	111	107	95	109	127	115	122	103
KSI	2,345	2,172	1,954	1,951	1,801	1,776	1,697	1,787	1,898	1,994	2,101
All severities	15,326	14,834	13,630	12,974	11,712	11,643	11,366	11,637	11,911	12,050	12,546
Motorcyclists[4] and passengers:											
Killed	498	547	605	583	609	693	585	569	599	588	493
KSI	6,442	6,908	7,374	7,305	7,500	7,652	6,648	6,508	6,484	6,737	6,049
All severities	24,610	26,192	28,212	28,810	28,353	28,411	25,641	24,824	23,326	23,459	21,550
Car drivers and passengers:											
Killed	1,696	1,687	1,665	1,749	1,747	1,769	1,671	1,675	1,612	1,432	1,257
KSI	21,676	20,368	19,719	19,424	18,728	17,291	16,144	14,617	14,254	12,967	11,968
All severities	210,474	205,735	206,799	202,802	197,425	188,342	183,858	178,302	171,000	161,433	149,188
Bus/coach drivers and passengers:											
Killed	18	11	15	14	19	11	20	9	19	12	6
KSI	631	611	578	562	551	500	488	363	426	455	432
All severities	9,839	10,252	10,088	9,884	9,005	9,068	8,820	7,920	7,253	7,079	6,929
LGV drivers and passengers:											
Killed	67	65	66	64	70	72	62	54	52	58	43
KSI	949	867	813	811	780	765	631	587	564	494	445
All severities	7,672	7,124	7,007	7,304	7,007	6,897	6,166	6,048	5,914	5,340	4,913
HGV drivers and passengers:											
Killed	60	52	55	54	63	44	47	55	39	52	23
KSI	560	540	571	500	524	429	406	395	383	363	240
All severities	3,444	3,484	3,597	3,388	3,178	3,061	2,883	2,843	2,530	2,476	1,930
All road users: [5]											
Killed	3,421	3,423	3,409	3,450	3,431	3,508	3,221	3,201	3,172	2,946	2,538
KSI	44,255	42,545	41,564	40,560	39,407	37,215	34,351	32,155	31,845	30,720	28,572
All severities	325,212	320,310	320,283	313,309	302,605	290,607	280,840	271,017	258,404	247,780	230,905

1 Casualties aged 0 -15.
2 Killed and seriously injured.
3 Casualties aged 16 and over.
4 Includes mopeds and scooters.
5 Includes other motor or non-motor vehicle users, and unknown road user type and casualty age.

☎020-7944 6595

8.3 Reported road accidents and accident rates: by road class and severity: 1998-2008

Number/rate per 100 million vehicle kilometres

	1998	1999	2000	2001	2002	2003	2004	2005	2006	2007	2008
Motorways											
Fatal	157	176	161	180	175	184	149	176	164	154	136
Fatal and serious	1,148	1,218	1,190	1,235	1,162	1,166	1,047	1,007	953	989	848
All severities	8,861	9,118	9,394	9,128	8,942	8,746	9,072	8,619	8,379	7,976	7,249
Rate [1]	*10*	*10*	*11*	*10*	*10*	*9*	*9*	*9*	*8*	*8*	*7*
Urban roads [2]											
A roads											
Fatal	588	572	599	610	622	624	527	489	526	469	420
Fatal and serious	9,724	9,001	9,099	8,737	8,405	7,842	7,116	6,440	6,615	6,430	6,149
All severities	69,793	67,999	69,036	67,216	64,013	61,525	57,708	53,780	50,483	48,661	47,207
Rate [1]	*84*	*81*	*83*	*81*	*76*	*74*	*68*	*64*	*60*	*59*	*58*
Other roads											
Fatal	555	573	543	558	488	520	504	510	500	452	412
Fatal and serious	11,696	11,085	10,679	10,499	10,162	9,551	8,871	8,699	8,682	8,404	7,952
All severities	85,507	84,313	83,574	81,348	78,584	75,143	72,639	71,570	68,173	64,731	60,354
Rate [1]	*80*	*77*	*76*	*73*	*68*	*64*	*62*	*61*	*58*	*54*	*52*
Rural roads [2]											
A roads											
Fatal	1,197	1,184	1,169	1,195	1,196	1,222	1,140	1,123	1,127	1,018	858
Fatal and serious	8,435	8,250	7,993	7,941	7,731	7,469	6,932	6,616	6,381	6,119	5,604
All severities	39,788	38,769	37,980	37,827	38,126	36,797	36,656	34,780	33,555	32,649	29,627
Rate [1]	*32*	*30*	*30*	*29*	*29*	*27*	*26*	*25*	*24*	*23*	*21*
Other roads [3]											
Fatal	633	593	613	600	639	695	656	615	609	621	515
Fatal and serious	6,680	6,581	6,433	6,165	6,127	6,096	5,745	5,167	5,239	5,093	4,907
All severities	34,451	33,320	32,488	32,290	31,544	31,559	31,175	29,899	28,546	28,085	26,144
Rate [1]	*58*	*56*	*54*	*54*	*50*	*50*	*48*	*46*	*42*	*40*	*36*
All roads [4]											
Fatal	3,137	3,138	3,108	3,176	3,124	3,247	2,978	2,913	2,926	2,714	2,341
Fatal and serious	37,770	36,405	35,607	34,764	33,645	32,160	29,726	27,942	27,872	27,036	25,462
All severities	238,923	235,048	233,729	229,014	221,751	214,030	207,410	198,735	189,161	182,115	170,591
Rate [1]	*52*	*50*	*50*	*48*	*45*	*43*	*41*	*39*	*37*	*35*	*33*
All A roads											
Fatal	1,788	1,782	1,782	1,826	1,821	1,847	1,669	1,612	1,653	1,487	1,278
Fatal and serious	18,201	17,388	17,204	16,761	16,168	15,328	14,055	13,063	12,997	12,550	11,755
All severities	109,807	107,474	107,544	105,548	102,378	98,436	94,429	88,599	84,050	81,316	76,839
Rate [1]	*52*	*50*	*51*	*49*	*47*	*44*	*42*	*40*	*37*	*36*	*34*
Other non-motorway roads											
Fatal	1,192	1,180	1,165	1,170	1,128	1,216	1,160	1,125	1,109	1,073	927
Fatal and serious	18,421	17,799	17,213	16,768	16,315	15,666	14,624	13,872	13,922	13,497	12,859
All severities	120,255	118,456	116,791	114,338	110,431	106,848	103,909	101,517	96,732	92,823	86,503
Rate [1]	*72*	*70*	*69*	*66*	*62*	*59*	*57*	*55*	*52*	*49*	*46*

1 Figures have been revised from those published in previous years, see Notes and Definitions in Section 7 for details.
2 The definition of urban and rural roads is different to that of built-up and non built-up shown in editions prior to 2003.
3 Urban and Rural accident figures for 1998-2007 have been revised.
4 Includes B, C and unclassified roads.
5 Includes cases where road class was not reported.

☎020-7944 6595

8.4 Reported road casualties by hour of day: 2008

(a) Weekdays

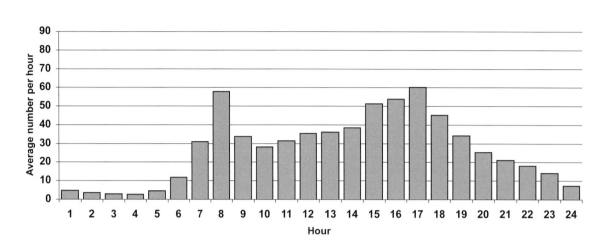

(b) Weekends

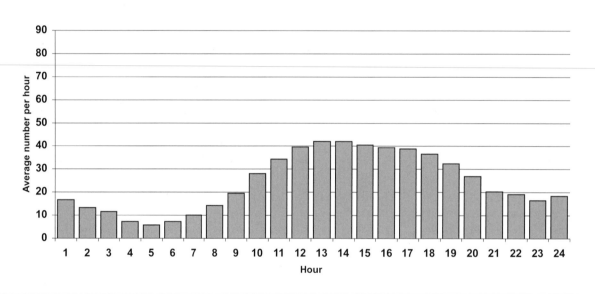

Note: The hours are defined as being the beginning of an hour,
i.e 1 being between 1 am and 2 am, and 12 being between midday and 1 pm, etc.

☎020-7944 6595

8.5 Reported road accidents: breath tests performed on car drivers and motorcycle riders involved in injury accidents: Great Britain: 1997-2008

Number/*percentage*

	1997	1998	1999	2000	2001	2002	2003	2004	2005	2006	2007	2008
Car drivers involved	338,924	337,794	329,866	329,846	321,900	314,568	299,333	291,842	281,810	267,991	255,891	236,923
Breath tested Number	157,373	173,610	175,916	172,840	163,540	159,782	151,442	149,430	149,687	146,564	146,024	132,708
Percentage of drivers involved	*46*	*51*	*53*	*52*	*51*	*51*	*51*	*51*	*53*	*55*	*57*	*56*
Failed breath test [1] Number	7,087	6,690	6,669	7,124	7,264	7,285	7,289	6,655	6,397	5,873	5,644	4,899
Percentage of drivers tested	*5*	*4*	*4*	*4*	*4*	*5*	*5*	*4*	*4*	*4*	*4*	*4*
Motorcycle riders involved	25,211	25,514	27,122	29,236	30,084	29,503	29,523	26,857	25,870	24,323	24,381	22,427
Breath tested Number	9,926	11,416	12,970	13,945	13,725	12,992	13,178	12,422	12,221	11,884	12,648	11,569
Percentage of riders involved	*39*	*45*	*48*	*48*	*46*	*44*	*45*	*46*	*47*	*49*	*52*	*52*
Failed breath test [1] Number	428	426	443	442	446	441	510	423	391	374	337	314
Percentage of riders tested	*4*	*4*	*3*	*3*	*3*	*3*	*4*	*3*	*3*	*3*	*3*	*3*

1 Failed or refused to provide a specimen of breath.

☎020-7944 6595

8.6 Motor vehicle offences: drinking and driving: summary of breath tests and blood or urine tests: England and Wales: 1998-2007

Number/percentage

	1998	1999	2000	2001	2002	2003	2004	2005	2006	2007
Screening breath test: number required (inc. refused/not able)	815,500	764,500	714,800	623,900	570,200	534,300	578,000	607,400	601,600	599,800
Of which: positive/refused[1]	102,300	94,100	94,600	99,500	103,500	106,300	103,000	104,300	105,700	97,600
Result (per cent)										
Positive	*13*	*12*	*13*	*16*	*18*	*20*	*18*	*17*	*18*	*16*
Negative	*87*	*88*	*87*	*84*	*82*	*80*	*82*	*83*	*82*	*84*
Refused/not able	..	..	..	..	..	..	..	..	..	..
Total	*100*	*100*	*100*	*100*	*100*	*100*	*100*	*100*	*100*	*100*

1 Includes persons unable to provide a breath test specimen.
2 Figures updated since publication of the TSGB 2007 edition.
3 Figures revised since publication of the 2004 bulletin.

☎020 7035 0299
Source - Home Office[4]

8.7 Motor vehicle offences: findings of guilt at all courts, fixed penalty notices and written warnings: by type of offence: England and Wales: 1998-2007

										Thousands of offences
	1998	1999	2000	2001	2002	2003[1]	2004	2005	2006	2007
Offence type:										
Dangerous, careless or drunken driving etc	190	183	176	172	171	177	231	275	322	267
Accident offences	21	19	18	18	18	19	18	17	16	16
Speed limit offences	962	1,001	1,154	1,386	1,538	2,041	2,076	2,087	1,933	1,591
Unauthorised taking or theft of motor vehicle	37	36	32	32	32	30	27	25	23	23
Licence, insurance and record keeping offences	817	807	785	769	819	953	957	844	747	641
Vehicle test and condition offences	277	261	243	226	228	241	227	187	152	116
Neglect of traffic signs and directions and pedestrian rights	271	245	232	218	213	264	258	245	245	239
Other offences relating to motor vehicles (except obstruction, waiting and parking)	353	320	268	255	239	280	354	380	352	344
All offences (except obstruction, waiting and parking)	2,927	2,872	2,911	3,076	3,259	4,005	4,147	4,059	3,789	3,237
Obstruction, waiting and parking offences[2]	2,139	1,828	1,611	1,341	1,180	1,059	896	584	499	453
All offences	5,066	4,700	4,523	4,417	4,439	5,244	5,043	4,643	4,288	3,690

1 These figures for 2003 have been revised.

2 Excludes Penalty Charge Notices issued by Local Authorities under Civil Parking Enforcement powers - see Notes.

3 For details on vehicle offences dealt with by the courts see Ministry of Justice Statistical Bulletin, "Criminal Statistics England and Wales 2007" and associated Supplementary Tables - "Volume 6 Offences Related to Motor Vehicles". Copies of this report and other publications can be downloaded free from the Ministry of Justice website at http://www.justice.gov.uk/publications/criminalannual.htm

4 For details on fixed penalty notices and written warnings see Home Office Statistical Bulletin, "Police Powers and Procedures, England and Wales 2007/08". Copies of this report and other publications can be downloaded free from the Home Office website at http://www.homeoffice.gov.uk/rds/police-powers.html

☎020 3334 4969

Source - Ministry of Justice[3]

☎020 7035 0299

Source - Home Office[4]

8.8 Railway accidents: casualties: by type of accident: 1998/99-2008

Number

		1998/99	1999/00	2000/01	2001/02	2002/03	2003 [1]	2004	2005	2006	2007	2008 [P]
Train accidents:												
Killed:	Passengers	0	29	10	0	6	0	5	0	0	1	0
	Railway staff	0	2	4	0	1	1	2	1	0	0	0
	Others	3	2	3	5	3	10	5	6	1	4	4
	Total	3	33	17	5	10	11	12	7	1	5	4
Major injuries:	Passengers	.	.	.	.	.	.	.	.	.	.	.
	Railway staff	2	3	6	6	0	0	5	0	2	3	2
	Others	.	.	.	.	.	.	.	.	.	.	.
	Total	2	3	6	6	0	0	5	0	2	3	2
Minor injuries:	Passengers	.	.	.	.	.	.	.	.	.	.	.
	Railway staff	29	20	36	17	23	12	21	20	17	9 [R]	8
	Others	.	.	.	.	.	.	.	.	.	.	.
	Total	29	20	36	17	23	12	21	20	17	9 [R]	8
Public injuries:	Passengers	40	290	178	21	128	53	76	22	20	95 [R]	10
	Railway staff	.	.	.	.	.	.	.	.	.	.	.
	Others	13	19	15	8	15	19	9	9	4	3 [R]	7
	Total	53	309	193	29	143	72	85	31	24	98 [R]	17
Accidents through movement of railway vehicles:												
Killed:	Passengers	17	14	7	10	14	8	3	5	4	6 [R]	2
	Railway staff	1	2	3	4	2	1	7	5	2	2	1
	Others	11	11	7	10	16	8	7	10	6	14 [R]	16
	Total	29	27	17	24	32	17	17	20	12	22 [R]	19
Major injuries:	Passengers	.	.	.	.	.	.	.	.	.	.	.
	Railway staff	35	37	25	26	26	35	48	28	25	36 [R]	43
	Others	.	.	.	.	.	.	.	.	.	.	.
	Total	35	37	25	26	26	35	48	28	25	36 [R]	43
Minor injuries:	Passengers	.	.	.	.	.	.	.	.	.	.	.
	Railway staff	246	289	296	293	313	299	328	311	333	274 [R]	313
	Others	.	.	.	.	.	.	.	.	.	[R]	.
	Total	246	289	296	293	313	299	328	311	333	274 [R]	313
Public injuries:	Passengers	668	569	610	573	556	584	547	580	525	546 [R]	485
	Railway staff	.	.	.	.	.	.	.	.	.	.	.
	Others	13	13	18	17	13	16	16	15	12	5 [R]	8
	Total	681	582	628	590	569	600	563	595	537	551 [R]	493
Accidents on railway premises:												
Killed:	Passengers	3	4	3	3	3	5	5	5	4	0	1
	Railway staff	3	1	1	1	4	3	1	0	2	0	2
	Others	1	0	1	2	1	1	0	1	2	0	2
	Total	7	5	5	6	8	9	6	6	8	0	5
Major injuries:	Passengers	.	.	.	.	.	.	.	.	.	.	.
	Railway staff	339	300	269	319	323	303	349	304	182	196 [R]	178
	Others	.	.	.	.	.	.	.	.	.	.	.
	Total	339	300	269	319	323	303	349	304	182	196 [R]	178
Minor injuries:	Passengers	.	.	.	.	.	.	.	.	.	.	.
	Railway staff	1,795	1,756	1,803	1,713	1,744	1,699	1,549	1,616	1,188	975 [R]	764
	Others	.	.	.	.	.	.	.	.	.	.	.
	Total	1,795	1,756	1,803	1,713	1,744	1,699	1,549	1,616	1,188	975 [R]	764
Public injuries:	Passengers	1,963	1,883	2,007	1,807	1,861	1,913	2,004	2,198	1,994	2,254 [R]	1,994
	Railway staff	.	.	.	.	.	.	.	.	.	.	.
	Others	75	53	51	67	55	60	44	36	57	34 [R]	43
	Total	2,038	1,936	2,058	1,874	1,916	1,973	2,048	2,234	2,051	2,288 [R]	2,037

8.8 (continued) Railway accidents: casualties: by type of accident: 1998/99-2008

Number

		1998/99	1999/00	2000/01	2001/02	2002/03	2003 [1]	2004	2005	2006	2007	2008 [P]
Overall totals:												
Killed:	Passengers	20	47	20	10	23	13	13	10	8	7 R	3
	Railway staff	4	5	8	5	7	5	10	6	4	2	3
	Others	15	13	11	17	20	19	12	17	9	18 R	22
	Total	39	65	39	32	50	37	35	33	21	27 R	28
Major injuries:	Passengers	.	.	.	.	.	.	.	.	.	.	.
	Railway staff	376	340	300	351	349	338	402	332	209	235 R	223
	Others	.	.	.	.	.	.	.	.	.	.	.
	Total	376	340	300	351	349	338	402	332	209	235 R	223
Minor injuries:	Passengers	.	.	.	.	.	.	.	.	.	.	.
	Railway staff	2,070	2,065	2,135	2,023	2,080	2,010	1,898	1,947	1,538	1,258 R	1,085
	Others	.	.	.	.	.	.	.	.	.	R	.
	Total	2,070	2,065	2,135	2,023	2,080	2,010	1,898	1,947	1,538	1,258 R	1,085
Public injuries:	Passengers	2,671	2,742	2,795	2,401	2,545	2,550	2,627	2,800	2,539	2,895 R	2,489
	Railway staff	.	.	.	.	.	.	.	.	.	.	.
	Others	101	85	84	92	83	95	69	60	73	42 R	58
	Total	2,772	2,827	2,879	2,493	2,628	2,645	2,696	2,860	2,612	2,937 R	2,547
Trespassers and suicides:												
Deaths		247	274	300	275	256	252	242	280	320 R	275 R	288
Injured		149	144	177	179	137	132	132	127	140	154 R	156

1 Prior to 2003 data covered financial years. See Notes and Definitions section at start of Chapter 8.

R There have been revisions to data since the last TSGB publication (see Notes and Definitions).

P 2008 figures should be treated as provisional since they will be subject to change next year as more information becomes available (see Notes and Definitions).

☎020 7944 8874

8.9 Railway movement accidents: passenger casualties and casualty rates: 1998/99-2008

Number/rate per billion passenger kilometres

	1998/99	1999/00	2000/01	2001/02	2002/03	2003 [2]	2004	2005	2006	2007	2008 [P]
Casualties: [1]											
Deaths	17	43	17	10	20	8	8	5	4	7 R	2
Public injuries	708	859	788	594	684	637	623	602	545	641 R	495
All casualties	725	902	806	604	704	645	631	607	549	648 R	497
Casualty rates:											
Deaths	0.4	0.9	0.4	0.2	0.4	0.2	0.2	0.1	0.1	0.1	0.0
Public injuries	16.2	18.6	16.9	12.5	14.3	12.9	12.4	11.6	9.9	10.9 R	8.1
All casualties	16.6	19.5	17.3	12.7	14.7	13.1	12.5	11.7	10.0	11.1 R	8.2

1 Passenger casualties involved in train accidents and accidents occurring through movement of railway vehicles.

2 Prior to 2003 data covered financial years. See Notes and Definitions section at start of Chapter 8. The casualty rates continue to be calculated using financial year rail passenger kilometre data because calendar year data is not available for all sources.

P 2008 figures should be treated as provisional since they will be subject to change next year as more information becomes available (see Notes and Definitions).

☎020-7944 8874

8.10   Railway accidents: train accidents: 1998/99-2008

Number

	1998/99	1999/00	2000/01	2001/02	2002/03	2003 [2]	2004	2005	2006	2007	2008 [P]
Collisions	121	94	106	101	69	61	60	27	20	26 [R]	36
Derailments	117	89	93	88	67	63	62	64	47 [R]	48 [R]	48
Running into level crossing gates and other obstructions	690	753	693	557	495	433	523	480	503	383 [R]	297
Fires	343	340	301	291	292	271	323	187	163	141	73
Damage to drivers' cab windscreens [1]	564	617	607	665	498	409	368	299	328	322 [R]	276
Miscellaneous	0	2	1	2	0	0	0	0	0 [R]	.	.
All accidents	1,835	1,895	1,801	1,704	1,421	1,237	1,336	1,057	1,061	920 [R]	730

1 Category now reportable under RIDDOR 95.
2 Prior to 2003 data covered financial years.
   See Notes and Definitions section at start of Chapter 8.
P 2008 figures should be treated as provisional since they will be
   subject to change next year as more information becomes available
   (see Notes and Definitions).

☎020-7944 8874
The figures in this table are outside
the scope of National Statistics
Source - ORR, previously HSE

9 Vehicles:

Notes and Definitions

.This section provides a range of data relating to vehicle registration and licensing, vehicle testing, driving license holding and car usage.

The following notes and definitions are relevant when considering the data presented within the section.

Vehicle registration and licensing: 9.1-9.8

Current taxation class groupings

The current taxation class groupings presented within this section are as follows:

Private and light goods (PLG):

This is by far the most common tax class, currently covering almost 89 per cent of licensed vehicles. This tax class primarily consists of cars and light vans but can include other vehicles used only for private purposes. Tax bands within PLG depend on engine size for vehicles first registered before March 2001, while for cars registered after March 2001, tax bands are based upon levels of CO_2 emissions, with lower rates for cleaner vehicles.

Motorcycles, scooters and mopeds:

This is a self-explanatory tax class, but excludes tricycles which have their own tax band. The rates of tax payable depend upon engine size.

Goods vehicles:

Vehicles that have a gross weight of over three and a half tonnes and are used for carrying goods are taxed in this class. Generally, the rate of tax payable depends on the maximum gross weight and the axle configuration of the vehicle. Since 1999, reduced rates have been available for vehicles that create less pollution.

Public transport vehicles:

This category covers buses and coaches with more than eight seats (excluding the driver) used for commercial purposes. Vehicles not used for commercial purposes would be licensed in the PLG tax class. The rate of tax payable is dependent upon the number of seats in the vehicle. As for goods vehicles, since 1999, reduced rates have been available for vehicles that create less pollution.

Crown and exempt vehicles:

This group includes vehicles which are exempt from vehicle excise duty. This can be for a variety of reasons, including vehicles driven by disabled drivers, emergency and crown vehicles and vehicles manufactured before 1973.

Special vehicles group:

This group includes works trucks, road rollers, mobile cranes, digging machines and showman's vehicles.

Other vehicles:

This group includes three wheeled cars and vans, recovery vehicles, general haulage vehicles and tricycles.

Changes in the taxation system over time

There have been several changes to the vehicle taxation system in recent years which are particularly important when interpreting the time series presented in Tables 9.1 and 9.2. These are as follows:

From 1 October 1982:

All general goods vehicles weighing less than 1,525 kgs in unladen weight were transferred from the 'goods' taxation group to the 'private and light goods' group. This has resulted in a discontinuity in the data presented for both taxation groups between 1981 and 1982.

From 1 October 1990:

All general goods vehicles weighing less than 3,500 kgs in gross vehicle weight were transferred from the 'goods' taxation group to the 'private and light goods' group. This has resulted in a discontinuity in the data presented for both taxation groups between 1989 and 1990.

From 1 July 1995:

Major changes were made to the taxation system with the intention of simplifying the taxation structure. These changes included:

* farmers and showmen's vehicles were transferred from the 'goods' taxation group into the 'other vehicles' group.

* cars and motorcycles over 25 years of age were transferred from the 'private and light goods' and 'motorcycles' taxation group to the 'crown and exempt' taxation group. Since 1998, only vehicles built before 1973 have been included in the 'crown and exempt' taxation group.

* public service vehicles with fewer than eight seats were transferred from the 'public transport vehicles' taxation group into the 'private and light goods' taxation group.

Due to these numerous changes, there is a discontinuity between the figures presented in Tables 9.1 and 9.2 for all taxation groups between 1994 and 1995.

Methods of measurement

Licensed vehicles:

Since 1978, data relating to the number of licensed vehicles has been calculated through an analysis of the records held centrally by the Driver and Vehicle Licensing Agency (DVLA) as at 31st December each year.

Prior to this, statistics on licensed vehicles were calculated through a sample of vehicle records held by local taxation offices and included vehicles licensed for at least one month during the third quarter of the year.

Newly registered vehicles:

Statistics relating to new vehicle registrations are calculated through a complete analysis of new registrations and include all vehicles newly registered in the calendar year.

Vehicle testing: 9.9-9.13

The statistics presented within these tables have been provided by the Vehicle and Operator Services Agency (VOSA), contact: (☎01792 454217.

Trailer tests:

Although there is no registration system for trailers which carry goods, there is still a requirement to have them tested each year under the DfT's plating and testing scheme.

MOT tests:

Since 2006/07, these statistics have been based on an analysis of all MOT tests carried out in the financial year. In 2005/06, the statistics were based on approximately 50 per cent of all tests carried out while, prior to this, the statistics were based on a 2 per cent sample of vehicle tests.

Passenger service vehicle tests:

EEC Directive 77/143 stipulated that all class VI (Public Service Vehicles) in use for more than one year must by 1 January 1983 have undergone a road-worthiness examination and be subject to an annual inspection thereafter. To meet this deadline, statutory testing of class VI vehicles commenced on 1 January 1982.

Heavy goods vehicle tests:

Vehicles subject to plating and testing have to undergo a test when they are 1 year old and are tested annually thereafter; the term 'first test'

refers to the first test of a vehicle in a particular year. The figures quoted cover the 52 week period ending on the Friday which precedes the first Monday in April.

Households with regular use of cars: 9.14

Data from 1961 onwards are derived from household surveys. Figures for earlier years are estimates. Also, see notes to Table 9.15.

Private motoring: 9.15 and 9.16

The mid-year estimates of the percentage of households with regular use of a car or van in Tables 9.15 (a) and (b) are based on combined data from the National Travel Survey (NTS), the Expenditure and Food Survey (previously the Family Expenditure Survey) and the General Household Survey (GHS), where available. The method for calculating these figures was changed slightly for 2006 onwards, to incorporate weighted data from the NTS and the GHS; previously these figures were based on unweighted data. Figures for 2005 have also been revised to incorporate weighted data.

Table 9.15 (c) by area type is based on data from the NTS only. Comparisons with Census data are also shown in Table 9.15 (a).

The percentage of driving licence holders in Table 9.16 is based on data from the NTS, and the estimated number of licence holders is based on the mid-year resident population estimates from ONS.

Annual mileage of 4-wheeled cars: 9.17

These figures are based upon annual estimates for each purpose (commuting, business and other private) per vehicle as reported by participants in the National Travel Survey (NTS). The data are for 4-wheeled cars only. Company cars provided by an employer for the use of a particular employee (or director) are included, but cars borrowed temporarily from a company pool are not.

Private motoring: 9.18

The statistics presented within these tables are provided by the Driving Standards Agency, contact: (☎02920 581218).

9.1 Motor vehicles licensed at end of year: 1950-2008

Thousands

Year	Private and light goods		Goods vehicles	Motor cycles etc	Public transport vehicles	Special machines/ Special concessionary[1]	Other vehicles	Special Vehicles group	Crown and exempt vehicles[1]	All vehicles
	Private cars	Other vehicles								
1950	1,979	439	439	643	123	262	24	.	61	3,970
1951	2,095	457	451	725	123	250	26	.	63	4,190
1952	2,221	477	450	812	119	270	29	.	86	4,464
1953	2,446	516	446	889	105	289	30	.	88	4,809
1954	2,733	566	450	977	97	307	32	.	88	5,250
1955	3,109	633	462	1,076	92	326	35	.	89	5,822
1956	3,437	685	471	1,137	89	336	37	.	95	6,287
1957	3,707	723	473	1,261	87	355	41	.	96	6,743
1958	4,047	772	461	1,300	86	367	46	.	96	7,175
1959	4,416	824	473	1,479	83	383	55	.	96	7,809
1960	4,900	894	493	1,583	84	392	65	.	101	8,512
1961	5,296	944	508	1,577	82	400	76	.	106	8,989
1962	5,776	1,002	512	1,567	84	401	83	.	107	9,532
1963	6,462	1,092	535	1,546	86	412	88	.	115	10,336
1964	7,190	1,184	551	1,534	86	421	90	.	120	11,176
1965	7,732	1,240	584	1,420	86	417	91	.	127	11,697
1966	8,210	1,283	577	1,239	85	399	87	.	142	12,022
1967	8,882	1,358	593	1,190	85	416	89	.	147	12,760
1968	9,285	1,388	580	1,082	89	409	92	.	157	13,082
1969	9,672	1,408	547	993	92	398	90	.	162	13,362
1970	9,971	1,421	545	923	93	385	89	.	121	13,548
1971	10,443	1,452	542	899	96	380	92	.	126	14,030
1972	11,006	1,498	525	866	95	371	95	.	128	14,584
1973	11,738	1,559	540	887	96	373	97	.	137	15,427
1974	11,917	1,547	539	918	96	380	96	.	149	15,642
1975	12,526	1,592	553	1,077	105	384	108	.	166	16,511
1976	13,184	1,626	563	1,175	110	387	117	.	156	17,318
1977	13,220	1,591	559	1,190	110	393	115	.	167	17,345
1978	13,626	1,597	549	1,194	110	394	111	.	177	17,758
1979	14,162	1,623	561	1,292	111	402	106	.	359	18,616
1980	14,660	1,641	507	1,372	110	397	100	.	412	19,199
1981	14,867	1,623	489	1,371	110	365	95	.	427	19,347
1982 [2]	15,264	1,624	477	1,370	111	371	91	.	454	19,762
1983	15,543	1,692	488	1,290	113	376	86	.	621	20,209
1984	16,055	1,752	490	1,225	116	375	82	.	670	20,765
1985	16,454	1,805	485	1,148	120	374	78	.	695	21,159
1986	16,981	1,880	484	1,065	125	371	73	.	720	21,699
1987	17,421	1,952	485	978	129	374	68	.	744	22,152
1988	18,432	2,096	502	912	132	383	83	.	761	23,302
1989	19,248	2,199	505	875	122	384	77	.	785	24,196
1990 [2]	19,742	2,247	482	833	115	375	71	.	807	24,673
1991	19,737	2,215	449	750	109	346	65	.	840	24,511
1992	19,870	2,198	432	684	107	324	59	.	903	24,577
1993	20,102	2,187	428	650	107	318	55	.	979	24,826
1994	20,479	2,192	434	630	107	309	50	.	1,030	25,231
1995 [2]	20,505	2,217	421	594	74	274	44	28	1,169	25,369
1996	21,172	2,267	413	609	77	254	40	48	1,424	26,302
1997	21,681	2,317	414	626	79	249	38	48	1,522	26,974
1998	22,115	2,362	412	684	80	243	37	47	1,558	27,538
1999	22,785	2,427	415	760	84	241	36	47	1,573	28,368
2000	23,196	2,469	418	825	86	233	34	46	1,590	28,898
2001	23,899	2,544	422	882	89	233	33	45	1,602	29,747
2002	24,543	2,622	425	941	92	.	32	46	1,855	30,557
2003	24,985	2,730	426	1,005	96	.	32	47	1,887	31,207
2004	25,754	2,900	434	1,060	100	.	32	50	1,929	32,259
2005	26,208	3,019	433	1,075	103	.	31	51	1,978	32,897
2006	26,508	3,137	446	1,094	107	.	31	54	1,991	33,369
2007	26,878	3,261	446	1,133	109	.	30	56	2,043	33,957
2008	27,021	3,303	436	1,160	111	.	29	56	2,091	34,206

1 The "Special concession" vehicles form part of the "Crown and exempt" taxation class from 2002
2 Changes to the taxation system have meant that there are some discontinuities in the series

☎020-7944 3077

9.2 Motor vehicles registered for the first time: 1951-2008

Thousands

Year	Private and light goods	Goods vehicles	Motorcycles etc	Public transport vehicles	Special machines and special concessionary[1]	Exempt and Other vehicles[1]	All vehicles
1951	136	85	133	8	34	18	414
1952	188	82	133	5	35	16	459
1953	295	97	139	5	34	14	584
1954	386	110	165	6	35	17	718
1955	501	154	185	6	39	22	907
1956	400	148	143	5	32	23	751
1957	425	141	206	5	40	20	837
1958	555	173	183	5	47	19	982
1959	646	192	332	5	49	30	1,253
1960	805	226	257	6	43	33	1,369
1961	743	220	212	6	46	31	1,259
1962	785	192	140	6	43	27	1,192
1963	1,009	206	166	6	48	31	1,466
1964	1,191	229	205	7	46	34	1,711
1965	1,123	229	151	7	45	46	1,601
1966	1,065	227	109	7	48	36	1,494
1967	1,117	222	138	7	54	39	1,575
1968	1,117	232	112	7	57	37	1,562
1969	987	240	85	7	49	33	1,402
1969 [2]	1,133	94	85	7	49	33	1,402
1970	1,248	85	105	8	49	30	1,525
1971	1,462	74	128	10	38	30	1,742
1972	1,855	75	153	10	48	44	2,184
1973	1,851	83	194	10	50	43	2,230
1974	1,400	68	190	8	46	40	1,750
1975	1,317	67	265	8	49	45	1,750
1976	1,402	64	271	9	52	41	1,838
1977	1,445	69	251	9	48	40	1,862
1978	1,746	80	225	9	50	41	2,151
1979	1,892	91	286	9	48	44	2,370
1980	1,679	75	313	9	37	44	2,156
1980 [2]	1,699	55	313	9	37	44	2,156
1981	1,644	40	272	8	33	35	2,030
1982 [2]	1,746	41	232	7	39	40	2,104
1983	1,989	47	175	7	42	48	2,308
1984	1,933	50	145	7	40	64	2,239
1985	2,030	52	126	7	40	55	2,309
1986	2,071	51	106	9	35	62	2,334
1987	2,213	54	91	9	38	70	2,474
1988	2,437	63	90	9	45	79	2,724
1989	2,535	65	97	8	43	81	2,829
1990	2,180	44	94	7	34	78	2,439
1991	1,709	29	77	5	26	77	1,922
1992	1,694	29	66	5	24	84	1,902
1993	1,853	33	58	5	30	94	2,074
1994	1,992	41	65	7	35	110	2,249
1995 [2]	2,024	48	69	5	33	127	2,307
1996	2,093	46	90	7	26	150	2,410
1997	2,244	42	122	7	22	162	2,598
1998	2,368	49	144	7	15	157	2,740
1999	2,342	48	168	8	25	174	2,766
2000	2,430	50	183	8	24	176	2,871
2001	2,710	49	177	7	27	169	3,138
2002	2,816	45	162	8	.	199	3,229
2003	2,821	48	157	8	.	197	3,232
2004	2,785	48	134	8	.	211	3,185
2005	2,604	51	132	9	.	226	3,021
2006	2,499	48	132	8	.	227	2,914
2007	2,539	41	143	9	.	265	2,997
2008	2,188	47	138	8	.	290	2,672

1 The "Special concession" vehicles form part of the "Crown and exempt" taxation class from 2002
2 Changes to the taxation system have meant that there are some discontinuities in the series

☎020-7944 3077

9.3 Motor vehicles licensed at end of year: by tax class, body type and engine size: 1998-2008

(a) Private and light goods tax class												Thousands
Year		1998	1999	2000	2001	2002	2003	2004	2005	2006	2007	2008
Body type cars classified by engine size												
Over	Not over											
	700cc	29	18	19	23	29	37	47	52	57	58	57
700cc	1,000cc	1,459	1,435	1,415	1,368	1,314	1,237	1,199	1,153	1,135	1,124	1,129
1,000cc	1,200cc	2,293	2,275	2,228	2,244	2,252	2,221	2,210	2,139	2,036	1,948	1,874
1,200cc	1,500cc	5,497	5,600	5,677	5,819	5,894	5,939	6,089	6,181	6,284	6,428	6,571
1,500cc	1,800cc	6,766	6,922	6,992	7,124	7,241	7,284	7,405	7,439	7,408	7,406	7,352
1,800cc	2,000cc	4,090	4,389	4,604	4,869	5,166	5,398	5,686	5,929	6,076	6,228	6,307
2,000cc	2,500cc	1,003	1,094	1,159	1,275	1,400	1,520	1,639	1,725	1,805	1,878	1,882
2,500cc	3,000cc	574	608	630	666	704	762	841	918	1,007	1,084	1,126
3,000cc		403	443	473	510	543	587	638	671	700	725	723
All engine sizes		22,115	22,785	23,196	23,899	24,543	24,985	25,754	26,208	26,508	26,878	27,021
Other vehicles		2,362	2,427	2,469	2,544	2,622	2,730	2,900	3,019	3,137	3,261	3,303
All private and light goods		24,477	25,212	25,666	26,443	27,165	27,715	28,654	29,226	29,645	30,139	30,324

(b) Motorcycles, scooters and mopeds tax class: by engine size												
Over	Not over											
	50cc	102	117	141	154	155	159	161	153	144	139	137
50cc	125cc	143	148	160	172	177	182	189	192	199	211	224
125cc	150cc	1	1	1	1	1	1	1	1	1	1	1
150cc	200cc	12	12	13	13	14	16	16	16	15	15	15
200cc	250cc	42	41	38	35	33	33	33	32	32	32	34
250cc	350cc	10	9	9	8	8	9	9	8	8	9	9
350cc	500cc	57	61	62	62	70	74	75	74	72	71	70
500cc		317	371	403	437	482	531	576	599	623	653	668
All over 50cc		582	642	685	727	786	845	899	922	950	992	1,022
All engine sizes		684	760	825	882	941	1,005	1,060	1,075	1,094	1,133	1,160

☎020-7944 3077

9.4 Motor vehicles licensed by tax class in 2008: by method of propulsion

						Thousands
Taxation class	Petrol	Diesel	Gas/Petrol-Gas	Gas Bi-Fuel/Gas Diesel	Hybrid-Electric	Other[1]	All
Private and light goods	20,140	10,075	30	31	47	-	30,324
ow: body type cars	19,959	6,966	27	21	47	-	27,021
Motorcycles, scooters and mopeds	1,158	1	-	0	0	1	1,160
Bus	1	110	-	0	0	0	111
Goods	1	435	-	0	0	0	436
Special vehicles group	-	53	1	1	-	-	56
Other non-exempt vehicles	12	17	-	0	0	0	29
Exempt vehicles	1,322	727	2	1	-	38	2,091
ow:							
former Special concessionary group	17	283	-	0	0	8	308
Total All Vehicles	22,634	11,419	34	33	47	39	34,206

1 Other comprises electricity, steam, new fuel technologies, electric diesel and fuel cells

☎020-7944 3077

9.5 Body type cars licensed: by government office region:[1] 2008

			2008			
			Body type cars in all taxation classes			
	1998 (thousand)	2007 (thousand)	(thousand)	Per 1000 population	Average vehicle age	Percentage first registered in 2008
North East	823	1,029	1,041	406	6.2	*6.7*
North West	1,778	3,215	3,219	469	6.4	*7.9*
Yorkshire and The Humber	1,805	2,219	2,257	436	6.5	*7.2*
East Midlands	1,699	2,125	2,157	490	7.0	*7.4*
West Midlands	2,288	2,737	2,755	512	6.7	*9.0*
East of England	2,429	2,875	2,898	512	7.4	*5.5*
London	2,371	2,588	2,605	345	7.6	*5.3*
South East	3,709	4,467	4,522	544	7.2	*7.4*
South West	1,131	2,677	2,709	523	7.8	*5.6*
Total England	20,001	23,932	24,164	473	7.0	*6.9*
Wales	1,131	1,433	1,442	484	7.1	*5.6*
Scotland	1,778	2,216	2,248	437	6.0	*7.6*
Great Britain [2]	23,293	28,228	28,390	479	7.0	*6.9*

1 Regions refer to location where each vehicle is registered

2 Totals for Great Britain include vehicles for which the region is unknown

☎020-7944 3077

9.6 Goods vehicles over 3.5 tonnes licensed by body type:[1,2] 2008

Thousands

	Over	3.5 t	7.5 t	12 t	16 t	20 t	24 t	28 t	32 t	33 t	37 t	38 t	All
Body type	Not over	7.5 t	12 t	16 t	20 t	24 t	28 t	32 t	33 t	37 t	38 t		weights
Rigid vehicles													
Box Van		57	3	6	16	1	3	-	-	-	-	-	86
Tipper		20	1	1	5	-	6	17	-	-	-	-	49
Curtain Sided		11	1	1	9	1	4	-	0	-	-	-	27
Dropside Lorry		12	1	1	5	-	3	-	-	-	0	-	23
Flat Lorry		8	1	1	4	1	5	1	-	-	-	-	20
Refuse Disposal		1	-	-	2	2	8	2	-	-	-	-	16
Insulated Van		6	1	2	4	-	2	-	-	-	-	-	15
Skip Loader		1	-	-	6	-	1	3	-	-	-	-	13
Goods		4	-	1	2	-	2	1	-	-	-	-	11
Tanker		-	-	-	2	-	3	1	-	-	-	-	8
Panel Van		7	-	-	-	-	-	-	0	0	0	-	8
Street Cleansing		2	-	2	-	-	-	-	0	0	0	0	5
Concrete Mixer		-	-	-	1	-	3	1	-	-	0	-	5
Tractor		-	-	-	-	-	1	-	-	-	-	2	4
Car Transporter		1	-	-	1	1	-	-	0	-	-	-	4
Livestock Carrier		3	-	-	-	-	-	-	0	0	0	-	4
Skeletal Vehicle		1	-	-	-	-	-	-	-	0	0	-	2
Not Recorded		1	-	-	-	-	-	-	0	0	0	-	2
Luton Van		2	-	-	-	-	-	-	0	0	0	0	2
Special Purpose		1	-	-	-	-	-	-	0	0	-	-	2
Tower Wagon		2	-	-	-	0	-	-	0	0	0	-	2
Van		1	-	-	-	-	-	-	0	0	0	-	2
Specially Fitted Van		1	-	-	-	-	-	-	-	0	0	-	1
Truck		1	-	-	-	-	-	-	-	0	-	-	1
Others/Unknown		2	-	1	1	-	1	1	0	-	-	-	6
Total		145	10	18	62	7	42	28	-	-	1	3	317
Articulated vehicles [3]		-	-	-	-	1	7	4	-	3	17	86	119
Total rigid and articulated vehicles		145	11	18	62	8	49	32	1	3	18	89	436

1 Goods Vehicles identified by tax class

2 Figures may not sum due to rounding

3 There is insufficient reliable data to separate articulated vehicles by body type

☎020-7944 3077

9.7 Goods vehicles over 3.5 tonnes licensed by axle configuration at end of year:[1] 1998-2008

Thousands

		Articulated vehicles			
Year	Rigid vehicles	Not over 28 tonnes	Over 28 tonnes	All	All vehicles
1998	310	13	98	111	421
1999	311	14	98	112	423
2000	311	14	100	114	425
2001	314	13	102	115	430
2002	316	12	104	117	433
2003	310	12	105	116	426
2004	316	11	107	118	434
2005	324	10	107	117	433
2006	325	10	111	122	446
2007	324	10	112	122	446
2008	317	9	111	119	436

1 Goods vehicles identified by tax class   ☎020-7944 3077

9.8 Goods vehicles over 3.5 tonnes gross weight by axle configuration:[1] 2008

Thousands

(tonnes)		Rigid				Articulated		
Over	Not over	2 axles	3 axles	4 axles	All rigid vehicles	2 axle tractive unit	3 axle tractive unit	All articulated vehicles
3.5	16	173.6	0.3	0.1	173.9	0.2	0.1	0.3
16	24	61.7	7.1	-	68.9	1.1	0.1	1.2
24	28	0.6	40.9	0.7	42.1	6.8	0.4	7.2
28	32	0.1	0.1	28.0	28.3	3.5	0.3	3.8
32	33	-	-	-	-	0.4	0.1	0.5
33	37	-	-	0.2	0.2	2.4	0.6	2.9
37	38	-	0.1	0.5	0.6	13.4	3.8	17.2
38		0.2	0.3	2.1	2.6	6.0	80.4	86.4
All weights		236.3	48.9	31.6	316.8	33.9	85.6	119.4

1 Goods vehicles identified by tax class   ☎020-7944 3077

Transport Statistics Great Britain 2009

9.9 Trailer tests by axle type: 1998/99-2008/09

Thousands

First / Annual tests in:	1998/99	1999/00	2000/01	2001/02	2002/03	2003/04	2004/05	2005/06	2006/07	2007/08	2008/09
1 axle	8.1	7.5	7.1	6.7	6.4	6.0	5.6	5.2	5.0	4.7	4.4
2 axle	98.1	89.8	82.2	74.1	68.9	63.9	58.4	53.9	49.0	45.9	42.6
3 axle	131.8	143.2	151.2	156.7	166.5	171.5	177.9	184.7	186.1	189.6	192.9
4 axle	0.1	0.1	0.1	0.1	0.1	0.1	0.2	0.2	0.2	0.2	0.2
5 axle	-	-	-	-	-	-	-	-	-	-	-
Total	238.1	240.6	240.6	237.6	241.9	241.5	242.1	244.1	240.3	240.5	240.1

☎01792 454296
Figures in this table are outside
the scope of National Statistics
Source - VOSA

9.10 Road vehicle testing scheme (MOT): test results 1999/00-2008/09

Thousands/*percentage*

	1999/00	2000/01	2001/02	2002/03	2003/04	2004/05	2005/06	2006/07 [1]	2007/08	2008/09
Motorcycles:										
Tested	513.8	567.8	568.4	584.9	745.0	801.0	873.2	951.0	955.7	1,012.9
Failed	114.4	112.9	113.1	108.2	134.0	166.5	164.1	163.4	176.5	195.6
Percentage failed	*22.3*	*19.9*	*19.9*	*18.5*	*18.0*	*20.8*	*18.8*	*17.3*	*18.5*	*19.3*
Cars and other passenger vehicles (up to 12 seats):										
Tested	22,035.0	22,775.0	22,768.0	22,781.0	22,509.0	20,695.0	22,665.0	26,281.9	27,180.1	28,040.2
Failed	7,403.8	7,212.8	7,281.2	7,084.9	6,622.1	5,951.9	7,516.4	8,750.9	9,586.0	10,178.5
Percentage failed	*33.6*	*31.7*	*32.0*	*31.1*	*29.4*	*28.8*	*33.2*	*33.3*	*35.3*	*36.3*
Private passenger vehicles (more than 12 seats):										
Tested	28.3	27.0	28.0	27.0	44.00	30.0	46.4	51.6	51.3	52.7
Failed	6.0	6.64	5.9	5.3	10.8	5.01	12.7	14.7	15.8	17.3
Percentage failed	*21.1*	*24.6*	*21.0*	*19.5*	*24.6*	*17.0*	*27.5*	*28.3*	*30.6*	*32.9*
Goods vehicles between 3,000 and 3,500 kg gross weight:										
Tested	282.0	283.0	284.0	376.0	495.0	634.0	437.4	521.3	555.5	585.3
Failed	93.9	89.6	97.5	132.0	167.3	209.0	190.5	226.3	249.5	267.1
Percentage failed	*33.0*	*35.9*	*34.4*	*35.1*	*33.8*	*33.0*	*43.6*	*43.4*	*44.9*	*45.6*
All vehicles:										
Tested	22,859.1	23,652.8	23,648.4	23,768.9	23,793.0	22,160.0	24,022.0	27,805.8	28,742.6	29,691.0
Failed	7,618.0	7,422.0	7,497.7	7,330.4	6,934.2	6,332.4	7,883.8	9,156.3	10,027.8	10,658.5
Percentage failed	*33.3*	*31.4*	*31.7*	*30.8*	*29.1*	*28.6*	*32.8*	*32.9*	*34.9*	*35.9*

1 MOT computerised figures are available from 2005/06 but computerisation
was only phased in at the vehicle testing stations during that year. This results in
the shortfall in volumes for 2005/06 in comparison to later years. Full records are
available from 2006/07, and up to 2004/05 a 2% Sample Survey was used. Figures
prior to 2006/07 are either incomplete or estimated and should be treated with caution.

☎01792 454217
Figures in this table are outside
the scope of National Statistics
Source - VOSA

9.11   Road passenger service vehicle testing scheme (PSV tests): 1998/99-2008/09

Thousands/*percentage*

Year	1998/99	1999/00	2000/01	2001/02 [1]	2002/03	2003/04	2004/05	2005/06	2006/07	2007/08	2008/09
First tests:											
Passed	62,950	67,219	67,016	65,899	65,458	67,528	67,425	69,270	69,447	70,777	73,003
Failed	12,332	11,216	11,583	14,290	14,515	13,832	13,045	12,086	12,237	11,046	10,725
Total tested	75,282	78,435	78,599	80,189	79,973	81,360	80,470	81,356	81,684	81,823	83,728
Re-tests:											
Passed	11,443	10,417	10,533	13,207	13,731	13,067	11,608	10,148	10,043	11,072	10,874
Failed	1,141	980	1,053	1,265	1,318	1,197	1,076	847	880	889	851
Total tested	12,584	11,397	11,586	14,472	15,049	14,264	12,684	10,995	10,923	11,961	11,725
Percentage failed:											
First test	*16.4*	*14.3*	*14.7*	*17.8*	*18.1*	*17.0*	*16.2*	*14.9*	*15.0*	13.5	12.8
Re-tests	*9.1*	*8.6*	*9.1*	*8.7*	*8.8*	*8.4*	*8.5*	*7.7*	*8.1*	7.4	7.3
All tests	*15.3*	*13.6*	*14.0*	*16.4*	*16.7*	*15.7*	*15.2*	*14.0*	*14.2*	12.7	12.1

1   Due to revisions of testing policy, from 2001/02 onwards fewer defects are now allowed to be
    rectified at the testing station, resulting in a decrease in passes, an increase in failures
    and an increase in re-tests.

☎01792 454296
Figures in this table are outside
the scope of National Statistics
Source - VOSA

9.12   Goods vehicles over 3.5 tonnes testing scheme (HGV Motor vehicles and Trailers): 1998/99-2008/09

Thousands/*percentage*

Year	1998/99	1999/00	2000/01	2001/02 [1]	2002/03	2003/04	2004/05	2005/06	2006/07	2007/08	2008/09
First tests:											
Passed	535.5	536.1	530.0	510.5	511.5	526.9	538.9	556.9	556.1	568.1	578.0
Failed	158.2	163.1	166.4	192.1	196.6	182.3	168.6	155.1	150.6	135.2	119.9
All	693.6	699.2	696.4	702.6	708.0	709.1	707.4	711.9	706.7	703.3	697.9
Re-tests:											
Passed	150.3	150.7	153.9	179.1	182.7	169.5	148.0	127.9	121.5	125.5	111.9
Failed	22.0	23.7	24.4	31.5	29.9	25.8	23.9	20.5	18.5	15.3	13.9
All	172.3	174.4	178.3	210.6	212.6	195.3	171.9	148.4	140.0	140.8	125.8
Percentage failed:											
First test	*22.8*	*23.3*	*23.9*	*27.3*	*27.8*	*25.7*	*23.8*	*21.8*	*21.3*	*19.2*	*17.2*
Re-tests	*12.8*	*13.6*	*13.7*	*15.0*	*14.1*	*13.2*	*13.9*	*13.8*	*13.2*	*10.9*	*11.0*
All tests	*20.8*	*21.4*	*21.7*	*24.5*	*24.6*	*23.0*	*22.0*	*20.4*	*20.0*	*17.8*	*16.2*

1   Due to revisions of testing policy, from 2001/02 onwards fewer defects are now allowed to be
    rectified at the testing station, resulting in a decrease in passes, an increase in failures
    and an increase in re-tests.

☎01792 454296
Figures in this table are outside
the scope of National Statistics
Source - VOSA

9.13 Road vehicle testing scheme (MOT): percentage of vehicles failing by type of defect: 2006/07-2008/09

	Percentage		
	2006/07 [1]	2007/08	2008/09
Motorcycles:			
Body	0.8	1.0	1.2
Brakes	5.8	5.9	5.8
Drive System	0.8	0.	1.0
Fuel and Emissions	1.4	1.4	1.3
Lighting and Signalling	8.7	8.9	8.9
Other	0.2	0.2	0.2
Road Wheels	0.4	0.4	0.4
Steering	2.3	2.2	2.0
Structure	0.8	0.8	0.8
Suspension	4.2	4.0	3.8
Tyres	2.5	2.6	2.6
Cars and other passenger vehicles (up to 12 seats):			
Body	8.0	8.4	8.6
Brakes	17.8	17.4	17.1
Fuel and Emissions	7.1	7.0	6.7
Lighting & Signalling	18.2	18.8	18.9
Other	0.9	0.9	0.9
Road Wheels	0.3	0.3	0.3
Seat Belts	1.8	1.7	1.8
Steering	2.7	2.7	2.7
Structure	2.4	2.3	2.3
Suspension	12.0	11.9	12.2
Tyres	7.5	7.9	8.1
Private passenger vehicles (more than 12 seats):			
Body	10.1	12.4	14.3
Brakes	19.0	19.5	19.7
Fuel and Emissions	4.7	4.5	4.5
Lighting and Signalling	16.0	17.1	18.5
Other	0.5	0.6	0.6
Road Wheels	0.1	0.1	0.1
Seat Belts	7.9	8.3	8.4
Steering	3.6	3.3	3.6
Structure	2.2	2.5	2.6
Suspension	6.8	6.8	6.8
Tyres	3.0	3.4	3.7
Goods vehicles between 3,000 and 3,500 kg gross weight:			
Body	20.1	20.5	20.1
Brakes	43.4	42.2	41.3
Fuel and Emissions	8.8	8.4	7.5
Lighting and Signalling	42.3	43.6	43.1
Other	1.3	1.3	1.2
Road Wheels	0.4	0.4	0.3
Seat Belts	4.5	4.5	4.5
Steering	7.2	6.6	6.2
Structure	6.5	6.2	6.0
Suspension	22.2	21.1	19.8
Tyres	7.6	7.8	7.6

1 MOT computerision was phased in at the vehicle testing stations during 2005/06.
Components with associated defects were changed significantly at this time
The first full year of data captured was in 2006/07 and as a result it is not possible
to match component details with those before that year.

☎01792 454217
Figures in this table are outside
the scope of National Statistics
Source - VOSA

9.14 Households with regular use of car(s): 1951-2007

For details of household car ownership by region and area type, see Table 9.15

Percentage

Year	No car	One car	Two cars	Three or more cars	All Households
1951	86	13	1	-	100
1952	84	14	1	-	100
1953	83	16	1	-	100
1954	81	17	2	-	100
1955	80	19	2	-	100
1956	78	20	2	-	100
1957	76	22	2	-	100
1958	74	24	2	-	100
1959	73	25	2	-	100
1960	71	27	2	-	100
1961	69	29	2	-	100
1962	67	30	3	-	100
1963	64	33	3	-	100
1964	62	34	4	-	100
1965	59	36	5	-	100
1966	55	39	6	-	100
1967	53	41	6	-	100
1968	51	43	6	-	100
1969	49	45	6	-	100
1970	48	45	6	1	100
1971	48	44	7	1	100
1972	48	44	8	1	100
1973	46	43	9	1	100
1974	45	44	10	1	100
1975	44	45	10	1	100
1976	45	44	10	1	100
1977	43	45	10	1	100
1978	44	45	10	1	100
1979	43	44	11	2	100
1980	41	44	13	2	100
1981	40	45	13	2	100
1982	40	44	13	2	100
1983	39	44	14	2	100
1984	39	44	14	3	100
1985	38	45	15	3	100
1986	38	45	15	3	100
1987	36	45	16	3	100
1988	35	44	17	3	100
1989	34	44	18	4	100
1990	33	44	19	4	100
1991	32	45	19	4	100
1992	32	45	20	4	100
1993	31	45	20	4	100
1994	32	45	20	4	100
1995	30	45	21	4	100
1996	30	45	21	4	100
1997	30	45	21	5	100
1998	28	44	23	5	100
1999	28	44	22	5	100
2000	27	45	23	5	100
2001	26	45	23	5	100
2002	26	44	24	5	100
2003	26	44	25	5	100
2004	25	44	25	5	100
2005	25	44	25	5	100
2006	24	44	26	6	100
2007	24	44	26	6	100

Note: Data from 1961 onward are derived from household surveys.
Figures for earlier years are estimates.

☎020-7944 3097
Source - Family Expenditure Survey, ONS;
General Household Survey, ONS;
National Travel Survey, DfT

9.15   Private motoring: households with regular use of cars

Historic details from 1951 are available in Table 9.14

(a) 1991-2007

Percentage

	No car	One car	Two cars	Three or more cars	All Households
Combined survey data[1]					
1991	32	45	19	4	100
2001	26	45	23	5	100
2002	26	44	24	5	100
2003	26	44	25	5	100
2004	25	44	25	5	100
2005	25	44	25	5	100
2006	24	44	26	6	100
2007	24	44	26	6	100
Census data					
1991	33	44	19	4	100
2001	27	44	23	6	100

(b) By Government Office Region: 2007 [1]

Percentage

	No car	One car	Two or more cars	All Households
North East	29	44	27	100
North West	26	42	32	100
Yorkshire and the Humber	27	42	30	100
East Midlands	20	45	35	100
West Midlands	21	42	37	100
East of England	15	45	40	100
London	38	43	18	100
South East	17	43	40	100
South West	17	45	38	100
England	24	43	33	100
Wales	23	46	31	100
Scotland	29	45	26	100
Great Britain	24	44	32	100

(c) By area type: 2008

Percentage/number

	Cars per Household	No car	One car	Two or more cars	All Households
London Boroughs	0.79	43	40	17	100
Metropolitan areas	0.98	32	41	26	100
Other urban areas with population:					
Over 250 thousand	1.16	23	45	32	100
25 to 250 thousand	1.15	24	44	32	100
10 to 25 thousand	1.15	23	45	32	100
3 to 10 thousand	1.38	16	42	42	100
Rural areas	1.49	10	43	47	100
Great Britain	1.14	25	43	32	100

1 Based on combined survey data sources - Family Expenditure Survey, ONS;
  General Household Survey, ONS; National Travel Survey, DfT.

☎020 7944 3097

9.16 Private motoring: full car driving licence holders by age and gender: 1975/1976-2008

Percentage/number (millions)

Year	Age								Estimated number
(a) All adults	17-20	21-29	30-39	40-49	50-59	60-69	70 or over	All adults	of licence holders
1975/1976	28	59	67	60	50	35	15	48	19.4
1985/1986	33	63	74	71	60	47	27	57	24.3
1989/1991	43	72	77	78	67	54	32	64	27.8
1992/1994	48	75	82	79	72	57	33	67	29.3
1995/1997[1]	43	74	81	81	75	63	38	69	30.3
1998/2000	41	75	84	83	77	67	39	71	31.4
2002	33	67	82	84	81	70	44	70	31.9
2003	29	67	82	83	80	72	44	70	32.1
2004	27	65	82	83	80	72	46	70	32.2
2005	32	66	82	84	82	74	51	72	33.3
2006	34	67	82	84	82	76	50	72	33.7
2007	38	66	81	83	82	75	52	71	33.8
2008	36	64	82	83	83	78	53	72	34.5[P]
(b) Male									
1975/1976	36	78	85	83	75	58	32	69	13.4
1985/1986	37	73	86	87	81	72	51	74	15.1
1989/1991	52	82	88	89	85	78	58	80	16.7
1992/1994	54	83	91	88	88	81	59	81	17.0
1995/1997[1]	50	80	88	89	89	83	65	81	17.2
1998/2000	44	80	89	91	88	83	65	82	17.4
2002	35	71	88	90	89	85	68	80	17.5
2003	33	73	87	90	91	87	69	81	17.8
2004	30	68	87	89	90	86	72	79	17.7
2005	37	69	86	90	90	88	73	81	18.1
2006	37	71	86	89	91	90	76	81	18.4
2007	41	69	86	88	90	87	75	80	18.4
2008	38	67	87	89	91	90	75	81	18.7[P]
(c) Female									
1975/1976	20	43	48	37	24	15	4	29	6.0
1985/1986	29	54	62	56	41	24	11	41	9.2
1989/1991	35	64	67	66	49	33	15	49	11.1
1992/1994	42	68	73	70	57	37	16	54	12.2
1995/1997[1]	36	67	74	73	62	45	21	57	13.1
1998/2000	38	69	78	76	67	53	22	60	14.0
2002	31	62	76	78	73	55	27	61	14.4
2003	25	62	77	77	70	58	26	61	14.3
2004	24	62	77	77	71	58	28	61	14.5
2005	27	62	77	79	73	61	35	63	15.2
2006	31	63	78	79	74	63	31	63	15.3
2007	34	62	76	78	74	63	36	63	15.4
2008	35	61	78	78	75	67	36	65	15.8[P]

1 Figures for 1995 onwards are based on weighted data

☎020-7944 3097

9.17 Annual mileage of 4-wheeled cars by type of car and trip purpose: 2008

Miles/percentage

	Business Mileage	Commuting mileage	Other private mileage	Total mileage	Proportion of cars in sample
All company cars	7,670	6,590	5,490	19,760	5
All private cars	680	2,440	5,010	8,130	95
All cars	1,020	2,640	5,040	8,690	100

	Business Mileage	Commuting mileage	Other private mileage	Total mileage	Proportion of company cars in sample
All 4-wheeled cars:					
1995/1997	1,710	2,830	5,160	9,700	7
1998/2000	1,590	2,940	5,030	9,550	8
2002	1,250	2,780	5,140	9,170	7
2003	1,230	2,840	5,160	9,230	6
2004	1,140	2,850	5,170	9,160	6
2005	1,090	2,840	5,080	9,010	6
2006	1,040	2,770	4,960	8,770	5
2007	1,070	2,740	5,060	8,870	5
2008	1,020	2,640	5,040	8,690	5

☎020 7944 3097

9.18 Private motoring: Car driving tests: 1998/99-2008/09

Thousands/*percent*

	1998/99	1999/00	2000/01	2001/02	2002/03	2003/04	2004/05	2005/06	2006/07	2007/08	2008/09
Applications											
received [1]	1,286	1,205	1,263	1,315	1,468	1,526	1,675	1,847	1,883	1,878	1,796
Tests conducted	1,166	1,130	1,015	1,216	1,344	1,399	1,668	1,834	1,784	1,769	1,717
Tests passed, by sex:											
Male	267	256	229	273	300	304	365	411	405	412	408
Female	268	240	214	254	283	295	340	370	367	370	369
Total	535	496	443	527	583	598	706	781	773	782	777
Pass rate, by sex:											
Male	*51*	*48*	*48*	*47*	*47*	*46*	*46*	*46*	*46*	*47*	*49*
Female	*42*	*40*	*40*	*40*	*40*	*40*	*39*	*40*	*41*	*41*	*42*
Total	*46*	*44*	*44*	*43*	*43*	*43*	*42*	*43*	*43*	*44*	*45*

1 These are gross figures and take no account of applications
  which do not mature into a test due to cancellations etc.

☎02920 581218
The figures in this table are outside
the scope of National Statistics
Source - DSA

10 International Comparisons:

Notes and Definitions

This section gives some broad comparisons between transport in the United Kingdom and transport in other major industrialised countries, based on statistics obtained from international publications. Although efforts have been made to achieve comparability, there are still hazards in international comparisons because of differences in the statistical methods and definitions, so the figures should be used with caution.

In most tables, the figures relate to either 1996 and 2006 or 1997 and 2007. For some countries recent data are not available and figures for earlier years are shown as best estimates with appropriate footnotes.

To ease comparisons, much of the data in the tables have been rounded, typically to three significant figures or fewer, but it should not be assumed that figures are always accurate to the precision shown.

Some United Kingdom (or Great Britain) figures differ from comparable tables in other sections of Transport Statistics Great Britain, as they conform to slightly different definitions for consistency with figures for other countries.

Data sources

The data are from a wide variety of sources. Population and Gross Domestic Product estimates are from National Accounts (OECD). Other data come from the EU publication Energy and Transport in Figures, and World Road Statistics (IRF), or from national statistics.

General Statistics: 10.1

Values at market exchange rates are series at current domestic prices converted to Euros by way of current exchange rates for those countries outside the Euro zone. Purchasing power parities are price relatives which show the ratio of the prices in national currencies of the same good or service in different countries relative to the EU27.

Road vehicles by type: 10.3

Stock of road vehicles: The number of road vehicles registered at a given date in a country and licensed to use roads open to public traffic. This includes road vehicles exempted from annual taxes or license fees; it also includes imported second-hand vehicles and other road vehicles according to national practices. The statistics should exclude military vehicles.

Passenger car: Road motor vehicle, other than a motor cycle, intended for the carriage of passengers and designed to seat no more than nine persons (including the driver). This, therefore, includes taxis and hired passenger cars provided that they have fewer than ten seats. This category may also include pick-ups.

Goods vehicle: Any single road motor vehicle designed to carry goods. This excludes articulated tractors and semi-trailers.

Motorcycle: Two-wheeled road motor vehicle with or without side-car, including motor scooter, or three-wheeled road motor vehicle not exceeding 400kg unladen weight. In most countries all such vehicles with a cylinder capacity of 50cc or over are included, as are those under 50cc which do not meet the definition of moped.

Moped: Two or three-wheeled road vehicle fitted with an engine with a cylinder capacity of less than 50cc and a maximum authorised design speed in accordance with national regulations.

Buses and coaches: Passenger road motor vehicle (including mini-buses) designed to seat more than nine persons (including the driver).

Road traffic: 10.4

The Great Britain figures are gathered from traffic counts as described in Section 7 of this volume: for Great Britain, the traffic measured includes that by Great Britain registered (national) vehicles together with a small amount by foreign vehicles on British roads. Other countries' figures are generally for national vehicles, but comparable statistics are not always available since not all countries have a regular monitoring programme. Some countries rely on roadside interviews, fuel consumption and vehicle ownership data to derive the road traffic statistics.

For Great Britain, vehicle kilometres for buses and coaches relate to vehicles with bus and coach body types as opposed to just those taxed as hackneys with nine or more seats. This differs from Table 10.3 and may differ from other countries.

Freight Transport: 10.5

Road traffic: Figures relate to national and international freight carried by vehicles registered in the country. For most countries these are not comparable with those published previously, as earlier figures related to all freight moved regardless of the nationality of the vehicle.

Inland waterway traffic: Includes all transport loaded and moved on a country's inland waterways on inland waterway craft. It excludes traffic on vessels passing from the sea to an inland waterway.

Rail traffic: Includes all traffic on the country's network.

Passenger transport: 10.6

There are substantial differences in methods used to estimate passenger kilometres, so that results give only a broad indication of variation between countries.

Carbon dioxide emissions from transport: 10.7

This table is based on data from submissions by member states to the United Nations Framework Convention on Climate Change (UNFCCC). The full data can be found at:

http://unfccc.int/national_reports/annex_i_ghg_inventories/national_inventories_submissions/items/4303.php

The data follow the Intergovernmental Panel on Climate Change (IPCC) definitions of emissions, and are on the by source basis. Land Use, Land Use Change and Forestry (LULUCF) emissions have been excluded from the totals for international comparisons, because treatment of this category can vary between countries. The data in Table 3.8(a) for UK 'net emissions all sources' includes LULUCF. Transport emissions of carbon dioxide are based on fuel purchases in the country in question.

Table 10.11 includes emissions from Crown Dependencies of Jersey, Guernsey and Isle of Man, and emissions from Overseas Territories. Table 3.7(a) includes emissions from Crown Dependencies but not from Overseas Territories.

Fuel prices: 10.8

The figures comparing the price of petrol and diesel are supplied by DECC, and are extracted from the IEA publication 'Energy Prices & Taxes'.

The use of the term Tax in part (b) of this table is necessary because some other European countries impose other taxes and fees on fuel. For the United Kingdom this includes just fuel duty and VAT.

The figures in Table 10.8 differ from those in Table 3.3 because of the differences in availability and timing of data collection. The international comparisons in Table 10.8 are based on averages over the year. Table 3.3 attempts to be as up to date as reasonably possible.

Principal fleets: 10.9

Fleets: Includes all trading ships of 100 gross tons and over, so that totals given here for the United Kingdom are not comparable with those given in Table 5.14 which includes trading ships in excess of 500 gross tons.

Airlines: 10.10

The figures in this table are supplied by International Civil Aviation Organisation (ICAO). A substantial proportion of the figures are estimated by ICAO on the basis of part-year data; the table therefore of use only as a guide. Airlines have been allocated to the country in which they are registered, apart from Cathay Pacific, which is based in Hong Kong, and which has been excluded from the United Kingdom figures. Traffic of the Scandinavian Airline System (SAS) has been divided 2:2:3 between Denmark, Norway and Sweden, respectively. The freight tonne-kilometres shown are those carried on freight-only flights.

Because they are not necessarily based on the same airlines each year, figures for some countries will not strictly be comparable over time.

Road deaths: 10.11

The data shown in this table are reproduced from the OECD International Road Traffic and Accident Database, International Transport Forum (ITF) and EU (CARE DATABASE).

International definition (Vienna Convention 1968) of road death: Any person who was killed outright or who died within 30 days as a result of the accident. Some countries use different definitions but adjustments are made for international comparability to a common 30 day basis.

10.1 General Statistics: 2007

	Population[2] (millions)	Area (1000 sq kms)	Population per square kilometre	Gross Domestic Product at current prices			
				At market exchange rates			At purchasing power parity[1]
				Euro (billion)	Euro per head of Population	1 Euro = [3]	Euro per head of Population
Great Britain	59.2	229	259	..	..	..	..
Northern Ireland	1.6	14	115	..	..	..	..
United Kingdom	60.8	243	250	2,047	33,670	0.68434	29,620
Austria	8.3	84	99	271	32,570	..	30,840
Belgium	10.6	31	344	335	31,530	..	29,390
Bulgaria	7.7	111	70	29	3,750	1.9558	9,270
Cyprus	0.8	9	84	16	19,980	0.58193	22,600
Czech Republic	10.3	79	131	127	12,320	27.766	19,960
Denmark	5.4	43	126	227	41,410	..	29,870
Estonia	1.3	45	31	15	11,380	15.6466	16,910
Finland	5.3	338	16	180	33,970	..	28,830
France	63.4	547	116	1,895	29,760	..	27,150
Germany	82.3	357	231	2,423	29,450	..	28,570
Greece	11.2	132	85	228	20,390	..	23,610
Hungary	10.1	93	108	101	10,060	251.35	15,580
Irish Republic	4.3	70	60	191	43,750	..	37,410
Italy	59.1	301	201	1,545	26,020	..	25,370
Latvia	2.3	65	35	21	9,280	0.7001	14,410
Lithuania	3.4	65	52	28	8,420	3.4528	14,810
Luxembourg	0.5	3	182	36	75,860	..	66,530
Malta	0.4	0	1,261	5	13,300	0.4293	19,330
Netherlands	16.4	42	394	567	34,620	..	32,580
Poland	38.1	313	122	311	8,150	3.7837	13,370
Portugal	10.6	92	115	163	15,380	..	18,950
Romania	21.6	238	94	124	5,740	3.3328	10,480
Slovak Republic	5.4	49	110	55	10,170	33.869	16,680
Slovenia	2.0	20	100	34	17,080	..	22,220
Spain	44.5	505	87	1,051	23,410	..	26,240
Sweden	9.1	450	20	331	36,210	9.2501	30,430
EU27	495.1	4,325	114	12,355	24,900	..	24,900
Norway	4.7	324	15	284	60,360	8.0165	44,420
Switzerland	7.5	41	181	312	41,520	1.6427	34,140
Japan	127.8	378	338	3,199	25,050	161.25	27,930
USA	301.6	9,827	31	10,027	33,230	1.3705	37,830

1 In terms of euros that have the same purchasing power
over the whole of the EU calculated weighted average
of the purchasing power of the national
currencies of EU Member States.
2 Some figures provisional
3 Exchange rate: 1 Euro = in national currency in 2007

☎020-7944 4442
The figures in this table are
outside the scope of UK National Statistics
Source - European Commission, Eurostat Yearbook,
European Economic Statistics; National Accounts (OECD)
Population Trends (ONS)

10.2 Road and rail infrastructure: 1996 and 2006

Thousand kilometres

| | Road network | | | | | | Rail network | | | | | |
| | All roads | | ow: motorways | | All roads per 1,000 square kilometres (kilometres) | | In operation | | ow: electrified | | Rail network per 1,000 square kilometres (kilometres) | |
	1996	2006	1996	2006	1996	2006	1996	2006	1996	2006	1996	2006
Great Britain	387	394	3.3	3.5	1,683	1,715	16.7	15.8	5.176	5.25	72	69
Northern Ireland	24	25	0.1	0.1	1,714	1,794	0.2	0.	..	..	15	15
United Kingdom	411	420	3.4	3.6	1,684	1,719	16.9	16.0	5.176	5.25	69	66
Austria	129	107	1.6	1.7	1,538	1,273	5.7	5.8	3.403	3.545	68	69
Belgium	145	152	1.7	1.8	4,751	4,992	3.4	3.6	2.467	3.002	111	117
Denmark	71	72	0.8	1.0	1,655	1,679	2.3	2.6	0.399	0.636	55	61
Finland	78	78	0.4	0.7	230	231	5.9	5.9	2.058	3.047	17	17
France	893	952	8.6	10.8	1,641	1,749	31.9	29.5	14.33	15.13	59	54
Germany	656	644	11.2	12.5	1,838	1,805	40.8	34.1	18.37	19.54	114	96
Greece	117	118	0.5	1.1	886	892	2.5	2.5	..	0.199	19	19
Irish Republic	93	97	0.1	0.3	1,316	1,373	2.0	1.9	-	0.052	28	27
Italy	470	..	6.5	6.6	1,559	..	16.0	16.6	10.25	11.73	53	55
Luxembourg	5	5	0.1	0.1	1,985	2,010	0.3	0.3	0.26	0.262	105	106
Netherlands	124	135	2.2	2.6	2,990	3,252	2.7	2.8	1.999	2.003	66	67
Portugal	..	83	0.7	2.5	..	902	2.9	2.8	0.627	1.435	31	31
Spain	345	..	7.3	12.1	682	..	14.3	14.7	6.879	8.73	28	29
Sweden	211	426	1.4	1.7	469	947	11.0	11.0	7.428	7.848	24	24
Bulgaria	37	40 [4]	0.3	0.4	331	363	4.3	4.1	2.71	2.806	39	37
Cyprus	10	12	0.2	0.3	..	..	.	.	-	-	-	-
Czech Republic	55	129	0.4	0.6	703	1,629	9.4	9.6	2.859	3.06	120	122
Estonia	15	58	0.1	0.1	339	1,273	1.0	1.0	0.132	0.131	23	21
Hungary	159	190	0.4	0.8	1,706	2,041	8.0	8.0	2.353	2.793	86	86
Latvia	56	70	.	.	863	1,079	2.4	2.3	0.271	0.257	37	35
Lithuania	66	80	0.4	0.3	1,016	1,231	2.0	1.8	0.122	0.122	31	27
Malta	2	..	.	.	6,667	..	.	.	.	.	-	-
Poland	375	..	0.3	0.6	1,199	..	23.4	19.4	11.63	11.83	75	62
Romania	193	..	0.1 [2]	0.2	813	..	11.4	10.8	3.96	3.979	48	45
Slovak Republic	42	44	0.2	0.3	870	897	3.7	3.6	1.516	1.577	75	74
Slovenia	15	39	0.3	0.6	732	1,899	1.2	1.2	0.499	0.503	59	60
Norway	91	93	0.1	0.3	282	287	4.0	4.1	2.4 [2]	2.552	12	13
Switzerland	71	71	1.2	1.4	1,722	1,727	3.2	3.6	..	3.563	78	86
Japan	1,148	1,190	5.9 [3]	7.4 [3]	3,036	3,148	26.5	20.1	17	15.7	70	53
USA	6,308	6,463	88.6	94.6 [4]	674	690	240.0	205.6 [4]	1.7	..	..	22

1. The definition of road types varies from country to country, the data are therefore not comparable.
2. 1995 data.
3. National expressways
4. 2005 data.

☎020-7944 3088

The figures in this table are outside the scope of UK National Statistics
Sources: EU Energy and Transport in Figures (EUROSTAT); IRF
Ministry of Land, Infrastructure and Transport, Japan

10.3 Road vehicles by type, at end of year: 1997 and 2007

Thousands

	Cars and taxis		Goods vehicles [1]		Motorcycles [1,2]		Buses and coaches	
	1997	2007	1997	2007	1997	2007	1997	2007
Great Britain	22,866	28,272	2,610	3,715	780	1,279	161	181
Northern Ireland	584	829	68	119	14	32	5	6
United Kingdom	23,450	29,101	2,678	3,834	794	1,311	166	187
Austria	3,783	4,246	726	373	576	668	10	9
Belgium	4,415	5,049	477	691	225	375	15	15
Denmark	1,788	2,068	346	537	94	197	14	14
Finland	1,948	2,570	267	395	167	377	9	12
France	26,090	31,443	5,100	5,476	2,298	2,535	82	94
Germany	41,372	41,184	2,481	2,503	4,547	5,550	85	75
Greece	2,401	4,799	939	1,256	..	1,299	26	27
Irish Republic	1,134	1,910	158	346	24	37	6	8
Italy	30,155	35,680	3,072	4,438	6,430	9,280	84	96
Luxembourg	237	322	19	33	30	40	1	1
Netherlands	5,931	7,392	727	1,010	373	585	11	11
Portugal	4,273	4,379	1,368	1,333	272	537	16	15
Spain	15,297	21,760	3,206	5,353	1,326	4,742	50	61
Sweden	3,701	4,258	321	504	279	528	15	13
Bulgaria	1,731	2,082	233	261	525	90	40	24
Cyprus	235	411	106	118	..	41	3	3
Czech Republic	3,392	4,280	247	555	..	860	21	21
Estonia	428	524	77	80	5	15	7	4
Hungary	2,297	3,012	315	459	..	136	19	18
Latvia	432	905	77	130	19	44	19	11
Lithuania	882	1,588	94	148	19	29	15	14
Malta	184	225	46	47	14	13	1	1
Poland	8,533	14,589	1,422	2,521	..	825	85	88
Romania	2,447	3,541	390	502	251	57	40	34
Slovak Republic	1,136	1,434	104	216	81	64	11	10
Slovenia	778	1,014	44	78	..	72	2	2
Norway	1,758	2,155	377	514	175	283	35	25
Switzerland	3,323	3,956	264	324	411	619	39	48
Japan	..	57,510 [3]	21,694 [4]	16,491 [3]	15,262 [4]	..	242 [4]	232 [3]
USA	129,749	135,933	77,307	110,497	3,826	7,138	698	834

1 There are differences in definitions between countries which limit comparisons.
2 Includes mopeds and three-wheeled vehicles but excludes pedal cycles.
3 2006 data.
4 1996 data.

☎020-7944 3088
The figures in this table are outside the scope of UK National Statistics
Source - EU Energy and Transport in Figures (EUROSTAT)
Ministry of Land, Infrastructure and Transport, Japan
Highway Statistics, USA

10.4 Road traffic on national territory: 1996 and 2006

Billion vehicle kilometres

	Cars and taxis		Goods vehicles [1]		Motor cycles [2]		Buses and coaches	
	1996	2006	1996	2006	1996	2006	1996	2006
Great Britain	359.9	402.6	72.4	94.3	3.8	5.2	5.0	5.4
Austria	..	60.7	..	10.4	..	1.2	..	0.5
Belgium	92.4	80.3	1.6	19.1	..	1.4	61.6	0.8 [3]
Denmark	34.8	..	6.1	..	0.4	..	0.6	..
Finland	36.0	44.6	5.9	7.0	..	..	0.6	0.6
France	372.0	420.0 [3]	103.0	125.0 [3]	4.0	8.5 [3]	2.3	2.5 [3]
Germany	519.1	578.0 [3]	53.9	57.3 [3]	13.4	13.0 [3]	3.7	3.5 [3]
Greece	37.3	..	26.0	..	7.7	..	1.4	..
Irish Republic	23.2	..	4.8	..	0.3	..	0.4	..
Italy	190.9	..	37.0	..	..	..	..	..
Luxembourg	3.1	3.8	0.5	0.6	- [4]	-	-	-
Netherlands	90.0	..	16.1	..	1.3	..	0.6	..
Portugal	41.3	..	44.9	..	3.3	..	0.7	..
Spain	112.9	..	19.5	..	0.7	..	2.1	..
Sweden	56.6	63.0	8.3	10.7	0.5	0.8	1.1	0.9
Bulgaria	..	..	..	..	..	..	..	..
Cyprus	..	..	..	..	..	..	..	..
Czech Republic	24.2	..	..	..	0.6	..	11.8	..
Estonia	4.3	6.4 [3]	1.5	..	..	..	0.2	..
Hungary	..	..	..	..	..	..	..	..
Latvia	..	9.5	..	2.3	..	..	..	0.2
Lithuania	..	7.2	1.9	1.8	..	0.1	0.2	0.1
Malta	..	..	..	..	..	..	..	..
Poland	80.5	..	32.9	..	3.3	..	5.1	..
Romania	..	..	..	..	..	..	..	..
Slovak Republic	8.6	..	0.3	..	0.1	..	0.4	..
Slovenia	7.1	9.8	0.8	1.6	-	0.1	0.1	0.1
Norway	25.4	..	3.9	..	0.7	..	0.3	..
Switzerland	45.0	52.4	5.4	5.6	1.8	2.1	0.1	0.1
Japan	464.1	..	266.9	..	..	..	6.7	..
USA	2,366.5	2,707.9	1,608.5	2,111.5	16.0	20.0	10.6	11.3

1 Including light vans.
2 Including mopeds and three wheeled
 vehicles but excluding pedal cycles.
3 2005 data.
4 1995 data.

☎020-7944 3088
The figures in this table are outside the scope of UK National Statistics
Source - IRF
Federal Highway Administration, USA

10.5 Freight moved by mode: 1997 and 2007

Billion tonne-kilometres

	Road [1]		Rail		Inland waterway excluding coastal and one port traffic		Inland pipeline (Oil) 50 km long and over	
	1997	2007	1997	2007	1997	2007	1997	2007
Great Britain	..	..	16.9	21.0	0.2	0.2	11.2	10.2
Northern Ireland	..	..	-	-	-	-	-	-
United Kingdom	169.2	171.5	16.9	21.0	0.2	0.2	11.2	10.2
Austria	28.6	37.4	14.2	21.4	2.1	2.6	8.0	7.2
Belgium	43.7	42.1	7.5	8.2	5.8	9.3	1.5	1.5
Denmark	21.5	21.0	73.9	1.8	.	.	3.8	4.6
Finland	25.7	29.8	9.9	10.4	0.1	0.1	.	.
France	181.4	219.2	54.3	42.6	7.1	9.2	22.1	21.7
Germany	245.9	343.5	73.9	114.6	62.2	64.7	13.2	15.8
Greece	26.1	27.8	0.3	0.8	.	.	.	.
Irish Republic	7.0	19.0	0.5	0.1	.	.	.	.
Italy	178.4 [2]	191.9	22.9	25.3	0.2	0.1	9.8	11.5
Luxembourg	4.4	9.6	0.6	0.4	0.4	0.3	.	.
Netherlands	70.6	77.9	3.4	7.2	41.0	41.9	.	.
Portugal	36.0	46.2	2.3	2.6	.	.	.	.
Spain	109.5 [2]	258.9	12.5	11.1	.	.	6.5	8.9
Sweden	35.1	40.5	19.2	23.3	.	.	.	.
Bulgaria	5.6	14.6	7.4	5.2	0.6	1.0	0.3	0.4
Cyprus	1.3 [2]	1.2	.	.	.	.	.	.
Czech Republic	30.6	48.1	21.0	16.3	0.1	.	2.1	2.1
Estonia	2.8	6.4	5.1	8.4	.	.	.	.
Hungary	14.9 [2]	35.8	8.2	10.1	1.4	2.2	1.8	3.0
Latvia	3.4	13.2	14.0	18.3	.	.	6.4	3.5
Lithuania	5.2	20.3	8.6	14.4	.	.	2.7	1.0
Malta	0.3 [2]	0.3 [2]	.	.	.	.	.	.
Poland	63.7	150.9	67.7	54.3	0.9	0.3	15.0	23.5
Romania	21.8	59.5	22.1	15.8	4.3	8.2	2.3	1.9
Slovak Republic	15.4	27.2	12.4	6.7	1.5	1.0	5.5	5.8
Slovenia	3.9 [2]	13.7	2.9	3.6	.	.	.	.
Norway	14.1	19.4	3.0	3.5	.	.	4.2	4.3
Switzerland	9.1	11.2	8.7	13.4	0.1	0.1	0.3	0.2
Japan	306.0 [3]	347.0 [4]	25.0	23.0 [4]	..	..	..	..
USA	1,621.4	1,889.9 [4]	2,031.0	2,705.1 [4]	520.0	486.0 [4]	900.1	853.6 [3]

1 Freight moved by vehicles registered in the country on national and international territory.
2 Estimated
3 1996 Data
4 2006 Data

☎020-7944 3088
The figures in this table are outside
the scope of UK National Statistics
Source - EU Energy and Transport in Figures (EUROSTAT)
Ministry of Land, Infrastructure and Transport, Japan

10.6 Passenger transport by national vehicles on national territory: 1997 and 2007

Billion passenger kilometres

	Cars		Buses and coaches		Rail excluding metro systems		Total of these modes	
	1997	2007	1997	2007	1997	2007	1997	2007
Great Britain	632.0	689.0	45.7	51.5	34.9	50.1	712.6	790.6
Austria	63.9	72.0	8.8	9.8	8.7	9.5	81.4	91.3
Belgium	100.4	112.5	13.1	18.5	7.0	9.9	120.4	140.8
Denmark	50.3	55.3	7.6	7.4	5.2	6.2	63.1	68.9
Finland	51.9	63.8	8.0	7.5	3.4	3.8	63.3	75.1
France	659.5	727.8	42.0	47.1	61.8	80.3	763.2	855.2
Germany	817.1	868.7	68.0	65.4	72.4	79.3	957.5	1,013.4
Greece	50.0	95.0	20.7	22.0	1.9	1.9	72.6	118.9
Irish Republic	28.0	42.0	5.5	7.3	1.4	2.0	34.9	51.3
Italy	638.8	720.2	90.0	104.1	46.4	49.6	775.2	873.9
Luxembourg	4.9	6.6	0.6	0.9	0.3	0.3	5.8	7.8
Netherlands	136.5	148.8	12.0	12.3	13.9	16.3	162.4	177.4
Portugal	47.2	74.0	11.6	10.9	4.6	4.0	63.4	88.9
Spain	267.6	343.3	44.0	59.2	17.8	21.9	329.4	424.3
Sweden	87.2	99.6	9.8	8.5	7.0	10.3	104.0	118.4
Bulgaria	19.5	34.0	15.0	11.3	5.9	2.4	40.4 [1]	47.7
Cyprus	3.6	5.5	1.1	1.3	.	.	4.7 [1]	6.8
Czech Republic	59.0	71.5	15.6	16.1	7.7	6.9	82.3	94.6
Estonia	5.8	10.0	2.2	2.7	0.3	0.3	8.3	13.0
Hungary	46.1	41.4	16.6	17.2	8.7	8.8	71.4	67.3
Latvia	9.0	17.5	1.7	2.6	1.2	1.0	11.9	21.1
Lithuania	20.0	39.1	3.2	3.6	0.8	0.4	24.0	43.2
Malta	1.7	2.1	0.4	0.5	.	.	2.2	2.6
Poland	132.0	239.3	33.1	27.4	19.9	19.5	185.1	286.1
Romania	40.0	60.0	13.5	12.2	15.8	7.5	69.3	79.6
Slovak Republic	18.6	26.0	13.5	8.7	3.1	2.2	35.1	36.8
Slovenia	19.0	23.1	4.4	3.2	0.6	0.8	24.0	27.1
Norway	46.5	54.8	4.3	4.2	2.6	2.9	53.3	62.0
Switzerland	77.1	88.2	5.4	6.0	12.1	17.0	94.5	111.2
Japan	704.0	724.0 [2]	93.0	89.0 [2]	395.2	396.0 [2]	1,192.2	1,209.0
USA	6085.0 [1]	7317.0 [1,2]	233.0	275.0 [2]	21.0	23.7 [2]	6339.0	7,615.7

1 Including light trucks/vans.
2 2006 data.

☎020-7944 3088
The figures in this table are outside the scope of UK National Statistics
Source - EU Energy and Transport in Figures (EUROSTAT)
Ministry of Internal Affairs and Communications, Japan

10.7 Carbon dioxide emissions from transport: by source: 1997 and 2007

Million tonnes of carbon dioxide

	Road transport		Railways		Civil aviation		Navigation		All domestic transport[1]		All sources[2]		Memo items[3] International bunkers-aviation		International bunkers-navigation	
	1997	2007	1997	2007	1997	2007	1997	2007	1997	2007	1997	2007	1997	2007	1997	2007
European Union																
United Kingdom[4]	117.0	122.0	1.7	2.2	1.5	2.1	3.8	4.9	124.4	131.8	552.4	546.4	45.5	69.9	8.3	7.2
Austria	15.7	23.2	0.1	0.2	0.1	0.1	0.1	0.1	16.2	23.9	67.2	74.2	1.5	2.2	..	..
Belgium	21.9	24.3	0.2	0.1	-	-	0.4	0.5	22.6	25.1	121.8	114.5	3.6	3.8	17.6	30.4
Denmark	11.0	13.2	0.3	0.2	0.2	0.1	0.8	0.5	12.3	14.0	64.5	53.2	2.0	2.7	4.4	3.6
Finland	10.6	12.3	0.2	0.1	0.3	0.3	0.5	0.6	12.3	14.0	62.4	66.1	1.0	1.7	1.3	1.5
France	122.7	127.4	0.8	0.6	5.7	4.6	1.7	3.0	131.4	136.0	400.3	397.1	11.4	17.1	8.2	9.3
Germany	166.1	144.1	2.1	1.3	2.6	2.3	1.3	0.5	176.1	151.9	914.3	841.2	16.1	25.3	6.9	9.9
Greece	14.8	19.8	0.1	0.1	1.0	1.3	1.8	2.1	17.8	23.4	93.7	113.6	2.4	2.9	9.9	10.0
Irish Republic	7.1	13.8	0.1	0.1	0.1	0.1	0.1	-	7.5	14.1	38.4	47.5	1.3	3.0	0.5	0.4
Italy	105.5	118.7	0.4	0.3	2.1	2.4	6.0	5.0	114.4	127.2	443.1	475.3	6.2	10.4	3.1	7.8
Luxembourg	3.7	6.6	-	-	-	-	-	-	3.7	6.6	8.8	11.8	0.8	1.3	-	-
Netherlands	29.7	34.5	0.1	0.1	-	-	0.4	0.6	30.3	35.2	171.1	172.7	8.7	11.1	38.4	51.4
Portugal	13.8	18.2	0.1	0.1	0.2	0.4	0.2	0.2	14.4	18.8	53.6	62.8	1.6	2.5	1.1	1.8
Spain	64.9	97.8	0.3	0.3	4.1	7.6	1.3	3.3	70.8	109.1	262.4	366.4	7.1	10.4	18.1	26.8
Sweden	17.4	19.4	0.1	0.1	0.7	0.6	0.4	0.4	18.6	20.6	56.9	51.6	1.6	2.2	4.3	7.4
Bulgaria	4.0	7.3	0.1	0.1	0.2	0.1	-	..	5.4	8.2	63.2	58.9	0.4	0.5	1.1	0.2
Cyprus	1.2	2.2	..	..	..	..	..	..	1.2	2.2	5.9	8.3	0.8	0.9	0.3	0.6
Czech Republic	10.4	18.0	0.3	0.3	0.1	-	-	-	11.1	18.5	131.8	129.9	0.5	1.1	..	..
Estonia	1.5	2.2	0.1	0.1	-	-	-	0.1	1.8	2.5	18.6	19.1	0.1	0.1	0.3	0.8
Hungary	6.9	12.2	0.3	0.2	..	..	-	-	7.2	12.4	61.1	57.8	0.5	0.7	..	..
Latvia	1.7	3.5	0.2	0.2	-	-	-	-	2.0	3.7	8.7	8.6	0.1	0.2	0.2	0.6
Lithuania	3.5	4.8	0.2	0.2	..	-	-	-	3.7	5.1	15.2	15.9	0.1	0.2	0.2	0.3
Malta	0.5	0.5	..	..	..	-	-	-	0.5	0.5	2.3	2.7	-	-	..	2.7
Poland	30.3	36.3	0.7	0.5	0.1	0.1	0.1	-	32.4	37.5	369.2	328.3	0.8	1.3	0.5	0.8
Romania	9.6	12.0	0.9	0.6	-	-	0.2	0.1	10.8	12.8	121.1	110.9	0.2	0.4	0.8	0.2
Slovak Republic	4.3	6.4	0.2	0.1	-	-	..	..	4.5	6.5	41.4	38.1	0.1	0.1	-	-
Slovenia	4.3	5.1	-	-	-	-	..	..	4.3	5.2	16.0	17.0	0.1	0.1	..	0.2

1 Includes a small amount of emissions from other transport sources.
2 The Land Use, Land Use Change and Forestry (LULUCF) category has been excluded from the totals, because treatment of this category can differ between countries.
3 Categories not included in the national emissions total.
4 Figures for the UK are slightly higher than those in Table 3.7 due to the inclusion of emissions from Overseas Territories.

☎ 020-7944 4129

The figures in this table are outside the scope of UK National Statistics

Source - UNFCCC

10.8 (a) Petrol and diesel in the European Union: current retail prices: 1998-2008[1]

Premium unleaded petrol (95 RON): per 100 litres   US Dollars

	1998	1999	2000	2001	2002	2003	2004	2005	2006	2007	2008
United Kingdom	108	113	121	110	110	125	147	158	168	189	196
Austria	90	87	87	81	82	99	118	130	137	154	179
Belgium	96	96	97	90	92	115	142	142	170	190	213
Denmark [2]	96	102	103	99	104	125	140	140	161	179	201
Germany	91	93	94	91	99	123	141	152	159	184	205
Finland	104	106	105	99	101	124	146	142	162	178	208
France	102	101	101	93	96	115	132	145	155	174	198
Greece	70	69	72	67	69	84	101	109	121	139	162
Irish Republic	84	80	82	80	81	98	118	129	140	153	179
Italy	101	102	100	94	99	120	140	152	161	178	202
Luxembourg	71	74	76	72	73	88	112	127	136	154	..
Netherlands	107	107	107	103	113	131	161	168	178	200	225
Portugal	90	86	80	81	83	109	128	142	164	181	203
Spain	74	75	76	73	77	92	108	119	128	142	162
Sweden	101	101	104	91	96	116	136	147	156	172	191

Lead replacement petrol [3,4] : per 100 litres

	1998	1999	2000	2001	2002	2003	2004	2005	2006	2007	2008
United Kingdom	118	125	130	115	115	131	155	..	..	..	..
Austria	..	..	..	..	..	..	..	..	..	..	..
Belgium	105	103	101	97	99	..	..	..	..	..	..
Denmark	..	..	..	..	..	..	..	..	..	..	..
Germany	..	..	..	..	..	..	..	..	..	..	..
Finland	..	..	..	..	..	..	..	..	..	..	..
France	107	106	108	100	103	124	142	..	..	..	..
Greece	75	75	76	71	74	89	108	117	130	147	173
Irish Republic	98	95	96	..	..	..	..	..	..	..	..
Italy	107	107	104	98	..	..	..	..	..	..	..
Luxembourg	80	..	..	..	..	..	..	..	..	..	..
Netherlands	..	..	..	..	..	..	..	..	..	..	..
Portugal	93	89	..	..	..	..	..	..	..	..	..
Spain	78	79	81	77	82	100	117	130	140	..	..
Sweden	106	105	107	..	..	..	..	..	..	..	..

Diesel: per 100 litres

	1998	1999	2000	2001	2002	2003	2004	2005	2006	2007	2008
United Kingdom	109	117	123	112	113	128	150	165	175	194	215
Austria	70	68	72	67	68	82	101	119	127	142	181
Belgium	69	68	75	70	68	84	109	109	135	150	183
Denmark	77	80	88	84	86	103	114	114	138	152	186
Germany	65	68	94	73	79	100	116	133	140	160	195
Finland	69	73	78	73	74	91	103	105	128	140	185
France	72	73	78	72	73	90	110	128	135	150	186
Greece	51	56	62	56	59	72	92	109	120	135	176
Irish Republic	79	75	78	73	73	91	110	129	137	148	186
Italy	79	81	82	78	81	99	117	138	146	159	196
Luxembourg	57	58	64	59	60	72	86	105	115	128	..
Netherlands	72	74	78	73	74	90	110	127	136	150	188
Portugal	59	58	60	60	61	80	98	116	133	149	185
Spain	79	60	64	62	65	78	94	111	119	131	165
Sweden	84	81	92	84	86	100	116	139	151	163	203

10.8 (b) Petrol and diesel in the European Union: Tax as a percentage of retail prices: 1998-2008[1]

Premium unleaded petrol (95 RON)											Percentage
	1998	1999	2000	2001	2002	2003	2004	2005	2006	2007	2008
United Kingdom	81	81	75	76	77	76	74	69	67	67	62
Austria	68	68	61	63	64	64	62	57	56	57	57
Belgium	76	74	66	67	69	67	66	66	61	61	59
Denmark [2]	72	73	67	68	70	70	68	68	62	61	60
Germany	75	74	69	72	73	74	71	67	65	65	63
Finland	78	74	67	68	70	72	68	70	64	63	62
France	81	79	70	71	74	74	72	67	64	64	61
Greece	67	63	53	55	56	55	52	49	47	49	48
Irish Republic	68	68	59	56	64	64	64	60	57	57	55
Italy	75	73	65	66	68	68	66	63	61	60	58
Luxembourg	66	64	56	58	59	59	60	56	54	54	..
Netherlands	75	73	66	69	68	71	67	66	64	63	61
Portugal	73	68	49	46	69	68	67	63	60	61	59
Spain	69	67	59	59	62	62	59	55	53	52	50
Sweden	76	73	67	68	70	70	68	65	63	63	62

Lead replacement petrol [3,4]											
United Kingdom	83	81	74	76	78	76	72	..	..	..	..
Austria	..	..	..	..	..	..	..	..	..	..	..
Belgium	77	76	64	64	67	..	..	..	..	..	..
Denmark	..	..	..	..	..	..	..	..	..	..	..
Germany	..	..	..	..	..	..	..	..	..	..	..
Finland	..	..	..	..	..	..	..	..	..	..	..
France	83	81	70	72	74	75	72	..	..	..	..
Greece	70	67	56	58	58	58	54	51	49	48	46
Irish Republic	70	69	61	..	..	..	..	..	..	..	..
Italy	76	74	66	68	..	..	..	..	..	..	..
Luxembourg	69	..	..	..	..	..	..	..	..	..	..
Netherlands	..	..	..	..	..	..	..	..	..	..	..
Portugal	74	67	..	..	..	..	..	..	..	..	..
Spain	71	69	60	60	63	62	59	55	52	..	..
Sweden	81	78	72	..	..	..	..	..	..	..	..

Diesel											
United Kingdom	82	81	74	74	76	74	72	67	65	65	58
Austria	63	62	54	55	57	57	55	50	50	52	48
Belgium	64	63	53	54	59	58	55	55	48	47	43
Denmark	64	61	56	59	60	61	60	60	53	53	49
Germany	68	67	61	63	66	67	64	58	56	56	51
Finland	67	63	54	55	57	58	56	56	49	49	47
France	75	73	62	64	66	66	64	57	55	55	50
Greece	65	64	52	54	55	54	48	43	42	43	40
Irish Republic	64	64	55	48	57	58	59	53	51	51	46
Italy	71	70	60	61	64	63	60	54	52	53	48
Luxembourg	63	60	50	52	53	53	50	44	43	44	..
Netherlands	67	65	56	57	59	59	57	52	50	50	48
Portugal	64	63	52	51	57	57	55	50	49	51	46
Spain	64	62	53	54	56	56	53	47	45	45	41
Sweden	62	60	55	55	57	59	59	55	53	54	51

1 There are revisions to some of the earlier data
2 Regular unleaded (92 RON) prices have been used from 2000 to date.
3 Refers to Four star petrol in earlier years.
4 The sale of Lead Replacement Petrol has been discontinued in most
   EU Countries

☎020-7944 4129
The figures in this table are outside
the scope of UK National Statistics
Source - Department of Energy and Climate Change

10.9 Selected trading fleets by type of vessel and flag at mid year: 1998 and 2008

Gross tonnage (million)

| | All trading ships of 100 gross tons and over | | of which: | | | | | | | |
| | | | Tankers | | Bulk carriers | | Container ships | | General cargo | |
	1998	2008	1998	2008	1998	2008	1998	2008	1998	2008
United Kingdom and Crown Dependencies	7.2	21.4	3.4	7.5	0.9	3.0	1.3	6.9	0.6	2.3
Denmark	5.7	9.4	1.6	2.4	0.5	0.4	2.4	5.7	0.7	0.5
France	4.2	5.8	2.4	3.1	0.4	0.2	0.6	1.6	0.3	0.1
Germany	7.4	13.1	0.2	0.6	0.0	0.2	5.8	11.7	1.0	0.2
Greece	25.3	36.6	12.8	21.6	9.1	10.6	1.1	2.5	0.9	0.4
Italy	6.1	13.1	2.2	4.1	1.4	2.2	0.4	1.1	0.9	2.3
Netherlands	4.4	7.2	0.6	0.7	0.2	0.2	1.2	1.5	1.9	3.7
Bahamas	25.9	43.9	12.5	22.0	4.8	7.6	1.0	2.0	5.9	6.9
Bermuda	4.9	9.0	2.8	4.4	1.2	1.8	0.5	0.8	0.2	0.1
China	15.3	24.2	2.2	5.0	6.5	10.4	1.4	3.5	5.0	4.8
Cyprus	23.3	19.6	4.1	4.7	11.4	8.9	2.2	3.8	5.1	1.7
Hong Kong	6.3	37.6	0.2	9.0	4.6	19.3	0.9	7.0	0.5	2.3
India	6.5	8.3	2.9	5.2	2.9	2.5	0.1	0.2	0.5	0.5
Japan	16.9	12.0	7.9	5.3	4.2	2.7	0.9	0.5	2.3	2.4
Liberia	59.8	79.8	32.7	35.7	17.2	14.6	3.8	25.5	4.3	3.9
Malaysia	4.9	6.8	2.1	5.3	1.4	0.3	0.6	0.7	0.8	0.5
Malta	23.6	30.9	9.7	10.9	9.1	13.6	0.7	1.7	3.9	3.6
Marshall Islands	6.0	37.4	3.4	22.0	1.5	9.7	1.0	4.1	0.1	1.5
Norway	22.0	16.6	13.0	8.9	3.8	2.5	0.1	0.1	4.0	4.1
Panama	92.8	173.9	26.3	43.3	39.3	74.6	11.3	29.3	14.3	23.6
Philippines	8.5	4.8	0.2	0.5	5.7	2.4	0.2	0.2	2.0	1.4
Russia	7.1	5.1	1.5	1.5	1.3	0.5	0.3	0.1	3.9	2.9
St Vincent and the Grenadines	7.8	5.4	1.4	0.4	3.0	2.0	0.1	0.2	3.1	2.8
Singapore	19.2	37.2	9.0	19.0	4.4	7.3	3.2	7.4	2.6	3.5
South Korea	6.1	13.0	0.6	2.5	3.4	7.6	1.0	1.4	1.1	1.2
Taiwan	5.6	2.6	0.9	0.8	2.4	1.2	2.1	0.5	0.2	0.1
Turkey	6.1	5.0	0.7	0.8	3.9	2.1	0.1	0.4	1.2	1.5
USA	10.1	10.6	4.6	2.7	1.3	1.2	2.8	3.2	1.2	3.1
World total [1]	500.3	770.7	180.3	273.8	161.1	225.2	51.1	133.2	88.6	106.9

1 Including other trading fleets not listed.

☎020-7944 4119

The figures in this table are outside the scope of UK National Statistics
Source - Lloyds Register - Fairplay

10.10   Selected outputs of airlines: 1998 and 2008

State of airline registration	Scheduled services								Non-scheduled services	
	International and domestic traffic									
	Aircraft kilometres flown (million)		Freight [1] tonne-kilometres flown (billion)		Passenger kilometres flown (billion)		International passenger kilometres flown (billion)		International and domestic passenger kilometres flown (billion)	
	1998	2008	1998	2008	1998	2008	1998	2008	1998	2008
United Kingdom [2]	886	1,508	4.7	6.3	152.0	232.6	145.0	223.6	84.1	78.9
Austria	123	159	0.3	0.4	12.0	16.5	11.5	16.3	1.8	2.4
Belgium	153	170	0.5	1.0	15.0	8.2	15.3	8.2	0	0
Denmark	59	63	0	0.2	5.1	6.5	4.7	6.8	0.1	1.2
Finland	95	148	0.3	0.5	10.7	17.9	9.5	17.0	2.4	5.2
France	559	1,000	4.6	6.1	90.9	150.1	59.9	130.0	0.1	1.9
Germany	636	1,548	6.2	8.4	90.4	220.8	82.9	211.1	31.4	8.9
Greece	72	87	0.1	0.1	8.5	9.0	7.5	7.2	0.0	0.6
Irish Republic	0	525	0.0	0.1	8.5	79.5	8.4	79.5	0.0	0.0
Italy	358	385	1.5	1.3	38.1	40.8	28.9	29.5	8.5	3.2
Luxembourg	39	96	2.2	5.4	0.5	0.7	0.5	0.7	0.0	0.5
Netherlands	337	538	3.8	4.9	57.6	94.4	57.6	94.4	0.0	4.0
Portugal	98	230	0.2	0.3	11.2	24.2	9.7	21.7	0.3	1.8
Spain	331	627	0.8	1.3	40.0	87.1	26.0	64.0	16.6	13.5
Sweden	127	135	0.3	0.2	10.0	12.8	7.1	10.3	0.4	4.8
Bulgaria	16	21	-	-	2.0	1.7	2.0	1.7	0.0	0.6
Cyprus	20	35	-	-	2.7	4.5	2.7	4.5	0.0	0.1
Czech Republic	32	76	-	-	2.6	6.3	2.6	6.3	0.3	4.4
Estonia	6	10	-	-	0.2	0.8	0.2	0.8	0.1	0.2
Hungary	34	54	-	-	2.5	4.1	2.5	4.1	0.0	0.2
Latvia	6	27	-	-	0.2	1.5	0.2	1.5	0.1	0.4
Lithuania	10	15	-	-	0.3	0.9	0.3	0.9	0.1	1.0
Malta	20	28	-	-	2.0	2.8	1.9	2.8	0.6	0.2
Poland	46	97	0.1	0.1	4.0	7.9	4.2	7.6	0.9	0.7
Romania	22	55	-	-	2.0	4.0	1.6	3.8	0.1	0.4
Slovak Republic	3	25	-	-	0.1	2.9	0.1	2.8	0.2	1.1
Slovenia	8	20	-	-	0.4	1.0	0.4	1.0	0.3	0.3
Norway	134	143	0.2	0.2	9.5	12.1	5.2	7.5	0.1	1.2
Switzerland	219	220	7.5	8.2	154.0	140.9	85.6	72.6	0.3	1.9
Japan	828	870	7.5	8.2	154.0	140.9	85.6	72.6	0.3	1.9
USA	9,114	11,880	25.6	39.3	984.9	1,275.2	273.4	390.9	13.0	16.1
Russian Federation	483	931	0.7	2.4	46.3	91.1	18.9	40.9	2.3	31.5

1 Excludes mail.
2 Source - UK Civil Aviation Authority (CAA).

☎020-7944 3088
The figures in this table are outside
the scope of UK National Statistics
Source - International Civil Aviation Organisation (ICAO)

10.11 International comparisons of road deaths for selected OECD countries: 1997-2008[1]

	1997	1998	1999	2000	2001	2002	2003	2004	2005	2006	2007	2008 [2]	Rate of road deaths in 2008 per 100,000 population [3]
Great Britain	3,599	3,421	3,423	3,409	3,450	3,431	3,508	3,221	3,201	3,172	2,946	2,538	4.3
Northern Ireland	144	160	141	171	148	150	150	147	135	126	113	107	6.0
United Kingdom	3,743	3,581	3,564	3,580	3,598	3,581	3,658	3,368	3,336	3,298	3,059	2,645	4.3
Austria	1,105	963	1,079	976	958	956	931	878	768	730	691	679	8.1
Belgium	1,364	1,500	1,397	1,470	1,486	1,306	1,214	1,162	1,089	1,069	1,067	922	8.6
Denmark	489	499	514	498	431	463	432	369	331	306	406	392	7.2
Finland	438	400	431	396	433	415	379	375	379	336	380	344	6.5
France	8,444	8,918	8,487	8,079	8,160	7,655	6,058	5,530	5,318	4,709	4,620	4,275	6.7
Germany	8,549	7,792	7,772	7,503	6,977	6,842	6,613	5,842	5,361	5,091	4,949	4,477	5.4
Greece	2,105	2,182	2,116	2,037	1,880	1,634	1,605	1,670	1,658	1,657	1,612	1,559	13.9
Irish Republic	472	458	413	415	411	376	337	374	399	365	338	279	6.3
Italy	6,713	6,314	6,688	7,061	7,096	6,980	6,563	6,122	5,818	5,669	5,131	4,739	7.9
Luxembourg	60	57	58	76	70	62	53	50	45	36	43	35	7.2
Netherlands	1,163	1,066	1,090	1,082	993	987	1,028	804	750	730	791	750	4.6
Portugal	2,210	2,126	1,995	1,860	1,671	1,675	1,546	1,294	1,247	969	974	882	8.3
Spain	5,604	5,957	5,738	5,776	5,517	5,347	5,400	4,749	4,442	4,104	3,823	3,102	6.9
Sweden	541	531	580	591	554	532	529	480	440	445	471	397	4.3
Bulgaria	915	1,003	1,047	1,012	1,011	959	960	943	957	1,043	1,006	1,061	13.9
Cyprus	115	111	113	111	98	94	97	117	102	86	89	82	10.4
Czech Republic	1,597	1,360	1,455	1,486	1,334	1,431	1,447	1,382	1,286	1,063	1,222	1,076	10.4
Estonia	280	284	232	204	199	223	164	170	169	204	196	132	9.8
Hungary	1,391	1,371	1,306	1,200	1,239	1,429	1,326	1,296	1,278	1,303	1,232	996	9.9
Latvia	525	627	604	588	558	559	532	516	442	407	419	316	13.9
Lithuania	725	829	748	641	706	697	709	752	773	759	739	498	14.8
Malta	18	17	4	15	16	16	16	13	17	11	14	15	3.7
Poland	7,310	7,080	6,730	6,294	5,534	5,827	5,640	5,712	5,444	5,243	5,583	5,437	14.3
Romania	2,863	2,778	2,505	2,499	2,461	2,398	2,235	2,418	2,461	2,478	2,794	3,063	14.2
Slovakia	788	819	647	628	614	610	645	603	560	579	627	606	11.2
Slovenia	357	309	334	313	278	269	242	274	258	263	293	214	10.6
Norway	303	352	304	341	275	312	282	259	224	242	233	255	5.4
Switzerland	587	597	583	592	554	513	546	510	409	370	384	357	4.7
Australia	1,768	1,755	1,758	1,817	1,737	1,715	1,621	1,590	1,637	1,598	1,617	1,466	6.7
Canada	3,064	2,934	2,972	2,927	2,779	2,931	2,766	2,725	2,925	2,892	2,754	2,431	7.3
Iceland	15	27	21	32	24	29	23	23	19	31	15	12	3.8
Japan	11,254	10,805	10,372	10,403	10,060	9,575	8,877	8,492	7,931	7,272	6,639	6,023	4.7
New Zealand	540	502	509	462	455	404	461	436	405	391	422	366	8.6
Republic of Korea	13,343	10,416	10,756	10,236	8,097	7,222	7,212	6,563	6,376	6,327	6,166	5,870	12.1
USA	42,013	41,501	41,717	41,945	42,116	42,815	42,643	42,636	43,443	42,708	41,259	37,261	12.3

1 In accordance with the commonly agreed international definition, most countries define a fatality as one being due to a road accident where death occurs within 30 days of the accident. The official road accident statistics of some countries however, limit the fatalities to those occurring within shorter periods after the accident. have been adjusted according to the factors used by the Economic Commission for Europe and International Transport Forum, to Numbers of deaths and death rates in the above table have been adjusted according to the factors used by the Economic Commission for Europe and International Transport Forum, to represent standardised 30-day deaths: Italy (7 days) +8%; France (6 days) +5.7%; Portugal (1 day) +14%; Republic of Korea (3 days) +15%

2 Provisional data.
3 Population taken from the OECD's International Road and Traffic Accidents Database and EUROSTAT and may differ from the figures in Tables 10.1 and 10.4.

☎ 020-7944 6595

Source: OECD, EUROSTAT, CARE, IRTAD and ITF

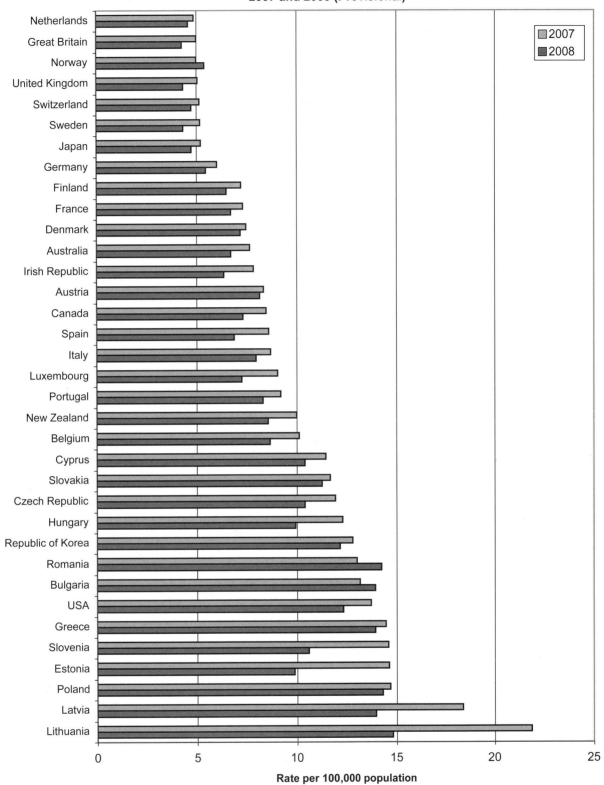

Chart 10.11 International comparisons: road deaths per 100,000 population: 2007 and 2008 (Provisional)

Rate per 100,000 population

Abbreviations used in Transport Statistics Great Britain: 2009 Edition

AAIB:	Air Accident Investigation Branch
ABI:	Association of British Insurers Also: Annual Business Inquiry for the employment data tables 1.17 and 1.18
ABP:	Associated British Ports
AES:	Annual Earning Survey
APEG:	Airborne Particles Expert Group
APTIS:	All Purpose Ticket Issuing System
BAA:	British Airports Authority
BEA:	(French) Bureau Enquetes Accidents
BERR:	Department for Business, Enterprise and Regulatory Reform
BIS:	Department for Business, Innovation and Skills
BR:	British Rail
BRB:	British Railways Board
BRF:	British Road Federation
BSOG:	Bus Service Operators Grant
BW:	British Waterways
CAA:	Civil Aviation Authority
CfIT:	Commission for Integrated Transport
CLG:	Communities and Local Government
CPI:	Consumer Prices Index
CSRGT:	Continuing Survey of Road Goods Transport
CTRL:	Channel Tunnel Rail Link
CVTF:	Cleaner Vehicles Task Force
DB:	Deutsche Bahn
DBFO:	Design, Build, Finance and Operate (contracts)
DDA:	Disability Discrimination Act
DECC	Department for Energy and Climate Change
DEFRA:	Department for Environment, Food and Rural Affairs
DfT:	Department for Transport
DLR:	Docklands Light Railway
DOE:	Department of the Environment
DPM:	Deputy Prime Minister
DiPTAC:	Disabled Person Transport Advisory Committee
DRS:	Direct Rail Services
DSA:	Driving Standards Agency
DVLA:	Driver and Vehicle Licensing Agency
EA:	Environmental Accounts
EC:	European Community

EEC:	European Economic Community
EPS:	European Passenger Services Ltd ex-BR subsidiary)
EST:	Energy Saving Trust
ETC:	European Transport Council
ETS:	Emissions Trading Scheme
EU:	European Union
EuroNCAP:	EU New Car Assessment Programme
EUTC:	European Union Transport Council
EWS:	English, Welsh and Scottish Railway
FDR:	Fuel Duty Rebate
FFG:	Freight Facilities Grant
FTA:	Freight Transport Association
GDP:	Gross Domestic Product
GLA:	Greater London Authority
GMDSS:	Global Maritime Distress and Safety System
GMPTE:	Greater Manchester Passenger Transport Executive
GOL:	Government Office for London
Grt:	Gross registered tonnage
GT:	Gross Tonnage
gvw:	gross vehicle weight
HA:	Highways Agency
HERL:	Heathrow Express Rail Link
HGV:	Heavy Goods Vehicle
HMRC:	Her Majesty's Revenue and Customs
HSC:	Health and Safety Commission
HSE:	Health and Safety Executive
ICAO:	International Civil Aviation Organisation
ICC:	International Climate Change
IEA:	International Energy Agency
Int:	International
IPCC	Intergovernmental Panel on Climate Change
IPS:	International Passenger Survey
IRF:	International Road Federation
IRFT:	International Rail Freight Terminal
KSI:	Killed or seriously injured
LA(s):	Local Authority(s)
LCA:	London City Airport
LCR:	ondon and Continental Railways
LDDC:	London Docklands Development Corporation
LEQ:	Equivalent Continuous Noise Level

LFS:	Labour Force Survey		RPI:	Retail Prices Index
LGV:	Light Goods Vehicle		RTFO:	Renewable Transport Fuel Obligation
LoLo:	Lift-on Lift-off			
LRT:	London Regional Transport		RTRA:	Road Traffic Reduction Act
LT:	London Transport		RVAR:	Rail Vehicle Accessibility Regulations
LTP:	Local Transport Plan			
LU:	London Underground		SACTRA:	Standing Advisory Committee
MAIB:	Marine Accident Investigation Branch		on	Trunk Road Assessment
			SBG:	Scottish Bus Group
MCA:	Maritime and Coastguard Agency		SIC:	Standard Industrial Classification (of Economic Activity)
MMC:	Monopolies and Mergers Commission.			
			SMMT:	Society of Motor Manufacturers and Traders
MML:	Midland Mainline (rail)			
MOT:	vehicle testing scheme		SOC:	Standard Occupational Classification
MPV:	Multi-purpose vehicle			
NAEI:	National Atmospheric Emissions Inventory		SPAD:	(train) Signal Passed at Danger
			SPTE:	Strathclyde Passenger Transport Executive
NATS:	National Air Traffic Services			
NBC:	National Bus Company		SRA:	Strategic Rail Authority
NDLS:	National Dock Labour Scheme		STAG:	School Travel Advisory Group
NEG:	National Express Group		STES:	Short Term Employment Surveys
NET:	Nottingham Express Transit			
NEXUS:	Tyne and Wear Passenger Transport Executive		SYPTE:	South Yorkshire Passenger Transport Executive
NTKm:	Net tonne kilometres		TAG:	Track Access Grant
NTO:	National Training Organisation		TCF:	Transport Card Forum
NTS:	National Travel Survey		TEN:	Trans European Network
OCJR:	Office for Criminal Justice Reform		TfL:	Transport for London
			TGWU:	Transport and General Workers Union
OECD:	Organisation for Economic Co-operation and Development			
			TMC:	Traffic Message Channel
ONS:	Office for National Statistics		TRL:	Transport Research Laboratory
OPEC:	Organisation of Petroleum Exporting Countries		TSO:	The Stationery Office
			TWA:	Transport and Works Act
ORR:	Office of Rail Regulation		TWPTE:	Tyne and Wear Passenger Transport Executive
OTIF:	International Railway Transport Organisation			
			UA:	Unitary Authority
PAYE:	Pay (tax) as You Earn		UNECE	United Nations Economic Commission for Europe
PCO:	Public Carriage Office			
PFI:	Public Finance Initiative		UNFCCC	United Nations Framework Convention on Climate Change
PHV:	Private Hire Vehicle			
PLG:	Private Light Goods (vehicle)		VAT:	Value Added Tax
PPM:	Public Performance Measure		VCA:	Vehicle Certification Agency
PPP:	Public-Private Partnership		VED:	Vehicle Excise Duty
PSV:	Public Service Vehicle		VI:	Vehicle Inspectorate
PTA:	Passenger Transport Area		VOSA:	Vehicle and Operator Services Agency
PTE:	Passenger Transport Executive			
RBSG:	Rural Bus Subsidy Grant		WHR:	Welsh Highland Railway
RDS-TMC:	Radio Data System - Traffic Message Channel		WYPTE:	West Yorkshire Passenger Transport Executive
RID:	Regulations concerning the International Carriage of Dangerous Goods by Rail			
RIDDOR:	Reporting of Injuries, Diseases and Dangerous Occurrences Regulations			
RITC:	Rail Industry Training Council			
Ro-Ro:	Roll-on Roll-off			

Index

Figures indicate table numbers.

CLIP TRANSPORT STATISTICS

CLIP Transport Statistics (CLIP-TS) is a sub-group of the Central and Local (Government) Information Partnership (CLIP), the main forum for discussion between central and local government on statistical matters.

Its formal terms of reference are:

- To act as a forum for consultation between DfT and local authorities on any transport statistics of interest to either side that are not dealt with by other groups; and on any gaps in the Department's coverage.

- To act as a point of contact between local authorities and DfT on statistical matters of common concern, including the statistics needed for the monitoring of Local Transport Plans, National Indicators, Regional Statistics and other relevant matters.

CLIP-TS is comprised of a Local Authority side and a DfT side. The LA side represents the Passenger Transport Authorities, Shire Counties, Unitary Authorities and London Boroughs. London Transport also attends in observer status.

Recent work of the group has centred on the information requirements for the transport National Indicators. This and other useful information will be shown on the group's website which can be found at:
http://www.clip.local.gov.uk/lgv/core/page.do?pageId=31640

Who sits on the group?

Anna Heyworth - Statistician, Regional and Local Transport Statistics, Statistics Travel Division, Department for Transport (Chair)
Penny Allen - Regional and Local Transport Statistics, Statistics Travel Division, Department for Transport (Secretary)
Claire Horton - Staffordshire County Council (LA Lead)
Tim Stamp - Divisional Manager, Statistics Travel Division, Department for Transport
David Robinson - Statistician, Statistics Roads Division, Department for Transport
Keith Oates - South Yorkshire Passenger Transport Executive
Keith Rogers - Solihull MBC
Mike Collop - Transport for London
Philip Heyes - Government Office for Yorkshire and the Humber
Ray Heywood - Leeds City Council
William Bryans - Surrey County Council
John Brown - Government Office: East
Belinda Godbold - Suffolk County Council

For further information contact:

> Clare Horton
> Transport Policy Officer
> Staffordshire County Council
> Development Services Directorate
> Riverway
> Stafford
> ST16 3TJ
>
> *Tel:* 01785 276636
> *Fax:* 01785 276621
> *Email:* clare.horton@staffordshire.gov.uk

TRANSPORT STATISTICS USERS GROUP

The Transport Statistics Users Group (TSUG) was set up in 1985 as a result of an initiative by the Statistics Users Council and the Chartered Institute for Transport (now known as The Institute of Logistics and Transport). From its inception it has had strong links with the government Departments responsible for transport.

The aims of the group are:

- To identify problems in the collection, provision, use and understanding of transport statistics, and to discuss solutions with the responsible authorities.

- To provide a forum for the exchange of views and information between users and providers.

- To encourage the proper use of statistics through publicity.

- To facilitate a network for sharing ideas, information, and expertise.

The group holds regular seminars on topical subjects connected with the provision and/or use of transport statistics. Recent seminars have included:

- Road Congestion Statistics

- GIS in Transport planning

- Road Safety Statistics

- UK Investment in Transport Infrastructure

- Active Traffic Management

- The Role of Motorcycling in the 21st Century

- Better Publicly Available Statistics On Vehicle Characteristics

- Concessionary Fares and the new Statistics and Registration Services Act

- Measuring the Importance of Shipping to the UK Economy

- National Passenger Survey

A Scottish seminar was also held.

A newsletter is sent to all members about four times a year. Corporate membership of the Group is £50, personal membership £22.50, and student membership £10. For further details please visit www.tsug.org.uk or contact:

> Nina Webster
> Walking and Accessibility Programme Manager
> Surface Transport Strategy
> 9th Floor (area green 7)
> Palestra, 197 Blackfriars Road
> London
> SE1 8NJ
>
> Tel: 020 3054 0874
> Email: nina.webster@tube.tfl.gov.uk

The TSUG also produces a Transport *Yearbook* which contains information on sources from governmental and non-governmental organisations, including some European sources. The yearbook is supplied free to TSUG members. Non-members can purchase a copy from The Stationery Office (TSO).

Transport Statistics Publications (as at November 2009)

TSO publications
(Transport Statistics Reports - priced)

Obtainable from:
TSO
Mail, Telephone, Fax and E-mail
PO Box 29, Norwich NR3 1GN
Telephone orders & general enquiries: +44 (0)870 600 5522
Fax orders: +44 (0)870 600 5533
E-mail: customer.services@tso.co.uk
Textphone: +44 (0)870 240 3701

TSO Shops – London, Belfast and Edinburgh

TSO@Blackwell and other Accredited Agents

Annual Reports
Transport Statistics Great Britain: 2008 Edition
(ISBN: 978-0-11-553030-2)
Maritime Statistics: 2008 (ISBN: 978-0-11-553096-8)
Reported Road Casualties Great Britain: 2008
(ISBN: 978-0-11-553089-0)

See also TSO's virtual bookshop at:
http://www.tsoshop.co.uk

DfT: Transport Statistics Publications
(Transport Statistics Bulletins - free)
Obtainable from:
Department for Transport
2/29
Great Minster House
76 Marsham Street
London
SW1P 4DR
+44 (0)20 7944 3098

Annual Bulletins – produced by Transport Statistics
Compendium of Motorcycling Statistics
National Rail Travel Survey
National Travel Survey
Public Transport Statistics Great Britain
Reported Road Casualties Great Britain: Main Results
Road Conditions in England (formerly NRMCS)
Road Statistics: Traffic Speeds and Congestion
Road Freight Statistics
Sea Passenger Statistics
Transport Trends
UK Seafarer Statistics
Vehicle Excise Duty Evasion
Vehicle Licensing Statistics
Waterborne Freight in the United Kingdom

Quarterly Bulletins – produced by Transport Statistics
Bus and Light Rail Statistics
☎ +44 (0)20 7944 4139
Provisional Port Statistics: Quarterly results
☎ +44 (0)20 7944 3087
Road Traffic and Congestion in Great Britain
☎ +44 (0)20 7944 3095
Road Goods Vehicles Travelling to Mainland Europe
☎ +44 (0)20 7944 4131
Reported Road Casualties Great Britain:
Quarterly Provisional Estimates
☎ +44 (0)20 7944 3078

NOTE: Prior to 1997, many of the Transport Statistics Bulletins were published as HMSO publications. Enquiries about back issues, or transport publications in general, should be made to Transport Statistics, 2/29, Great Minster House, 76 Marsham Street, London SW1P 4DR. ☎ +44 (020)7944 3098

See also the Transport Statistics website at:
http://www.dft.gov.uk/pgr/statistics

Notes

Notes